CRISIS COUNSELING

A CONTEMPORARY APPROACH

Second Edition

ELLEN H. JANOSIK

Jones and Bartlett Publishers

Boston London

Editorial, Sales, and Customer Service Offices
Jones and Bartlett Publishers
One Exeter Plaza
Boston, MA 02116
1–800–832–0034
617–859–3900

Jones and Bartlett Publishers International
P.O. Box 1498
London W6 7RS
England

Library of Congress Cataloging-in-Publication Data

Janosik, Ellen Hastings.
    Crisis counseling : a contemporary approach / Ellen H. Janosik. —
2nd ed.
        p.   cm.
    Includes bibliographical references and index.
    ISBN 0-86720-641-1
    1. Mental health counseling.   2. Crisis intervention (Psychiatry)
I. Title.
RC466.J36   1994
616.89'14—dc20   93-11333
                                                                    CIP

Printed in the United States of America
97 96 95 94 93   10 9 8 7 6 5 4 3 2 1

Contents

Preface

The nature and extent of contemporary crises have altered in the last few years, and that alteration is the impetus for this second edition of *Crisis Counseling: A Contemporary Approach.* The appeal of the first edition depended, in part, on its timeliness and its relevance to modern life. During the last few years, vast changes have taken place throughout the world, and change rarely ushers in a halcyon interlude. Instead, people living in the latter part of the twentieth century must confront long-standing problems and complex new problems. As always, the four horsemen of the apocalypse—war, famine, disease, and death—still ride among us. Inevitably, there are crises that disrupt whole nations, crises that disable communities, and crises that disturb individuals and their families.

Like the first edition, this book is intended for care providers from various disciplines, such as medicine, nursing, social work, psychology, and counseling, who endeavor to help people deal with the conflicts and demands of modern life. Crisis intervention is not limited to members of the health professions. Therefore, this book should also be useful to teachers, managers, and members of the clergy who are often called upon to be crisis workers, even when this is not part of their job descriptions.

The basic premise of this edition is unchanged, namely that crisis work consists of the systemic application of tested principles to situations in which the equilibrium of an individual, family, or group is seriously impaired. Some care providers believe that crisis intervention is inappropriate for persons already suffering physical or psychiatric disability. However, the disequilibrium attributable to crisis is often superimposed on long-term disability or impairment. In such circumstances, crisis intervention can be an appropriate and effective treatment modality.

There is no way to avoid crisis entirely, either in one's own life or in the lives of others. This means that everyone has, at one time or another, experienced crisis. It also means that virtually everyone, regardless of role or occupation, has been called upon to act as a crisis counselor. Crises are so recurrent and so universal that they are indeed part of the human condition. It is possible to state categorically that crisis is a natural phenomenon rather than an indication of weakness or pathology.

Several chapters have been added to make this book more comprehensive than the first edition. Part One, Crisis Theory, now contains four chapters. This was done to make each theoretical chapter more focused and more explicit. In Part Two, Individuals in Crisis, crises of adulthood are now organized according to three stage-specific patterns dealing with the early, the middle, and the later years of adult life.

The AIDS epidemic and the implications of HIV tests received relatively little attention in the first edition because the overwhelming proportions of the AIDS crisis were not yet apparent. As the AIDS epidemic spread, groups and communities were adversely affected. Nations found, to their horror, that the virus traveled easily across their borders. No longer confined to any age, gender, or sexual predilection, the AIDS epidemic has become synonymous with global crisis. Chapter 14 deals, at length, with the devastating effects of the HIV virus on individuals, families, and entire communities.

Some forms of crisis are atypical in that they do not fit neatly into the crisis paradigm. However, persons experiencing atypical crises react in identifiable ways, and often respond to crisis counseling. Present-day awareness of post-traumatic stress reactions goes far beyond the military environment in which symptoms were first identified. Chapter 15 emphasizes the connections between post-traumatic stress reactions and preventive measures formulated in wartime, which the community mental health movement adopted.

Early treatises on crisis work tended to be unidimensional and simplistic. In reality, crisis theory and intervention are closely associated with psychodynamic, developmental, interpersonal, and sociological frameworks. Both students and practitioners should understand this association if they are to use crisis counseling effectively. Since crises often arise in the context of diverse biopsychosocial problems, this book has ramifications for anyone interested in providing holistic care. It strongly emphasizes the importance of selection criteria, but also suggests that crisis work can be adapted to many people and many situations.

This edition offers guidelines for choosing a generic or a specific approach in crisis work. Crisis counseling specific to the persons involved may cause heightened anxiety and therefore should be influenced by the urgency of the crisis and the capacity of the client to tolerate anxiety. Generic crisis work usually allays anxiety immediately; specific crisis work is growth producing, but its exploratory facets may escalate anxiety for a time.

The contemporary aspects of the book permit treatment of current problems, such as joblessness, incest, and rape. These and other issues are analyzed as precipitants of crisis. A related feature of this book is insistence that the client in crisis should not be regarded in isolation but rather as part of a social gestalt. This means that the external and internal causes of crisis are significant, and that client and context should be assessed. Although specificity in crisis work requires greater theoretical knowledge and clinical expertise, this approach does not negate the basic principles of crisis counseling. This edition should enable thoughtful practitioners to engage in active, time-limited crisis work based on psychological, physiological, and sociocultural connections between the crisis event and the responses of the participants.

At one time, certain principles were considered appropriate for *all* crisis events. Crisis workers now try to include in their assessment not only the characteristics of the crisis, but also the characteristics of the persons involved. In earlier publications, it was stated that only the circumstances or nature of the crisis should be addressed. This book, however, advocates a comprehensive approach that assesses the crisis, the people in crisis, and their reciprocal interactions.

Ellen H. Janosik

PART
ONE

CRISIS THEORY

1

Nature of Crisis
Recognizing the Signs

Humanity transcends nationality. We're human beings before we are anything else.

John Hume

Crisis is such a common occurrence in the lives of individuals, families, and groups that it seems to be part of the human condition. People constantly encounter changes, demands, and challenges in life that cause them to feel unsure and anxious. To understand the inherent nature of crisis, one must realize that there are both similarities and differences in the way people react to their experiences. To begin with, no event is perceived or received in exactly the same way by those who are involved because every participant and onlooker attaches a special, unique meaning to whatever has happened. Whether we are central or peripheral figures in an event, all of us try, in our own way, to impose order and meaning on our experiences in order to understand their significance. More than the event itself, it is the individual's or family's interpretation of events and the attached meaning that influences subsequent actions.

ETIOLOGY OF CRISIS

The etiology of crisis includes a meaningful event that is followed by unsuccessful efforts to deal with the event. Failure to deal with the event successfully leads to negative consequences. Caplan (1964) described *crisis* as a reactive state provoked by hazardous events that threaten important life goals or values. When a hazardous event does not respond to customary problem-solving tactics, a period of disorganization follows. During the period of disorganization, various efforts to cope continue, but these are impeded by psychological dysfunction. Eventually, reorganiza-

3

tion and equilibrium are regained, but the resolution of the problematic event may or may not be in the best interests of the individual or family.

Crisis theory and intervention are chiefly concerned with the recognition, assessment, and management of the critical event and the crisis experience. In order to appreciate the range and limits of crisis theory, it is necessary to define certain terms precisely. A *hazard* consists of any event that endangers the adaptation or adjustment of an individual, family, or community. Hazardous events may come in the form of interpersonal change such as loss of a significant person through death or divorce. They may also take the form of social change, such as the loss of a meaningful role due to retirement. The hazardous event may consist of changes in the environment such as moving to a new home or facing a natural disaster. Physiological changes arising from illness, aging, or disability are other types of hazardous events that have the potential to generate crisis. Examples of various hazardous events are shown in Table 1–1.

There is widespread belief that certain life events are inherently more stressful than others, and therefore are more likely to precipitate a crisis. It is difficult to measure the effects of a hazardous life event in numerical terms, although Holmes and Rahe (1967) endeavored to do so. Their formulations have been widely circulated. Other researchers have found an association between a large number of stressful life experiences and the subsequent incidence of chronic illness. Wilder and Plutchik (1985) expressed doubtfulness on the merits of quantifying hazardous life events

TABLE 1–1 Classification and Examples of Hazardous Life Events

Classification	Examples
Significant developmental milestones	Becoming a teenager Entering college Leaving home Getting married Becoming a parent
Significant decisions	Changing careers Divorcing Remarrying Relocating Retiring
Significant challenge and change	Experiencing illness Suffering an accident Confronting economic reverses Facing disaster or catastrophe

when they noted that one cannot measure the impact of life events in terms of physical dimensions, such as numbers, decibels, or volts. In every person a complex process mediates between any event and the individual's response to it. This mediation process influences the emotional reaction to the event, the cognitive interpretation of it, and behavioral activities that may or may not be adaptive. In crisis counseling, as in most forms of psychotherapy, it is more useful to explore the mediation process that is operating than to assign numerical quotas to hazardous events.

Our interpretation of events and our responses are influenced by our previous history, by our personality structure, and by whatever resources are available to us. The impact of a series of hazardous events is likely to be cumulative. Many challenging events might be manageable if they arrived singly or infrequently, but they can prove overwhelming when they occur within a short period of time. This presents a powerful argument for deferring decisions or avoiding additional changes in one's life in the aftermath of any critical event.

In dealing with hazardous events and with the rigors of daily life, most people tend to adopt a fairly consistent pattern. This is because they cling to behaviors that have worked well for them in the past. Some individuals and families can use a wide spectrum of coping behaviors, while others limit themselves to a paltry few. Members of the latter group are more prone to crisis and require outside help. At the same time, even competent, resourceful people may find themselves in crisis and be unable to solve their own problems.

Psychological deficits and psychiatric disorders, in and of themselves, do not constitute crisis but they may intensify vulnerability by curtailing coping behavior. For our purposes, *coping behavior* refers to the psychological and psychosocial processes used by individuals and families to maintain or restore equilibrium or balance. Coping behaviors encompass, but are not restricted to, the defense mechanisms; they include both internal (psychological) and external (psychosocial) behaviors that people employ.

All individuals have a breaking point at which they become disorganized and dysfunctional due to certain situations. However, the threshold of the breaking point varies greatly, even among people caught up in the same experience. For some capable individuals and families, the breaking point is seldom reached, even in very difficult circumstances. Such people have an armamentarium of coping skills that enables them to handle challenging events with confidence and resourcefulness. Even for the most competent person, however, there may be times when customary solutions prove inadequate. Old problem-solving methods fail and new ones do not seem readily available. As a result, the failure to cope sets the stage for the turmoil that is characteristic of crisis.

The failure of their usual solutions causes people considerable emotional distress. They then begin to experience the "uncanny" emotions of dread, fear, and anxiety that Harry Stack Sullivan (1953) so vividly described. People can no longer view the hazardous situation realistically; instead, they magnify the most ominous details and dimensions of their situation. Their negative emotions soon take over and intrude on virtually every aspect of their lives. Inevitably, their perception of reality is altered.

CONTRIBUTIONS TO CRISIS THEORY

A notable contributor to crisis theory was Gerald Caplan (1964), whose interest in crisis work stemmed from his experiences with institutionalized children in Israel after the Second World War. It was Caplan who described crisis as a human reaction to impediments to life goals when such obstacles resist problem solving. Preceding any crisis, according to Caplan, is a hazardous event or situation that is subjectively interpreted as a threat to one's instinctual needs or meaningful existence.

Other contributions to crisis theory came from Erich Lindemann (1944), whose work distinguished adaptive and maladaptive grief. In his study on the reactions of survivors and relatives of victims of a nightclub fire in Boston, Lindemann found that the first six weeks after bereavement was a critical time during which the resolution of grief could be either adaptive or maladaptive. Crisis theory was enriched by the conceptualizations of Caplan and Lindemann. Clinical applications of their work are presented in Chapters 2 and 4.

REALITY TESTING AND CRISIS

Crisis is marked by a search for alternative coping measures as people try unsuccessfully to resolve their problems on their own. Recurrent failure causes people to regress and to resort to increasingly maladaptive tactics. Haunted by circumstances and beset by failure, people feel that their lives are out of control and unmanageable. They sense that they are living in a dangerous world, and that they can no longer rely on their own abilities. In effect, events have transpired that have drastically changed their view of themselves and their lives. Indeed, there are notable similarities between the altered perceptions of people in crisis and the disruption of reality experienced by people in an acute psychotic state. In both instances, a disruption of reality has taken place due to partial failure of the ego function known as *reality testing.*

Reality testing is the ability to differentiate external stimuli from internal stimuli. Persons capable of reality testing can make distinctions between what is happening around them, and thoughts and feelings generated within themselves. Therefore, their responses and interpretations are largely based on what is taking place in the real world. As a result, their reactions to events are more or less rational and appropriate. Reality testing is a term borrowed from psychodynamic theory; it can be used to explain the emotional, cognitive, and behavioral errors characteristic of persons in crisis. Anna Freud (1953) formulated a list of defense mechanisms, explaining that people use a variety of protective or defensive measures, some of which are more functional than others. Some major defense mechanisms are as follows:

- *Repression.* The inability to remember or be consciously aware of material or content that is unacceptable to the individual. For example, a person who cannot acknowledge hostility toward a relative may "forget" the relative's birthday.
- *Displacement.* The transfer of emotion from one target to another. A man who is angry with his wife may control his feelings at home but yell at his office secretary.
- *Reaction formation.* The transformation of unacceptable feelings into behavior indicating opposite emotions. A mother who is excessively loving and conscientious may, at a deeper level, feel angry and frustrated by her family's demands.
- *Isolation.* The separation of an idea from its emotional component. A college student may dismiss feelings of homesickness but often think of family reunion.
- *Undoing.* An effort to cancel or retract certain actions, real or imagined. Undoing may be attempted through apology, atonement, or ritualistic behavior. The classic example is Lady Macbeth who could not wash the blood from her hands despite repeated, ritualistic cleansing.
- *Rationalization.* The formation of reasonable explanations that may or may not be true, for certain actions. It helps individuals conceal their actual motives from themselves and others. An example is the alcoholic who says he needs to drink because his job is so high pressured.
- *Intellectualization.* This resembles rationalization but is more subtle. It involves the use of intellectual processes to avoid emotional involvement. A couple may substitute intellectual discussion for open disclosure of their feelings about one another.
- *Denial.* Partial or complete rejection of an event or of the emotional reaction to an event. Denial may be adaptive or maladaptive, depending on the situation. Dealing with loss, for example, often begins by denying the loss or minimizing one's emotional reaction to it.
- *Projection.* This enables individuals to attribute their own feelings and desires to others. A student who dislikes a teacher may assume that the teacher is hostile to him.
- *Regression.* This permits people to return to an early level of functioning to avoid the tension and demands of a later stage. The five-year-old child with a new sibling may return to an earlier stage of dependency.

- *Introjection.* The erasure of differences between an individual and a beloved other. A person who internalizes all the characteristics of another loses the sense of having a separate identity. Sometimes after losing a loved one, a survivor may adopt the interests and/or mannerisms of the deceased to reduce awareness of loss.
- *Identification.* Refers to imitating the attributes of a person one admires. This resembles introjection but is less profound. The daughter of a famous actress who tries to emulate her mother's career is using the identification mechanism.
- *Sublimation.* The expression of psychological needs in ways that are socially acceptable. A woman who expresses her loving needs by nurturing day care children is using the sublimation mechanism. Sublimation of the aggressive drive is evident in the behavior of a young man who becomes a competitive, successful athlete.

CHRONOLOGY OF CRISIS

To understand the impairment of reality testing and the distortions that ensue, it is helpful for the counselor to develop chronology depicting the emergence of the hazardous event, its significance, and the coping attempts undertaken by the individual or family. The chronology is a bridge between what really occurred and the distortions currently experienced by those in crisis. It not only enhances the crisis counselor's understanding but, when shared with those seeking help, can be used to reinforce reality.

Crisis is a frequent, but not an inevitable, consequence of hazardous life events. Many times life changes are successfully dealt with and challenges are met. When situations respond to problem solving, crisis is averted. Negative emotions recede and equilibrium is preserved; the danger element is introduced when the hazard is unresponsive to whatever solutions are tried. As one after another solution fails, emotional distress increases and distress mounts within the frustrated individual or family. When this pattern appears, the persons involved lose the ability to engage in rational, reality-based thinking. Focused thoughts and actions are adversely affected. They are replaced with erroneous thoughts that interfere with the ability to appraise the actual situation and respond accordingly. A state of general disorganization prevails, which only intensifies distress. Their distorted thoughts cause the situation to assume gigantic proportions. Figure 1–1 depicts the chronology of crisis.

The cognitive distortion inherent in crisis means that the power to assess a situation, to plan effectively, and to predict consequences is greatly reduced. A person in crisis is distracted, incoherent, and often irritable. Extreme emotional reactions cause cognitive errors, and the

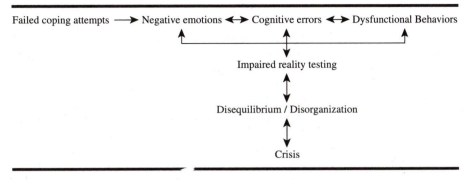

FIGURE 1–1   Chronology of Crisis

cognitive deficits heighten emotional reactivity. Some individuals deal with their distress through withdrawal or regressive behaviors. One form of regressive behavior is belief that problems will be solved without effort or that a miraculous rescuer will appear on the horizon. Occasionally, an individual's distress takes the form of physical symptoms such as insomnia or anorexia.

Because emotional reactivity represents a root cause of crisis, it is advisable for a crisis counselor to permit a certain amount of emotional discharge or catharsis. This may encourage regressive tendencies if it is unduly prolonged. Therefore, the extent of emotional catharsis should be time limited and carefully monitored. Following this, attention should be directed to correcting cognitive distortions. By correcting cognitive errors, counselors encourage the restoration of reality testing and emotional control.

People in crisis are seldom able to make a rational connection between a precipitating situation or event, the subjective distress that followed, and their eventual disequilibrium. Therefore, the counselor should make connections. The actual dimensions of the crisis must be outlined before a solution can be found. As far as possible, an individual's sense of helplessness, hopelessness, and entrapment should be alleviated. Only when the situation is reduced to manageable proportions for the individual can cognitive and emotional distortions be corrected. The counselor should be prepared to deal with the individual's initial defensiveness and unwillingness to grapple with the problem. Here again the correction of cognitive errors helps lower defensiveness and makes the individual more willing to see the true proportions of the problem.

Cognitive distortion is a global term but its manifestations and its consequences are quite specific. The irrational thinking that accompanies cognitive distortion can be identified in the illogical, self-defeating communication of persons in crisis. The following are examples of cognitive distortions that require attention and should be targeted for correction.

- *Overgeneralization* consists of making a global assumption based on one incident. An example is a wife who feels unloved and misunderstood when her husband asks her to put gas in the car.
- *Magnification* causes the problems and demands of any task or situation to be greatly exaggerated. An example is the worker who is competent and well motivated but feels inadequate when asked to perform.
- *Minimization* causes individuals to belittle and doubt their own ability, regardless of a record of success. Minimizing one's own worth often accompanies magnifying the skills and abilities of other people.
- *Polarized thinking* produces all-or-nothing thought patterns. One day the individual believes that he is a star performer; the next day the same individual believes that he is a hopeless failure, all in the absence of reliable evidence.
- *Selective concentration* involves focusing on a single detail, ignoring other details, and interpreting an entire situation on the basis of one detail. An example is a teacher who thinks the entire lesson failed because one student in the back row was briefly inattentive.
- *Unsubstantiated judgments* refers to reaching conclusions in the absence of solid, substantiating evidence. An example is an individual who concludes that an old, trusted friend is disloyal despite contrary indications.

In correcting cognitive errors, the counselor examines the extent of the problem, appraises the results of attempted solutions, and encourages individuals to search for alternative measures. This down-to-earth analysis in itself offers considerable relief to distraught people in crisis. On the subject of cognitive distortion, Horowitz et al. (1984, p. 328) wrote, "Patients often have a tendency to speak of themselves in irrational terms, yet can learn to speak of themselves in more rational ones. . . . Patients may learn to modify their states of mind through an inner dialogue, learned, rehearsed in therapy sessions in which they counteract some repetitive, irrational assumptions of inferiority or blame."

With the discharge of some emotion and the correction of cognitive distortion, the counselor and those in crisis are ready to work on solving the problem. In crisis counseling, as in other forms of therapy, goals and interventions must be acceptable to persons seeking help. The starting point is the need expressed by the individual or family. This cannot be ignored or discounted, even when the counselor can see more pressing needs.

Persons in crisis are aware of their failure to cope. This makes them more receptive to new ways of functioning. Yet the same disorganization that increases their receptivity also increases the probability of regression or apathy, at least in early counseling sessions. When a therapeutic alliance develops between the counselor and the counselee, defensiveness lessens and cooperation becomes possible. Defensiveness on the part of people in crisis may stem from a wish to demonstrate how hard they have already tried to solve the problem.

Catharsis generated by structured emotional expression facilitates the return of reality testing. The counselor should promote self-control as soon as possible by stating that extreme feelings are understandable but unproductive because they absorb energy that might be put to better use. Persons who wallow in self-pity or self-blame can honestly be told that their situation will not always seem so hopeless.

Often the person in crisis seeks help from a friend or relative, or someone not professionally prepared to play a counseling role. Although anyone able to establish a caring, supportive relationship may provide crisis counseling, a word of warning is in order. All counselors, professional and nonprofessional, must guard against overidentification with the troubled individual. Additionally, if the situation is beyond the expertise of the counselor, appropriate referrals should be made quickly. Willingness to listen without censuring or blaming is essential for anyone from whom troubled people seek help. Instilling hope is another counseling tool available to professionals and nonprofessionals alike. Because the crisis distortions are three-dimensional, interventions almost always include emotional, cognitive, and behavioral elements.

While accepting some discharge of distressing emotion, the counselor tries to move from emotional catharsis to cognitive restructuring. This begins with identifying the precipitating event. Sometimes the event is readily apparent, but sometimes neither the counselor nor the troubled person can point to a recent occurrence that triggered the crisis. It may then be necessary to search for the precipitating hazard. Sometimes a single event can be found, but sometimes an accumulation of moderately distressing occurrences have caused the crisis.

The following lists summarize the basic concepts of crisis theory and responsive interventions, based on cognitive correction, that were presented in this chapter. The cognitive framework links thoughts, emotions, and behaviors; its goal is to reestablish rational thinking, subdue extreme emotions, and promote positive actions.

Principles of Cognitive Correction:
- How people interpret a situation determines their reaction to it. For example, people who believe themselves in danger react defensively or aggressively to protect themselves.
- How people interpret a situation influences emotional reactions. Situations that seem overwhelming evoke strong emotions.
- Crisis is characterized by distortions leading to dysfunctional behavior:
  - Angry, resentful people adopt *fight* tactics.
  - Frightened, anxious people adopt *flight* tactics.

- Helpless, dependent people adopt seeking or *approach* tactics.
- Hopeless, depressed people adopt *avoidance* tactics, thinking they are beyond help.

Facilitating Cognitive Correction:
- Permit moderate amounts of emotional expression but limit the extent.
- Help individuals make connections between preceding events and current reactions.
- Ascertain what individuals have already done in response to the situation.
- Suggest alternatives in the form of positive steps that may not have been taken.
- Identify stresses in the recent past, their duration, their consequences, and their relationships to other stresses that occurred earlier.
- Explore current coping skills, level of functioning, and access to support systems.
- Use all available means in the social and community network to expand each individual's repertoire of coping behaviors.

•CLINICAL EXAMPLE:
EMOTIONAL, COGNITIVE, AND BEHAVIORAL
DISTORTION IN RESPONSE TO PARENTAL ILLNESS

Trudy Preston is a twenty-two-year-old married woman who moved to an Eastern city from Phoenix, Arizona, a year ago, after marrying a serviceperson stationed in the East. Trudy and her husband, George, had gone through high school together. Their families were well acquainted and approved of the marriage, although Trudy's parents were reluctant to accept the fact that their only daughter was moving fifteen hundred miles away. Even though she was devoted to her husband, Trudy found it hard to leave her family, especially her mother, with whom she had enjoyed a close, warm relationship. Trudy had two older brothers but their interests coincided with those of their father, not their mother.

At first homesick, Trudy soon adjusted well to the move. She enjoyed taking care of her small apartment, cooking, and acting as housewife. After a few months she obtained a part-time job in the post exchange on the military base. The job supplemented George's pay and helped Trudy make friends. Things were going well for the young couple until Trudy's father called shortly before Thanksgiving to tell them that Trudy's mother had suffered a "nervous breakdown" and had been admitted to a psychiatric hospital. The news upset Trudy so much that she became hysterical, and canceled the plans to spend a fall weekend in the country with George. This outing had been eagerly anticipated by them both.

In the days that followed, Trudy did not regain her composure. The news of her mother's breakdown reminded Trudy of her mother's illness after a spontaneous miscarriage that had occurred when Trudy was ten or eleven years old. At that time her mother had been seriously depressed. She was hospitalized briefly, medicated, but remained apathetic and withdrawn for months afterward. Turning inward, Trudy's mother took no interest in her family. Conditions in the home deteriorated so much that Trudy's grandmother moved in to care for the children and the household. Her mother's illness lasted for months only, but her grandmother remained in the home for two years. She was an efficient manager, but she was strict with the children, especially Trudy. She constantly exhorted them to be quiet, to help with chores, and never, never worry or upset their mother.

Trudy's reaction to her mother's illness was excessive and disproportionate. She felt guilty for feeling happy in her new life when her mother was undoubtedly lonely. Even though her father reassured her by phone that her mother was making progress, Trudy began to torment herself with the fixed idea that her mother would never get well. Every phone call from Phoenix alarmed her more; she insisted that her father spoke of her mother's recovery merely to keep Trudy from worrying. Trudy's pessimism about her mother's illness increased and she began to blame herself for causing her mother's illness, saying, "She got sick because I was selfish enough to leave home. And she won't get well until I return."

Trudy's concerned husband promised that they would both go home at Christmas time, and this calmed her for a few days. Then she began to say that she could not wait for Christmas because her mother might be dead by then, and they would never see each other again. Her anxiety mounted until she was unable to continue working, even though the lost income meant that they might not be able to afford the Christmas visit. By this time Trudy was spending most of her time staring into space and was always on the verge of tears. She had no interest in taking care of the apartment of which she had been so proud. George tried to be understanding but every day he became more frightened and bewildered by Trudy's behavior. He urged Trudy to call her mother directly and see for herself that her mother was recovering. His suggestions were unheeded. On one occasion she told George that it didn't matter whether they visited Phoenix at Christmas because by then she and her mother would both be dead. At this point George made an appointment for Trudy to see a therapist at an Army mental health facility, and escorted her there.

The opinion of the Army psychologist assigned to Trudy was that she was experiencing a situational reaction that had precipitated crisis. She had been happy in her marriage and had adjusted well to living so far from her parents. Trudy was meticulous and compulsive in discharging her responsibilities to people she loved. Her distress on hearing of her mother's illness brought back memories of the difficult period in her childhood when she felt abandoned by her mother and relegated to the stern care of her grandmother. In Trudy's worry about her mother she projected her childhood feelings of abandonment onto her mother. As a child she longed for the return of her mother; as a young adult she remembered this early disquiet and assumed that her mother was experiencing the same misery.

Trudy rejected the accurate reports from her father. She was told daily that her mother was improving. On one level she was aware that her own state of health was excellent, yet all she could dwell on was the great distance separating the two of them. Her regressive behavior consisted of ruminating endlessly about her situation, rejecting reassurance, and sabotaging her husband's efforts to arrange a Christmas reunion.

The therapist saw the couple together in one session, saw Trudy alone several times, and arranged for a final session with both partners. He helped Trudy understand that separating from her parents and beginning a new life with George was a legitimate task. There was no reason to burden herself with feelings of guilt or disloyalty, nor to assume that she was responsible for her mother's psychiatric problems, now or in the past. Through the aegis of Army Relief, arrangements were made for Trudy to travel to Phoenix a week before Christmas, and for George to join her for the holiday. As soon as travel plans were made, Trudy decided to return to work in order to buy gifts for her family. The therapist asked Trudy to check in with him once after she returned and let him know how the visit went.

Critical Guidelines

The therapist did not directly address Trudy's emotional, cognitive, and behavioral distortions, yet all intervention aimed at reducing her erratic and unrealistic responses to her mother's illness. The therapist did not delve into Trudy's lingering resentment of her mother's early illness. Instead, the therapist focused on the here-and-now aspects of her reactions to the current illness. The importance of the marital bond was reinforced by emphasizing George's unfailing support. Trudy's use of projection was discouraged by questioning her belief that she caused her mother's present hospitalization. Her accomplishments as a wife and homemaker were acknowledged, but fantasies of her omnipotence in causing her mother's symptoms were discounted.

The therapist working with Trudy was well aware of her obsessive personality and her use of a primitive defense mechanism such as projection. However, he was impressed with her history of good adjustment during successive life stages. By recognizing her overall social stability and her commitment to her marriage, the therapist was able to establish a therapeutic alliance that enabled her to manage the conflict between her obligations as a wife and as a daughter (Frieswyk et al., 1986). The therapist's suggestion that Trudy see him at least once after visiting her parents would provide additional data about Trudy's ability to mediate between internal distortion and external reality.

The thrust of crisis intervention for Trudy was her need and her right to accomplish the developmental tasks of a young adult (Budman & Stone, 1983). This approach enabled the therapist to describe Trudy's predicament as an impediment to the normal developmental progression to which she was entitled. There were hysterical and histrionic aspects to Trudy's behavior, and manipulative components as well. Repeated allusions to the developmental theme promoted clarification and acceptance by Trudy and her husband, and discouraged their fears of psychopathology. McKenzie (1988) believes that brief intervention is more effective when focal themes are kept in the foreground. This promotes adjustment to the current life situation.

SUMMARY

This introductory chapter describes the emotional, cognitive, and behavioral distortions that compose the disequilibrium of individuals in crisis. The crisis counselor is urged to adopt an approach that deals with the triad of distortions. The social environment and the support systems available to an individual are important in the development and in the effective resolution of any crisis. Immediate relief of the distress and disorganization characteristic of crisis is more important than exploring historical causes. Although the disorganization experienced by persons in crisis challenges the counselor, it also makes people more amenable to therapeutic suggestions about coping abilities.

Reality testing is an adaptive ego function that enables people to distinguish inner and outer stimuli. Impaired reality testing is an aspect of crisis that impedes problem solving. Restored reality testing follows the correction of distortions that prevent people in crisis from perceiving their actual situation.

Sometimes people in crisis are really afraid that they are going crazy. If this happens, the crisis counselor may indicate that many others in a similar situation might feel the same way, and that the individual's distress is understandable. Cognitive and behavioral improvement are unlikely to occur until the counselor provides opportunity for the client to express strong emotion. This emotional catharsis should be monitored, but it usually makes the person in crisis more receptive to measures designed to alter dysfunctional thoughts and actions. There are two major goals in crisis counseling. The goals are interdependent. One goal is to modify any distortions that are operating; the second goal is to ease internal distress to facilitate problem solving.

The clinical illustration described various emotional, cognitive, and behavioral errors characteristic of persons in crisis, and presented the circumscribed interventions the counselor applies.

REFERENCES

Budman S.H., and J. Stone. "Advances in Brief Psychotherapy, A Review of Recent Literature." *Hospital and Community Psychiatry* 34(1983): 939–946.

Caplan, G. *Principles of Preventive Psychiatry* New York: Basic Books, 1964.

Freud, A. *The Ego and Mechanisms of Defense.* New York: International Universities Press, 1953.

Frieswyk, S.H., J.G. Allen, D.B. Colsen, et al. "Therapeutic Alliance: Its Place as a Process and Outcome Variable in Dynamic Psychotherapy Research." *Journal of Consulting and Clinical Psychology* 54(1986): 32–38.

Holmes, T.H., and R.H. Rahe. "The Social Readjustment Rating Scale." *Journal of Psychosomatic Research* 2(1967): 213.

Horowitz, M.J., C. Marmar, J. Krupnick, et al. *Personality Styles and Brief Psychotherapy.* New York: Guilford Press, 1984.

Lindemann, E. "Symptomatology and Management of Acute Grief." *American Journal of Psychiatry* 101(1944): 141–148.

McKenzie, K.R. "Recent Developments in Brief Psychotherapy." *Hospital and Community Psychiatry* 39(1988): 742–752.

Sullivan, H.S. *The Interpersonal Theory of Psychiatry.* New York: Norton, 1953.

Wilder, J.F., and R. Plutchik. "Stress and Psychiatry." In *Comprehensive Textbook of Psychiatry,* 4th ed., edited by H.I. Kaplan and B.J. Sadock. Baltimore: Williams & Wilkins, 1985.

2

Parameters of Crisis
Defining the Limits

Mishaps are like knives that either serve us or cut us as we grasp the blade or the handle.

James Russell Lowell

Crisis is a time-limited condition and crisis counseling is a short-term form of intervention. The state of crisis is so distressing that it is thought to be incompatible with continued existence. Internal distress erodes adaptational powers, but it tends to make people more willing to try new ways of coping. In a sense, crisis often acts as a catalyst, stimulating alternative coping methods that may be positive or negative in the long run. This is what is meant by the statement that crisis represents an opportunity as well as a threat. When successfully negotiated, crisis can ultimately become a source of renewed strength and competence. Usually the acute disorganization produced by crisis ends, one way or another, four to ten weeks after the appearance of the precipitating hazardous event.

Although distress and disorganization may fade within a relatively short time, the aftermath of crisis is unpredictable. Outcomes may vary greatly in desirability, ranging from creative problem solving to regressive behaviors that aggravate the original predicament. Crisis may lead to chronic impairment that lasts for many years. We see this in incest or rape victims, who may suffer lifelong dread of sexual intimacy or lasting feelings of shame. We see it also in some disaster or holocaust victims, who feel forever guilty for having survived when others perished. For many people distress and disorganization may abate, but the crisis is never resolved once and for all time. Instead, the memory of the hazardous event lurks just below the surface, always available to be revived in ways that complicate later experiences. The phenomenon in which the anniversary of a loss revives old grief is very familiar. The crisis known as

17

Post-Traumatic Stress Disorder (PTSD), which sometimes follows episodes of violence, ebbs and rises for long periods of time. In PTSD, intervals of relative tranquility are interrupted by times of severe distress that may be activated by visual, olfactory, or auditory stimuli. However, the abatement of acute crisis seems to follow a natural sequence. Intervention alone does not end a crisis, but it certainly affects the outcome.

The short-term aspects of crisis counseling have undoubtedly expanded its use. Yet there may be a worrisome disparity between the increased use of crisis intervention and adequate understanding of crisis theory. It is not enough for health care providers to have a vague idea of crisis theory principles or to confuse crisis work with other forms of brief therapy. Health care providers need a clear understanding of crisis theory, and they should know how and when to offer crisis intervention.

In addition to time limitations, crisis counseling is also limited in scope. Insight is not the goal of crisis intervention, nor is the improvement of interpersonal relationships, although these results may be apparent after crisis intervention. Behavior modification is not a primary objective of crisis intervention, except as a means of dealing with the crisis itself. Attention is consistently directed to the perceived and actual dimensions of the crisis, and to alternative behaviors that will resolve the critical impasse. Sometimes the parameters of crisis counseling seem narrow and restricted, but concentrating on the current problem is advisable. At the termination of crisis intervention, appropriate referrals may be made for additional counseling that may have a broader perspective.

CLASSIFICATION OF CRISES

Crises may be classified in several ways. A general schema is one that classifies crises as either developmental or situational. Situational crises are more individualistic, less predictable, and less universal. Erikson (1963) described eight developmental tasks of the individual life cycle that must be accomplished if healthy maturation is to take place. Duvall (1977) conceptualized eight developmental tasks that must be undertaken during the life span of a family (see Chapter 8). It can be stated without exception that every individual developmental task initiates a journey into new terrain and brings with it the potential for crisis. In addition, crisis may arise when the critical tasks of individual family members conflict with the critical tasks of other family members, or of the family system as a whole.

Situational crises include unforseen events and circumstances, unrelated to specific developmental tasks, that are so hard to manage that they cause biopsychosocial disorder in people's lives. Groups and communities must periodically deal with situational crises in the form of natural disasters and human-derived catastrophes. At the same time that contemporary forces push people toward crisis, viable support systems comprised of relatives and neighbors are more fragmented and less available than they were in more traditional times.

STRESS AND CRISIS

Crisis is a term that is commonly but incorrectly applied to everyday annoyances and frustrations. Sometimes the terms *stress* and *crisis* are used interchangeably even though stress is actually a temporary or prolonged condition that requires people to adapt to circumstances or expectations shaped by the self or others. Stress is rarely a simple stimulus-response situation, but is rather an interactive process in which one's perception of the rewards in relation to the energy expended is an intervening variable. This individualistic perception implies that an appraisal is followed by an interpretation of the situation, which may be positive, negative, or somewhere in between. It is the appraisal and the ensuing judgment that determine whether one's adaptation to the situation is experienced as distress (pain) or eustress (pleasure) (Selye, 1956). Therefore, similar conditions may be construed as positive or negative according to the subjective perceptions of the person adapting to stress.

Stress makes demands on people that may be physiological, social, psychological, or any combination of the three. Although response to stress may appear to be successful, the mobilization of energy that stress requires often may extract a price in the form of psychophysiological symptoms. Selye (1956) described three stages of stress response that together constitute a general adaptation syndrome (GAS): *alarm, resistance,* and *exhaustion.* The stress responses characteristic of the three-stage GAS are shown in Table 2–1. In some respects crisis may be considered an acute variant of stress that is so extreme that the individual or group becomes fully disorganized and unable to function. Exposure to stress may cause losses in one's ability to function, but not lead to total disorganization. Prolonged efforts to adapt to stress often cause the emergence or worsening of organic pathology.

TABLE 2–1   General Adaptation Syndrome

Stage	Characteristic Responses
Alarm	Stress activates the mobilization of adaptive mechanisms.
Resistance	Stress requires sustained, high-level use of adaptive mechanisms.
Exhaustion	Stress depletes adaptive mechanisms through prolonged use.

EMERGENCY AND CRISIS

There is a tendency to confuse crises with emergencies, but it is possible to differentiate between the two. *Emergencies* may be described as sudden, distressing events in which the persons involved know that prompt action is needed; they may or may not try to help themselves. Unless relieved rather promptly, an emergency may lead to serious consequences, physiological or psychological, or both. Nevertheless, emergency situations usually respond to any form of outside assistance such as reassurance, distraction, control, or rescue. Any form of aid that reduces the fears, responsibilities, or demands of the participants is likely to be effective.

If a man stands on the ledge of a tenth-floor window and threatens to jump, he presents an emergency. After he has been coaxed to leave the window ledge, the emergency is over. However, the man remains suicidal; he is now in a state of crisis, which requires appropriate intervention.

During the disorganization that accompanies acute crisis, some people solicit help from relatives, friends, and professional counselors, while others search on their own for alternative solutions. Their search is hampered by distortions and irrationality that accompany disequilibrium. Sometimes the alternative solutions are adaptive and sometimes they are not. Alternative solutions that are not especially adaptive consist of avoiding the worrisome event, ruminating over the problem, or denying one's own distress. Here the danger potential of the crisis continues to outweigh the growth potential, for maladaptive coping not only impairs current problem solving, but also threatens future problem-solving ability.

An illustration of opportunities and dangers present in a crisis situation may be found in the alternative behaviors of a heroin addict whose supply source suddenly becomes unavailable. For the addict, drug dependence is not a crisis until the loss of a supply source creates a hazard of major proportions. After the addict tries vainly to obtain the drug from friends on the street, several courses of action are open. The addict can respond to the situation by seeking treatment and voluntarily entering a detoxification, withdrawal, or methadone maintenance program. Another recourse is to turn to alcohol, which is legal, available, but also destructive. A third course of action might be to attempt armed robbery to obtain money for a new supplier, and to be apprehended by the police. In choosing the first course of action, the addict embraces the opportunity offered by the crisis. In choosing the second course of action, the addict merely substitutes one addictive behavior for another. The third course is the most maladaptive, since the addict compounds the crisis by moving wholly outside the law. In some ways the addict's recourse to an act of violence and subsequent involvement with the law superimposes a second crisis on the first. Table 2–2 shows the juxtaposition of opportunity and danger in the crisis faced by the heroin addict.

In a more ordinary situation, a young mother with a new baby and two preschool children might find herself unable to manage her daily tasks. An adaptive solution would be for the mother to discuss her distress with her husband, obtain outside assistance, and arrange for a few hours away from the children each week. A less adaptive solution would be for the mother to set priorities that permit her to attend to the basic needs of the children but leave no time for meaningful interaction with her husband. A maladaptive solution, fraught with danger for parents and children, would be for the overwhelmed mother to neglect the legitimate needs of the children, withholding food and attention from them as her feelings of inadequacy and desperation grow. For this family, the addition of the new baby comprises a hazard; crisis may be precipitated if the new baby is hospitalized for failure to thrive and the neglect of the older children comes to the attention of professionals in the health care system.

Often there is a dormant period between the arrival of a hazardous event and the disequilibrium generated by rising distress. During the dormancy period, which may last from several hours to several weeks, attempts are made to deal with the problem. Intervention made at this time may avert disequilibrium or reduce its severity. When the problem is solved through a person's own efforts or with outside intervention, possibilities of future crises lessen.

A hazardous event in the form of life change, transition, or challenge may be new in the experience of an individual or be a repetition of previous events. When coping methods that worked before prove ineffectual, the failure causes anxiety, confusion, indecision, and preoccupation

TABLE 2–2 Alternative Behaviors of an Addict in Crisis

Crisis Event	Coping Behavior	Outcome
Addict experiences subjective distress when supply of an illegal substance is curtailed.	Addict seeks treatment for addiction.	Adaptive solution: coping skills increase.
	Addict substitutes alcohol for unavailable illegal drug.	Questionable solution: coping skills unchanged.
	Addict attempts armed robbery to obtain money for a new supplier and is arrested.	Maladaptive solution: coping skills are impaired and crisis worsens.

with the problem. Often the failure of attempted coping behavior activates memories of earlier failures, all of which add to feelings of disquiet.
It is not the hazardous event that causes crisis, but the event coupled with
inability to cope. The insoluble nature of the hazardous event is compounded by feelings of entrapment. Despite their best efforts, people find
themselves in situations that are beyond them, and the disparity between
external demands and the resources of the individual or group may be
quite painful.

Crisis, in many respects, is less compelling than emergency, which is
immediate and unforeseen. Entering school, marrying, or changing jobs
do not constitute emergencies but may bring challenges that lead to crisis.
Some clinicians believe that an emergency exists if immediate intervention is warranted. If the person in distress can wait twenty-four hours, a
crisis is present rather than an emergency. It is possible for an emergency
to be superimposed on a crisis. An example of this is an individual who
has been trying to deal with a critical situation and becomes so discouraged that he is seriously suicidal. Usually a crisis represents a situation
that has been building up over time. Unlike emergencies, which tend to
respond to almost any remedial measure, crises require a search for
alternative ways of coping, and collaborative problem solving. In the
previous example, the suicide risk can be considered an emergency that
demands immediate attention. Even after the suicide risk has abated, the
critical situation remains and must be resolved. Table 2–3 illustrates the
sequence that occurs when an emergency is transformed into a crisis.

GRIEF AND CRISIS

Differences between normal grief and its less normal counterpart, depression, have been noted. Neither grief nor depression is a pleasant experience, but the latter is more pathological. One feature common to both
experiential states is that they are reactions to loss, either real or symbolic.
Precursors of grief are often apparent and therefore more identifiable than
precursors of depression. As a rule, *grief* is a reaction to the sustained loss
or absence of any person or object that is highly valued. Thus the grief of a
mother for a lost child, of an athlete for an unattained trophy, or a student
for the security of home and parents have much in common. In grieving,
all people mourn the loss of something meaningful; thus people who
grieve are those who have learned to love, to form attachments, and to
acquire values and identifications.

Loss is present in depression also, but it is less likely to be perceived
realistically. Even though the depressed person's reaction to loss seems
excessive or disproportionate to the actual loss, it is essential for crisis
workers to accept the client's viewpoint. What seems inconsequential to

TABLE 2-3 Stages of Emergency and Crisis

Stage I

Emergency → → Shock, Disbelief, Distress, Panic

Intervention →

Honeymoon phase → → Hope, Compliance, Gratitude

Relief, rescue, or hazardous event

Stage II

Hazardous event →

Uncertain outcome → → "Uncanny" emotions, Awe, Fear, Dread

Disintegration → → Shame, Guilt, Anger, Helplessness, Hopelessness → Focal awareness, Selective inattention

Crisis → → Bewilderment, Confusion, Noncompliance, Confrontation, Conflict → Chaos

Continued

23

TABLE 2–3 *Continued*

Stage III

Crisis intervention →	Reintegration
	↓
Collaboration	Change
Problem solving	↓
Anticipatory guidance	Acceptance of change → coping skills improve
	Refusal of change → coping skills decrease
Alternatives	Partial acceptance of change → coping skills unaltered
	↓
Consensual validation	

Source: Adapted from Sullivan (1953), Lindemann (1944), and Caplan (1964).

24

others may be a profound deprivation for the client. A minor facial scar, imperceptible to observers, may engender deep depression in an adolescent but cause only mild regret in a housewife. Loss of autonomy, loss of function, or loss of role may cause grief reactions in some individuals and pervasive depression in others. What then is the difference between the two experiential states, either of which may be precipitated by loss?

Rubin (1981) stated that the central task after losing a loved one is the loosening of emotional ties to the beloved. This task of object detachment follows a predictable sequence. The acute grief reaction lasts from three to twelve weeks, after which mourning may continue for a period of one to two years. At the end of this longer period, detachment from the loved one is thought to be concluded. Persistent and intense grieving beyond this time is assumed to indicate incomplete relinquishment of the loved one. The distinction between normal grieving and depression is based on the functioning level of the bereaved and the length of time that has elapsed since the loss. This conceptualization agrees with the psychoanalytic definition of mourning as a reaction to the loss of the beloved and a process of gradual detachment (Freud, 1953).

The work of Lindemann (1944) indicated that there were patterned grief responses after the death of a loved one. When a tragic nightclub fire in Boston brought death and injury to many young people celebrating a football victory, Lindemann, who was then working at Massachusetts General Hospital, interviewed a number of survivors and relatives of persons killed or injured. He found that overcoming the loss of a loved one depended on meaningful grief work, the purpose of which was the disengagement of the griever from the deceased, followed by readjustment and the ability to form new interpersonal relationships. The implications of this extensive investigation were that experiences of loss are difficult for everyone, but become crises for persons who are particularly vulnerable because of earlier life experiences, personality attributes, or both.

Lindemann's theoretical constructs on loss and grief work have proved durable and have been incorporated into many crisis intervention programs. A few years after the nightclub fire, Lindemann established the Human Relations Center in Wellesley, Massachusetts, which became a model community mental health center. By providing crisis intervention to persons confronting hazardous situations and by educating a wide variety of professionals and paraprofessionals, the Human Relations Center was able to help large numbers of persons who had no psychiatric diagnoses but were in crisis. In this environment, crisis theory and practice flourished, and interventions designed for people in crisis contributed to growing interest in short-term therapeutic approaches.

Crisis theory and practice have enhanced our understanding of non-pathological behavior, particularly responses to loss. A pattern of grief reaction that is simultaneous rather than sequential is observable in behaviors characteristic of persons suffering loss. Such behaviors include the following manifestations:

- Preoccupation with the lost one.
- Identification with the lost one.
- Expressions of guilt and hostility.
- Some disorganization in daily routine.
- Some evidence of somatic complaints.

Most of the foregoing behaviors accompany normal grieving, particularly during the acute period. The same behaviors may indicate morbid or pathological grief reactions whenever they become excessive or protracted. Lindemann found that morbid grief reactions may also take the form of denied grief, delayed grief, or aberrant behaviors. Distorted grief reactions may be expressed through overactive, excessively cheerful behaviors, or through incorporating the loved one by adopting mannerisms or symptomatology typical of the one who was lost. Another indication of a morbid grief reaction is withdrawal from previously beloved persons or activities whenever this withdrawal persists beyond the expected stage of acute grieving.

Lindemann noted a connection between detachment from the deceased and personality changes in the griever. During the time of acute grief, extreme personality alterations may be considered normal since they can be attributed to the process of detaching from the beloved. Linking the detachment process to personality changes in the griever led Rubin (1981) to formulate a chronological description of this dual process.

- *Disturbed equilibrium.* Loss of the loved one causes intrapsychic, behavioral, and social disequilibrium. Hence the task of grief work and mourning is to restore equilibrium in these areas.
- *Grief work.* During the acute or crisis stage of grief, considerable behavioral and personality changes may be discerned. Such changes indicate that the first requisite of effective grief work has been met, namely, to accept the fact of the loss and begin to detach from the loved one.
- *Mourning.* As grief becomes less acute, grief work gives way to quiet mourning. Detachment proceeds, and changes in behavior and personality either subside or moderate.
- *Restored equilibrium.* Detachment from the loved one is accomplished to the utmost possible extent. Personality and behavioral changes have either disappeared or become entrenched. Equilibrium has been restored, but perhaps not to preloss levels.

Belief that grief has a beginning and an end is prevalent among health care professionals. Many investigators have postulated various stages of grief, generally consisting of *shock, despair, guilt, withdrawal, acceptance,* and *adjustment.* Engel (1964) identified normal grieving as having three stages:

1. Shock and disbelief as denial is used.
2. Awareness and recognition as denial fails.
3. Ritualization and restitution.

There is also belief that when acute grief lasts beyond a few months, chronicity develops due to failure of the detachment process. Silverman and Worden (1992) noted that young children who lost a parent devoted considerable energy to staying connected to the deceased. They did this through dreams, by speaking of the dead parent, thinking of the dead parent, or by preserving keepsakes that belonged to the dead parent. These behaviors were interpreted by the investigators either as efforts to keep the dead parent alive or to make the loss seem real. Such efforts to maintain a connection have sometimes been labeled *dysfunctional* and *problematic.* Dietrich and Shabad (1989) have stressed the need to disengage from the lost one. Other experts disagree, noting that while the parent died, the relationship did not (Siegel et al., 1990). Similar attempts to preserve connections have been observed in parents after the death of a child. Preoccupation with the deceased expressed by talking about the deceased, by reminiscing, and by valuing momentoes may help grief-stricken adults and children adjust to a new social context. This is a process crucial to the normal grief and mourning task (Worden, 1991).

For crisis counselors, the period of acute grief has the greatest impact but prolonged or chronic mourning is also significant. For some individuals the crisis of grief is not resolved once and for all. It may seem dormant, but it is always present and available to be reactivated later in ways that may generate or intensify another crisis. The phenomenon in which the anniversary of a loss revives earlier grief is all too familiar. Thus, related crises may occur periodically even after a loss seems to have been successfully worked through. Neither acute grief nor chronic mourning is always dispelled permanently.

The value of sequential stages of grief and mourning is that observed behaviors can be identified and described. Baker et al. (1992) claimed that stage or phase conceptualizations are oversimplified and are of little clinical value. Instead, they offer a series of time-specific tasks that must be achieved. *Early phase tasks* begin as soon as the individual learns of the death. This phase includes an understanding of what has happened and the use of any protective or defensive mechanisms that guard against the psychological impact of the loss. *Middle phase tasks* include working through the loss and the pain it brings. *Late stage tasks* include reintegration of identity and resumption of age-appropriate developmental tasks. Although the subjects in this study were children, the tasks to be accomplished in each stage are applicable to adults also. Clinical interventions can be tied to the stage of grief the mourner is experiencing. This task-oriented model interprets grieving behaviors as adaptive rather than pathological. Table 2–4 describes the stage–specific tasks of grieving presented by Baker et al.

There is some value in knowing stages of grief, but more important is awareness that differences between normal and abnormal grieving are differences of intensity and not differences of kind. Grief work is painful but indispensable if the crisis of loss is to be resolved. Among the interesting speculations on this topic is the idea that prolonged depression may be a defense against active grieving, since grief work demands painful awareness of loss before restitution can begin.

Identification of crisis stages emerged from clinical observation of individuals and families reacting to disability or bereavement. Although the reactive stages presented by various theoreticians are not always congruent, there are overlapping areas of agreement. Expressions of grief may be individualistic, but, in general, early responses to crisis tend to be defensive. The first impact of crisis due to loss or change activates protective maneuvers, which may take the form of stereotyped or automatic behaviors. The mother of a boy killed in a motorcycle accident will finish the family laundry as if the act of completing ordinary work refutes the fact of the loss. Families whose household effects are destroyed by fire or flood may react numbly, drawing comfort from possession of a single

TABLE 2–4   Phase/Stage-Specific Grief Tasks

Phase/Stage	Significant Tasks
Early grief	Understand that someone has died. Relate the implications to oneself. Engage in protective acts toward self and family members.
Middle grief	Acknowledge reality of the loss. Accept emotional reaction to the loss. Explore and reevaluate the lost relationship. Confront the pain caused by the loss.
Late grief	Restore sense of selfhood and identity. Resume age-appropriate developmental tasks. Invest in new relationships. Cope with periodic resurgence of pain.

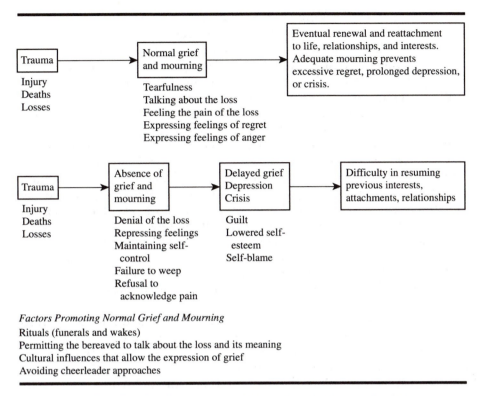

FIGURE 2-1 Comparison of Normal and Abnormal Grief

scorched or water-damaged photograph. Defensive fight-flight behaviors are followed by growing recognition of loss, which precedes the process of adaptation. A crisis sequence as general as defense, acknowledgement, and adaptation has the advantage of wide applicability and requires fewer exceptions than do more particularistic schema. Murphy (1988) reported that bereaved persons suffered mental distress for up to three years, and that the deceased continued to be important for much longer periods. Normal and abnormal grief are compared in Figure 2–1.

INTERVENTION TECHNIQUES

As problem-solving efforts fail, people in crisis tend to withdraw or give up rather than continue a search for solutions. Engel (1964), in the context of depression, called such behavior the "conservation withdrawal" of energy. In crisis situations many people apply their energies not to problem solving, but to relieving their internal distress. The crisis counselor must therefore oppose any feelings of helplessness or ineffectuality expressed by those seeking help. Even in the first therapeutic encounter the counselor must try to mobilize and channel any available resources.

Unless the counselor explores the symbolic meaning of the critical event, it is difficult to understand the intensity of reactions that are being displayed. Frequently, the symbolic meaning of the crisis far outweighs reality. A family man passed over for promotion may in his disappointment discount his impressive accomplishments and feel totally worthless. A depressed mood follows that threatens his family life and his job performance. A college freshman far from home may develop sudden physical symptoms that make leaving school acceptable to the student and the family. An elderly woman may suffer a period of disorientation after moving to a new neighborhood. In each case the response to the situation seems excessive until the symbolic meaning is understood. Even after exploring the meaning of the precipitating event and clarifying its dimensions, the subjective experience of the client should be considered valid. The counselor's assessment should include the amount of confusion and disorganization present, any angry or aggressive impulses toward the self or others, the presence or absence of external supports, and indications of internal strengths.

Crisis counselors should first guide individuals and families toward mastery of whatever immediate circumstances are causing the most distress. Although some emotional expression is allowable, it is advisable even in early sessions to call attention to extreme or irrational feelings on the grounds that these interfere with problem solving. Behavioral distortions should also be questioned, not only the client's behavior, but also the client's interpretation of the behavior of others. Emphasis on rational thinking and on sound reality testing are ongoing. Reducing the immediate turmoil is a prerequisite for problem solving.

In crisis counseling, services should be flexible and accessible, but the primary focus is the crisis situation. The contract for crisis treatment is usually short term, extending no longer than the duration of the crisis. During counseling sessions, which may vary in length from fifteen minutes to an hour, the crisis worker is actively involved but not excessively directive. Although the active stance of the crisis worker may incline clients toward dependency, the dependency is negated by the short-term nature of the relationship. Sometimes crisis contracts are open ended, but the majority are limited to six or eight sessions. An excellent rule for the crisis worker is to avoid making decisions for clients and to restrict interventions to what clients are unable to do without help. Restored functioning and resolution of the crisis through expanded coping behavior is sought. A minimum goal of crisis work is to maintain precrisis levels of functioning. A more ambitious goal is to improve precrisis levels of functioning.

Frequency of meetings is a decision made primarily by the crisis worker. If distress is extreme or, if there is a question of self-destructive-ness or of violence toward others, daily meetings may be necessary. On the other hand, if a reliable support network exists or if the crisis worker wishes to foster autonomy or self-determination, weekly meetings may be deemed sufficient. In all instances, the genuine interest and concern of the crisis worker should be conveyed to the client. Assurances that the crisis worker may be reached by phone are much appreciated by persons in crisis, many of whom do not telephone but are reassured because they are able to call if they choose. For many clients, the phone number of the crisis worker is a talisman that guards against fear of imminent disaster.

Generic or nonspecific crisis intervention is within the ability of many people who are not members of the health care professions, but considerable caution is necessary. Crisis intervention can be quite demanding, especially when people are in a very disorganized state. The crisis counselor, whether professional or nonprofessional, must guard against being manipulated into reinforcing the distortions that are present. Giving specific advice is unwise, and persons seeking help should always be free to follow or to reject advice without jeopardizing the therapeutic relationship. The only times that advice or admonition should be firmly given are those preventing harm to the self or others. Before initiating crisis intervention, the counselor must assess suicidal and homicidal risks, and take appropriate action. This may necessitate family involvement, hospitalization, or communication with police officials.

The crisis counselor must be wary of expecting too much from clients too soon, or of showing disappointment when suggestions are not followed. Including other sources of help in the therapeutic plan discourages dependency and gives clients some options. Self-help organizations are useful adjuncts to crisis work because they demonstrate coping behaviors of people with similar experiences. As crisis counseling proceeds, and new coping methods are introduced and applied, the counselor should make suggestions regarding appropriate resources and referrals.

For many people in crisis the generic, circumscribed approach is sufficient. It is a brief but relatively intense form of work whose purposes are clearly defined. Termination sometimes seems premature to clients, but they have been advised from the start that intervention will be time limited. The temporary nature of acute crisis requires adherence to time limits of the therapeutic contract. It is rarely advisable for a crisis counselor to be involved for more than eight to ten weeks. After that length of time there will be subtle changes in the interactions between counselor and client; interventions can no longer be classified as crisis work. If referrals for additional therapy are indicated, these should be made after the original crisis has subsided and equilibrium has been restored.

Crisis intervention is a circumscribed, time-limited approach; it is a brief but relatively intense modality whose purposes are clearly defined. Termination may sometimes seem premature to clients and even to crisis counselors, but the temporary nature of acute crisis demands adherence to this provision of the therapeutic contract. Shortly before termination, the therapist and client review the problem-solving process and recognize any improvement in coping abilities. If referrals for longer work are indicated, these should be made after the original crisis has subsided and equilibrium has been restored.

CRISIS PREVENTION MODELS

Primary Crisis Prevention

Primary crisis prevention may be defined as crisis work that deals with variables affecting people at risk. The assumptions on which primary crisis prevention is based depend on clinical, investigatory, and epidemiological studies that indicate the incidence (new cases) and prevalence (total cases) of crisis in certain populations. In primary crisis prevention, the aim is to reduce the incidence of crisis in populations at risk by modifying external variables and reinforcing internal coping strengths.

Some life problems are more likely than others to precipitate crisis, just as some individuals are more crisis-prone than others. Precipitating events may be generated by conditions in the external environment or by internal developmental, physiological, and psychological forces. Cultural values, religious beliefs, and social customs may exacerbate or attenuate the crisis potential of certain events. Still, it is possible to predict various situations that are likely to pose hazards for relatively large numbers of people. Interestingly, it is the experience of change itself that is considered hazardous, regardless of any intrinsic positive or negative effects. A career advancement that entails new responsibilities may be as disruptive to equilibrium as a demotion.

Primary crisis prevention provides intervention before the arrival of change through counseling or teaching that emphasizes anticipatory planning. Some life changes arrive without warning, but other impending changes allow time for advance preparation. Populations at risk for crisis are found in perinatal clinics, hospitals, schools and colleges, nursing homes, and facilities for the elderly. Primary crisis prevention may be offered on an individual, group, or community basis. Through anticipatory guidance, people are given the opportunity to select and practice behaviors that are likely to be helpful in the imminent situation.

The premise of anticipatory guidance is that knowledge is strength and that individuals facing crisis are better equipped if they have an idea of what may lie ahead. Increasingly the docile, submissive patient is recognized by health professionals as a person who may have a relatively difficult adjustment to illness. More demanding patients who ask insistent questions about their condition and seek information about proposed treatments frequently achieve a better adjustment than do patients who appear acquiescent or passive. Childbirth education classes that include both of the prospective parents are an example of widely accepted anticipatory guidance. A primary prevention approach used by community nurses working with potential child abusers is to teach parents about the developmental progress of young children. In this way the unrealistic expectations of the parents are reduced and appropriate responses to natural childish behavior can be rehearsed in advance.

Research of Bowlby (1969, 1973, 1980) and others (McCartney & Galanopoulos, 1988; Phillips et al., 1987) centered on attachment and separation between mothers and children. Such studies have resulted in the greater involvement of parents with their ill or hospitalized children, even when treatment schedules must be adjusted. The substitute grandparents program is another primary prevention program that benefits old and young people and reduces the prevalence of crisis stemming from intergenerational distrust. Other examples of primary prevention include premarital counseling by the clergy, bedside teaching by nurses, and orientation programs offered by colleges.

Primary crisis prevention often follows Maslow's hierarchy of needs (1962) by including in its purview physical resources, such as food and shelter, that are necessary for survival; psychological resources, such as love and security, that are necessary for self-esteem; and social resources that encourage the self-actualization necessary for fulfillment.

Secondary Crisis Prevention

Secondary crisis prevention consists of early intervention with persons in crisis in order to restore equilibrium promptly and reduce the severity of distress. During periods of crisis people feel helpless, and their motivation to find solutions is high. Unless remedial crisis counseling is offered early, many people try to manage somehow until they regain equilibrium of sorts, and are no longer amenable to therapeutic interventions. It is during the acute period of crisis that the counselor's influence is the greatest.

During secondary crisis intervention, the individual's disorganization is obvious. What may be less obvious is the effect of the crisis on the entire family. Because the context in which crisis appears is important, secondary crisis measures should include assessment of the strengths and weaknesses of the family system. More often than not it is the family system in which the crisis developed and in which it must be resolved. After the dimensions of the crisis have been noted, and various distortions identified, the client and the crisis counselor jointly develop a plan of action. Here the crisis counselor may be as active as necessary, but no more so. Suggestions may be made, but coercive direction is inadvisable. Solutions must be acceptable to the family and not just to the crisis counselor. One of the most valuable services a crisis counselor can provide is to instill hope within distraught people. Since every crisis inevitably comes to an end, this assurance can be given without reservation.

Throughout the intervention process, attention is paid to whatever strengths and abilities the individual and family possess. Preoccupation with defeat and failure dampens hope. This does not mean that reassurance should be unrealistic, nor should the crisis counselor try to dispel all anxiety. Some anxiety can propel the client toward adaptive problem solving, provided anxiety does not become overwhelming.

Even though secondary prevention involves persons who are already in crisis, group and community programs can be used to their advantage. Parents Anonymous is a group program for actual and potential child abusers. Gamblers Anonymous is a group program for compulsive gamblers trying to overcome the habit. These programs resemble Alcoholics Anonymous, which combines group support with a structured format. Pregnant teenagers comprise another population that is often the recipient of secondary prevention. For this population the most effective programs offer primary and tertiary prevention, in addition to secondary measures needed during the immediate crisis of labor and delivery. Postnatal counseling concerning sexuality, contraception, parenting, and education fall under the rubric of primary and secondary crisis prevention.

Tertiary Crisis Prevention

Tertiary crisis prevention endeavors to reduce any residual impairment that may result from a poorly resolved crisis. Since the thrust of crisis work is to improve functioning rather than personality change, it is possible to educate persons outside the health professions to the need for primary and tertiary intervention and to involve them to a considerable degree. Teachers, scout leaders, and athletic coaches are examples of people who can learn to identify and help persons embarked on a crisis course. These informal care providers can also help individuals who have recently moved from a crisis state to restored homeostasis. If community agents are sensitized through training programs, the media, or ongoing communication with health professionals, they can become important adjuncts in crisis prevention.

•CLINICAL EXAMPLE:
STAGE-RELATED INTERVENTION
FOR A GRIEF REACTION

> For weeks Harriet and Phil had looked forward to attending their fifth college reunion. The morning of their departure they drove to Phil's parents, who had agreed to care for their two-year-old

child, Anabel. On the way their small car collided with a truck and was demolished. Harriet and the child suffered minor injuries; Phil was seriously hurt and was pronounced dead on arrival at the local hospital. Harriet reacted quietly when told of Phil's death. Her child and Phil's parents were very distraught, but Harriet was able to comfort and console them to some extent in the hours after the accident. Some observers commented on the flat, automatic aspect of Harriet's behavior. On an intellectual level she was aware that Phil was gone but her emotions seemed frozen. She made most of the funeral arrangements with the help of other family members, and expressed strong desires to have the kind of funeral "Phil would have wanted."

At the grave site, Harriet lost her composure for the first time. She became agitated and hysterical, screaming violently and throwing herself across her husband's coffin. Relatives pulled her away as she wept and shouted, "No, no—you must come back to me." Harriet had chosen not to have her child come to the cemetery so Anabel did not witness her mother's outburst. By the time the funeral group returned home Harriet was quieter, although she seemed remote and unresponsive to those who expressed their sympathy. The next day she stayed in her room, leaving Anabel in the care of a friend. She spent most of her time in the lounge chair Phil had loved. Dry eyed, she talked about feeling responsible for Phil's death because she had wanted so much to attend the reunion. Her anger was directed toward herself and even toward Anabel. She seemed resentful when well-meaning sympathizers reminded her that she still had a child to live for.

For about a week Harriet refused to leave the bedroom she had shared with Phil. She took no interest in her appearance nor in the grief that Anabel and Phil's parents felt. Harriet's sister became worried by this behavior and consulted the pastor who had officiated at the funeral. It was he who suggested that grief counseling might be helpful.

Critical Guidelines

Because Harriet had no psychiatric history and because her husband's tragic death was so recent, crisis intervention was considered the treatment of choice. In dealing with Harriet, the crisis counselor formulated interventions related to the early tasks of grief resolution. Harriet's initial tasks included gaining an understanding of what had happened and overcoming her feelings of personal responsibility for Phil's death. Until the funeral she had been numbed by what had happened and she was able to deny her loss by comforting family members who shared her loss. Only at the cemetery, when her husband's body was lowered into the ground, did Harriet realize the permanence of her loss. She felt ashamed of her histrionic behavior and resolved not to lose control again. Her retreat to her room was an attempt to remain composed by avoiding any references to Phil's death. Instead of drawing closer to grieving family members, Harriet isolated herself. She was angry with herself, with Anabel, and with Phil's parents because they were alive and he was not.

Harriet's inability to cry and her unstated resentment of Anabel concerned the counselor. Her intense anger and her guilt for feeling angry frightened Harriet. She was afraid that if she gave way to grief, these bewildering feelings would become obvious to everyone. Counseling sessions dealt with Harriet's mixed feelings of love and rage at supportive family members. She was assured that such feelings were not unusual, that grief work was hard and painful, and that her inability or unwillingness to weep and accept sympathy were adding to her trauma. In the safety of counseling sessions Harriet was able to acknowledge her loss by crying and by verbalizing her conflicted feelings. The counselor encouraged Harriet not to withdraw from others, but to share her need for help. Her dealings with Anabel were especially destructive because Harriet had distanced herself from her daughter when the child was already feeling deprived and abandoned.

Before terminating the therapeutic contract with Harriet, the counselor invited Anabel and Phil's parents to the last session. Here the emphasis was on reuniting the family, on remembering the deceased, and on sharing memories. Although grief counseling was provided for only two months, Harriet was functioning at a more normal level. She was given the option of joining a support group for the recently widowed but had not yet made a decision.

Studies of bereavement indicate that grief-related pain may persist for years after a loss, especially if the death was sudden and tragic. No precise point has been established for full recovery from grief. Time may be a healer but it is not always a predictable element. It is the process or the way in which people handle grief rather than the duration that is most significant. In times of mourning prompt crisis counseling helps people understand their feelings and integrate the loss into their life experience.

Harriet's indecision to join a support group immediately was understandable in light of her grief stage. Instead of turning away from family members she had learned to turn toward them. After a loss like hers it is not unusual for family members to become dependent on one another for understanding and relief. In time Harriet will become less preoccupied with her grief and more willing to establish relationships with other people. Through counseling Harriet was able to reach out to her daughter, whose suffering was as great as her own. The loss of a parent activates great fear in children, who often feel they may be abandoned by the surviving parent. Even though Anabel was tenderly cared for by relatives, she needed to hear from her mother that she is cherished and will not be abandoned. The plight of Anabel was aggravated by her mother's behavior and inability to look beyond her own grief.

It is normal for people who have suffered loss to withdraw to some extent, but not totally or for long periods of time. One of the most common signs of a worrisome grief reaction is stoicism, or the failure to cry or express sadness about the death. Extreme regression and apparent refusal to display grief, even with trusted friends or family members, are signals that crisis intervention may be necessary.

•CLINICAL EXAMPLE:
INTERVENTION IN A GRIEF CRISIS

Joel Benson, aged thirty-five years, married, and the father of three children, was attacked about 2 A.M. by unknown persons and beaten savagely. His wallet and car were taken by the assailants. Joel was left unconscious on a city street, his inert body soon concealed by falling snow. The next morning he was found by police and taken by ambulance to a nearby hospital, where he was pronounced dead on arrival. Joel's body lay unclaimed in the city morgue for two days until his brother arrived to make an identification.

Family grief for Joel's death was intensified by the circumstances in which he died. A police investigation revealed that Joel had been on his way home after being with another woman. Because of the severe beating he suffered, his body was badly mutilated, so much so that no family except his brother viewed the body before burial. The decision was made jointly by Joel's wife and his brother. Despite the discovery of Joel's extramarital affair and the sordid circumstances of his death, Joel's wife mourned for her husband. Unlike Joel's wife, his mother was told no details of her son's death except that he had been robbed, knocked unconscious, and died of exposure. The two women closest to Joel, his wife and his mother, remained separate and self-contained in their grief; but both of them appeared to overcome the acute crisis of loss successfully. Joel's wife, in particular, comforted and was comforted by the presence of her children.

About six months after the tragedy, Joel's mother began to behave strangely. Even though she had attended the funeral service and seen the casket interred, she began to question whether her son was really dead. Within a short time she became convinced that her son was still alive. She reasoned that the blow on his head had caused amnesia and that Joel was somewhere in the city waiting for her to find him. Her daughter-in-law and her surviving son tried vainly to persuade her that Joel was actually dead. She began to see men on the street, in shops, and in automobiles who resembled her lost son. She followed men who reminded her of her son, sometimes trying to engage them in conversation until closer contact showed them to be strangers. Eventually her actions became so bizarre that she was referred to a community mental health center for help.

Critical Guidelines

The goal set for Joel's mother was to help her recognize the death of her son, to experience the pain of permanent loss, and to immerse herself in active grieving for a time. Only then would she to able to complete the detachment process. The well-meant protection of her family was interpreted as an influence that helped perpetuate her denial. In addition, the subterfuge of the family contributed to her accurate conviction that important information was being withheld from her.

A time-limited crisis model was used to facilitate grief work for Joel's mother. All the adult members of the Benson family were invited to a series of six weekly meetings coordinated by a crisis worker. At these sessions Joel's death was discussed frankly and openly. Family members explained their motives for not being candid with Joel's mother and admitted that their decision was ill advised. During the meetings the family talked and wept together. Joel's widow talked about the bitterness she felt toward her husband, even though she grieved for him. Joel's brother described the battered body of his brother and his own lonely ordeal of going to the city morgue to identify the corpse. The sixth meeting of the series was attended by the entire family, including Joel's children. Encouraged by the crisis worker, the family arranged to meet at the cemetery on a sunny day. Together they planted flowers on the grave as Joel's mother began the painful work of acknowledgment, detachment, and restitution.

SUMMARY

Crisis should not be confused with stress and emergency situations, neither of which contains the growth potential of crisis resolution. The disequilibrium characteristic of crisis may lead to productive outcomes, such as improved coping ability and less dysfunction. In formulating crisis theory, the contributions of Lindemann (1944) and Caplan (1964), among others, emphasize the usefulness of crisis intervention, and its applicability in primary, secondary, and tertiary preventive models. Generic crisis work is relevant for individuals, families, and communities who are in a temporary state of disequilibrium. It is an intense, time-limited modality directed to the resolution of a particular problem or situation.

Crisis theory has enhanced our understanding of grief and mourning as necessary and adaptive reactions to loss. Several theorists have proposed sequential models of grief reactions but many are merely descriptive. Recent studies offer task-related stages of grief. Stage-related tasks indicate the readiness of mourners to accomplish grief work and move on. Clinical interventions can then be presented that are compatible with the stage of task accomplishment that the mourners are experiencing.

REFERENCES

Baker, J.E., M.A. Sedney, and E. Gross. "Psychological Tasks for Bereaved Children." *American Journal of Orthopsychiatry* 62(1992): 105–116.

Bowlby, J. "Attachment." In *Attachment and Loss,* vol. I. New York: Basic Books, 1969.

———. "Separation." In *Attachment and Loss,* vol. II. New York: Basic Books, 1973.

———. "Loss." In *Attachment and Loss,* vol. III. New York: Basic Books, 1980.

Caplan, G. *Principles of Community Psychiatry* New York: Basic Books, 1964.

Dietrich, D.R., and P.C. Shabad *The Problem of Loss and Mourning.* Madison, Connecticut International Universities Press, 1989.

Duvall, E.M. *Marriage and Family Development,* 5th ed. Philadelphia: Lippincott, 1977.

Engel, G.H. "Grief and Grieving." *American Journal of Nursing* 64(1964): 93–98.

Erikson, E.H. *Childhood and Society.* New York: Norton, 1963.

Freud, S. *Mourning and Melancholia,* Complete Works, vol. 14. London: Hogarth and the Institute of Psychoanalysis, 1953.

Lindemann, E. "Symptomology and Management of Acute Grief." *American Journal of Psychiatry* 101(1944): 141–148.

Maslow, A. Toward a Psychology of Being New York: Van Nostrand 1962.

McCartney, K., and A. Galanopoulos. "Child Care and Attachment: A New Frontier the Second Time Around." *American Journal of Orthopsychiatry* 58(1988): 16–24.

Murphy, S.A. "Mental Distress and Recovery in a High Risk Bereavement Sample Three Years After Untimely Death." *Nursing Research* 37(1988): 30–35.

Phillips, D., K. McCartney, S. Scarr, and C. Howes. "Child Care Quality and Children's Social Development." *Developmental Psychology* 23(1987): 537–543.

Rubin, S. "A Two Track Model of Bereavement: Theory and Application in Research." *American Journal of Orthopsychiatry* 51(1981): 101–109.

Selye, H. *The Stress of Life.* New York: McGraw-Hill, 1956.

Siegel, K., V.H. Raveis, B. Bettes, et al. "Perceptions of Parental Competence While Facing the Death of a Spouse." *American Journal of Orthopsychiatry* 64(1990): 567–576.

Silverman, P.R., and J.W. Worden. "Children's Reactions in the Early Months After the Death of a Parent." *American Journal of Orthopsychiatry* 62(1992): 93–104.

Sullivan, H.S. *The Interpersonal Theory of Psychiatry.* New York: Norton, 1953.

Worden, J.W. *Grief Counseling and Grief Therapy: A Handbook for Mental Health Practitioners,* 2nd ed. New York: Springer, 1991.

3

Analyses of Crisis
Expanding the Framework

By speaking of our misfortunes we often relieve them.

Pierre Corneille

No one discipline or school of thought can claim crisis theory as its own, for the theory has been derived from a variety of sources. The result, therefore, is an eclectic framework that is deceptively simple but is drawn in part from general systems theory, psychoanalytic theory, adaptational theory, and interpersonal theory.

SYSTEMS THEORY AND CRISIS

The terrain of human behavior is so vast that a single perspective can reveal only certain features. Although somewhat reductionistic, systems theory has the virtue of showing relationships and interdependence among people, and between people and events. A systems approach to human behavior is comprehensive enough to organize disparate concepts into a coherent framework, even though the multiple structural and functional aspects of human relationships may not be fully addressed. In a discussion of family systems, Carter and McGoldrick (1980) noted the importance of simultaneously adopting a horizontal and a vertical perspective. A horizontal view encompasses the everyday stress and tensions of family life, whereas a vertical view encompasses intergenerational patterns of relating and functioning. Among the organizational strengths of systems theory are the following concepts:

- Systems theory differentiates functional and dysfunctional behaviors. This distinction facilitates identification of individual and family interactions for which corrective feedback may be necessary.

41

- Systems theory interprets much of human behavior as an adjustment between social demands and personal needs. Developmental changes and situational stressors confronting individuals and families require an ongoing process of adjustment and adaptation within a system or among several systems.
- Systems theory includes external influences (input) and internal responses (output) that affect the social, biological, and psychological expressions of human behavior.

Each of the concepts helps orient students of human behavior, even though systems theory is probably most effective when it is buttressed by other frameworks. Therapeutic interventions based on a systems approach address complex relationships in order to help individuals, families, and groups adjust to conditions or alter conditions in ways that produce greater satisfaction for the participants.

Tension

Tension is a useful systems concept that is related to stress and stressors. When tension is excessive, pressure arises within and between interrelated components of the system. A state of tension results that can become unbearable, causing components of the system to break down, or connections between components to be severed. Human beings can experience tension physiologically through organs or organ systems, or psychologically through subjective discomfort. Tension results in a sense of restlessness and urgent desire for relief from feelings of anxiety. Thus tension may be described as an intervening variable connecting anxiety to behaviors motivated by a conscious or unconscious search for relief from anxiety.

PSYCHOANALYTIC THEORY AND CRISIS

Psychoanalytic concepts that attempt to explain the mysteries of human behavior are more individualistic and deterministic than the concepts of systems theory. In psychoanalysis, the technique of free association is used by the therapist to bring repressed experiences to conscious awareness to achieve insight, alter behavior patterns, and improve the quality of life. The phenomenon of transference allows the therapist to become a screen on which the client projects unconscious distortions originating in the past, thus permitting the enactment of a corrective emotional experience that releases psychological energy previously unavailable to the client.

Early psychoanalytic work was of relatively brief duration, but gradually the process became lengthier. The technique of free association demands passivity and neutrality from the therapist, which, along with transference, prolongs the therapeutic process, for there is virtually no limit to the distortions of early life that utilize images of mother, father, siblings, and others projected on the analyst so as to promote insight. *Insight* refers to the ability to establish connections between behaviors and their underlying motivation. The acquisition of insight during psychoanalysis is a cognitive and emotional process achieved through free association, transference phenomena, and the therapeutic reenactment of earlier experiences as the client's resistance to change is moderated and maladaptive behaviors relinquished.

During the 1920s some attempts were made to shorten the time needed for psychoanalysis. Ferenczi (1926) modified traditional analysis by introducing calculated interventions that encouraged clients to disclose their fantasies and provoked frustration in the client so as to heighten willingness to change. Rank (1929) devoted considerable attention to the traumatic experience of birth and advocated nine gestational months of psychotherapy to counter the adverse emotional experience of leaving the womb. Despite the advocacy of Ferenczi and Rank, Freud was opposed to shortening the length of psychoanalysis. His stance impeded the movement toward briefer therapeutic encounters and strengthened adherence to psychoanalytic treatment, which sometimes seemed endlessly prolonged.

Almost two decades later, Alexander and French (1946) proposed other drastic revisions of the psychoanalytic protocol followed by most traditionalists. What the revisionists sought was the substitution of active, brief psychotherapy for the tedious methods of classic psychoanalysis then in vogue. Their suggestions were ignored for a time even in the face of growing demand for mental health services. It was not until the work of Lindemann and Caplan became known that brief psychotherapy was considered to have intrinsic value.

Although Freud questioned the merits of brief therapeutic encounters, he formulated two hypotheses that are of inestimable value in understanding crisis theory. One was the principle of *psychic determinism,* which challenged the premise that human behavior is accidental or random. Psychic determinism is a theory of causality that assumes that all behavior is purposeful and meaningful, and that the causes of behavior originate in the previous experiences of individuals, regardless of conscious awareness of the reasons for their behavior. Another formulation helpful in understanding crisis theory is the concept that psychic energy is finite and limited in amount. This concept, along with psychic determinism, helps to explain the disequilibrium of crisis that develops when customary coping skills fail and psychological energy is depleted.

ADAPTATIONAL THEORY AND CRISIS

Among other theorists, Rado (Weiner, 1985) rejected psychic determinism as the overriding causation for human behavior. Although the importance of the past was not entirely rejected by Rado, therapeutic emphasis was placed on the immediate experience. The impact of previous experience was acknowledged, but new and adaptive behaviors were introduced and practiced until they became natural and spontaneous for the client. Insight was sought, not through free association, but through acquiring and adapting new behaviors. The activities of learning and perfecting new behaviors were regarded as more essential than insight alone, which was not considered a primary goal but merely a milestone in the advance toward adaptive functioning. Rado also recognized the psychological effects of pain and pleasure on human beings, and identified the presence of interactive variables other than instinctual drives and childhood experience in molding behavior. Many clinicians today are associated with adaptational goals that emphasize the reciprocal interactions of individuals with their environment. Among the interactive variables seen as contributing to maladaptation are the following attitudes:

Overdependence on other people.
Overreliance on intellectualization.
Overattachment to limited sources of gratification.

Failure to adapt to changing circumstances may precipitate disorganization in certain individuals. Therefore, therapeutic interventions are aimed at improving and refining adaptational skills. The therapist acts as teacher and educator for the client. In return the client becomes an active learner in a cognitive and affective process of adapting and growing.

Adaptational theory has many positive implications for crisis work. First, adaptation avoids the health-illness polarities of the medical model and offers instead a meaningful way to differentiate minimal, adequate, and maximal adjustment. In using an adaptational approach, one may describe a functioning person as someone whose physical and psychological equipment sustains a comfortable sense of security and well-being. A dysfunctional person is one whose physical and psychological equipment does not permit successful adaptation. This failure imposes various threats to well-being and sometimes imperils survival.

It is possible to identify prevailing behavioral patterns in individuals, although most persons have a repertoire of available responses from which to choose. Moreover, several dysfunctional behaviors may be expressed either simultaneously or sequentially. For example, an employee experiencing frustration on the job may displace anger to family members or friends who are unlikely to retaliate. In addition, hostility may be projected to co-workers in the mistaken belief that they are antagonists. These psychological defenses of displacement and projection may be expressed through belligerence, withdrawal, depression, or defeatism. Essential to effective adaptation is the ability to learn from, but not be controlled by, past experience; to appraise the demands of the moment; and to respond selectively to the current situation. Although constrained to some extent by individual potential and social resources, adaptiveness is considered a behavior that can be acquired or improved through appropriate intervention.

INTERPERSONAL THEORY AND CRISIS

Interpersonal relationships from infancy through adulthood were a major concern of Sullivan (1953), who saw human personality as the product of a network of social arrangements. The self-system of every individual is based on the reflected appraisals of others, and psychological disturbances are considered to be reactions to difficult life situations. In his work, Sullivan used direct communication between client and therapist, avoiding free association. One of the most profound tenets of this interpersonal framework is the theorem of *reciprocal emotion,* which states that persons who think well of themselves tend to think well of other people, while persons deficient in self-esteem tend to perceive other people as equally unworthy. Individuals who lack a sense of self-worth project their feelings of worthlessness to others. The result is that they believe themselves to be surrounded by enemies inhabiting a harsh and treacherous world. Such individuals are often victims of self-fulfilling prophecy. Anticipating injury, they search for it and are seldom disappointed. Expecting not to be successful, they have a propensity for meeting failure and disappointment.

When children are highly valued and treated tenderly, they experience the self as good. When children are subjected to harshness and disapproval, they think of themselves as bad, with consequent feelings of worthlessness, anger, and anxiety. These children develop malevolent attitudes toward a world that always seems threatening. Their basic perceptions have been determined by negative interpersonal experiences that propel them into similar experiences in later life. Sullivan attributed anxiety to the ever-present need for approval from significant persons. If approval is forthcoming, a child experiences a pleasurable state of euphoria, which Sullivan termed the *absence of anxiety.* It is the child's attempt to obtain approval and preserve euphoria, combined with attitudes emanating from significant persons, that help determine susceptibility to anxiety.

In work based on interpersonal theory, the clinician is neither screen nor teacher but a participant observer. Throughout the therapeutic encounter both clinician and client are engaged in an unfolding relationship in which the client's interactional patterns are identified. Verbal and nonverbal components of the encounter are used to point out behaviors and experiences that have brought the client to the present impasse. The interpersonal framework uses the therapeutic session as an intricate transaction that is structured by the clinician. In utilizing an interpersonal approach to crisis work, a clinician may adopt the following guidelines for structuring the sessions:

- Ascertain the presenting problem brought to the session. For example, the presenting complaint of a troubled wife may be her husband's infidelity, but the actual problem is the couple's inability to tolerate their middle years without the presence of children in the home. In this event the presenting problem will be the initial focus of attention. If the couple is willing, the underlying problem may be addressed later.
- Estimate the relative amount of pleasure and pain currently experienced by the client or clients, as well as the sources of gratification and frustration experienced in daily life.
- Investigate attributes and abilities that clients either value or devalue in themselves. For instance, a college honors student might discount academic achievement and consider scholarship effete compared with being a member of a varsity team.
- Observe the defensive behaviors used by clients to maintain feelings of security. Defensive behaviors might include selective inattention, focal awareness, denial, repression, projection, and rationalization. All issues that elicit security behaviors are deserving of attention, even if they are not directly confronted during crisis intervention.
- Adhere to the short-term contract required in crisis work but make referrals for more intensive help if necessary after the crisis has been resolved.

ROLE OF ANXIETY IN CRISIS

A major factor in the disequilibrium of crisis is the presence of anxiety, which has been described as the most unpleasant human experience, with the possible exception of loneliness (Sullivan, 1953). *Signal anxiety* was the term Freud used to denote a response to anticipated threat that signaled ego forces to oppose the threat. Simply stated, signal anxiety represents internal mobilization against perceived external dangers. *Castration anxiety* is another psychoanalytic term applied to anxiety that produces guilt and activates the superego; it can be generalized to include any fear of punishment or reprisal. *Separation anxiety,* as described by Rank (1945), is an experiential state first encountered at birth and repeated periodically throughout life until final separation occurs in the form of death. A connection between anxiety and hostility was identified by Horney (1939), who believed that anxiety originated in fears of interpersonal rejection. Erikson (1963) distinguished between fears of recognizable peril and anxiety, which is likely to be disproportionate to the actual threat.

Despite semantic differences, there is agreement that anxiety is a distressing state characterized by diffuse feelings of apprehension, uncertainty, and imminent disaster. The causes of anxiety are variously ascribed to separation, isolation, alienation, disapproval, fear of punishment, withdrawal of love, and disruption of meaningful relatedness. Any circumstance that constitutes a threat to inner security, whether psychological or biological, is likely to generate an uncomfortable amount of anxiety.

Anxiety appears in varying amounts and with varying frequency. For some individuals, anxiety is a characterological trait rather than an occasional state or condition. The turmoil of the anxiety-prone person has been aptly described by Freud, who wrote that for some persons there is "a quantum of anxiety in a free floating condition which in any state of expectation controls the selection of ideas and is ever ready to attach itself to any suitable ideational content" (Thompson, 1957). In other words, diffuse anxiety tends to find any means to perpetuate itself in susceptible individuals. Chronic anxiety is of long duration and relatively low intensity. Acute anxiety is of shorter duration and relatively high intensity. For anxiety-prone persons, periods of acute anxiety are all too common, and chronic anxiety is a respite between frequent periods of greater discomfort. These individuals have fluctuating levels of discomfort with acute periods of severe anxiety superimposed on chronicity.

Anxiety has the power to generate energy, but when levels are excessive the energy becomes undirected and disintegrative. (See Table 3–1.) Mild anxiety, however, releases energy that can be directed toward problem solving. Moderate anxiety causes decreased efficiency, whereas more severe anxiety leads to frustration and feelings of entrapment. When anxiety is severe enough to be called *panic*, all available energy is directed toward escape. If escape is impossible, there is temporary disintegration of personality that may evoke destructive behavior toward oneself or others. Disequilibrium that accompanies crisis is a reflection of anxiety that hovers between severe and panic levels.

For all persons in crisis, anxiety is a common denominator that can become the impetus for disequilibrium. Since restoration of equilibrium is essential, the crisis worker must offer enough reassurance to foster a sense of relative safety and security. Excessive solicitude is likely to encourage regression; nevertheless, the competence and assurance of the crisis worker can be used to transmit confidence to the client as problem

TABLE 3-1   Anxiety: Levels, Characteristics, and Interventions

Euphoria	Mild Anxiety	Moderate Anxiety	Severe Anxiety	Panic
Absence of anxiety. Sense of well-being.	Alertness and vigilance.	Reduced perception, concentration, communication.	Selective perception and attention. Subjective distress.	Perceptual distortions. Inability to communicate. Inability to function.
Interventions Maintain connections to reality.	Reconcile demands of the situation and expectations of the individual. Trace connections between causes and manifestations of anxiety.		Encourage motor activity. Facilitate cognitive and affective expression (walking, talking, crying).	Provide structure and direction until anxiety decreases.

Source: Adapted from Sullivan (1953) and Peplau (1952).

solving begins. Prolonged interrogation is less meaningful than interacting with the client while assessing the disequilibrium. The anxious person may display forgetting, circumstantiality, and selective inattention. In describing the chronology of events, a client may be unreliable concerning details. Usually unreliability indicates disorganization rather than conscious intent to deceive. Contradictory statements also indicate disorganization rather than deception.

In crisis work, assessment is ongoing. This principle is important to keep in mind because the disorganization of the client may preclude extensive investigation. The history of a hazardous event, review of failed coping attempts, and assessment of resulting disequilibrium provide a natural sequence as the crisis worker guides the client from the disordered present to the immediate past. Clients may or may not know exactly what led to the crisis, nor why they feel overwhelmed with anxiety. Hope and some expectation of success are necessary to motivate clients who are in crisis. Because mild levels of anxiety are facilitative, as opposed to severe levels, which are disruptive, a central task of clinicians working with anxious clients is to help clients tolerate mild levels of anxiety and utilize anxiety as a constructive, rather than a destructive, force. Delineating the outlines of the actual crisis and exploring problem-solving efforts of the immediate past are interventions that help clients reduce anxiety to manageable levels. The timing of interventions is important, for there are limits to the ability of clients in crisis to move rapidly toward insight or to understand dynamic interpretations of the causes for their difficulties.

Physiological outlets are available for expressing anxiety, usually by means of a hyperactive sympathetic nervous system. Sweating, tachycardia, pupillary changes, hyperventilation, and gastrointestinal symptoms are some of the ways in which anxiety finds physiological expression. Anxiety is akin to fear, but when fear becomes anxiety there is a shift from recognition of a known threat to an inner apprehension that may overwhelm the individual. One cannot run away from anxiety just as one cannot run away from guilt, because both are internal experiences that operate independently of external reality.

The clinical implications of anxiety have been studied by a number of nurse-theorists, and the concept of anxiety has been accepted as a valid nursing diagnosis. The most extensive investigation of anxiety by a nurse-theorist was done by Hildegarde Peplau. In work that has become a prototype of nursing theory, Peplau developed an operational definition of the term *anxiety,* discussed causes and effects of anxiety, and outlined four progressive levels of anxiety, along with appropriate interventions at each level (Peplau, 1952).

Preferred behavioral patterns often constitute a means of handling anxiety. Therefore, behavior can be both a manifestation of anxiety and a defense against the discomfort it brings. During the disequilibrium of crisis, individuals are frustrated as well as anxious. The cause of frustration is the inability to resolve the crisis successfully, and the effect of frustration is a feeling of deprivation or entrapment. Responses to frustration are individualistic. Some frustrated persons will experiment with one solution after another, searching for new ways of coping as soon as ineffective methods are discarded. Other individuals procrastinate, becoming irresolute and indecisive. Not infrequently, frustrated persons grow angry, projecting their feelings of inadequacy to the crisis worker, who is then labeled inept, or displacing their feelings on any other available target. Other frustrated persons measure their own worth against events over which they have little control and attribute their predicament to their own deficiencies. Self-deprecation is counterproductive, since it gives rise to feelings of helplessness and hopelessness. Behaviors apparent during the disequilibrium of crisis are often variations of the following patterns:

1. *Fight-flight behavior:* Blaming, avoidance.
2. *Conflicted behavior:* Ambivalence, irresolution.
3. *Helpless behavior:* Dependency, passivity.
4. *Hopeless behavior:* Regression, surrender.

Fight-flight behavior may take the form of blaming others (fight) or of evading responsibility (flight). Conflicted behavior may be expressed through ambivalence or through tendencies to fulfill obligations partially but not entirely. Helplessness takes the form of overt dependency and reluctance to participate in problem solving. Hopelessness produces surrender behavior and regression expressed through apathy and withdrawal. Identification of prevailing behavior patterns is an essential part of assessment during meetings between clients and crisis workers.

TYPES OF CRISIS WORK

Treatment methods in crisis work are similar to other forms of treatment that attempt to alter behavior within a short time period. Not all crisis intervention comes under the rubric of psychotherapy, but there are broad distinctions that can be applied to both. In general, brief psychotherapy may be divided into two classifications based on objectives and the characteristics of clients for whom they are suitable. Sifneos (1967, 1980) described two types of brief psychotherapy: (1) anxiety provoking or dynamic, and (2) anxiety suppressive or supportive. The criteria for patient selection, the intervention strategies, and the outcome objectives of the two types of treatment are quite divergent.

Short-term Anxiety-provoking Treatment

Essential to short-term anxiety-provoking treatment is the belief that a certain level of anxiety is needed to motivate clients to examine the underlying dynamics or causes that produce maladaptive behaviors. Although the clinician monitors proceedings so that overwhelming anxiety is avoided, confrontation and interpretation are employed to explore the client's customary behavioral responses. It is not necessary or even desirable that interventions be unduly harsh, but it is important that they be more than merely supportive. Improved functioning can sometimes be obtained through exploratory interventions that promote introspection, identify similarities between the current situation and earlier situations, and make connections between present and previous behavioral responses.

Anxiety-provoking brief treatment can be further divided into therapy that lasts from two months up to one year, and crisis work that lasts up to two months. In anxiety-provoking crisis work, the client is in a state of temporary disorganization because of a developmental or situational impasse. Interventions are directed toward alleviating the crisis by examining the circumstances, behaviors of the present and the immediate past, and the accompanying emotional experience. As with all crisis work, the therapeutic contract covers a period of six to eight weeks, at which point the crisis will have abated. Treatment may then be terminated or a referral made for additional help that is not crisis oriented. All forms of anxiety-provoking treatment, whether limited to six weeks or lasting a year, include within their purview some degree of behavioral or psychological change and also offer anticipatory guidance for the future. For purposes of clarification, traditional psychoanalysis is a form of anxiety-provoking therapy that may last several years.

Certain requirements must be met before short-term anxiety-provoking treatment is attempted. First, the clinician must have comprehensive knowledge of psychodynamics. Although this type of therapy is offered by psychiatrists, psychologists, social workers, and psychiatric nurses, it should be performed only by experienced individuals who possess a graduate degree in their discipline and have access to qualified supervision or consultation.

Selection of candidates for anxiety-provoking brief therapy should be done very carefully. In this form of treatment, clients must have sufficient psychological strength to withstand increased levels of anxiety, since anxiety is used to induce clients to alter their behavioral responses. According to Sifneos (1967, 1980), clients suitable for anxiety-provoking treatment should meet the following criteria:

Clients must have at least average intelligence.
Clients must have at least one meaningful relationship.
Clients must have an identifiable problem.
Clients must be interested in solving the problem.
Clients must be willing to set realistic goals.
Clients must be able to express emotion or affect.

Anxiety-provoking Crisis Intervention

Sometimes called *exploratory crisis work,* anxiety-provoking crisis intervention attempts to maintain or improve the client's coping skills by means of techniques that emphasize the following issues:

Rapport between client and clinician.
Review of sequence leading to crisis.
Analysis of coping behaviors and skills.
Introduction of alternative coping methods.
Anticipatory guidance for future crisis events.

During the period of anticipatory guidance, current problems are related to earlier problems and to similar experiences likely to occur at a future time. Opportunities are provided to plan and rehearse new behaviors that are likely to avert crisis or facilitate future problem solving.

Selection criteria for candidates being considered for anxiety-provoking crisis work resemble criteria used in exploratory work of longer duration. Both types of anxiety-provoking work attempt to produce limited change in a context that considers more than the current circumstances. Both utilize a review of previous problems and a preview of future problems to resolve present problems. In both forms of anxiety-provoking treatment, emphasis is on learning and problem solving through exploration of reciprocal transactions and regulation of anxiety as a force for change.

Short-term Anxiety-suppressive Treatment

Supportive or anxiety-suppressive treatment may also be divided into brief treatment that lasts from two months to one year, and crisis treatment that lasts up to six or eight weeks. Supportive or anxiety-suppressive treatment, regardless of its exact duration, is usually selected for somewhat disturbed persons who have a history of poor adjustment and inadequate social relationships. Such individuals require prompt symptomatic relief, which is best provided by supportive interventions. In this approach, the clinician tries to mitigate as soon as possible the elements causing disorganization in a client who is susceptible to further decompensation. Emotional support, environmental manipulation, and reassurances are essential, whether supportive work is limited to the time of crisis or extended over the course of a year.

Since reduction of distress is mandatory for vulnerable clients, supportive treatment may be offered daily or several times a week during the initial phase of the therapeutic contract. Sessions may last only fifteen minutes or they may be longer, depending on the assessment of the client's needs. It is helpful for the crisis worker to demonstrate availability and genuine commitment to the client. The minimizing of anxiety is extremely important. Although previous difficulties may be touched on, more attention is paid to the current situation. The regulatory functions of the clinician are devoted to lowering anxiety levels, relieving subjective distress, and resolving immediate problems.

Anxiety-suppressive Crisis Work

Vulnerable clients in the throes of a crisis are appropriate candidates for anxiety-suppressive crisis intervention. In these circumstances, priority is given to relieving anxiety and restoring function so that problem solving around critical issues may begin. Supportive crisis work may be used to help individuals surmount situational or developmental tasks that have caused or may cause severe decompensation. As in all crisis work, it may be advisable after expiration of the acute period to refer clients for additional help. Occasionally an individual who has received supportive crisis intervention may be strengthened sufficiently to tolerate later treatment of an exploratory or anxiety-provoking nature.

Generic vs. Individual Crisis Work

The choice of anxiety-provoking or anxiety-suppressive treatment depends largely on the characteristics of the client. Another methodological distinction can be made based on the nature of the crisis and the qualifications of the care providers. If the crisis is of a universal or developmental nature and if the care provider is not an expert in psychodynamic theory, a generic route to crisis intervention may be selected. In generic crisis work, attention is paid only to the crisis episode, and similar interventions are applied to all affected members of a group or to all persons facing similar crises. An example of generic crisis work is the encouragement of active grieving in virtually all persons who have suffered loss, regardless of the idiosyncratic experiences of the persons involved. The individual approach to crisis work demands an assessment of the unique needs of each client so that interventions are formulated that are specific to the individual and the circumstances. Anxiety-provoking crisis intervention is invariably an individualized form of treatment, since the deliberate heightening of anxiety requires the presence of a skilled therapist. Anxiety-suppressive treatment may be either generic or individualized, depending on the relative amount of attention paid to dynamic factors, and on the place of the current crisis episode within the context of the psychological experience and reciprocal behaviors of the client. Table 3–2 shows the distinguishing features of anxiety-suppressing and anxiety-provoking treatment approaches.

•CLINICAL EXAMPLE:
ALTERNATIVE TREATMENT APPROACHES FOR THE ANXIOUS CLIENT

Jim Hall was an eighteen-year-old high school graduate referred to a mental health center by the emergency department of an urban hospital. Shortly after finishing high school, Jim applied for work with the U.S. Postal Service, an agency in which his father was a valued employee with twenty-five years of continuous service. While waiting to begin the written examination required for employment, Jim suffered a severe anxiety attack. His somatic symptoms of sweating, trembling, tachycardia, and hyperventilating were extreme enough for bystanders to believe that Jim was having a heart attack. An ambulance was called and Jim was taken to the nearest hospital, where his symptoms soon subsided. Jim was kept under observation for forty-eight hours. When medical tests revealed no organic disorder, Jim was

TABLE 3–2 Anxiety-provoking and Anxiety-suppressing Treatment Approaches

Type of Treatment	Duration	Goals	Client Characteristics
Anxiety-provoking brief therapy	2 months to 1 year	Problem solving Exploration Psychological growth Behavioral change Anticipatory guidance	Psychological stability Social resources Average intelligence or more emotional expressiveness
Anxiety-provoking crisis therapy	6 to 8 weeks	Problem solving Situational change Exploration Behavioral change Anticipatory guidance	Psychological stability Social resources Average intelligence or more crisis disequilibrium emotional expressiveness
Anxiety-suppressive brief therapy	2 months to 1 year	Support reassurance Symptom relief Problem solving Behavioral change Anticipatory guidance	Emotional vulnerability Possible deterioration
Anxiety-suppressive crisis work	6 to 8 weeks	Support reassurance Symptom relief Situational change Problem solving Anticipatory guidance	Emotional vulnerability Crisis disequilibrium Imminent deterioration

discharged and referred to a crisis team working in a mental health center. The group was an interdisciplinary unit that functioned as a treatment and referral team for persons without previous psychiatric history.

Jim's anxiety attack was interpreted as a response to his ambivalence about being a post office employee. Questioning Jim about his high school years led to a rhapsodic description of his interest in camping and the outdoors. Jim expressed strong dislike for the confines of cities and said that his ambition was to work as a forest ranger. However, he had never considered this ambition to be realistic, nor had he ever been led to believe that one's job should be rewarding, except in monetary terms. One worked in order to live, and it was a foregone conclusion that one's life work would be routine and monotonous. Jim had watched his father on his daily rounds, carrying a heavy mail bag and trudging endlessly over the same city streets. The prospect of the same job intimidated Jim, but he hesitated to oppose his father's wish that he take advantage of the security offered by a post office job. In discussing treatment for Jim, two alternative approaches were considered by the crisis team.

Alternative One: Anxiety-suppressive Crisis Work. The crisis worker encouraged Jim's fondness for the outdoors and his timid wish for a career that would allow him to express this interest. A likable young man of average intelligence, Jim was encouraged to investigate fields of employment that were more to his liking. The oldest of four children, Jim felt a sense of urgency about finding a job quickly. He was somewhat intimidated by his forceful father. Therefore, the crisis worker invited Jim's parents to two of the eight sessions that had been arranged.

During the meetings that Jim's parents attended, the crisis worker became an intermediary, supporting Jim's ambitions and reassuring Jim's father that viable economic opportunities existed outside the postal service. With the help of the crisis worker, parents and son were able to communicate more easily. A referral to a respected vocational counseling program was made for Jim. During the last session, when Jim met alone with the crisis worker, he reported that he was now investigating job opportunities in national parks. His father no longer insisted that Jim take a job at the post office and had remarked jokingly that "forest rangers and mail carriers all worked for the same boss—Uncle Sam."

Alternative Two: Anxiety-provoking Crisis Work. In this approach, Jim's anxiety attack was interpreted as maladaptive behavior used because Jim was unable to express his feelings appropriately. Considerable attention was given to interactions between Jim and his father. Although it was true that Jim's father was opinionated, it seemed to the crisis worker that the problem lay less in the father's forcefulness than in Jim's timidity. The crisis worker listened attentively as Jim described his love of the outdoors and tentatively suggested that perhaps Jim was less comfortable with other people than he would like to be. Jim admitted that he felt inept socially except when he was camping or hiking outdoors. There he always felt confident and in his element.

The crisis worker and Jim established a contract for eight sessions, at the end of which renegotiation would occur. The parents were invited to one session, and with Jim's collaboration the following goals were formulated:

1. Explore the possibility that Jim's love of outdoor life might be an avoidance tactic.
2. Examine the feelings and experiences that caused Jim to feel socially inadequate.
3. Support Jim's right to choose his own vocation and provide guidance.

4. Encourage Jim to express his career preferences to his parents, especially his father.
5. Refer Jim to a vocational counselor to help clarify career choices.

By the end of the crisis contract, more than Jim's career options had been explored. Jim was persuaded that he should become more assertive and autonomous. Clear communication channels were opened between Jim and his parents, but major responsibility for keeping the channels open was given to Jim. Jim's father was not labeled an overbearing tyrant, but a worried parent who did not understand Jim's ambitions but might be willing to listen. The choice of a vocation was described as Jim's inalienable right, but the search for opportunities was also his.

Because this approach was anxiety provoking and specific to Jim, a decision was made that Jim required further help after expiration of the crisis contract. When Jim terminated with the crisis worker, he was already meeting with a vocational counselor, and aptitude tests had been arranged. A referral was made to a social learning group composed of other young people near Jim's age. By the end of eight weeks, the crisis situation had been resolved and Jim faced the immediate future with new allies and new coping skills. He felt anxious about joining the social learning group but believed the effects would be beneficial. At the time of termination, the crisis worker assured Jim of the worker's continued availability but expressed confidence and respect for Jim's newfound insight.

Critical Guidelines

Most mental health facilities are staffed with therapists and counselors who use various orientations in their work. Ideally, every client would be assigned to a particular form of treatment based on the presenting problem and the client's needs. Oliver et al. (1988) found that there was relatively little research on the connection between clients' characteristics and their assignment to a particular form of therapy. A number of studies have shown that certain demographic characteristics such as race, educational level, and socioeconomic status influence the kind of treatment offered to individuals and families.

In choosing anxiety-provoking approaches for a person in crisis, therapists must use careful assessment and unstructured interviewing to determine whether an individual is capable of tolerating this form of intervention. In the early phases of acute crisis, no client should be subjected to anxiety that is deliberately escalated by the therapeutic approach. Only after anxiety has subsided and rapport has been established can accurate assessments be made of the client's tolerance for exploratory interventions. The safest course in crisis counseling, as in most forms of therapy, is to begin with anxiety-suppressive interventions and to adopt an alternative approach only if clients have sufficient ego strength, are motivated, and are likely to benefit.

Anxiety-provoking intervention is not for the inexperienced therapist even if the client is an appropriate candidate. In such instances referral to another therapist is advisable. Some clinicians who possess skills and expertise necessary for anxiety-provoking therapy regard it as a form of primary or tertiary prevention. Primary prevention has the objective of anticipating future hazards and preparing the client to deal with them. Tertiary prevention has the objective of minimizing disability by reinforcing new ways of coping.

Piha (1988) observed that persons with a previous psychiatric history were less able to manage demanding situations than persons with no psychiatric history. Since anxiety-provoking therapy makes special demands on clients, the approach should be limited to persons with considerable psychological strength. The choice of anxiety-provoking over anxiety-suppressing therapy depends on the stage of the crisis. Even more important is the assessment of the client's overall resources, interpersonal, environmental, and psychodynamic. Table 3–3 shows the cognitive, emotional, and behavioral reactions to anxiety.

Most people modify their behavior according to their circumstances. Even those who function well, however, have a preferred style of reacting and interacting. This preferred style is determined by social learning, temperament, personality traits, cultural expectations, and other influences. In general, rising anxiety tends to reinforce an individual's preferred interactional style. Table 3–4 describes the strengths and weaknesses characteristic of interactional styles.

SUMMARY

Crisis theory draws from a number of theoretical sources. General systems theory, psychoanalytic theory, adaptational theory, and interpersonal theory have contributed to the crisis treatment framework. In the disequilibrium that accompanies crisis, anxiety is always present and the discomfort of anxiety provides an impetus for change. Some people are more able than others to tolerate anxiety, thus the ability to tolerate high levels of anxiety is a major factor in selecting an anxiety-provoking or an anxiety-suppressing treatment approach for a person in crisis.

During the most acute phase of disequilibrium, few persons can tolerate additional anxiety, but as problem solving begins some individuals are capable of responding well to anxiety-provoking interventions that are exploratory in nature. Selection of an anxiety-provoking treatment plan should be determined on the basis of client selection and clinical expertise. Choice of an individualized method of crisis treatment rather than a generic method should follow the same criteria.

TABLE 3-3 Cognitive, Emotional, and Behavioral Reactions to Anxiety

Levels of Anxiety	Cognitive/Behavioral	Cognitive/Emotional	Corrective Interventions
Mild anxiety +	Alertness Vigilance	Noises seem louder. Restlessness Irritability	Recognition of anxiety as a warning sign that something is not going as expected. This can be done by: 1. Observing what goes on. 2. Describing what goes on. 3. Analyzing what was expected. 4. Analyzing how the expectations and what went on differed. 5. Formulating what can be done about the situation in terms of changing the situation or changing the expectations. 6. Validating with others.
Moderate anxiety ++	Reduced power to perceive and communicate. Increased tension	Concentration on problem. Someone talking, may not be heard. Part of the room may not be noticed. Muscle tension, pounding heart, perspiration, stomach discomfort.	Recognition that in moderate and severe anxiety the focus is reduced and connections may not be seen between details and that anxiety provides energy which can be reduced to mild anxiety and then used to find out what went wrong.

Severe anxiety +++	Only details are perceived. Physical discomfort. Emotional discomfort.	Connections between details are not seen. Headaches, nausea, trembling, dizziness. Awe, dread, loathing, horror.	Moderate to severe anxiety may be reduced by: 1. Working at a simple, concrete task. 2. Talking to someone who can listen. 3. Playing a simple game. 4. Walking. 5. Crying.
Panic ++++	A detail perceived is elaborated and blown up.	Inability to communicate or function.	The person experiencing panic needs help in getting more comfortable. In this stage, learning cannot be expected to take place.

59

TABLE 3–4 Interactional Styles

Interactional Style	Strengths	Weaknesses
Passive/dependent	Willing to trust others. Aware of their own needs. Able to rely on others. Seek and accept help.	Expect a great deal from others. Sacrifice independence for fear of losing people they need. May substitute substance dependence (alcohol) for personal dependence.
Passive/aggressive	Willing to trust others. Aware of their own needs. Able to rely on others to some extent.	Resent their need for others. Express anger indirectly toward those they need. May substitute substance dependence (alcohol, drugs) for personal dependence.
Masochistic	Sacrifice self for others. Willing to serve others. Willing to defer own needs. Prefer hurting the self to hurting others.	Extreme self-sacrifice leads to anger and bitterness. May hurt others if they feel unappreciated (sadomasochism).
Obsessive/compulsive	Strong need for order. Need to be in control. Careful with details. Comfortable with routines and schedules.	Unable/unwilling to accept help. Trust self more than others. Uncomfortable with strong emotion. Prefer personal distance to closeness with others.
Hysterical	Comfortable with strong emotions. More interested in the "big picture" than in details. Enjoy changes in routines and schedules. Enjoy being the center of attention. Often dramatic, interesting, and creative. Usually balance dependency and autonomy.	Unreliable in completing difficult tasks. Reluctant to share the limelight. Vacillate between managing own life and wanting to be cared for.

REFERENCES

Alexander, F., and T. French. *Psychoanalytic Theory.* New York: Ronald, 1946.

Carter, E.A., and M. McGoldrick. *The Family Life Cycle.* New York: Gardner, 1980.

Erikson, E. *Childhood and Society.* New York: Norton, 1963.

Ferenczi, S. *Further Contributions to the Theory and Technique of Psychoanalysis.* London: Hogarth, 1926.

Freud, S. *Problems of Anxiety.* New York: Norton, 1938.

Horney, K. *New Ways in Psychoanalysis.* New York: Norton, 1939.

Oliver, J.M., H.R. Searight, and S. Lightfoot. "Client Characteristics as Determinants of Intervention Modality and Therapy Progress." *American Journal of Orthopsychiatry* 58(1988): 543–551.

Peplau, H. *Interpersonal Relations in Nursing.* New York: Putnam, 1952.

Piha, J. "Psychosocial Coping in Young Adulthood of Male Child Psychiatric Outpatients: Implications of Early Treatment." *American Journal of Orthopsychiatry* 58(1988): 524–531.

Rank, O. *Will Therapy and Truth and Reality.* New York: Knopf, 1945.

Sifneos, P.S. "Two Different Kinds of Psychotherapy of Short Duration." *American Journal of Psychiatry* 123(1967): 1069–1074.

Sifneos, P.S. "Brief Psychotherapy and Crisis Intervention." In *Comprehensive Textbook of Psychiatry,* 3d ed., vol. 2, edited by H.I. Kaplan, A.M. Freedman, and B.J. Sadock. Baltimore: Williams & Wilkins, 1980.

Sullivan, H.S. *The Interpersonal Theory of Psychiatry.* New York: Norton, 1953.

Thompson, C. *Psychoanalysis: Evolution and Development: A Review of Theory and Therapy.* New York: Grove, 1957.

Weiner, M.F. "Theories of Personality and Psychopathology: Other Psychodynamic Schools." In *Comprehensive Textbook of Psychiatry,* 4th ed., edited by H.I. Kaplan and B.J. Sadock. Baltimore: Williams & Wilkins, 1985.

4

Categories of Crisis
Choosing an Approach

Where there is much desire to learn, there of necessity will be much arguing, much writing, many opinions; for opinion in good men is but knowledge in the making.

John Milton

As a structured framework, crisis theory is relatively new, although families, friends, and communities have always provided assistance in times of crisis. Indeed, whenever one distraught person turns to another for help or advice, a form of crisis intervention occurs. Present-day clinicians working in acute care settings, in birthing centers, in schools, in outreach clinics, and in hospices all participate formally and informally in the problem-solving activities that crisis work requires. It is often difficult to apply rigid standards to the selection of crisis clients, for in many respects this population is self-selected. The problem is compounded by the fact that crisis work is not restricted to professionals trained in therapeutic techniques nor to settings in which backup service is readily available. What is essential, then, is for crisis workers to have an understanding of how principles of crisis intervention may be applied, and how crisis work can supplement other treatment modalities. Specific concepts and strategies have developed from the ways in which crises have always been resolved, augmented by empirical observations of contemporary groups and individuals who find themselves in crisis.

The framework supporting crisis theory represents a shift in emphasis from the intrapsychic experience of the individual to the interaction of the individual with others or with the environment. Even though the crisis event is foremost, it always involves an individual responding in a particular way to particular circumstances. Crisis work begins with prompt assessment, and throughout the assessment process the crisis worker in action and words should acknowledge the existence of an immediate, compelling problem and the importance of finding a solution. It remains necessary, however, to assess the crisis in the context of the individual's life situation and psychosocial experience. Among clinicians and theoreticians, there is widespread agreement that crisis is an individualized response that results from the meaning of the event rather than from the obstacle itself. Even though crisis work deals primarily with the here and now, adequate assessment, planning, and implementation must consider not only the problem, but also the psychodynamic experience of the client.

As crisis theory became formalized, attempts were made to differentiate types of crisis. Using one set of criteria, two major types of crisis have been identified: (1) developmental or universal crises, and (2) situational or episodic crises. *Developmental crises* are maturational events that are expected but which produce changes that necessitate new coping methods. *Situational crises* result from unexpected episodes that also produce change and necessitate new coping methods. In a somewhat similar triadic classification, Schneidman (1973) described crises as *intertemporal,* or characteristic of a transitional life stage; *intratemporal,* or characteristic of an attained life stage; and *extratemporal,* or unrelated to any particular life stage.

DEVELOPMENTAL CRISES

The foremost explicator of developmental crises was Erikson (1963), who identified essential developmental tasks to be accomplished during the life cycle. It was his contention that there are eight life stages, each with its own critical task. Within each life stage there is a period of ascendance during which the critical task for that stage must be surmounted. Ascendancy stems from the combined urgency of social, psychological, and physiological forces acting on the individual. Failure to accomplish early critical tasks impairs ability to deal adequately with later tasks and contributes to psychological vulnerability.

Momentous occasions, such as graduating from college, getting a job, marrying, or becoming a parent, have been called *marker events* (Sheehy, 1976). Although marker events are crucial, they do not of themselves comprise developmental stages. Developmental stages result from subtle feelings and pressures arising within individuals; even when marker events are absent from the life of an individual, the impetus for developmental advancement remains. Thus, changes resulting from market events may lead to disequilibrium, but so may the absence of marker events. When marker events do occur, the consequences affect the internal (psychological) and external (social) experience of the individual. Sheehy noted that marker events and their consequences caused alterations in four areas of interior perception:

1. Changes in the inner sense of self in relation to others.
2. Changes in the inner sense of balance between security and danger.

3. Changes in the inner consciousness of time and its passing.
4. Changes in the inner awareness of vitality as opposed to stagnation.

The life stages proposed by Erikson comprise a psychosocial developmental model that supports and expands the psychosexual developmental model formulated earlier by Freud. Although expressed in terms of conflict resolution and instinctual drives, the psychosexual model conveys the idea of critical tasks. This idea is reinforced by conceptualization of defense mechanisms, such as fixation and regression, that imply maladaptive developmental progression (Freud, 1933, 1946). A comparison of the psychosexual and psychosocial models is shown in Table 4–1.

In the Erikson model, the primacy of each critical task is specific to one stage, but adaptive resolution of the task depends on many factors. This model is less deterministic and more comprehensive than the Freudian model. Even though the mastering of critical tasks does not necessarily produce crisis, the transitional state of ascendance is a time of increased susceptibility. Intrinsic in the paradigm of critical tasks are the following assumptions:

1. Individuals develop according to progressive steps leading to wider spheres of interaction.
2. Development is determined by a variety of internal and external forces acting on individuals.
3. Families and communities maintain equilibrium by monitoring the rate and sequence of individual development.

Although described in conceptual terms, critical tasks can be translated into universal experiences, such as separation, individuation,

TABLE 4–1 Freudian Psychosexual and Eriksonian Psychosocial Developmental Models

Psychosexual Stage	Conflict	Psychosocial Critical Task
Oral	Dependency	Trust vs. mistrust
Anal	Control	Autonomy vs. shame and doubt
Phallic	Competition	Initiative vs. guilt
Latency	Competence	Industry vs. inferiority Identity vs. role diffusion
Genital	Intimacy	Intimacy vs. isolation Generativity vs. stagnation Ego integrity vs. despair

marriage, parenthood, aging, and death. Many similarities exist between the terms *critical tasks* and *marker events;* however, critical tasks represent abstract, internal experiences, whereas marker events tend to be concrete and external. Role expectations and ceremonial rites of passage, such as weddings, graduations, and anniversary celebrations are among the practices society uses to monitor individual development. Erickson sometimes applied the word *crisis* to the stages of his developmental model, but *critical task* is more accurate. When critical tasks are successfully accomplished, the needs of the individual and society are met. The result is an absence of crisis. Failure or inadequacy around critical tasks increases the probability of crisis whenever later tasks are ascendant.

Even though most developmental tasks can be anticipated and prepared for in advance, many are never fully resolved. Resolution of critical tasks is rarely completed but is a continuous lifelong process. All changes impose new demands on people; when individuals cannot find ways to cope with developmental or situational change, disequilibrium and crisis may follow. In dealing with expected change, anticipatory guidance is an intervention strategy that may be used to prepare for impending events. This strategy was described by Caplan (1964) as a form of "emotional inoculation," which is effective in building psychological defenses against the hazards of prospective change. Since critical tasks are stage specific, it is possible to predict change and to identify vulnerable populations. One example of a target population is very young mothers who must deal with parenthood before their adolescent task of identity has been completed. In most cases, adaptive resolution of development tasks depends on the previous experience of the individual, motivation and coping skills brought to the task, and access to appropriate assistance support.

POPULAR MYTHS ABOUT CRISIS INTERVENTION

- *Myth One.* Crisis intervention is appropriate only for psychiatric emergencies.
- *Myth Two.* Crisis intervention is limited to a single therapeutic session.
- *Myth Three.* Crisis therapy is practiced only by paraprofessionals.
- *Myth Four.* Crisis intervention offers only temporary stabilization until more lasting help can be given.
- *Myth Five.* Crisis intervention can be considered only a primary prevention method.
- *Myth Six.* Crisis intervention requires no special knowledge or expertise if the clinician is experienced in more traditional therapeutic approaches.

Source: Adapted from Ann W. Burgess and Bruce A. Baldwin. *Crisis Intervention Theory and Practice* (Englewood Cliffs, New Jersey, Prentice-Hall, 1981).

SITUATIONAL CRISES

Most situational crises are considered extratemporal in that they occur randomly and are independent of any developmental stage. Because they are seldom anticipated, situational crises take people by surprise. As with developmental crises, adequacy of coping skills acquired previously influences adaptive crisis resolution. Any change in one's life or circumstances, whether positive or negative, may precipitate crisis. In a study that established mean scores for certain life changes, the death of a spouse constituted the greatest stress, followed by divorce and marital separation. Personal injury or illness was found to be a significant cause of stress, as was any change in financial status. Lower on the scale but still consequential were such disparate events as job losses and outstanding personal achievements. Clusters of change within a short time span were found to increase the likelihood of crisis arising within a year, usually in the form of physical illness (Holmes & Masuda, 1973; Holmes & Rahe, 1967).

COMPOUND CRISES

The term "compound crisis" describes the experience of some clients currently undergoing a traumatic event that is intensified by memories of previous losses that had receded from consciousness until reactivated by present circumstances (Horsley, 1988). Many care providers not practicing in mental health settings will encounter the phenomenon of compound crisis in clients facing illness or injury to themselves, or a family member, whose inability to cope is related to unresolved events of the past. The memory of past crises intrudes on the present; the difficulties of the present situation are compounded by old griefs, so that the energy needed to deal with the new problems is depleted and recuperative powers are doubly threatened. Clients dealing with a compound crisis often are extremely sensitive to incidents that seem trivial to staff members. They may become withdrawn, very demanding, or apparently uncooperative. With such clients the care provider should call upon a psychiatric specialist who will help upset staff members deal with their reactions to the difficult client and, in some instances, explore with the client the meaning of the maladaptive behaviors.

Clients displaying extreme reactions to the current situation may or may not be suffering compound crisis. Exploration of past events in the life of the client helps determine whether unresolved grief is present. Sometimes there is no history of previous trauma or loss. At other times there have been previous crises, but the client is able to discuss them with appropriate emotionality, showing neither uncontrolled nor deficient reactions. When clients are dealing primarily with the current situation, they may be angry and anxious, but they are able to think about the future. When clients are dealing with compound crisis they are more apt to respond to the present situation with depression, apathy, or surrender, rather than anxiety. The result of compound crisis is lack of energy or desire to meet the challenge of the current situation.

The following is a therapeutic model for intervention with an individual experiencing a compound crisis.

- Examine the current situation to determine what factors in the present crisis are evoking past experiences of trauma or loss.
- Search for similarities and differences between present and past conditions.
- Focus on past and present stressors in ways that reinforce the client's strengths; express confidence in the client's coping skills.
- Help the client identify his or her preferred methods of coping now and in the past.
- Use cognitive interpretations to help the client understand the influence of past experiences on current reactions.
- Within the limited scope of the crisis model, encourage the client to move from the past to the present.
- Permit the client to express residual grief and sorrow for past events, thereby reducing the intensity of memories of previous crises.
- Refer the client for follow-up counseling if previous and current distress cannot be dealt with adequately in the time allowed.
- Interpret the client's behavior as an indication of compound crisis rather than as a weakness or a desire to be troublesome.

•CLINICAL EXAMPLE:
ILLNESS AS A COMPOUND CRISIS

Mrs. Franklin was hospitalized on a surgical unit for a radical mastectomy. She was forty-five years old, the wife of a prominent business man, and the mother of three teenage children. She had handled her ordeal extremely well in the opinion of her surgeon and the nursing staff. Her demands on staff were minimal and she was regarded as an ideal patient. The Franklin family was a close one and the children visited daily after school. Mr. Franklin was unable to visit every day because of business pressures, but he came in several times a week. His wife's room was full of gifts and flowers sent by the family and friends. Only the immediate family was permitted to visit, at Mrs. Franklin's request, and she had asked not to have her phone connected. Although her primary nurse was concerned about Mrs. Franklin's withdrawal, she was reassured by the fact that her client seemed bright and animated whenever her husband and children visited.

As the days passed the nurse became more and more concerned. When it was suggested that Mrs. Franklin walk a little to regain her strength, she complied but walked only within her own room. She kept her door closed, spoke politely to staff, but initiated no conversation except with her own family. The primary nurse was experienced enough to recognize signs of deepening depression and was not surprised to find her cooperative client crying bitterly one morning. Mrs. Franklin said she was merely tired after a sleepless night, but when her nurse suggested that Mrs. Franklin might like to talk with a mental health nurse, the client agreed.

When the nurse specialist visited, she expected Mrs. Franklin to talk about her changed body image and misgivings about her sexuality. Introducing these topics caused Mrs. Franklin to smile ruefully and dismiss the subject with a wave of her well-manicured hand. It was only when the nurse specialist introduced the topic of the Franklin children that the client's defenses began to crumble. The nurse realized that this was an area that needed to be explored and asked about the children's reaction to their mother's surgery. The question caused the client to talk about her fears of dying and abandoning her children at a time when they still needed her. She said that she had grown up in a motherless home and it was the last thing she wanted to happen to her own children. She described her feelings as a child of ten when her mother had died. She remembered being the object of much solicitude that had quickly diminished as people were caught up in their own affairs. Her grandmother, a stern and straitlaced woman, had come to live with Mrs. Franklin, who was an only child. She remembered being told that she mustn't cry for her mother because her father would be unhappy and he was doing his best to be both mother and father. Mrs. Franklin also had memories of being dressed in a funny, old-fashioned way as a child, of never having a birthday party, and of being more restricted than other youngsters her age.

Critical Guidelines

As a result of her own childhood, Mrs. Franklin had resolved to make her husband and family as comfortable and happy as possible. She had evidently succeeded, for the devotion shown by her husband and children was remarkable. From her remarks it was evident that Mrs. Franklin was reliving her own emotionally barren childhood and foreseeing the same fate for her children. The nurse specialist recognized that Mrs. Franklin was suffering a compound crisis related to her own surgery and to her memories of a mother who had died.

Listening to Mrs. Franklin talk about her mother's death, the nurse specialist realized that the client's emotional reactions stemmed from her painful association of her current situation with the past. While accepting the reality of the client's feelings about her mother's death, the nurse specialist pointed out the differences in the two situations. Mrs. Franklin's mother had succumbed to pneumonia at a time when antibiotic drugs were unknown. The client's condition was discovered by mammography at a very early stage and the prognosis was excellent. The only real similarity in the two situations was that two mothers, a generation apart, had become ill. The energy that Mrs. Franklin had devoted to being a wise and giving mother was still there and could be used to assist her own recovery. In addition, the energy of the Franklin family was available to be mobilized on her behalf if she chose to use it. The nurse specialist suggested that shutting herself of from friends and showing only her heroic side to her family deprived everyone of an opportunity to be supportive. The nurse specialist met several times with Mrs. Franklin. In the meetings the client grieved openly for her mother and even began to smile at her grandmother's quirks and demands. The nurse specialist continued to emphasize the importance of dealing with the present situation. She pointed out to the client that she had been strengthened as well as weakened by her childhood experiences, and that the present situation could be dealt with more easily if it were not clouded by bitterness about the very different circumstances of the past.

APPLICATION PRINCIPLES

Assessment

It is axiomatic that the basic question in crisis assessment is not "Why has the client come?" but rather "Why has the client come now?" The distress of clients in crisis often causes incoherence to the extent that emotional catharsis may be necessary before any information can be elicited. In beginning the assessment, the crisis worker should trace a chronology of events by asking what happened, when various events occurred, who was involved, what actions were taken before seeking assistance, and what were the effects of those actions. Sometimes there is no recognizable precipitating event in the recent past, and questions must then address the more distant past. In the absence of a clear precipitator, there may be a number of seemingly trivial events that accumulated and pushed the client into disequilibrium.

As soon as the anxiety of the client has been allayed to the point that meaning can be comprehended, the nature and limits of crisis work should be explained. Since accurate and relevant information is essential, it may be necessary to question other persons in addition to the client. This questioning should be done with the knowledge and, if feasible, the concurrence of the client. When the client can understand the proceedings, the short-term nature of crisis work should be explained. A contract for crisis intervention seldom exceeds eight weeks, and the client should be told that the major problem will probably be solved by that time and that crisis treatment will terminate. Possibilities of other forms of assistance may be suggested and the promise of appropriate referrals may be extended, but the crisis worker will indicate that additional help will be forthcoming from a different source. There are some workers who prefer not to mention further assistance, believing that knowledge of this possibility reduces the client's active participation in crisis resolution. Because the crisis worker assumes an active role, there is danger that some clients will become dependent. This danger is negated by discussing the limits of crisis work, by bringing up the subject of termination as early as possible, and by using auxiliary resources, such as family, friends, and community agencies.

During assessment, any suicidal or homicidal thoughts of the client must be appraised. Direct questioning is recommended in assessing suicidal or homicidal potential. Clients should be asked whether thoughts are entertained of harming the self of others. If the answer is affirmative, additional questions should deal with the seriousness of intentions, the comprehensiveness of any plan, and the availability of means to carry out the plan. There is a fallacious idea that bringing up the question of suicide or homicide may "put ideas in the client's head." This notion attributes more power to the clinician than actually exists. Indeed, if a worker is reluctant to bring up these issues and discuss them openly, the client will feel inclined to conceal any such intentions. If the client admits to having a well thought out plan and if means are accessible, immediate hospitalization should be considered. A history of a previous suicide attempt is significant, as are such variables as age, sex, and social isolation.

More women than men attempt suicide, but more men accomplish suicide. The risk of suicide increases with age, although adolescents are high suicide risks because of their impulsivity. Among women, suicide is accomplished more frequently by housewives and widows. Men tend to use methods that are violent, such as hanging or shooting themselves; women tend to ingest pills or inhale toxic substances, such as carbon monoxide. Suicidal persons who seek professional help are likely to be ambivalent about ending their own lives and, therefore, tend to respond to supportive therapeutic measures. Crisis intervention is effective for suicidal persons who are ordinarily stable but have been thrown into disequilibrium by sudden stress. Chronically depressed persons, alcoholics, psychotics, and withdrawn persons without reliable social networks are not appropriate for crisis work. A suicidal person is frequently an individual who requires a long-term, meaningful relationship with a caring person. Such persons may regard short-term intervention and termination after eight weeks as another abandonment.

Violent and assaultive individuals are usually brought to psychiatric emergency departments by the police. Although clinicians sometimes feel more comfortable when police or security guards are present, there are grounds for excluding them from the treatment area as soon as rapport with the client has been established. However, if there is reason to believe that the client cannot maintain control, the continued presence of police or security guards is indicated. Some persons express verbal threats to the safety of others but have not carried out their threats. As with suicidal persons, the specificity of the plan and the accessibility of means should be appraised. Although there are instances in which impulse control is lost without warning, it is more likely that the crisis has been foreshadowed by past behaviors. If there is a history of violent behavior in the client's past, or if the present situation is complicated by addiction, sociopathy, or neurological or psychiatric disorder, crisis intervention is not appropriate. As a rule, violent and assaultive persons require emergency treatment followed by long-term therapy. For some individuals, custodial care is indicated for the protection of the community. In acute situations, psychiatric evaluation, medication, and external controls in the form of competent professionals and paraprofessionals are usually sufficient to calm agitated persons. Disposition and further treatment are determined by the client's history, the wishes of the family, and the safety of society.

Planning

At times, crisis intervention is generic and wholly restricted to external factors impinging on the individual. In these instances the inner world of the individual may not need to be considered. Psychodynamic issues concerned with earlier emotions and responses may be largely ignored as current behavioral manifestations are inspected. At other times, the crisis worker is advised to explore core developmental issues and to assess general coping skills rather than the skills used in coping with the present crisis. These are more complex techniques that require knowledge of psychodynamics to understand individual responses to episodic struggles and frustrations.

Every crisis involves an individual, a family, or a community that responds in a particular way to particular circumstances. During the crisis counseling sessions, the worker acknowledges in words and actions, the existence of a compelling problem that is causing distress. The focus of crisis work is on the search for a solution to the immediate problem.

The contract for crisis counseling is usually short-term, lasting for the six- to eight-week duration of acute crisis. The counseling sessions may vary in length from fifteen minutes to an hour. The client and the counselor jointly decide on how often to meet. If distress is extreme or if the client has poor impulse control and may be destructive to himself or others, daily meetings may be necessary. A worker may consider it appropriate to give the client a phone number where she can be easily reached. If the client has a reliable support network, weekly or biweekly meetings may be sufficient. During the sessions, the crisis caregiver is actively involved but does nothing for the client that the client is able to handle himself. Some clients may become dependent on the nurse or other crisis worker, but the dependency is not too worrisome because crisis intervention and the period of the therapeutic contract are brief.

Sometimes people working on a long-term basis with a family or individual will observe that a crisis situation has developed. It may be necessary for a worker to alter the approach being used and to become more active in order to facilitate resolution of the crisis. A worker may then have to resume the previous approach in which involvement was less intense. One way to accomplish this is to introduce other professionals into the care plan, so that any dependency on a worker can be gradually reduced.

For people engaged in helping clients in a crisis, a primary rule is not to make decision *for* them but to became involved in making decisions *with* them. Restoration of equilibrium through improved coping behavior is the maximal goal of crisis work. A minimal goal is to help the clients return to at least precrisis functioning levels, but there are occasions when even this lesser goal is not achieved. Table 4–2 shows alternative outcomes in resolving crisis.

Implementation

Having assessed the proportions of the crisis and the locus of causation, the crisis worker is able to develop a treatment plan that deals solely with external factors or with a combination of external and internal factors. Assessment and planning are activities that are maintained throughout crisis work, particularly when the distress of the client has impeded these activities initially. Regardless of the approach used, implementation of crisis work begins with goal setting and establishing a contract. Ideally, the client and the crisis worker should mutually agree on the goals to be reached. It is essential that these be clearly stated so that the direction of treatment is understood and accepted. In addition, evaluation of treatment outcomes is possible only if treatment goals are clearly defined.

Working together, client and crisis worker agree on goals and define the boundaries of the relationship. Baldwin (1980) described boundaries as being definitional and contractual. Defining the problem introduces the idea of cognitive, affective, and behavioral dysfunction in relation to the crisis. Definitional boundaries go far to alleviate the confusion of the client and constitute a strategy that expedites problem solving. Contractual boundaries involve goal setting, establishing a time frame, and discussing shared responsibility. The constraints of a short-term crisis contract must not be allowed to keep the worker from avoiding total responsibility. Occasionally people in crisis become wholly dysfunctional. Here the worker may be more directive than usual, although directness is more therapeutic than excessive directiveness. Specific suggestions may be in order and are usually made in a supportive way. The attitude of the worker can be crucial, for interest and empathy instill

---

TABLE 4–2   Alternative Outcomes in a Family Crisis

A demanding elderly woman, no longer able to continue living alone, moves in with her married daughter and the daughter's family.

Type of Solution	Coping Strategy	Outcome
Functional	The daughter, her husband, and the children discuss relocating the mother. They agree that family life will go on as usual, with all members taking some responsibility for the mother. The daughter and husband share results of the family conference with the elderly mother. They discuss common expectations.	*Improved coping skills:* Preliminary agreement and planning prepare the family for change. Future turmoil and dissension are avoided.
Questionable	The daughter tries to interact with the family as if nothing has changed. She does this by placating her mother, her husband, and her children, as she has always done. Her motto is "Peace at any price" even if this requires considerable self-sacrifice on her part.	*Unchanged coping skills:* Family equilibrium is preserved. The family and elderly mother are comfortable. Daughter feels entrapped by her mother's demands and her family's needs, as she often has since her marriage.
Dysfunctional	The daughter aligns herself with her mother and against her family. She struggles to satisfy all her mother's whims and argues constantly with her husband. Eventually her husband moves out of the house; the marriage is in serious trouble. The family is in crisis.	*Impaired coping skills:* Family is in a state of disequilibrium. The children are enraged, and the husband is estranged. The mother is content, but her daughter is unhappy.

---

hope that the problem can be solved. Along with offering guidance, the crisis worker must try to replace feelings of helplessness with optimism and involvement. Alienation intensifies the distress of clients, and social supports other than the crisis worker should be introduced. Expanding the support network may consist of involving relatives and friends, or of recruiting other professionals.

Critical Guidelines

Restoration of function means that the cognitive, emotional, and behavioral distortions of crisis have been corrected to the point that the client is no longer in a condition of disorganization and disability. Restoration of function also means that the client, however slowly, has regained energy to meet the basic demands of everyday life and is beginning to enjoy some simple pleasures without being overcome by guilt or regret. The crisis counselor who keeps this realistic goal in mind should find the following suggestions useful (Weiss, 1987):

- Accept the client's feelings about the current situation even if they seem excessive or inappropriate. Offer assurance that the feelings are understandable without commenting on how the client should feel. For example, the crisis counselor might comment on the difficulty of making decisions or just getting through the day when the client is so upset.
- Explain to the client whey she feels so overwhelmed. Many clients in crisis wonder why they cannot function; some of them even worry that they may be "crazy." For example, the crisis counselor might review the sequence of events the client has experienced and indicate that here is the reason the client feels helpless and inadequate.
- Instill hope in the client by stating that the present emotional distress need not last forever. It can be helpful to describe gradual stages of recovery that are likely to follow initial distress. For example, the crisis counselor might say, "After an experience like yours many people say it takes a long time to get readjusted and even longer before they can manage as well as they did before."
- Give the client permission to recover and move toward normalcy and restored function. Some clients feel that loyalty to a lost person or place, or resentment at changes or injuries suffered makes recovery impossible. For example, the crisis counselor should acknowledge that the client may proceed at his own pace, but should not become immobilized because of guilt or anger. The counselor might also suggest that the client not only needs to begin to function again, but has the right to recover and move on.
- Help the client interpret recovery as simply a return to effective functioning rather than a return to the status quo. Indicate that recovery is not the same as forgetting or forgiving, both of which may be a long time coming.

Evaluation

Although acute crisis is self-limiting, the residual effects are long-term. The fact that severe disorganization abates within a short period complicates the evaluation of outcomes. Restoration of equilibrium takes place even when precrisis levels of functioning do not return. Reequilibrium may mask deteriorated functioning until time elapses and other life events arrive to test the client's coping skills.

Golan (1980) described a group of individuals who experienced community catastrophes superimposed on normal transitional events. At the time of the disaster, harried crisis workers used generic interventions that seemed effective at the time, but merely produced a state of pseudoequilibrium. The results of later evaluation led inescapably to the conclusion that the crisis approach used had been too narrow and that for some persons the disaster had obscured psychological problems that were more extreme.

Baldwin (1980) wrote that the problem of inadequate crisis resolution might be attributed to poor understanding of differential approaches to crisis intervention. Only a well-prepared clinician can view crisis through the client's perspective and respond simultaneously to the immediate and long-term aspects of the problem. Frequently the distress caused by crisis induces clients to avoid peripheral issues that have been present for a long time and have depleted the client's ability to cope with the current crisis. As a result, the ebbing crisis is replaced by pseudo-equilibrium in which the client appears able to function, only to have variations of the same crisis arise in the future.

Evaluation of crisis outcomes is a complicated matter that begins when the contract is made. At that point the objectives of treatment are outlined, and attention is paid to accomplishing the stated goals. Since equilibrium is restored within a short time, equilibrium per se is not a variable that can be used to evaluate outcomes. Comparing a client's gains with the original goals is one way to evaluate progress. Subjective accounts by the client or by concerned family members may or may not be reliable sources of evaluative data. What is more valuable is to compare postcrisis coping skills with precrisis coping skills, and to use anticipatory guidance to prepare clients for future stress. Warnings must be issued about evaluating outcomes of crisis intervention only at the time of termination without subsequent evaluation measures. Any effort to engage in outcome evaluation of crisis work should include retrospective and anterospective examination of the client's coping abilities.

Locus of Causation

An excellent system for classifying crises has been devised to facilitate crisis assessment and planning (Baldwin, 1978). This classification system describes six types of crisis, each of which moves from lesser to greater degrees of psychopathology. As the gravity of psychopathology increases, the causes of crisis become internal rather than external, and the approach of the crisis worker is modified accordingly. In using this

Recovery from crisis does not mean forgetting what happened.
Recovery from crisis does not mean that you and your life are
unchanged.
Recovery from crisis means a return of energy for everyday living.
Recovery from crisis means a resumption of attachment to others.
Recovery from crisis means renewed ability to feel satisfaction, even joy.
Recovery from crisis means that distress is not fixed or endless. It may,
however, return from time to time, triggered by an anniversary, a
memory, or a chance remark.

categorization, the crisis worker must engage in a multifactorial assessment process that considers not only the dimensions of the crisis, but also the psychosocial perspectives of the client. Even though the exigencies of the crisis situation dominate treatment, psychological and interpersonal phenomena intrude.

Baldwin designated the six types of crisis that help determine external and internal causes of crisis, estimate relative amounts of psychopathology, and plan corresponding interventions. In the following section, the categories that Baldwin used are described and appropriate treatment plans are suggested. A brief clinical example of each type of crisis is included.

TYPOLOGY OF CRISES

1. Dispositional crises.
2. Transitional crises.
3. Traumatic crises.
4. Developmental crises.
5. Psychopathological crises.
6. Psychiatric emergency crises.

•CLINICAL EXAMPLE:
DISPOSITIONAL CRISIS

Betty Lou was an efficient young secretary whose fiancé had married another girl two weeks before the date of their formal wedding. In the following month her behavior alternated between hysterical weeping and angry outbursts. She felt disappointed and humiliated. Unable to sleep or eat, her performance at work became so erratic that her job was in jeopardy. Thoughts of committing suicide crossed her mind. She denied serious intent but wanted to make her ex-fiancé feel guilty. At times Betty Lou had fantasies of committing acts of vandalism on his expensive car. Reluctantly, Betty Lou accepted her employer's suggestion that she seek help at a family service agency. Her job depended on this ultimatum.

Category	Causation	Plan
Class 1	Crisis caused by external or situational factors. Acute episodic distress of a temporary nature.	Clarify and define the situation. Provide information and guidelines. Offer support and guidance. Solicit peer interaction. Reinforce social networks.

•CLINICAL EXAMPLE:
TRANSITIONAL CRISIS

Jim and Lucy had made sound financial plans for retirement from the hardware store where both had worked for many years. After a holiday cruise with Jim, Lucy settled down to enjoy being a full-time homemaker. She joined a gourmet cooking class, played cards with old friends, and relished her new leisure. Jim, on the other hand, was restless and discontented. He visited the hardware store daily, criticized decisions, and countermanded orders until his son-in-law threatened to quit the business. At home Jim was taciturn and irritable. He stopped attending his lodge meetings, lost his appetite, and began to have trouble sleeping. Lucy became so worried about her husband that she was no longer able to enjoy the activities that she had looked forward to in retirement. In desperation, Jim's wife and daughter prevailed on him to accept pastoral counseling, since this was the form of assistance most acceptable to Jim.

Category	Causation	Plan
Class 2	Crisis caused by predictable life transitions that could have been anticipated. Retirement signified gains for the wife but losses for the husband.	Clarify and define the transition. Explore its meaning and implications. Contrast the role changes of the spouses. Involve both spouses in counseling. Search for alternative behaviors. Encourage some shared activities. Encourage some independent activities. Introduce anticipatory guidance.

•CLINICAL EXAMPLE:
TRAUMATIC CRISIS

The Mills family, consisting of husband, wife, and two children, lived in a trailer on the outskirts of town. One winter night an overworked heater in the trailer caught fire. Awakened by smoke, Joe managed to lead his wife and small sons to safety. When he returned for the family dog, Joe became trapped inside the trailer. The dog jumped out a small window but Joe died in the fire. His wife, Donna, showed no signs of grief but reacted stoically to her loss. She refused, however, to let her sons out of her sight. They slept in the same bed with her and were no longer permitted to attend the nursery school they had enjoyed so much. Donna moved in with her parents but was withdrawn and uncommunicative even with them. Two months after the tragedy, Donna showed no signs of working through her grief. Donna's worried mother asked a trusted community nurse who had supervised the health of the children to visit.

Category	Causation	Plan
Class 3	Crisis caused by sudden traumatic event that could not be anticipated. Surviving spouse was unable to express appropriate grief, and could not detach from the lost one. She reacted by withdrawing from social interaction. Having lost the role of wife, she focused on the mothering role. Her single-minded attention to the children hampered their adjustment. An unexpected, sudden death is often hard to deal with because there is no time for anticipatory intervention. The traumatic circumstances of the death inhibited the grief work of the surviving spouse.	Encourage acknowledgment of loss. Recognize meaning of loss. Permit spouse to express painful feelings of anger and guilt for having survived. The mother's overprotectiveness of the children is maladaptive for everyone concerned. Instead of restricting their world, mother needs to help the children deal with the loss and to resume usual activities. Acceptance and recovery on the part of mother can begin with directing her attention to their needs as well as her own. Crisis intervention should include the following interventions:

Encourage grieving and help Mrs. Jones detach from her dead husband.
Encourage reminiscing.
Permit expression of guilt feelings.
Expand social interactions.
Promote wholesome involvement from the children.
Reduce phobic restriction of children's activity.

•CLINICAL EXAMPLE: DEVELOPMENTAL CRISIS

When Bill was a college freshman, his father died suddenly. His mother was a homemaker who had never worked outside the home and who had depended on her husband to make decisions for her. Bill's college was about five hundred miles from his hometown. He was shocked and grief stricken by his father's death but was even more dismayed when his mother begged him to move back home and attend a local college. Bill had adjusted well at school and resented the prospect of becoming "the man of the house" for his mother. Yet he found it difficult to say "no" to her. He was able to return to school to finish the semester, but the idea of returning home was so disturbing that his academic standing was affected. He confided in one of his professors, who suggested that Bill make an appointment with the counseling service. Bill's dilemma was especially difficult because the college he was attending was his father's alma mater. His father had been proud of Bill's college record and had been instrumental in convincing Bills' mother that their son would benefit from not being too close to home. Bill's mother had no real financial worries; other family members, including Bill's married sisters, lived close to her.

Category	Causation	Plan
Class 4	Bill was making progress in his developmental task of separating from his family until the death of his father. This meant that Bill had lost an ally and a role model. His mother had other resources on which to rely but was determined that Bill would fill the place of her deceased husband. Thus, Bill's developmental task was impeded and his mother was able to avoid coming to terms with her loss.	Encourage a sibling alliance between Bill and his two sisters. Help Bill's mother to accept the death of her husband, to grieve, and to gradually begin making new attachments. Encourage Bill to continue his present task of making his own way in the world and establishing an identity. Help all the siblings to participate in comforting their mother so that Bill will not be the only child to whom she turns for solace.

•CLINICAL EXAMPLE: PSYCHOPATHOLOGICAL CRISIS

Paul was brought into the emergency department of a hospital when he was found lying in the traffic lane of a busy highway. A thirty-year-old male, Paul was disheveled, mute, and very frightened on admission. Identification cards on his person showed him to be the resident of a halfway house for chronic psychiatric patients discharged to community care. When reached by phone, a staff member came to the hospital to give information and reassure Paul. The staff member stated that a few weeks before, Paul had been referred to a rehabilitation program for vocational training. At the time he seemed eager to become self-sufficient and self-supporting. In the program Paul's progress was excellent, and the counselors hoped that he would learn to handle a real job. The morning on which Paul was found lying on the street had been stressful for him. Another client enrolled in the program accused Paul of stealing his lunch. A zealous counselor suggested that Paul began thinking of leaving the halfway house and finding his own apartment. The same morning Paul was assigned complicated work that was unlike the simple tasks he had been performing. The accumulation of incidents caused Paul to become anxious and confused. He left the rehabilitation building without telling anyone, walked about aimlessly for a while, and decided that he could not meet the expectations that others had for him. Wishing to run away or withdraw entirely, Paul lay down in the highway. He wanted to give up and be cared for; the suicide gesture was Paul's way of communicating his feelings of despair.

Category	Causation	Plan
Class 5	Crisis caused by internal psychopathology. Psychopathology precipitates or complicates the crisis. Excessive demands caused high anxiety. Fear of failure produced a wish to regress. Ambivalence between desire to achieve and desire to be safe created inner conflict.	Acknowledge preexisting psychopathology. Limit crisis intervention to stabilizing or restoring function. Discourage dependency and further regression. Coordinate crisis work with long-term treatment plan. Make referrals for additional treatment as indicated.

•CLINICAL EXAMPLE: PSYCHIATRIC EMERGENCY CRISIS

Ben was a municipal employee who lost his job when public funds were cut. Never an outgoing man, Ben had always had difficulty getting along with fellow workers. He accused them of going through his desk, disarranging his files, and talking about him. After losing his job, Ben became more irrational. His suspicions grew and affected family relationships. He began drinking excessively and was verbally abusive at home. At other times he seemed indifferent and despondent, lost in his own thoughts, and unresponsive to others. Ben began to berate his children. He accused his wife of having lovers, claimed that the phone was tapped, and that neighbors were spying on him. He said that FBI agents tracked him when he left the house because his loyalty was under investigation. Because Ben had always been suspicious of others, his wife considered his behavior to be an exaggeration of normal tendencies increased by loss of his job. She was unprepared for his violent outburst one day when he grabbed a hunting rifle and ran from the house shouting that he was going to take care of his enemies in city hall. Reluctant to involve the police, Ben's wife phoned a relative. The relative immediately called the police, who issued an alert. Ben was apprehended not far from city hall, where his stalking movements and his rifle had already attracted attention. A police officer trained in crisis work was able to disarm Ben and persuade him to come into custody peacefully. Ben's wife was notified and agreed to accompany her husband to a medical center for his psychiatric evaluation and disposition.

Category	Causation	Plan
Class 6	Crisis caused by a psychiatric state of paranoid psychosis, loss of control, and feelings of incompetence. Alcohol abuse. Suicidal ideation and homicidal threats.	Assess the situation promptly. Intervene to protect the individual and others. Obtain medical, psychiatric, and other backup resources. Take the individual into custody. Hospitalize if necessary. Coordinate crisis work with long-term treatment. Make referrals for additional care as indicated.

CRISIS ASSESSMENT TOOL

Initial Steps

1. Collect data that indicate the dimensions of the problem, using various sources of information.
2. Formulate a dynamic hypothesis concerning the problem and the coping responses of the client.
3. Assess the problem in terms of intrinsic and extrinsic factors, and determine a therapeutic approach.
4. Involve the client in problem-solving activities.
5. Negotiate a contract that sets clear, reachable goals.
6. Explain that treatment will be terminated according to the terms of the contract.

General Procedures

1. Obtain demographic data.
2. Define the problem in realistic terms.
3. Assess the mental status of the client(s).
4. Assess the physical status of the client(s).
5. Assess the psychosocial status of the client(s).
6. Assess coping skills of the client(s).

Coping Skills Assessment

1. How does the client deal with anxiety, tension, or depression?
2. Has the client used customary coping methods in the current situation?

3. What were the results of using customary coping methods?
4. Have there been recent life changes that interfered with customary coping methods?
5. Are significant persons contributing to continuation of the problem?
6. Is the client considering suicide or homicide as a way of coping? if so, how? When?
7. Has the client attempted suicide or homicide in the past? Under what conditions?
8. Assess the extent of suicidal or homicidal risk presented by the client. Hospitalization may be necessary as a protective measure.

Planning and Problem Solving

1. Is the present crisis new or a reenactment of similar events that occurred in the past?
2. What alternative methods might have been used to avoid development of the present crisis?
3. What new methods might be used to resolve the present crisis?
4. What supports are available to strengthen new problem-solving methods?

Anticipatory Guidance

1. What sources of stress remain for the client?
2. How might the client deal with problematic issues in the future, based on the current repertoire of coping skills?
3. How might the current repertoire of coping skills be maintained or expanded?
4. With termination of the contract for crisis intervention, is further referral or follow-up care necessary?

SUMMARY

Several typologies are available to classify different crises. One typology relates crises to critical life tasks and uses categories of intertemporal, intratemporal, or extratemporal conditions of crisis. Another typology separates six types of crises, differentiated according to the progressive amounts of pathology present in the client. In this typology, attention to psychodynamics is essential in assessment and planning, beyond the presenting problem. Regardless of the typology used to classify a crisis, the importance of assessing suicidal potential cannot be overstated. Age, sex, suicide plan, and availability of means are some of the major variables used for suicide assessment. Sometimes a client may be assaultive or violent. When dealing with these persons, additional help is needed, especially if the client does not trust the crisis worker or if impulse control is dubious.

Evaluation of outcomes in crisis work poses difficulties even though restoration of equilibrium occurs within a short time. The adequacy of coping skills after the problem is resolved cannot be determined immediately, but must wait until behavior during future periods of stress can be ascertained. The possibility of pseudoequilibrium must be considered, particularly when generic crisis interventions overlook individual psychodynamics.

REFERENCES

Baldwin, B.A. "A Paradigm for the Classification of Emotional Crises: Implications for Crisis Intervention" *American Journal of Orthopsychiatry* 48: 538–551, 1978.

Baldwin, B.A. "Styles of Crisis Intervention: Toward a Convergent Model." *Journal of Professional Psychology* 11(1980): 113–120.

Burgess, A.W. and Baldwin, B.A. *Crisis Intervention Theory and Practice* Englewood Cliffs, New Jersey: Prentice Hall 1981.

Caplan, G. *Principles of Preventive Psychiatry.* New York: Basic Books, 1964.

Erikson, E. Childhood and Society. New York: Norton, 1963.

Freud, S. *New Introductory Lectures on Psychoanalysis.* New York: Norton, 1933.

———. *The Ego and Mechanisms of Defense.* New York: International Universities Press, 1946.

Golan, N. "Using Situational Crises to Ease Transitions in the Life Cycle." *American Journal of Orthopsychiatry* 50 (1980): 542–550.

Holmes, J.H., and R.H. Rahe. "The Social Readjustment Scale." *Journal of Psychosomatic Research* 2 (1967): 213.

Holmes, T., and M. Masuda. "Life Change and Illness Susceptibility." In *Separation and Depression,* edited by J.P. Scott and E.C. Senay. Washington, D.C.: American Association for the Advancement of Science, 1973.

Horsley, G. "Baggage from the Past." *American Journal of Nursing* 88 (1988) 60–63.

Schneidman, E. "Crisis Intervention: Some Thoughts and Perspectives." In *Crisis Intervention,* edited by G. Spector and H. Claiborn. New York: Behavioral Publications, 1973.

Sheehy, G. *Passages.* New York: Dutton, 1976.

Weiss, R.S. "Principles Underlying a Manual for Parents whose Child was Killed by a Drunk Driver." *American Journal of Orthopsychiatry* 57 (1987): 431–440.

PART
TWO

INDIVIDUALS
IN CRISIS

5

Children in Crisis
The Early Years

Children's griefs are little, certainly, but so is the child, so is its endurance, so is its field of vision, while its nervous impressionability is keener than ours. Grief is a matter of relativity; the sorrow should be estimated by its proportion to the sorrower; a gash is as painful to one as an amputation is to another.

Francis Thompson

Any examination of the impact of crisis on the lives of children must incorporate developmental issues relevant to them and their families. Children have individual resources for coping with crisis, and, within the context of their family and community, additional resources are available as well. Children's developmental levels, however, make them potentially vulnerable to poor and ineffective ways of dealing with crisis that family and community members may use.

Children's individual or *internal* resources include established attachments to and relationships of trust with adult caretakers. In addition, children's level of cognitive development affects their perception and interpretation of a crisis situation as well as their ability to express needs either by words or behavior. A child's temperament and repertoire of past experiences, if any, in dealing with crises are brought to bear on a current crisis. Health status is also relevant to a child's ability to mobilize other resources.

The most thorough formulation of cognitive development in children was offered by Piaget (1969). Knowledge of the cognitive limitations of young children is important for counselors assisting them in dealing with the crises of change and loss.

External resources can be arbitrarily subcategorized into those proximal and those distal to the child. The primary proximal resource is the child's nuclear family. Parents and siblings bring their bonds with the child and their own history of success or failure in dealing with crisis to any new crisis situation. In addition, the degree to which the temperament styles of parent and child mesh also affect the parents' availability as resources. Extended family members are also potential resources, as are nonrelated adults who may be neighbors, teachers, family friends, or parent surrogates for the child. School-aged children may find their friends to be of help if they share a common experience.

Among the child's distal external resources are health care providers, including physicians, nurses, psychologists, counselors, and other members of human service professions, such as the clergy. In addition, the child's participation in group activities, such as church youth groups and Scouts, can provide either direct or indirect assistance in coping with crisis.

These developmental and interpersonal elements will be considered individually and in greater depth. Their separate and collective relevance to assessment, management, and evaluation will be demonstrated in vignettes and in more detailed clinical examples.

ATTACHMENT

Socialization of a newborn infant begins with the infant's transition from an absolute physical and physiologic attachment to the mother in utero to the attachment of affectional bonding. Bowlby (1979) attributed this extrauterine attachment to social behavior. Social behavior begins at birth (Thomas, 1981).

Forming the First Bond

As the dependent member of the pair, the infant receives care from the mother, and thus she influences their attachment behavior. However, the relationship is reciprocal. The frequency and the nature of the infant's responsive interaction with the mother affects the care that she gives. Both members are active in establishing their attachment. While the mother has a variety of care-giving activities from the onset of their relationship, infants have roles that alters as their abilities increase. Initially, the infants' actions brings the mother and keeps her near. These actions include crying, smiling, and sucking, and the later addition of calling and specifically using her name. By four months of age, the infants' visual perception allows them to discriminate their mother from others and to engage her in these ways. Eventually, infants' actions bring them to the mother and keep her close as they follow and cling to her.

Other Aspects of Bonding

As infants widen the range of their attachment behaviors, they also broaden the cast of persons with whom they form attachments. These attachment bonds with other adults differ from the attachment bond with the mother. These other behaviors appear later, and they are less strong and less consistent than the behaviors directed to the mother. In reviewing studies, Bowlby (1969) reiterated that the attachment to mother was not diminished in intensity when attachment behaviors were also exchanged with other adults. Elsewhere in the same book, Bowlby indicated that children with more intense attachments to their mothers are in fact more likely to establish many reciprocal bonds with other adults in their milieu.

The display of these behaviors has a fluid quality. Even in the younger infant, there is variation within a day and from one day to another in the consistency and intensity of demonstrated attachment. Some of the variability is accounted for by the child's physiological state. When children are hungry, tired, unhappy for some reason, or ill, they are more likely to cry for mother or follow and cling to her. Until age three, children exhibit strong attachment to the mother with great regularity. After age three, attachment behaviors occur less frequently and with less urgency but still comprise a major part of the preschooler's behavior. At the same time, children are more tolerant of the mother's absence if they are with other familiar attachment figures. They may even seek consolation from a nonhuman source—the so-called "security blanket." Litt (1981) described such transitional objects as not being part of the child's body and used by parents not using pacifiers and bottles for oral gratification. Many mothers were aware of the object's functions and even had encouraged its use. Such use had specified limitations, however. The object was used only at bedtime or only in the house.

Disturbance of Attachment Bonds

The disruption of a bond at any stage in its existence can cause problems for a child. Clearly, the greatest disruption is the loss of a parent through separation, divorce, or death. When the experience of losing an adult to whom the child is intensely attached occurs repeatedly, the child is left with a sense of being unloved, abandoned, and rejected.

Spitz (1945, 1946) described the effects of such a disruption. In his article on hospitalism, however, Spitz attributed these physical and mental effects to a lack of stimulation from care-giving adults and other aspects of the environment. He noted not only a susceptibility to illness that resulted in a high mortality rate, but also a decline in the developmental quotients of the children. Later it was found that the syndrome called early or anaclitic depression improved in part with restoration of the mother to the child. The somatic effects included susceptibility to infection and decline in developmental progress together with weight loss and insomnia in some children. Spitz listed other symptoms according to their increasing severity. Apprehension progressed to sadness and weepiness. Slowing of the child's development intensified to a slowed reaction to stimuli, slowed movement, dejection, and general unresponsiveness. In this instance, Spitz identified the separation from the mother as the etiological factor and documented the partial reversal of the decline in developmental quotient on her restoration to the child.

It is noteworthy that not all of the children separated from their mothers developed these symptoms. Spitz believed that the depression was obviated for those children by a better match of child and mother-surrogate having occurred.

Bowlby (1973, 1979) widened the description of the results of such a loss to include the fear of abandonment by the remaining parent, a yearning for the person who is gone, and anger that the person cannot be found. The child searches for the lost person and tries to identify who is responsible for the loss or who is impeding the return of the person. The yearning for and anger at the lost attachment figure must be expressed either in words or behavior if this grieving is to be resolved. Children need the aid of another trusted person who can take their perspective of the loss and respect their conflicted feelings.

Attachment and Protest Behavior

Research on children reared under different conditions in the United States and elsewhere shows that protest reaction to separation rarely occurs before nine months of age, peaks at about thirteen months, and gradually declines (Fish & Belsky, 1991). Even though distress over separation seems to abate with age, some children continue to protest separation from mother or the significant caretaker even in the early school years. Differences in distress over separation have often been attributed to the child's temperament and to aspects of the parent-child attachment. Belsky and Rovine (1987) noted that any early childhood distress over separation will be determined by temperament, whereas later distress is more likely determined by attachment issues. In research designed to substantiate the interactive importance of temperament and of attachment in separation distress expressed by children at three, twelve, and thirty-six months of age, it was found that it was the securely attached children who were most likely to protest separation (Sroufe, 1988). From this it is possible to assume that protest behavior and intolerance of separation may represent effective coping behavior for some children. The data of Fish and Belsky (1991) refuted the general assumption that intolerance of separation, especially in the preschool years, always reflects insecurity, immaturity, and temperament vulnerability. It is possible that one consequence of secure attachment is a child's ability to express distress of separation by means of open protest behavior. Supporting this premise is German research (Fish & Belsky, 1991) showing that three year olds with a history of secure attachment were more likely to express sadness at failing a task than those with insecure attachment. Providing sensitive, responsive care figures can do much to strengthen attachment, which for many children fosters the open expression of feelings, positive and negative. In contrast, mothers and caretakers who fail to provide attachment security convince their children that protest behavior will not have the desired result of alleviating their distress. Parental disapproval of emotional expression by distressed children has been associated with lower academic competence (Roberts & Strayer, 1987). The crucial role of caretakers in accepting and channeling protest behavior in children is supported by research (Kopp, 1989).

Reciprocity persists in all interactions between parent and child, as each influences the other. The child's variations in responsive behavior affect a parent's responsive behavior and attitudes toward the child. At times the helplessness and dependency of the child can elicit negative parental responses as well as positive ones. Parents' perception of a child's needs greatly determines their availability or unavailability to the child. If parents ignore the impact of circumstances and context on a child's behavior, they are less able to recognize a child's potential for change. Lacking developmental knowledge, parents may hold expectations that are unrealistic for a child to meet; and knowledgeable parents may lack sufficient resources to meet a child's needs.

Children's difficulties are exacerbated in families in which the parents themselves have been deprived, are poorly educated, and are currently stressed. Some parents provide a chaotic and irrational home life where parents convey the attitude that the world is dangerous and no one is to be trusted. In a more positive light, some families offer a resourceful environment where children learn to trust themselves and one another, and where change is accepted as a fact of life. These families establish relationships with the children that are characterized by warmth and readiness to help the children deal with new situations as they arise.

Coping begins with recognizing the promising as well as the threatening elements in a situation. The motivation and ability of a child's family to respond creatively to life stress and change permits a child to progress developmentally, socially, and affectively.

•CLINICAL EXAMPLE: CRISIS OF ATTACHMENT

At age twenty, Valdeen had just had her second baby, another daughter. Her two and a half year old, Becky, was a cheerful, sociable preschooler with a well-developed vocabulary.

The second pregnancy was unplanned. Valdeen had faithfully taken her birth control pills. Not realizing that she had conceived, she continued the pills through the first four months of her pregnancy. She and the children's father had discussed their alternatives. They had both been working and saving money to buy a house and get married. Postponing those plans was disappointing but neither one wanted a second trimester abortion.

Rose, the new baby, had a cleft palate and other difficulties beyond her feeding problems, but Valdeen had not been given a clear idea of what they were. In addition, one doctor had said that the baby had a cleft palate because Valdeen had taken birth control pills when she was already pregnant. Several caretakers had indicated disbelief when Valdeen had reiterated her claim of faithfully contracepting.

Because of Rose's feeding problems, community health nursing services had been requested for Valdeen's family. Valdeen and Becky had spent a large part of each day at the hospital to be with Rose and to feed her. Valdeen felt the hospital staff believed her irresponsible because of the birth control pill issue, and they had not given her encouragement to hold and cuddle Rose. She had once been scolded for picking Rose up soon after a feeding. When the community health nurse asked Valdeen if anyone at the hospital had asked her how *she* was feeling physically or emotionally after Rose was born, Valdeen's eyes filled with tears.

The nurse encouraged Valdeen to weep and begin to express her anger, frustration, and grief. Valdeen was receptive to daily home visits "to help you and Becky and Rose all get settled in together and give you some moral support."

The nurse's initial evaluation included recognizing the stability of Rose's feeding problems, and the greater need for Valdeen to deal with her affective issues and to form attachment bonds with Rose. Valdeen had felt disparaged by the hospital staff and guilty that her misuse of birth control pills had caused Rose's problems. The nurse assessed Becky to be a well-stimulated, well-loved, and well-cared-for child. Valdeen had carefully prepared Becky for the coming of a new sibling. The nurse chose to emphasize the fine job that Valdeen was doing with Becky to help restore her self-esteem. The nurse planned to monitor the reciprocity of affection between Valdeen and Rose, and to evaluate the involvement of the girls' father, Terrence.

Despite her own fatigue and worry, Valdeen was able to draw on her experience with Becky to make a commitment "to give my little Rose blossom what she needs." Becky had a role as Mommy's helper and big sister. Terrence got too nervous if some of Rose's feeding came out her nose or if she choked, but he was increasingly helpful with Becky's care and very supportive of Valdeen.

Despite the family's rallying, at age five weeks, Rose had to be rehospitalized after only five days at home. During Rose's ten-day hospitalization, the community health nurse actively advocated for the family with the hospital personnel, so that more information was shared with Valdeen and Terrence. The nurse had also done some searching and shared with Valdeen that she had found no evidence that birth control pills had caused Rose's problems. The physician in charge of Rose's care later confirmed this opinion.

When Rose was discharged, Valdeen noticed a change. "She doesn't want to be held. She cries and stiffens. If she isn't eating, she seems happier in her crib. She won't even try to smile anymore." The nurse recognized the baby's behavior as being the result of her hospitalization and separation from her mother. She interpreted the behavior to Valdeen as the baby's forgetting what it was to be home with her mother and needing to learn it again.

With that encouragement, Valdeen spent much of the next few days holding Rose, talking and singing to her, and smiling at her. Rose continued to stiffen and cry at first, but, by the third day, the baby would occasionally give a hint of a smile. Her eating was also much improved.

Rose continued to improve for several days at home but was again rehospitalized. She was again improving rapidly in the hospital and was nearly ready to be discharged when she aspirated regurgitated formula during the night and died. The community health nurse visited several times to help the family with grief work and to express sadness at their loss.

After the initial numbness subsided, Valdeen and Terrence planned a modest wake and funeral service for Rose. Becky seemed to adjust quickly to Rose's absence and played normally. She was told that Rose had died and would not come home with them anymore. Nevertheless, she continued to ask about Rose and when she would come home. Valdeen surmised that Becky did not understand what being dead meant. She decided not to cry in front of Becky.

The nurse confirmed Valdeen's appraisal of Becky's understanding and encouraged her to answer Becky's questions with simple answers. She also advised Valdeen to talk to Becky about her own grief and sadness because Rose died. She stated that Becky might ask her mother if she herself or her mommy or daddy were going to die, too. The nurse reiterated her statement about giving simple responses and reassuring Becky that Valdeen and Terrence would not leave her.

About a month after Rose's death, the nurse's visits were discontinued. Valdeen planned to return to her part-time job and Becky would go to her regular day care center. The community health nurse reassured Valdeen of the nurse's availability if questions or problems arose.

Because of the suddenness of Rose's death, the crisis was markedly escalated. The parents were aided in their mourning by knowing the circumstances of the baby's death and planning and participating in funeral services for her. Terrence and Valdeen accepted both Becky's need to know that Rose had died and Becky's limited cognitive ability to comprehend death as adults do. They also perceived the possibility that Becky might wonder about her own or her parents' death.

Critical Guidelines

The initial crisis arose because Rose had insufficient opportunity to become attached to her mother. Valdeen responded well to the initial crisis. She was not prepared to deal with Rose's depression after being hospitalized and separated from home. Professional intervention was needed to help Valdeen cope with Rose's deterioration.

Rose's death was a crisis for the whole family. The parents needed to work through their grief. Additional guidance was needed to ease their feelings of guilt. They needed developmental information in order to understand Becky's concept of death. Since Becky was an easy-going child, the parents might have overlooked her feelings because of their own distress.

Cognitive Development

Just as socialization begins at birth, so does learning. Infants respond to visual patterns almost from birth. Newborns can react to sound and can localize the direction from which sound originates. Furthermore, as is true of attachment processes, cognitive learning involves the infant and the adult caretaker(s), since the child's responses influence the caretaker's interactions with the child (Thomas, 1981). Elkind (1974, 1988) described a child's attachment to parents as the stable foundation supporting a child's entry into social and cognitive learning. Because the contribution of significant adults is so crucial to the development of children, it is important to know something of how and when children learn.

Adults tend to think of children as miniature adults. They impose rules that are too complex for children to understand and demand behaviors of which children may be developmentally incapable.

One young mother was committed to the idea that her toddler learn to read before entering kindergarten. Luckily, she responded to the suggestion that coercion would be unwise. Being read to and watching her parents read would be sufficient to instill in the child an interest in books without subjecting her to literary forced feedings.

In keeping with the erroneous idea of the child as a miniature adult, parents attribute adultlike understanding and intention to their young child's use of "dirty words," swear words, expressions of contempt, or wishes that a person were dead. At most, the child realizes that such words or phrases are powerful in some way. This realization is based on prior reactions of others rather than on understanding the meaning of the words.

Parents may err in attributing intent to a child's actions. Eighteen-month-old Jason had been exploring the office while his mother and the nurse practitioner discussed his current health status. Intrigued by the nurse's shiny support stockings, Jason zeroed in to check things out and ran both his hands up her leg to her skirt hem. His deeply embarrassed mother snatched him up and told him to "stop acting mannish." Jason's mother required considerable discussion with the nurse to convince her that Jason's intent was not a sexual gesture but merely to touch something shiny.

Based on a desire to raise polite, well-mannered children, parents may try to impart rules of behavior to their young children. It does not work because the child is not able to discern situations when the rules apply (Elkind, 1974). A common example is the use of "thank you." The child has been given a gift; the parent's question "What do you say?" is responded to with silence. The parent is frustrated because the child did not learn the rule. The child is frustrated because he cannot yet learn the rule and has annoyed the parent.

Stages of Cognitive Development

Jean Piaget was a Swiss psychologist who conducted extensive observational studies of children in an attempt to understand their stages of intellectual and cognitive development. On the basis of observation, interviews, and experiments, Piaget postulated four stages of cognitive development in children, lasting from birth to the beginning of adolescence. Although he gave normative ages to the stages, Piaget (1969) emphasized the range of individual differences in rates of development and therefore presented chronological ages simply as a guide (Table 5–1).

TABLE 5–1 Piaget's Cognitive Development Stages

Stage	Age	Characteristics
Sensorimotor	Birth–18 months	Child learns about self and surroundings through sensory and motor exploration and experience; learns through trial and error.
Preoperational	18 months–7 years	Child develops language skills, acquires understanding of symbols, recognizes object permanence, learns to separate and classify.
Concrete operational	8 years–11 years	Child uses and manipulates numbers, understands spatial relationships, learns to think logically and to reason.
Formal operational	12 years–Adulthood	Adolescent understands abstract concepts, expands ability to think logically and to reason, formulates and tests hypotheses.

Piaget termed the first stage of cognitive development the *sensorimotor stage*. During the first eighteen months of life, an infant uses her senses to learn about the world. By means of sight, hearing, taste, touch, and smell the infant explores her environment. Eventually she learns patterns of behaviors and looks for ways to test and replicate these patterns, and she gradually learns to predict actions based on the consequences of previous actions. For example, she may learn that dropping a bottle on the floor causes adults in the vicinity to retrieve the bottle and return it to her, an action that she finds gratifying. Such primitive sequences of cause-and-effect behavior are the foundation for future problem solving and lead to more complex intellectual development.

During the *preoperational stage*, the thinking of the young child is quite rigid and inflexible, partly because the child is *egocentric* and unable to appreciate ideas and viewpoints that differ from his own.

At this age, the child comes to realize that even though he cannot see a hidden object or a person who has left the room, the object or person continues to exist. Thus, he attains *object permanence*, the understanding that people and objects exist apart from the self. To the child in the sensorimotor stage, people or objects that are out of sight have disappeared permanently as far as he is concerned. Therefore, when a toy is taken away from him and concealed, he will not look for it. The child at the preoperational stage, on the other hand, will search for a concealed toy, demonstrating object permanence.

Another characteristic of the preoperational stage is the use of symbols in the child's thinking and communicating. At this stage the child realizes that a single word or sign can represent more complex ideas and meanings. Bringing a ball to father is an invitation for father to play with the child; putting on a coat signifies a desire or readiness to go outdoors. Pumpkins signify Halloween and the flag signifies one's country. From such basic signs, the child learns the significance of symbols.

Between the ages of eight and eleven, the child is in the *concrete operational stage*. During this stage the child can use and manipulate numbers and begin to understand spatial relationships. These are the years when the concept of moral judgment begins to develop and when the cognitive skills of the child are burgeoning, although abstract thinking is not yet present. When asked to explain the meaning of the proverb "Never change horses in the middle of a stream," the child will give a literal interpretation, explaining that a rider changing horses in the middle of a stream would fall in and get wet. The child would be unlikely to generalize the meaning to other situations or to extract the message that anyone who starts a project and changes the original plan risks failure.

The fourth stage of cognitive development, the *formal operational stage,* begins at about age twelve. This is the most sophisticated cognitive level. The individual becomes capable of abstract thinking and is able to formulate and test hypotheses. Problem solving at this stage is sequential and orderly, and reasoning processes are logical and usually consistent.

Childhood Concepts of Death

At the beginning of the sensory-motor period (newborn to 18 months), infants have an innate grasp reflex with which they begin to manipulate objects. The reflex activity undergoes progressive change by contact with objects having a variety of different shapes, textures, temperatures, and weights (Thomas, 1981). Grasping and manipulating objects gradually becomes intentional and selective. Elkind (1974) stated that the cognitive task of this period is the conquest of the object. This conquest involves the transition from an object's ceasing to exist for children unless they are in some current sensory contact with it, to an object's existing as a mental symbol when they are not in sensory contact with it. Thus, children of two years or less believe objects and people do not exist unless they can be seen, touched, or heard by the child.

When children are between two and six years, they are in the pre-operational stage. They expand their use of symbols by acquiring language and beginning to use symbolic play. For a child in this stage, an object can have only one name. Once they have affixed a name to a person or object they are reluctant to employ other names that are more conventional. Thus 'an umbrella may continue to be called a "bumbershoot" despite corrections by parents or siblings. Special names are consistently used to refer to significant persons or objects.

From age two on, children ask many questions if they are permitted to do so. By age four they want to know the origin and purpose of things around them. "Where did it come from?" or "What is it for?" are questions they ask repeatedly. At this age children begin to be concerned about death. "What is death?" and "Why do people die?" Most of these children do not see death as final, but as a temporary state.

At some time between ages five and nine, children come to realize that death is final. However, they also personify death and therefore, they feel that death can be outwitted and eluded. This concept still locates death as being outside the person. Thus, children's perception of death is gradually modified by cognitive development. Very young children view death as temporary and when confronted with the death of a loved one believe that the person will return at some future time. School-aged children recognize the difference between life and death but tend to believe that only other people die. By eight or nine years of age, children are aware of personal mortality but perceive death as possible rather than inevitable. Magical thinking is often used by children to ward off threats of illness or injury. Some youngsters take reckless risks to master their fears. They may accept dares and challenges that permit them to scoff at danger and deny their growing awareness of sharing the destiny of all living things.

In explaining death to children, it is advisable to be factual and honest. Euphemisms and evasions tend to confuse children. Statements to the effect that "Grandpa is happier where he is now" seem strange when uttered by weeping family members. Preparing children to deal with death can be facilitated by candid discussion of the cyclical nature of human existence. Such discussion is a form of anticipatory guidance that may be painful for adults but helpful for children, whose cognitive and experiential understanding of death is limited. When any family member dies, the reminiscing and mementos that ease mourning for adults can be adapted to help children accept and understand.

Entry into the stage of concrete operations occurs at about age seven or eight and this stage persists until about age eleven. To their parents' delight, children's intense question asking is over. Their thinking is now more adultlike in that they can deal with two elements or relationships of a situation at the same time. In confronting death these children can see the difference between the inevitable death of an elderly person and the untimely death of a younger person. Furthermore, in their mastery of recognizing classes of things, children can complete the primary school exercise of inspecting several items and picking out the one that does not belong—that is, the item not in the same classification as the others.

In discussing children's cognitive ability at this stage Elkind coined the term "cognitive conceit" and applied it to the new discovery by children that adults can be wrong and the resulting assumption that adults must be wrong about almost everything. Although children suppose adults to be in error much of the time, they also believe that most adults have good intentions in spite of not being very bright (Elkind, 1974).

Piaget's theoretical framework can also be used in trying to teach, reassure, and care for children of various ages, whatever the setting. Knowing that a young child cannot use or understand symbols will remind nurses to interact in a fashion appropriate to the child's age and cognitive abilities. The use of games, dolls, and puppets to explain various procedures to hospitalized children is one example of the application of Piaget's ideas. His framework is also helpful in understanding why separation from the mother is particularly distressing for children in the sensorimotor stage, who believe that absent persons and objects cease to exist.

INDIVIDUAL LIFE TASKS

0–18 months	Trust vs. mistrust	• Consistent loving care fosters trust • Inconsistent harsh care fosters mistrust • Some mistrust remains in every adult
1–3 years	Autonomy vs. shame and doubt	• Desire arises to control own thoughts and actions • Success leads to sense of control over body and environment
3–6 years	Initiative vs. guilt	• Need to explore world via senses, actions, imagination • Conscience begins to develop, guiding initiative • Negative relationships with parents promote guilt
6–12 years	Industry vs. inferiority	• Understands and accepts rules • Engages in productive work • Starts and completes tasks • Excessive parental expectations induces feelings of inferiority
12–18 years	Identity vs. role diffusion	• Attempts to rework problems of earlier stages • Demonstrates interest in members of opposite sex • Tries to integrate past and present experiences • Copes with changing body image • Searches for identity and a place in society
18–25 years	Intimacy vs. isolation	• Achieves sufficient identity to establish intimacy • Accepts personal commitments • Tries to understand others and to be understood by others • Isolation results when intimacy is not attained
25–55 years	Generativity vs. stagnation	• Tries to guide and eventually release the next generation • Is concerned with maintaining family and cultural values
55 years on	Ego integrity vs. despair	• Renounces self-love and unrealistic ambitions • Becomes aware of human continuity • Gratitude for the gift of life reduces fear of death

Source: Adapted from Erikson *Childhood and Society* (1963).

Temperament

Attachment processes, social learning, and cognitive development are thought to begin at birth. Similarly, a child's temperament becomes apparent in the neonatal period. Just as attachment behaviors are variable over time, so are manifestations of temperament. Thomas and Chess (1977) defined *temperament* as a behavioral style expressed over time. The origins of behavioral style or temperament may lie in genetic influences as these are influenced by social experiences. Parents and siblings, peer groups, teachers, extended family members, and neighbors all convey environmental and familial influences to children (Thomas, 1981).

Individuality in behaviors of newborn infants appears in the regularity or irregularity of their eating patterns, in the intensity of motor activity, in their responses to stimuli, and in their willingness to modify their reactions. Thomas and Chess (1977) formulated nine traits of temperament from which they developed three constellations of children: (1) the easy child, (2) the slow-to-warm-up child, and (3) the difficult child. All three constellations may be considered within normal limits. Not every child definitely fits into one of the constellations and no child remains in the same constellation at all times. The individuality of each child persists in spite of trait or temperament categorization. The nine traits constituting temperament characteristics include the following:

1. Level of motor activity (proportion of active and inactive periods).
2. Rhythmicity or regularity (cycles of eating, sleeping, and elimination).
3. Approach–withdrawal responses (initial response to new stimuli).
4. Adaptability (readiness to modify responses to new stimuli).
5. Responsiveness threshold (amount of stimulation needed to elicit a response).
6. Reaction intensity (energy level of response).
7. Mood quality (proportion of positive, friendly behavior to negative, unfriendly behavior).
8. Distractibility (alteration of ongoing activity by presence of extraneous stimuli).
9. Attention span and persistence (attention span refers to amount of time in which child engages in an activity; persistence refers to continuing an activity in the face of obstacles to continuation).

According to Thomas and Chess (1984), individuality of temperament is well-established by two to three months of age. However, temperament in the sense of behavioral style changes over time, with some traits showing less durability than others. In addition, as children develop, their behavioral repertoire expands and the same temperamental characteristics may be expressed in different ways. For example, establishing daily routines may offer fewer opportunities to display slow adaptability while promoting rhythmicity and regularity.

It is clear that a child's temperament interacting with certain environmental circumstances can precipitate a crisis, such as the disruption of the relationship between a parent and child.

Thomas and Chess were interested in seeing whether behavioral problems of their subjects in late childhood and adolescence could be predicted on the basis of temperament; they found that the most important predictor of adjustment or maladjustment was not the temperament of the child but the "fit" or "consonance" between the child and the family environment. Consonance was considered present when parental expectations and demands were in accord with the child's capacities, motivation, and behavioral style. For example, a boy might have a constellation of behaviors that earned him the label of "difficult" by the investigators, but if his parents accepted that his behaviors were different from those of an "easy" child and rose to the challenge without rejecting their son, the child's adjustment would be eased.

Thomas and Chess (1977, 1981) pointed to the importance of *goodness of fit*, which results from compatibility between the child and the environment. Compatibility or consonance exists when environmental expectations and demands are in accord with the child's capacities, motivation, and behavioral style. All parents bring their particular values and attitudes to child rearing. Their responses to the child depend greatly on harmony or goodness of fit between the child's temperament and parental expectations. It is also helpful if family standards conform to those of the community, the school, and other social institutions.

Sometimes a child's temperament interacting with environmental factors can precipitate a crisis in the form of disruption in the relationship between parents and children. Dissonance between environmental circumstances may exist in a large, busy family in which easy-going children are ignored because they are relatively undemanding. In some instances these children are overlooked and their ability to make strong attachments is impaired. At the same time, children in such families who cannot shift easily from one activity to another may be labeled as stubborn rather than merely persistent.

Various stimuli present in the environment are qualitatively different for children of different temperaments. Children who hesitate to approach new experiences or situations differ from their active, busy counterparts who plunge headlong into every event. Nevertheless, both types of responses may be considered normal.

Children's temperaments influence attachment formation and cognitive development. Their emotional attachments are the foundation from which they perceive and influence their environment. Within the framework of their cognitive development they can elect a different way of dealing with environmental demands or of eventually selecting a different kind of environment.

Temperament and Stress

During childhood children and their families encounter stressful life events, such as illness, relocation, and the loss of a significant person through death or divorce. Stress is also engendered in the daily operations of children and their families through time pressures, obligations, and what Kanner et al. (1981) termed *daily hassles.* A number of variables have been identified that reduce the impact of stresses being expressed behaviorally. High levels of social support constitute a mediating variable. Another mediating variable is temperament, and environmental responses. Carey (1981) noted that temperament–environment interactions are involved in such childhood problems as colic, night waking, minor developmental delay, school performance, and frequency of accidents and illness. They are also likely to be factors in failure-to-thrive, child abuse, obesity, and other psychosomatic syndromes. In a study of relationships among stress, temperament, and behavior, Wertlieb et al. (1987) found several areas of significance. The following temperament characteristics were associated with behavioral symptoms in children: high activity level, low adaptability, withdrawal from new stimuli, high intensity, unpleasant or unhappy mood, lack of persistence, and irregularity and unpredictability of behavior. The data also indicated that chronic stresses caused by poverty led to daily hassles that may be as stressful to children as major adverse life events. How particular temperament attributes place certain children at risk has not yet been clearly documented. Available data lend empirical support to the idea that temperament is a significant influence in the socioemotional functioning of children and in the outcome of stress reactions. Lerner and East (1984, p. 158) wrote that "temperament may be a quite salient moderator of a person's reactions to stressors" by interacting "with key contextual moderators, such as social support."

FAMILY AS A RESOURCE

The parents as caretakers of children provide them with their first and most intense attachments, their first opportunities to manifest temperament, and their first learning experiences. As children develop, their siblings will influence them. Thomas and Chess (1977) indicated that each child has a different family experience because of ordinal position, age at the birth of any siblings, and sex. Younger children may model the behavior of older siblings and of the parents. For example, Chrissie, at age two, was frustrated with her toilet training. She could not understand why aiming her belly button at the toilet to urinate only resulted in wet sneakers when (by her observations) it seemed to work just fine for her daddy and big brother!

Grandparents, aunts, uncles, cousins, and other extended family members are not merely persons with whom the child establishes additional attachments. They are also the repository and conveyors of the family's history and accumulated wisdom. That wisdom often relates to how problems were solved and crises managed in the past. In addition, adult members of the family provide access to resources, such as human services agencies or health care facilities, to which the child alone could not gain entry.

COUNSELING CHILDREN

Grownups like to think of childhood as a jolly time when most parents or parent surrogates love and protect their children. This is not always true. Even in stable families, children inhabit an inner world of uncertainty and puzzlement, which is aggravated by urgent maturational tasks. Because infants and young children are so dependent on adults to attend to their needs, teaching adults who are responsible for children about maturational tasks and developmental stages is a primary prevention strategy. Dysfunctional behavior patterns in children can be worsened or alleviated, depending on parental expectations. Parents and others who do not recognize developmental time frames may attempt to hasten or impede processes that are within the normal range.

If the behavior problems of children assume crisis proportions, practitioners can use principles of secondary intervention. When it appears that a parent is the instigator of the problem, practitioners can model effective adult-child interactions. By explaining and demonstrating basic concepts of stimulus, response, reward, and conditioning, practitioners can indicate those adult actions that initiate, reinforce, or reduce undesirable behavior in children. The difference between limit setting and punishment is a subtle one for parents who rely only on scoldings and spankings to change children's behavior. It is extremely important to show parents the value of positive reinforcement (rewards) in eliciting improved behavior. For some parents praise is harder to bestow than criticism. Such parents need to learn that approving gestures will not necessarily threaten discipline or erode their authority.

•CLINICAL EXAMPLE:
CRISIS OF SEPARATION

Mrs. Louise Selby, her husband, and four sons had recently moved to the city from their home of long standing in a mountain town. The move was prompted by hard times at home and the lure of employment for the husband. The family had no nearby relatives and had neither opportunity nor desire to make friends in the neighborhood. Mrs. S. described feeling like a "foreigner" in her mixed neighborhood of black, hispanic, and white families. Her three school-aged sons had frequent fights with other children in the area but were tentatively beginning to make friends at school. Then the school nurse told Mrs. S. that one of the boys had intestinal parasites. All the children needed testing and treatment. The cost of health clinic visits and medication further taxed the family's meager resources.

A community health nurse had made several home visits to support Mrs. S. in her efforts to coordinate the baby's health needs and the social needs of the entire family. Mrs. S. seemed unusually harried and short-tempered with the baby and, with the nurse's encouragement, divulged that her husband had escalated his drinking recently. They had argued more, and Mr. S. had left the family a few days ago and did not plan to return.

The family was nearly out of food, the rent was due in several days, and Mrs. S. had no money. "And to make it worse, I got the kids underfoot all the time. I say 'go play' and they go for ten minutes! And Billy's started wettin' the bed."

Mrs. S. needed to share her anger and frustration. Because of the trust established with the nurse, she was also able to admit her sadness and her fear. She felt totally abandoned by her husband in a hostile environment.

She had some awareness that the children also had similar feelings. As the eldest child, ten-year-old Billy had been "the apple of his dad's eye." He may have felt the loss of his father more. His being told "you're the man of the family now" probably added to his unspoken fears that mother also would leave. His onset of enuresis—the behavior of a much younger child— was a behavioral plea that mother not leave.

With the nurse's help, Mrs. S. was able to see Billy's actions and some behavior of the younger children as related to their father's departure. That made her more angry at Mr. S. Nonetheless, she was able to verbally reassure the children. "I'm not leavin'—we're a team. And Daddy didn't leave 'cause of you. He's mad at me, not you. He loves you." Billy's bedwetting diminished as his sense of security increased.

Because her resources were so marginal, Mrs. S. chose to return to the mountain town where both she and the boys had access to the support of a large extended family and friends.

Prior to his departure, Mr. and Mrs. S. had argued loudly. Among the accusations exchanged was Mr. S.'s complaint that nothing he did satisfied his wife and that she and the children "are draggin' me down, not letting me get my head above water." The children, of course, overheard.

As the eldest son and his father's favorite, Billy thought that he had done something wrong to make his father leave. He accepted his father's statement. He reinterpreted the parents' discord to see himself as the cause of it, not his father's shaky self-esteem and alcoholism. Although Billy could neither acknowledge his father's problems nor fully accept that marital discord caused the disruption, he was able to assimilate his mother's commitment to the children.

Billy's eight-year-old brother coped with the departure of his father by accepting the message that Billy was "the man of the family" now. Missing his father, he followed Billy constantly. The older boy found this a nuisance, but he tried to respond to his brother's distress.

The five-year-old boy in the family had endless questions about his father's absence. Because his mother became upset by the questions, the five year old turned to Billy for comfort. The youngest child, eleven months of age, continued his usual habit of looking and calling for "Da," especially in the evening when his father usually arrived home from work. He persisted with this for almost two weeks after his father left. For a much longer period he was reluctant to let his mother out of his sight and repeatedly called to her to reassure himself of her presence.

School personnel were especially interested in the two older children. As a result, they met regularly with a school counselor. A social worker from the local health clinic visited the home to help Mrs. S. deal with various community agencies. The worker was not successful in persuading Mrs. S. to make friends in the neighborhood, but her visits and those of the nurses helped the family to feel less isolated and abandoned.

Critical Guidelines

The mother and children in this family experienced two drastic separations within a short period of time. There was separation from a familiar community, followed by the father's desertion. Anxiety levels of all family members was extremely high. In addition, the mother was overwhelmed by her new role as a single parent. In their old community she would have access to the advice and friendship of other women. The first consideration in working with this family was to help the mother deal with the immediate problems. A welfare worker gave assistance so that rent was paid, and the family received a subsistence allowance for food. A community worker was made available to accompany Mrs. S. to a parents' meeting at her boy's school where the school program was explained. Although she continued to be reclusive, Mrs. S. found that the visit did reduce her fears of the unknown. Aid was given to help the family return to their former community.

In general, an ecological approach was used with the family. Once the survival needs of her children were met, Mrs. S. became more receptive to explanations of her children's feelings. Even though she chose to return to her home community, the crisis situation became a learning experience for Mrs. S. and strengthened family ties.

SUMMARY

Crisis in children's lives should be examined in light of the developmentally relevant resources available to the child for crisis resolution. Attachment, cognitive development, and temperament of children influence and are influenced by family reciprocity and interaction. Additionally, the concepts of attachment and separation by their presence or absence clarify situational precipitators of crisis in children. Theories of cognitive development and studies of temperament in children also help to explain some of the differential responses of children in crisis.

REFERENCES

Belsky, J., and M. Rovine. "Temperament and Attachment Security in the Strange Situation: An Empirical Rapprochement." *Child Development* 58(1987): 787–795.

Bowlby, J. "Attachment." In *Attachment and Loss*, vol. 1. New York: Basic Books, 1969.

―――. "Separation." In *Attachment and Loss*, vol. 2. New York: Basic Books, 1973.

―――. *The Making and Breaking of Affectional Bonds*. London: Tavistock, 1979.

Carey, W.B. "The Importance of Temperament-Environment Interaction for Child Health and Development." In *The Uncommon Child,''* edited by M. Lewis and L. Rosenbaum. New York: Plenum Press, 1981.

Elkind, D. *Children and Adolescents: Interpretative Essays on Jean Piaget.* New York: Oxford University Press, 1974.

―――. *The Hurried Child.* Menlo Park, California: Addison-Wesley, 1988.

Erikson, E. *Childhood and Society.* New York: Norton, 1963.

Fish, M., and J. Belsky, "Temperament and Attachment Revisited: Origin and Meaning of Separation Intolerance at Age Three." *American Journal of Orthopsychiatry* 61(1991): 418–427.

Kanner, A.D., A. Harrison, and D. Wertlieb, "Comparison of Two Modes of Stress Measurement: Daily Hassles and Uplifts vs. Major Life Events." *Behavioral Medicine* 4(1981): 1–39.

Kopp, C.P. "Regulation of Distress and Negative Emotions: A Developmental View." *Developmental Psychology* 25(1989): 343–354.

Lerner, R.M., and P.L. East, "The Role of Temperament in Stress, Coping, and Socioemotional Functioning in Early Development." *Journal of Infant Mental Health* 5(1984): 148–159.

Litt, C.J. "Children's Attachment to Transitional Objects: A Study of Pediatric Populations." *American Journal of Orthopsychiatry* 51(1981): 131–139.

Piaget, J. *Origins of Intelligence in Childhood*. New York: International Universities Press, 1969.

Roberts, W., and J. Strayer "Parents' Responses to the Emotional Distress of Their Children: Relations with Childrens' Competence." *Developmental Psychology* 23(1987): 415–422.

Spitz, R. "Hospitalism: An Inquiry into the Genesis of Psychiatric Conditions in Early Childhood." *Psychoanalytic Study of the Child* 1(1945): 53–73.

————. "Anaclitic Depression." *Psychoanalytic Study of the Child* 2(1946): 313–342.

Sroufe, L.A. "The Role of the Infant Caregiver Attachment in Development." In *Clinical Implications of Attachment*, edited by J. Belsky and T. Nezworski. Hillsdale, New Jersey: Lawrence Erbaum, 1988.

Thomas, A. "Theory and Review: Current Trends in Developmental Theory." *American Journal of Orthopsychiatry* 51(1981): 580–609.

Thomas, A., and S. Chess. *Temperament and Development*. New York: Brunner/Mazel, 1977.

————. *The Dynamics of Psychological Development*. New York: Brunner/Mazel, 1981.

————. "Genesis and Evolution of Behavioral Disorders from Infancy to Early Adult Life." *American Journal of Psychiatry* 141(1984): 1–9.

Wertlieb, D., C. Weigel, T. Springer, and M. Feldstein, "Temperament as a Moderator of Childrens' Stressful Experiences." *American Journal of Orthopsychiatry* 57(1987): 234–245.

6

Adolescents in Crisis
The Teen Years

*We are so largely the playthings of fate in our fears.
To one, fear of the dark, to another of physical pain,
to a third of public ridicule, to a fourth of poverty, to
a fifth of loneliness—for all of us our own particular
creature lurks in ambush.*

Hugh Walpole

For adolescents, as for younger children, developmental issues play a
large role in precipitating crises. At the same time developmental maturation may improve a teenager's capacity for crisis resolution, especially if
family support is available. In exploring the expanded social sphere of
adolescents, it is appropriate to discuss such important factors as attachment, temperament, and cognitive development.

ATTACHMENT

Bonds of affection between parents and child weaken somewhat during
the young person's adolescence. Nonetheless, Bowlby (1969) indicated
that the attachment persists at relatively intense levels throughout life,
with individual variations in range of intensity. Attachments with siblings in part reflect the teen's ordinal position among the children. For
example, an older teen may take a parent surrogate role with one or more
younger siblings. On the other hand, the teen may become closer to one or
more older siblings whose role may be as mentor or guide. Teenagers
form bonds with other adults that may approach the intensity of bonds
with parents. Thus, teachers, counselors, the school nurse, neighbors,
leaders of community teen groups (such as clergy), and others in human
service professions may become very accessible as resources. Rutter
(1979) tied the establishment of such bonds to successful past attachments and the trust that results. As with prior attachments, the effectiveness of newer attachments is predicated on the quality, strength, and

109

security of the relationship. Progression from junior to senior high school usually results in association with a larger peer group. Sexual attraction also accounts for increasing association with and attachment to peers, since dating often begins with group activities. Peer group discussions may informally promote problem-solving skills as teens share the similarities and diversities of their experiences and thoughts (Ricks, 1980). Perception of this broadening social milieu of the teenager gives perspective to the degree of distress the teenagers experience when families move to a different geographic location.

The shift in attachments and social relationships is exemplified by the adolescent's decrease in time spent with the family and increase in time spent either away from the family altogether or in solitude. Gradually, teenagers become transportation-oriented: bicycles, roller skates, skateboards, cars, or almost anything else that will move them from one place to another!

Some adolescents are estranged from their parents. They account for some portion of the teenagers who run away from home each year. Several transactional modes may occur in families. Two modes contain an element of estrangement. The expelling mode involves the neglect and rejection of the teen. Parents abdicate their caretaker roles, setting no limits for the young person. In the expelling mode, parents are fairly active in encouraging the teenager to move out. The expelling mode is used by parents who are consumed by their own life issues, such as marital problems. The delegating mode is another mechanism by which the adolescent is cued to behave in ways that give vicarious pleasure to the parents. Here the teenager does what the parents cannot do. This mechanism may also include acting out the parents' delinquent tendencies. In other instances, teenagers run away because of a crisis of their own. This departure becomes a plea for the parents to rescue them and induce them to return. When such a desperate act is performed to initiate parental involvement, the young person may have a long history of inadequate parental care. Thus, the current crisis is complicated by the chronic one. Periodic physical distancing is often accompanied by disagreement of the teenager's and parents' opinions about clothing, hair length, or other aspects of appearance, as well as the reasonableness of curfews or other limits.

A pattern of antisocial behavior can sometimes be discerned early in life. In some families the child of five to ten begins to show signs of excessive defiance, temper tantrums, unruliness, and hostility. One of the consistent findings in the lives of delinquent adolescents is a constellation of unfavorable family characteristics. Parents of teenagers who display antisocial behaviors have a higher-than-average history of alcoholism, criminality, and marital conflict. The mothers frequently lack close emotional ties to their children and tend to ignore the delinquent behavior. The fathers tend to be strict and to use physical forms of punishment. Although disorganization is common in the families of delinquents, it is by no means a requirement. Antisocial behavior is expressed by adolescents from all socioeconomic levels, from intact nuclear families and one-parent families. In short, there is no clear-cut, simple formula to identify delinquent-pro-ducing families (Hartman, et al., 1987).

TEMPERAMENT

The adolescent's temperament or behavioral style continues, as did the child's, to respond to environmental expectations and demands. Thomas (1981) spoke of the proportional dominance of change and continuity. When the environment is stable and when the person's behavior reinforces the stability of environmental components, continu-ity is maintained.

In speaking about consistency of temperament over time, Thomas (1981) defined five variations along a temperament-environment contin-uum. These are clear consistency, sporadic consistency of various aspects of temperament, distortion by other factors of the way temperament is expressed, consistency in temperament with change in the quality of temperament and environment interaction, and clear-cut change in a temperamental trait. Because environmental factors and an individual's abilities and motivations do not remain stable over time, the levels of their impact on temperament will vary. Therefore, a person's tempera-ment does not show linear continuity over time. As a result, a teenager's behavior may offer only occasional remnants of childhood temperament constellations. While past behavior cannot fully predict future actions, some knowledge of an adolescent's prior behavior style, and experiences and the current challenges to be faced can be valuable.

COGNITIVE DEVELOPMENT

In Chapter 5, we saw that children at the stage of concrete operations become able to discern appearance from reality. Concrete operational children view what is physical and external as being real. With accession to formal operations, adolescents come to include their internal subjective experiences as part of reality. The ability to take the perspective of another person evolves in the transition from concrete to formal operations.

Kohlberg and Gilligan (1971) found the age at which formal opera-tional thinking is consistently manifested to be variable, depending in part on socioeconomic status. They found that clear formal operational reasoning was used to complete a task by 53 percent of the sample who were between sixteen and twenty years of age. The highest display occurred in the group aged twenty-one to thirty years, of whom 65 percent were reasoning at formal operational levels. Clearly, a segment of the population probably does not attain the capacity for abstract thought, whereas some other persons may be inconsistent in their ability to deal with abstractions. Formal operational thinking is not solely a function of IQ but reflects the influence of culture and the adolescent's life history. On moving into formal operational thinking, teenagers find that their hypotheses are arbitrary. As they learn hypothesis testing, they also find that some of their hypotheses are wrong (Elkind, 1974). They become self-critical and shift to aspire to adult standards. Furthermore, in being able to examine all the possibilities in a situation, teenagers develop the ability to take the perspective of others.

Early in this nascent perspective taking, however, young teenagers project their interests and concerns onto others. The stereo is played loudly in part because they are sure that everyone else in the house loves that record, that song as much as they. The physical and physiologic changes of early adolescence focus teenagers' attention on their own bodies and their appearance. They think most people are also preoccupied with them, their behavior, and their appearance. Elkind (1974, 1978) referred to this cognitive process as the construction of an imaginary audience. He speculated that this sense of being under constant observation contributes both to teenagers' being very self-conscious and to their increase in seeking privacy and solitude.

From their sense of being the objects of other people's interest, adolescents generate a perception of themselves and of their feelings as being exceptional. Elkind (1974) described a number of manifestations of what he termed the *personal fable.* Among these examples were both the keeping and the content of diaries by some teens, and the evolving of religious belief in a relationship of guidance and support from a personal God. An associated notion of not being subject to the laws of nature is displayed in their expectation that they will not die or that their sexual intercourse without contraception will not result in pregnancy. The personal fable fades as adolescents share their ideas, perceptions, and experiences with other teenagers. They find they are individuals but not unique in the sense of having either special privileges or exemptions from the consequences of risk taking.

In the progression into formal operational thinking, teenagers gather wider ranges of possibilities in dealing with any given situation. Elkind noted their consequent difficulty in making decisions. In part, the difficulty lies with teenagers' inability to assess the appropriateness or the priority of their alternatives (Elkind, 1978). The dilemma is in part responsible for the young teenagers' tendency to follow the dictates of their peer group. They may also baffle their parents by asking for advice and then ignoring it. It is likely to minimize confrontations if parents can include the adolescent in the process of evaluating factors relevant to limit setting, such as curfews. It is equally clear that if decisions are left totally up to young teenagers, they may flounder in the sea of alternatives. An unspoken parental expectation that teenagers can easily accept parental views and give them priority over their own is unrealistic.

MORAL JUDGMENT

Kohlberg (1968) proposed a theory of moral development that sees the individual as going through a fixed series of states. This theory is based on a longitudinal study of males ranging in age from ten to twenty-eight. Data collection procedure consisted of reading the subjects stories that depicted moral dilemmas, asking them to solve them, then questioning subjects about their reasons for arriving at particular solutions. Kohlberg's emphasis was on the subjects' reasoning processes in solving the moral dilemmas, not on the solutions themselves. A coding and scoring system was used that allowed researchers to classify and analyze the proposed solutions. As a result of this long-term investigation, Kohlberg identified three levels of moral development, each of which is further divided into two stages (called *orientations*), making a total of six. The accompanying box outlines the stages and levels of moral development proposed by Kohlberg.

KOHLBERG'S MORAL DEVELOPMENT STAGES

Preconventional Level

Stage 1. Punishment and obedience orientation
Stage 2. Instrumental relativist orientation

Conventional Level

Stage 3. Interpersonal concordance or good boy/nice girl orientation
Stage 4. Law and order orientation

Postconventional Level

Stage 5. Social contract legalistic orientation
Stage 6. Universal ethical principle orientation

One of Kohlberg's basic assumptions is that the progression of moral development does not vary in any way. That is, each individual must proceed through each of the given stages in sequence and cannot omit a stage while advancing to higher levels of moral development.

Each stage of moral development has its own particular orientation; ambiguity arises as individuals begin to question their present orientation stage. This questioning is resolved as individuals move to the next stage and find that the new orientation settles or reconciles their previous questions. If a person finds that his present stage is not adequate to resolve a moral dilemma, he will gravitate toward the next highest stage.

Preconventional Level

Kohlberg described the first level, or *preconventional level,* as one at which the child is responsive to cultural labels of good and bad, right and wrong, but interprets these labels in terms either of the physical or psychological consequences of action (punishment, reward, exchange of favors) or of the physical power of those who enunciate the rules and labels. This level describes most children up to the age of early adolescence; however, some adults are fixated at this level, too. At this first level, actions are judged according to expected consequences.

Fear governs the actions of a person at stage 1 of the preconventional level called the *punishment and obedience orientation.* Kohlberg's theory would explain the antisocial actions of criminals as behaviors of a stage 1, preconventional level. Kohlberg called stage 2 the *instrumental relativist orientation.* At this stage a person decides issues based on what satisfies her own needs and sometimes considers the needs of others. Persons operating at stage 2 of the preconventional level perceive society as made up of others like themselves, and they believe that if they extend help to others, they are likely to be helped in return. Because the person at this stage believes that all people are alike, she will begin to question why one person should have more rights than another. Thus, stage 2 marks the beginning of a sense of fairness. Nonetheless, self-interest remains important, and fear of authority is reduced. To obtain compliance from persons at this stage, it may be necessary to demonstrate how they will benefit from a given situation or transaction.

Conventional Level

The move from the preconventional level to the *conventional level* is accompanied by accepting group values, and recognizing the importance of group rules and sanctions. The personal consequences of an action are no longer the only criteria by which to judge its goodness or morality. Instead, an action is judged by how well it meets the standards or expectations of others in a group or social order. When individuals identify with a group, the esteem and approval of others begins to displace tangible rewards as dominant motivators of behavior. Another feature of the conventional level is cohesiveness or wishes to belong to a group. At this level group standards of conformity and loyalty are readily adopted. Most teenagers operate at the first phase (stage 3) of the conventional level. This helps explain their preoccupation with fads and popular heroes. Gradually, they realize that society is composed of diverse groups whose values and customs must be considered. This realization causes them to progress to the second phase (stage 4), at which time they respect authority and order. They tend to assume that no person or group is above the law; Kohlberg declared that most adults remain fixed at this stage of moral development.

Postconventional Level

Before advancing to this level behavior is guided by fear of punishment (stage 1), desire for rewards (stage 2), group norms (stage 3), or adherence to rules and laws (stage 4). At this last level individuals make a distinction between public welfare and personal freedom. They believe the existing laws may be questioned, and that the status quo may be challenged without creating anarchy. At the same time laws cannot be discarded simply because they are personally objectionable.

This last and highest stage of moral development encourages internalized respect for honor, justice, and the rights of all. The individual operating at this level will go far to avoid violating self-imposed principles, even at the cost of unpleasant consequences, such as imprisonment or social ostracism. In Kohlberg's view, this stage is an ideal seldom reached.

Critics of Kohlberg's work assert that he did not give equal attention to both sexes, and that he considered the word *child* to refer only to boys. Gilligan (1982, 1983) proposed that there are two modes of moral reasoning. One mode, as described by Kohlberg, is based on logic, justice, and rights; the other is based on caring, circumstances, and relationships.

Gilligan has concluded that men and boys are apt to define themselves in terms of autonomy and achievement, whereas women define themselves in terms of relationships. In her ongoing work Gilligan has found that many girls emerge from adolescence with a poor self-image, and lowered expectations for themselves. Among girls, race seems to be a significant factor. More black girls have been found to be relatively self-confident in high school compared with white and Hispanic girls. White girls lose their self-assurance earlier than Hispanic girls. Without making broad generalizations, Gilligan states that it is during the teen years that girls begin to doubt themselves. At eleven years of age they are full of self-confidence, but by age fifteen or sixteen they have begun to doubt themselves (Gilligan et al., 1989).

Gilligan's work is relevant to crisis among adolescents for two reasons. (1) It acknowledged the complexity of the many facets of human development, and (2) it included the influence of gender in considering adolescent behavior and motivation.

SOMATIC CHANGES

Physical maturation accompanies the cognitive and moral development of children and adolescents. Teenagers today, male and female, reach physical maturity earlier than young people of previous generations. This trend is generally attributed to improved nutrition and hygiene as well as declines in infant mortality (Bellack & Edlund, 1992). Today, North American males reach full stature at age twenty compared with age twenty-five in 1900. Tanner and Davies (1985) noted that the onset of completion of puberty varies considerably among eleven-, twelve-, and thirteen-year-old girls and among thirteen-, fourteen-, and fifteen-year-old boys. This variation is illustrated by data on age at menarche. The trend has been for age at menarche to drop three or four months every decade. Currently the median age at menarche is 12.5 years compared with 13.5 years in 1950.

The hallmark of adolescence is puberty, a physiological process during which the reproductive system begins to function. For girls, puberty begins with the appearance of breast buds and pubic hair. Axillary hair appears later than pubic hair. The height spurt follows, and menarche usually occurs after the girl has had her greatest acceleration in height. Early menstrual cycles are often anovulatory and irregular in occurrence. Each girl's individual cyclic timing of ovulation and menstruation becomes established somewhat later in adolescence. The sequence of pubertal changes for boys usually commences with the growth of the testes and scrotum. The skin of the scrotum becomes more wrinkled and darkens. Pubic hair appears, and the penis enlarges both in length and circumference. The boy's height spurt occurs. Axillary hair becomes evident about two years after pubic hair. Facial hair, growing first at the corners of the upper lip, begins concurrently with axillary hair, as does the growth of body hair. Voice changes may be marked or gradual and occur fairly late in the sequence.

These events of puberty are potentially problematic for some. For example, at the time when his testes and scrotum had enlarged but his penis had not yet begun to grow, one particular teenaged boy noticed the change in size proportion. His interpretation, however, was that his penis was shrinking. His concern had been elicited by the comments of the coach about the expected and normal increase in teens' interest in their body changes and sensations, including exploration by masturbation. The coach reassured him that he was growing normally and indicated that his penis would start to grow larger about the time he noticed hair growing in his genital area.

Physical changes progress fairly steadily throughout childhood and are assimilated into the child's body image relatively easily. As the rate of physical change normally increases in adolescence, however, assimilation processes have difficulty keeping pace. Again, the young person may feel helpless in the face of these changes. The psychological component of body image is crucial; adolescents' self-esteem and coping mechanisms are tested as they struggle to adapt to the changes. Being different carries an implication of being inferior and may affect children who mature earlier or later than their peers. Sibling comparison and rivalry may also contribute to concerns with body image, as in instances in which a younger sibling begins pubertal changes before the older teen. Also, younger adolescents may begin the sequence of change after an older sibling but, because of variation in tempo, may move through and complete development earlier than the older teen. Frequently, many of the late-developing adolescents have deep concerns about whether their bodies will ever develop properly. Concurrent worries about sexual development are reflected in hidden concerns about sexual functioning. In addition, adolescents may cause their sense of inadequacy on a perceived defect that may be relatively minor or a variation of normal.

SEXUALITY IN ADOLESCENCE

Somatic growth brings the teenager's physical size to adult levels, whereas the changes of puberty bring internal and external physical characteristics closer to the appearance and function of an adult of the same gender. Much of the cause of these changes is the preparation of the young person's body for sexual and reproductive functioning.

Chilman (1977) described human sexuality as having physical and psychosocial aspects. Physical aspects include bodily characteristics and the capacity for specific sexual behaviors. The psychosocial component encompasses learning, values, norms, and attitudes about sexual behaviors, as well as gender identity and related beliefs and attitudes about oneself and others as males or females in society. Usually a person's gender identity or sense of being either male or female is developed by age three. The other elements of sexuality evolve over time, subject to influence by the person's past and present experiences, and societal norms. Much of the development of adolescence is geared toward achieving adult sexuality.

Early adolescence is marked by close friendships with teens of the same sex, often involving group activities. Chilman (1977) stated that sex play occurs fairly frequently in groups of boys aged eight to thirteen. Their activities include mutual masturbation, exhibitionism, and voyeurism. In early adolescence, about 10 percent of boys may engage in sex relations at least once with another male. However, only about 3 percent engage in long-term homosexual relationships. The data for girls indicate that about 5 percent are involved in early adolescent homosexual activity, with less than 2 percent participating in long-term involvements.

Research studies have tried to evaluate differences between adolescent girls who are sexually active and those who are not. A relationship has been established between adolescent sexual activity and the use of alcohol, tobacco, and other drugs (Franklin, 1988). A study done in California, which controlled for race of the subjects, found that sexual activity was significantly related to race and socioeconomic status (SES), with black and low-SES girls more likely to be sexually active (Gibbs, 1986). Interestingly, white females were more likely to use drugs but less likely to be sexually active. A conclusion was reached that race, going steady, and cigarette smoking were the strongest predictors of early sexual activity.

A number of investigators agree that smoking and drug abuse may have unique importance during adolescence for the following reasons:

- This type of behavior is an attempt to grasp otherwise unattainable goals.
- The behaviors are learned ways of handling personal frustration and anticipated failure.
- The behaviors express rejection of more conventional society.
- The behaviors ease developmental transition and signify membership in the peer subculture.

It is apparent that teenagers who begin to smoke and drink at an early age tend to adopt other so-called adult activities in the teen years (Franklin, 1988; Zelnik & Kantner, 1980). Family structure is another factor in teenage pregnancy since girls in father-absent households are more likely to become pregnant than girls in two-parent homes (Buchholz & Gol, 1986).

Other studies indicate that for girls the motivation stems from a wish to please the sexual partner, although they apparently experience less sexual pleasure. Ladner (1971, p. 209) attributed the early sexual activity of low-income black girls to their search for a feeling of "belonging and feeling needed by their boyfriends . . . and a sense of identity and utility." Quay (1981) suggested that, especially for girls, dependency needs, unhappiness at home, and a wish for affection underlie early coitus and pregnancy.

Piaget (1969) asserted that adolescents are undergoing a shift from concrete to formal operational thinking. Consistent contraceptive behavior demands thinking on the level of formal operations. Not all adolescents are capable of abstract thinking on the causes and consequences of their actions. Only those adolescents who have advanced to this level of thinking can prepare for sexual encounters, avoid impulsive coitus, and acquire and apply the information needed for responsible sexual behavior.

An adolescent still at the stage of concrete operations has limited understanding of the meaning of the ovulation, conception, and child-birth processes. Another consequence of being in the concrete operational stage is extreme egocentrism, which allows the adolescent to feel special and invincible. This personal fable of their own uniqueness reinforces adolescent attitudes that bad things happen to other people but not to them.

The male partner's role is an essential factor in considering contraceptive behavior among adolescents. Zelnik and Kantner (1980) reported that about 40 percent of sexually active females depend on male use of contraceptives. Among the many different reasons teenagers gave for getting pregnant were: (1) wanting a baby, (2) holding on to a boyfriend, (3) thinking it might be "fun" to have a baby, (4) punishing her parents, and (5) wanting to be loved by the baby (Resnick et al., 1990).

Programs at the level of individuals, families, and communities must be developed if the teenage pregnancy rates are to be lowered. Attention must be paid to adolescents prone to early initiation into sexual activity. This means identifying families most likely to foster precocious sexual activities in their adolescents, and understanding community norms that reinforce patterns of early sexual activity and parenthood. Hofferth (1985) conducted a literature review on the impact of family planning programs on the sexual activity, contraceptive use, and fertility of adolescents. She concluded that adolescents engaged in smoking, drinking, or drug use, and adolescents with poor academic performance were most at risk and should be a target group for primary prevention. Ideally, such programs would help girls identify educational and vocational goals, and assist them in comprehending the limiting effects of adolescent motherhood. Outreach efforts of these programs would try to involve males. Franklin (1988) adds that the widespread problem of joblessness should be part of any agenda addressing teenage pregnancy. In light of this, a worthy goal of any program trying to reduce teenage pregnancy is to decrease high school dropout rates and enable more adolescents to be competitive in the labor force.

A number of school districts across the country have established student health clinics within high schools, where students have access to services that they might not otherwise seek. Staffed by nurse practitioners and part-time physicians, the clinics usually accept referrals from school nurses, teachers, parents, and the students themselves. The school-based clinics utilize support services of school guidance counselors, nutritionists, psychologists, and community health care providers. Most of the clinics provide services ranging from emergency care to physical assessment, immunization, counseling, and follow-up supervision. Information on school-based clinics is available from the Support Center for School-Based Clinics, 5650 Kirby St., Suite 242, Houston, Texas 77005. The Support Center is underwritten by the Center for Population Options, Washington, D.C. (Desrosiers, 1989).

There is a tendency for some young people to regard spontaneous sexual intercourse as an outcome of feelings too strong to control. Impulsive sexual activity is not considered wholly wrong as long as premeditation was not present. The premise is that "good" girls may sometimes be swept away by passion but should not be condemned harshly for this lapse. Conversely, "bad" girls are those who engage in planned sexual activity in which some form of contraception is used. When these ideas are expressed, the counselor must refute the fallacious notion that: (1) sexual intercourse that takes place on the impulse of the moment is acceptable and relatively guiltless, and (2) sexual intercourse that is planned and protected is more reprehensible than sexual intercourse that is unplanned and unprotected.

In identifying general factors that inhibited sexual behavior among their male subjects, Offer and Offer (1977) listed fear of interpersonal closeness, fear of rejection, constraints of social norms, and lack of opportunity. The first three inhibitors seem comparable to the first two reasons given by the Canadian young women for their abstinence. In their study with a group of female virgins in Canada, Herold and Goodwin (1981) found that as a reason for abstaining from premarital intercourse, the belief that it was wrong ranked third. The two most common reasons given were: (1) the teen felt that she was not ready to have intercourse, and (2) she had not met a suitable partner. These young women were in their late teens.

Some teens bolster their low self-esteem through a love-sex relationship or counteract their sense of inadequacy through hostile, manipulative, exploitive sexual embezzlement. While *embezzlement* may seem a strange term in connection with sex, it is supported by studies which noted that young, sexually active adolescent girls were very likely to engage in sex behavior largely to please their boyfriends and did not enjoy it themselves (Chilman, 1977, 1983). This revelation may partially explain the findings of Zelnik and Kantner, that sexually experienced teenaged women had intercourse infrequently; 48 percent had not had intercourse in the four weeks prior to interview for the study. Infrequent intercourse may in turn partly explain the trend away from birth control pills to less reliable contraceptive methods, noted by Zelnik and Kantner (1980). The shift to less reliable contraception or to no contraception may also reflect decision making based on the personal fable. They saw teens as applying the laws of probability to their own sexual activity in an ignorant way, believing pregnancy was not possible because "we only did it a few times." If intercourse has not resulted in pregnancy, teenaged women may then surmise that they cannot get pregnant.

Follow-up studies indicate that programs that assist young mothers to complete their education are associated with increased use of contraception and fewer subsequent pregnancies (Phipps-Yonas, 1980). Elective abortion tends to be the recourse of older pregnant females and of those in higher socioeconomic classes. Decisions either to abort or to carry pregnancy to term seem to be related to influence from the mother or boyfriend. Not infrequently the individual who succumbs to pressure from others for abortion will soon conceive again and carry the subsequent pregnancy to term. In the short run, those who have been persuaded to abort seem less able to cope with the stress of the procedure than those who choose freely. In general, anxiety and depression are more associated with delay than with abortion itself. There is, however, no easy way to deal with the crisis of an unwanted and unexpected pregnancy at any age.

The rising incidence of teenage pregnancy has led to federal, state, and local programs that focus on pregnancy prevention, pregnancy decision making, and postpregnancy outcomes. One strategy has been to suggest adoption as an alternative to abortion or teenage motherhood. The majority of respondents in a retrospective study cited external reasons such as pressure from parents, physicians, and social workers as the primary reason for placing the children for adoption. A small minority cited personal reasons such as age, education, or unpreparedness for parenthood as major reasons for adoption (Deykin, et al., 1984).

In a study of adolescents who carried their pregnancy to term, a majority described abortion as morally unacceptable or against their religious faith. A small minority said that it was "too late" for an abortion by the time the pregnancy was confirmed, or by the time the teenager acknowledged it. Resnick et al. (1990) warned that the complexity of pregnancy decision making does not lend itself to simple explanations. Family composition, social status, and future aspirations are a few of the external influences on pregnancy decision making. In addition, a host of internal influences such as moral and cognitive development, along with subconscious dynamics, are also present. Practitioners can clarify the dilemma of pregnant adolescents by providing accurate information. Despite time constraints, practitioners need to encourage pregnant teenagers to consider carefully the consequences of whatever decision they and their families select.

Studies of pregnancy decisions indicate that choosing abortion or childbirth involves complex and contradictory judgments. Wanting a baby some day and disliking elective abortion are obvious reasons for continuing an unplanned pregnancy to term. In a comparison of decision making among pregnant adult and minor females ranging in age from thirteen to twenty-six years, with subjects under seventeen considered minors, the following differences were noted:

- More adult females consulted a physician or counselor in making a decision even though all subjects were cognizant of counseling services.
- Minor females were more preoccupied with fantasies of motherhood and less concerned with practicalities.
- Adult females were more likely to question their ability to care for the child.
- Minor females were more concerned with possible deformity of the child.
- Minor females were more concerned with the effect of their decision on their families.
- More adult females stated they "wanted" an abortion; more minor females stated they "had" to have an abortion.

The study showed no significant difference in the contraceptive knowledge of adult and minor females, but younger subjects were disinclined to use oral contraceptives lest their parents discover possession of the pills. Minor females were less likely to blame themselves for the pregnancy and more likely to blame their partner. The most compelling difference between the adult and minor females was the fact that decisions of minors were externally determined, whereas adult women justified their decisions in terms of their own needs.

A research team found that all the unmarried pregnant women in their sample, whose ages ranged from fifteen to forty-four years, initially resented their pregnancy, alleging that this was a poor time for them to bear a child. The women expressed concerns for the social and economic damage that having a child might cause. The pregnant women in the study who chose abortion tended to have higher educational and vocational aspirations, while those who chose childbirth were passive and fatalistic in their belief that no action of theirs would alleviate the situation or improve their lives.

Accessibility to contraception and abortion is not the fundamental issue. The real question is how to guide young people toward sexually responsible behavior and convince women that biology need not be destiny. When counseling unmarried pregnant females, it is not advisable to be directive about such decisions as marrying the father or terminating the pregnancy. Marriage between the pregnant mother and the putative father is usually a middle-class option, with the majority of lower-class expectant mothers choosing single parenthood.

•CLINICAL EXAMPLE:
CRISIS OF ADOLESCENT SEXUALITY
AND UNWANTED PREGNANCY

Sarah was seventeen. She had come to the health care facility for birth control pills saying, "We got scared a few weeks ago when my period was four days late." The nurse practitioner found Sarah's physical exam to be entirely normal and instructed her on appropriate use of her birth control pills and common minor side effects that might occur. Sarah refused the offer of foam and condoms, indicating that since she would begin the pills soon she could easily abstain in the interim. The nurse encouraged Sarah to call her if she had any questions or problems with using her birth control pills.

At her follow-up appointment eight weeks later, Sarah was her usual cheerful self. She told the follow-up interviewer that she had not begun taking the birth control pills because her period had not come. Sarah was not worried. "You know, my periods get like that sometimes if I'm real busy; we've got my brother's wedding coming up in two weeks and besides we haven't done anything since I was here last."

The couple had last had intercourse a few days before Sarah's physical exam and Sarah could not remember if they had "used anything." A second pelvic exam was done and it confirmed the urine pregnancy test. At this news, Sarah became panicky, crying and saying that she wished she was dead. Sarah was immediately referred to the health care social worker, who helped the girl become calmer. The social worker was very supportive, saying, "Sarah, I know this is a real shock for you and you are very upset right now. But you don't need to feel so desperate. You have some options and some choices to make. We'll talk about that in a few minutes. For right now, why don't you let those tears come. I'll sit with you, if it's ok with you, so you don't feel so alone."

After crying for a while, Sarah regained composure and was ready to talk about her choices in dealing with her pregnancy. She thought that her boyfriend would support any decision she made and also felt that her mother's youngest sister would be understanding. When Sarah mentioned her aunt as a possible ally, the social worker suggested that the aunt be present when Sarah disclosed her condition to her mother. She followed this suggestion, and the presence of a third person reduced recriminations.

After both her parents were told, Sarah continued to visit the clinic and talk to the nurse and the social worker. Both professionals used the visits to point out the wisdom of using contraception for every sexual encounter to avoid pregnancy. Sarah's alternatives to have the baby and keep it, to have the baby and give it up for adoption, or to terminate the pregnancy were reviewed. Both professionals refrained from directive suggestions, saying that Sarah, her family, and her boyfriend must make the decision. The consequences of each course of action were discussed. Within the first trimester a decision was reached that the pregnancy be terminated. Sarah's aunt and mother accompanied her to the clinic for the procedure, and Sarah went to her aunt's home for aftercare.

After the procedure was done, the nurse again discussed various contraceptive methods with Sarah, adding that, although legally permitted, abortion was the least acceptable method of birth control from a psychological, physiological, and ethical standpoint. Moreover, reliance on abortion to undo the results of thoughtless sexual acts encouraged political and public dissent.

An appointment was scheduled for the time Sarah would have delivered had she chosen to continue the pregnancy, a time when women who have undergone spontaneous or induced abortion usually need help with their feelings. At this visit, Sarah seemed older and quieter but not regretful of her choice. The relationship with her boyfriend had survived the ordeal of unwanted pregnancy. Sarah now used contraception consistently and had shared her experience with her girlfriend in order to help her be more realistic about sexuality.

Critical Guidelines

Many esoteric explanations have been proposed for the rising numbers of inappropriate and unplanned pregnancies in modern life. Some young women undoubtedly view pregnancy as a way of negotiating a rite of passage into adulthood, only to find themselves isolated from their peers and alienated from their families. Among young parents there is rarely much awareness of the long-term responsibilities of parenthood nor realistic planning for the future. Time factors compound the difficulties present in this extreme crisis of decision. If time constraints are pressing, frequent preliminary sessions should be arranged in order to promote decision making. A model for conflict resolution has been formulated to be used in deciding pregnancy outcome (Bracken et al., 1978). In this model, cognitive and affective activities are identified:

- Acknowledgment of the pregnancy and the emotions it evokes.
- Formulation of alternatives and possible actions.
- Consideration of merits and disadvantages of various alternatives.
- Commitment to the decision made, with opportunity provided for emotional catharsis.

The initial counseling sessions should deal with issues categorized as retrospective, immediate, and prospective. For each category certain relevant questions should be asked:

Retrospective Issues:
- What were the circumstances surrounding the pregnancy? Is the pregnancy the result of rape or incest? Were the partners involved in a long-term relationship?

Immediate Issues:
- Is the putative father still involved with the expectant mother? What are his feelings about the pregnancy? Is he pro-abortion, anti-abortion, or neutral?
- What is the most compelling reason for considering abortion? Fear of parenthood? Financial worries? Commitment to career goals?
- What is the most compelling argument against abortion? Religious beliefs? Parental disapproval? Other emotional entanglements?

Prospective Issues:
- What are the most formidable aspects of carrying the pregnancy to term? What would it be like to deliver the baby and keep it? What would it be like to deliver the baby and give it up for adoption?
- What are the most formidable aspects of abortion? Physical fears? Emotional consequences? Anxiety? Guilt? Remorse? Relief?

Decisions about sexuality are difficult for adolescents, especially if they believe they have no understanding adults to help them. Because they tend to distrust adults, adolescents are susceptible to misinformation circulated by peers. Unsure of themselves, young people are subject to exploitation, and at times sexual activity may be used by young women to manipulate and coerce young men.

An instance of such manipulation occurred in the life of Bill, an eighteen-year-old mechanic. Debbie, a girl Bill dated, became pregnant and claimed the baby was his, although she had other sexual partners from time to time. Bill wanted "to do the right thing" but was reluctant to marry Debbie. As a result of her entreaties, Debbie and Bill began to live together. When the baby was born, Bill tried to live up to the responsibilities he had accepted but by the time the baby was six months old, Bill felt trapped. He and Debbie argued about everything; she was an indifferent mother and they disagreed about how to care for the child. Bill's job paid poorly, but Debbie refused to consider taking a part-time job to help with expenses. Difficulties were made worse because Bill suspected that Debbie had used her pregnancy to "get what she wanted—a dependable wage earner like me." Furthermore, Bill had come to believe that Debbie cared very little for him or for the child. His depressed state of mind came to the attention of his employer, who valued Bill's services. Bill's employer advised him to seek counseling, along with legal assistance to ascertain his rights and responsibilities toward the child, whom he loved.

IDENTITY

Adolescence is generally recognized as a turbulent period of life. The individual is maturing physically, intellectually, socially, and sexually at a rapid rate. In an interval of about seven years, the individual travels the territory between childhood and incipient adulthood. It is a strange and intense journey over an unknown terrain (Erikson, 1968). Most adolescents progress without undue difficulties, although the period is often stressful for parents as well as children. Perhaps the major task for adolescents is the establishment of identity as they move away from their family of origin. In the process of establishing a separate identity, they sometimes acquire problematic behaviors. The task of creating a separate identity is complicated by the fact that most adolescents must accomplish it while continuing to live with their family of origin, on whom they are likely to be financially dependent. At this point the adolescent is asking himself such existential questions as "Who am I? What shall I do with my life? Where will I fit in?" While the adolescent is asking these questions and differentiating from his family, his peer group assumes a position of great importance. Fads, stereotyped activities, and group-approved behavior become highly influential, often more than parental viewpoints.

Childhood identifications achieved by exposure to roles modeled within the family precede identity formation (Erikson, 1968). Teenagers selectively take on and leave out parts of those roles and combine the parts in new ways under the influence of their social milieu. Sider and Kreider (1977, p. 844) defined identity as "the adolescent's awareness of who he is as well as his perception of the assessment of others regarding who he is." A positive identification with parents and participation in the process of family decision making are among the most salient factors in the establishment of a strong identity. As we have seen in other aspects of development, the tempo of progress toward identity formation may be variable.

No one has written more sensitively on the process of identity formation and identity confusion than Erikson (1963, 1968), who formulated the concepts of identity foreclosure and moratorium. *Foreclosure* consists of a premature stabilizing of identity that results from the demands of others rather than self-discovery. The lure of foreclosure for teenagers lies in their avoidance of the work of choosing among a range of options the life style, vocation, values, and relationships that are most meaningful to them. There is potential for crisis in premature foreclosure. The young person who ignores internal aspirations and impulses, and yields to external forces tends to eventually become quite dissatisfied with life.

For some young people, affiliation with causes and cults of one kind or another provides an easy answer to the issue of identity foreclosure. The emotional intensity associated with a cause or a group generates a sense of belonging achieved through obedience or devotion. Joining a zealous group or becoming a strong adherent of a cause confers self-esteem on many teenagers who have not yet established an authentic identity for themselves (Ricks, 1980).

Erikson (1968, p. 157) described a *moratorium* as a delay period granted to someone who is unready to meet an obligation. He defined moratorium as "a delay of adult commitments, and yet it is only a delay. It is a period that is characterized by a selective permissiveness on the part of society and of provocative playfulness on the part of youth, and yet it often leads to deep, if transitory commitment by the youth . . . Each society and each culture institutionalizes a certain moratorium for the majority of its young people."

•CLINICAL EXAMPLE:
CRISIS OF IDENTITY FORECLOSURE

For most of her life Jean had tried hard to be a dutiful daughter, and do as her mother, grandmother, and the church elders dictated. When she became pregnant at age fourteen, they said, "Marry your child's father." Jean behaved as she usually did, and obediently married the man who had impregnated her. Her husband was ten years older than Jean. Although he was not physically abusive, he had little regard for Jean's feelings and soon began telling her what to do. She complied with his commands and advice just as she had her family's.

By age nineteen, Jean had a daughter in kindergarten and a newborn son. Another son, born when Jean was sixteen, had died in infancy. She and her husband were active in a fundamentalist church. At the recent birth she suffered depression with two episodes of psychotic behavior that almost necessitated short-term hospitalizations. There were two major elements to her distress. The first was a reworking of the anger and grief over the death of her first son and her resulting fears for the newborn son. The second element was her sense of confinement in her foreclosed identity. As she said to her community health nurse, "Mama, Big Mama (her grandmother), Sam (her husband), the church elders, and mothers . . . they all be telling me 'do this, do that.' They still call me Jeanie! Shit! I'm Jean! And Jean's gonna do what *she* wants to do! I'd like to finish grammar school . . . and then I'd like to go to high school, and maybe get a job." The plan for her recovery addressed both the grief work and identity foreclosure. Her husband was helped to understand her need for doing some of her adolescent development and the necessity of his being more active in the care of their children to facilitate her growth.

Critical Guidelines

Erikson (1968) indicated the usefulness of a psychosocial moratorium, which he saw as a prolongation of adolescence. Ricks (1980) described the moratorium as keeping one's options open. The adolescent avoids commitment to long-range components of identity. He experiments in affiliating with different groups and in assuming different identities within those groups. Ricks stated that the maintenance of the moratorium is often a conscious effort for adolescents in college.

•CLINICAL EXAMPLE:
CRISIS OF IDENTITY RESOLUTION

Jenny is the oldest child in a conservative, devout, middle-class family. Her father is a prosperous corporate lawyer and her mother is an active club woman and avid golfer. Jenny did not question family values until she left home and became a college freshman. The college she chose was known for liberal thinking of its faculty and students, many of whom were political activists. At college Jenny was influenced by the opinions of the people around her. Gradually she stopped attending church services because she no longer found them relevant. She became involved in a number of student organizations that took a strong stand on controversial issues, and she began marching in demonstrations, chanting, carrying signboards, and engaging in sit-ins. When she went home at vacation time, Jenny argued heatedly with her parents, who were shocked by most of the causes Jenny supported. She, in turn, criticized her parents for their affluence, their smugness, and their indifference to poverty and social injustice. Her school performance suffered because of her new interests, providing another source of contention between Jenny and her parents.

Relations between Jenny and her parents were strained until the beginning of her junior year, when she informed them that she had decided to go to law school after graduation. However, she warned her father that she was not at all interested in corporate law because such lawyers were "social parasites." Instead, Jenny would become a lawyer who protected the rights of the poor and humble, even if this was less profitable than corporate law. Although her parents did not agree with their daughter's extremism, they were relieved that she had chosen an occupation that seemed acceptable.

Critical Guidelines

Jenny herself was satisfied with her decision, and the family conflict abated. There were even times when she and her father could discuss legal matters without becoming enraged at each other. In effect, Jenny had resolved a maturational crisis, even though the resolution was a stormy, tumultuous time for the family. She had challenged her parents' outlook on politics, religion, and occupational choice. The sessions with her parents were difficult for everyone, but the questioning process Jenny undertook was important to her identity achievement as she identified and became committed to a value system of her own. The sequence Jenny followed in her search for identity can be summarized in six steps:

1. Group influences at college
2. Challenge to family values
3. Acquisition of new values
4. Family crisis
5. Commitment to individual values
6. Achievement of individual identity

Body Image

Most adolescents are intensely preoccupied and concerned with their body image. They monitor the somatic changes in themselves, and make comparisons with the bodies of peers and with the physical ideals of society. In some adolescents, especially females, attention to one's body takes on compulsiveness that far exceeds the established limits of normalcy. One particular expression of body image distortion is the condition called *anorexia nervosa.*

Anorexia nervosa is a physiological disorder, psychogenic in origin, that is accompanied by self-induced dieting that eventually exceeds the boundaries of conscious control and becomes compulsive. The syndrome includes episodes of fasting, gorging, vomiting and purging, a compulsive preoccupation with food, weight, and dieting that is demonstrated in a never-ending struggle with the environment and with persons in the environment.

The anorectic young woman believes that there is little she can do to experience feelings of mastery, so she looks for one area that she can control. Ultimately she discovers this mastery by controlling what she eats. As the disorder progresses she no longer experiences sensations of hunger yet continues to be preoccupied with preparing and discussing food. Most anorectic persons are high achievers in school and display compulsive behaviors regarding academic achievement.

Bruch (1979) insisted that the anorectic is as obsessed with food as the obese person, and that fasting and overeating are symptoms of the same disorder. Brumberg (1990) explained that cultural forces send contradictory messages to adolescent girls, who comprise the majority of anorectics. On one hand, they are confronted with an abundance of food and encouraged to enjoy it. On the other hand, they are told to control their bodies by means of dieting and exercising. In Western countries the search for thinness is unending. The disorder known as anorexia often begins with an effort to lose a few pounds that eventually gets out of control.

The disorder known as *bulimia* is characterized by alternate periods of binging and self-induced vomiting. The incidence of bulimia is less well-established than that of anorexia nervosa because bulimics usually maintain weight within normal limits.

Anorexia nervosa can be a life-threatening disorder; when the individual has become a skeletal figure, she is often unable to eat. She has ignored sensations of hunger for so long that they are no longer significant. At this point hospitalization is necessary for survival, and a combination of strategies may be used. Behavior modification is effective in some cases, combined with individual and family counseling. Depression is thought to be associated with anorexia and with bulimia; therefore, antidepressant medication is sometimes used. Once an individual has regained sufficient weight so that the problem is no longer life threatening, outpatient treatment is feasible. Individual counseling, family therapy, and support groups are the customary adjuncts to treatment. In working with persons who have an eating disorder, practitioners must deal with collateral issues: low self-esteem, anxiety, and ambivalence. The objective is not merely for the individual to maintain normal weight, but to develop the capacity to handle her own life.

The etiology of anorexia nervosa remains controversial but external pressures are thought to play a role, particularly the high value placed on slimness in Western society. According to Bruch, anorectic persons display three characteristics: (1) distorted body image, (2) distorted perception of sensations of hunger and fatigue, and (3) an underlying sense of being ineffective. Bruch attributed the disorder to parental neglect or inappropriate response to the child's needs. The parents may be over-controlling and/or overprotective, causing the child to doubt her own value and competence. As a consequence of the control imposed by parents, the child comes to experience herself and her body in a distorted way (Bruch, 1988).

Eating disorders are most prevalent among women, and their onset seems to coincide with physiological changes unique to women. When excess amounts of body weight are lost, the adolescent girl may feel more able to return to her carefree childhood years, especially if, as often occurs, weight loss is accompanied by cessation of menstrual periods.

The deprivation to which anorectic persons subject themselves causes the same physiological changes that would appear in any starving person. Eventually, during repeated fasting, the transmission of physiological messages signaling hunger seems to be lost. Anorectic behavior then moves beyond conscious control and becomes resistant to change. In some respects, the term anorexia is misleading; although anorectic persons deny themselves food, they do not actually lose their appetites until the condition has advanced to severe stages. In earlier stages the person is preoccupied with food, often collecting recipes and cooking for others but not ingesting food herself.

Marcus and Weiner (1989) presented anorexia nervosa as a selection of different activities that allow the anorectic person to deal with certain psychosocial events in daily life. The premise of this explanation is that variations in eating are socially learned and reinforced. They conclude that all atypical eating habits, such as anorexia, bulimia, and even unusual food preferences, occur within family contexts. Instead of dwelling on the psychopathology of persons with anorexia nervosa and assuming this population to be homogeneous, these investigators identified six psychosocial transactional patterns in anorexia nervosa: negativistic, attention centering, distracting, childlike, attractive, and self-punishing. The behavior patterns listed are not personality types nor do they account for all variations of anorexia nervosa. They do, however, describe the behaviors of most young girls with anorexia nervosa living with their families of origin. Marcus and Weiner warned that the six transactional patterns did not apply to males or to older females with the disorder.

The *negativistic* pattern is marked by overt refusal to eat. The person who simply plays with food is within the *attention centering* pattern; in the *distracting* pattern, not eating is attributed to a small appetite. The *childlike* pattern is evident in those who have limited or picky food preferences. *Dieting* is the socially accepted term for food refusal in the *attractive* transactional pattern and *fasting* is the term used for food refusal in the *self-punishing* pattern. Anorexia nervosa is generally thought to be a family problem. Analyzing the way food refusal is expressed helps explain family reactions to the disorder and provides some direction for practitioners.

Managing Anorexia Nervosa

Anorexia nervosa is a crisis when it assumes life-threatening proportions. When hospitalization is necessary, the therapeutic regimen varies with the facility. Behavior modification is often used, with the program tailored to the needs of the adolescent. The physical care of a person with anorexia nervosa is only part of the treatment. Family counseling is often necessary for younger persons and marital therapy for older ones. All of them need help in realizing that they can exert control over their life without starving themselves. Even when the immediate crisis of survival has been met, persons with anorexia nervosa usually need long-term psychological help.

Managing Bulimia Nervosa

The bulimia nervosa condition is usually managed on an outpatient basis. Interventions are directed first to stopping the cycle of binging, vomiting, and purging. The client is encouraged to discover better ways of coping with feelings of anxiety and depression. Therapy centers on the idea that it is one's own distorted thinking that engenders bad feelings about oneself, rather than the actual situation. Counseling helps the client develop better feelings about herself, and reinforces belief that she has the power to change her behavior.

Besides individual counseling, support or self-help groups are beneficial. Bulimic persons are accustomed to using deceit and secrecy in their dealings with others, partly to hide the behavior of which they are ashamed. Establishing trust with these clients and helping them to trust other people are appropriate therapeutic goals. Behavior modification may be used to change eating habits by substituting other activities for binging and vomiting. Cognitive therapy to help correct the emotional, behavioral, and thought distortions that perpetuate the cycle is also relevant for these clients.

Counseling Adolescents

Adolescence is a period when malleable, tractable children often become rebellious and challenging. It is essential, then, to differentiate the normal turbulence of adolescence from actual crisis. In a true crisis situation, family equilibrium is so threatened that outside intervention is usually necessary. Adolescent crises may be classified as follows (Dixon, 1979).

1. Inability to meet and resolve some developmental task, frequently related to sexuality, identity, or body image.
2. Inability to accept or adapt to rules and demands of society.
3. Inability or unwillingness to accept family rules and values.

As a general rule, permission from one or both parents is a requirement for offering professional counseling to an adolescent. An exception to the rule is school-related problems appropriate for school personnel to handle. Because adolescents struggle between dependence and independence, the counselor should endeavor to seem neutral. Without siding with adults in the picture nor succumbing to adolescent manipulation, the counselor tries to build rapport. This is sometimes met with resistance on the part of the adolescent, but the counselor facilitates rapport with supportive behavior and a willingness to listen to all sides, especially to the adolescent whose feelings may have been discounted until now.

The counselor also tries to reinforce reality testing. This includes helping the adolescent distinguish what is actually happening (objective perception) from what he believes is happening (subjective interpretation). Since the adolescent may initially resist the correction of cognitive errors, such corrections should be made after a trusting relationship has been established. By maintaining neutrality and objectivity, the counselor can mediate between society and the immature impulses of a troubled adolescent. Because adolescents are at the mercy of their impulses and because their self-image tends to be fragile, counselors must be alert to the possibility of destructive acts the adolescent may direct toward the self or other people. Extra caution is needed in assessing impulse control and destructive potential of the adolescent. Supervision and consultation are advisable when the counselor is relatively inexperienced. In doubtful instances, referral to more traditional therapeutic modes is indicated.

SUMMARY

Adolescents experience many changes in their relationships with themselves and with others. The emerging ability of adolescents to make decisions based on abstract thinking is often questionable. Adolescents experience considerable difficulty in the realm of moral judgment. Current investigations seem to argue for the existence of two modes of moral decision making: one that reflects Piaget's "normal logic," and another that acknowledges the influence of context and interdependence on thought and decision. Additional research points to the widespread inconsistencies, fantasies, and apparent irresponsibility that adolescents manifest in regard to sexuality.

The search for identity causes some teenagers to select a negative identity that opposes accepted values, while others accede to pressures to conform. In any case, a potential for crisis is present when adolescents eventually become dissatisfied with a life based on external demands. A psychosocial moratorium in which crucial decisions are deferred for a time can be a useful expedient during the adolescent years, even though the end of the moratorium may reactivate a developmental or existential crisis. Adolescents are often conflicted about such issues as identity, sexuality, and body image; any of these issues, if unresolved, may precipitate a crisis.

REFERENCES

Bellack, J.P., and B.J. Edlund, (edited by). *Nursing Assessment and Diagnosis* 2nd ed. Boston: Jones and Bartlett, 1992.

Bowlby, J. "Attachment." In *Attachment and Loss,* vol. 1. New York: Basic Books, 1969.

Bruch, H. *The Golden Age: The Enigma of Anorexia Nervosa.* Cambridge, Massachusetts: Harvard University Press, 1979.

_____. "Anorexia Nervosa: Therapy and Theory." *American Journal of Psychiatry* 138(1988): 12–14.

Brumberg, J. *Fasting Girls: The Emergence of Anorexia Nervosa* Cambridge, Massachusetts: Harvard University Press, 1990.

Buchholz, E., and B. Gol. "More than Playing House: a Developmental Perspective on the Strengths in Teenage Motherhood." *American Journal of Orthopsychiatry* 56(1986): 347–359.

Chilman, C. *Adult Sexuality in a Changing American Society: Social and Psychological Perspectives.* Washington, D.C.: U.S. Department of Health, Education, and Welfare, 1977.

─────. *Adult Sexuality in a Changing Society,* 2nd ed. New York: Wiley, 1983.

Desrosiers, M.C. "A Nursing Response to the Teenage Pregnancy Epidemic" *RN* 4(1989): 22–24.

Deykin, E.Y., L. Campbell, and B. Patti. "The Postadoption Experience of Surrendering Parents." *American Journal of Orthopsychiatry* 54(1984): 271–280.

Dixon, S.L. *Working with People in Crisis.* St. Louis, Missouri: Mosby, 1979.

Elkind, D. *Children and Adolescents: Interpretive Essays on Jean Piaget,* 2nd ed. New York: Oxford University Press, 1974.

─────. "Understanding the Young Adolescent." *Adolescence* 13(1978): 256–270.

Erikson, E. *Childhood and Society.* New York: Norton, 1963.

─────. *Identity, Youth, and Crisis.* New York: Norton, 1968.

Franklin, D.L. "Race, Class, and Adolescent Pregnancy: An Ecological Analysis." *American Journal of Orthopsychiatry* 58(1988): 339–354.

Herold, E.S. and M. Goodwin "Reasons Given by Female Virgins for Not Having Premarital Intercourse" *Journal of School Health* 51 (1981) 496–500.

Gilligan, C. "New Maps of Development: New Visions of Maturity." *American Journal of Orthopsychiatry* 52(1982): 199–212.

─────. *In a Different Voice.* Cambridge, Massachusetts: Harvard University Press, 1983.

Gilligan, C., J.V. Ward, J.M. Taylor, and B. Bardige. *Mapping the Moral Domain.* Cambridge, Massachusetts: Harvard University Press, 1989.

Hartman, C.R., A.W. Burgess, and A. McCormick. "Pathways and Cycles of Runaways: A Model for Understanding Repetitive Runaway Behavior." *Hospital and Community Psychiatry* 38(1987): 292–298.

Hofferth, S. *The Effects of Programs and Policies on Adolescent Pregnancy and Childbearing.* Bethesda, Maryland: National Institute of Child Health and Development, 1985.

Kohlberg, L. "Moral Development." In *Encyclopedia of Social Science.* New York: Macmillan, 1968.

Kohlberg, L., and C. Gilligan. "The Adolescent as Philosopher: the Discovery of Self in a Postconventional World." *Daedalus* 100(1971): 1051–1086.

Ladner, J. *Tomorrow's Tomorrow: the Black Woman.* New York: Doubleday, 1971.

Marcus, D., and M. Weiner. "Anorexia Nervosa Reconceptualized from a Transactional Perspective." *American Journal of Orthopsychiatry* 59(1989): 347–353.

Newman, B., and P. Newman. "The Concept of Identity: Research and Theory." *Adolescence* 13(1978): 157–166.

Offer, J., and D. Offer. "Sexuality in Adolescent Males." *Adolescent Psychiatry* 5(1977): 96–107.

Phipps-Yonas, S. "Teenage Pregnancy and Motherhood." *American Journal of Orthopsychiatry* 50(1980): 403–431.

Piaget, J. *The Origins of Intelligence in Children.* New York: International Universities Press, 1969.

Quay, H.C. "Psychological Factors in Teenage Pregnancy." In *Teenage Parents and Their Offspring,* edited by K. Scott, T. Field, and E. Robertson. New York: Grune and Stratton, 1981.

Resnick, M.D., R.W. Blum, J. Bose, M. Smith, and R. Toogood. "Characteristics of Unmarried Adolescent Mothers: Determinants of Childrearing Versus Adoption." *American Journal of Orthopsychiatry* 60(1990): 577–584.

Ricks, D. "A Model for Promoting Competence and Coping in Adolescents and Young Adults." In *Social Competence of Children,* edited by M. Kent and J. Rolf. Hanover, New Hampshire: University Press of New England, 1980.

Rutter, M. "Protective Factors in Children's Responses to Stress and Disadvantage." In *Social Competence of Children,* edited by M. Kent and J. Rolf. Hanover, New Hampshire: University Press of New England, 1979.

Sider, R., and S. Kreider. "Coping with Adolescent Patients." *Medical Clinics of North America* 61(1977): 839–854.

Tanner, J.M., and P.S. Davies. "Clinical Longitudinal Standards for Height and Height Velocity of North American Children." *Journal of Pediatrics* 107(1985): 317–329.

Thomas, A. "Theory and Review: Current Trends in Developmental Theory." *American Journal of Orthopsychiatry* 51(1981): 58–69.

Zelnik, M., and J. Kantner. "Sexual Activity, Contraceptive Use and Pregnancy among Metropolitan Area Teenagers." *Family Planning Perspectives* 12(1980): 230.

7

Adults in Crisis
The Early Years

The art of living does not consist in preserving and clinging to a particular mood of happiness, but in allowing happiness to change its form without being disappointed by the change.

Charles Langbridge Morgan

Individuals entering adulthood presumably have separated from their families of origin, but experiences within those families have entered and shaped the developing adult. The epigenetic principle proposed by Erikson (1963) and others (Lidz, 1980) stated that the critical tasks of the life cycle must be mastered during their time of ascendance if future tasks are to be resolved satisfactorily. Even though the epigenetic principle is less strictly applicable to adult life, later success depends greatly on earlier accomplishment. The epigenetic principle contains the possibilities of progression, regression, and fixation as critical tasks are approached. Many individuals are caught up in conflict between a wish to move forward and a wish to remain secure. Although regression and fixation may be carried to pathological extremes, they often represent temporary expedients adopted before moving on to the next developmental phase.

Early adulthood is a time for decisions regarding career, marriage, and parenthood. Commitments cannot be postponed indefinitely even though behavioral regression or fixation sometimes constitutes a moratorium used to delay decisions about future actions (Erikson, 1963). Middle adulthood is a period of achievement and success, of disappointment and failure, or of mixed experiences. The transition from middle to late adulthood is accompanied by recognition that achievements of the past may not be repeated, and that maintaining the status quo for a while is the most that can be expected. For persons who have not achieved all that they wanted, middle adulthood may be a time of learning to appreciate what was achieved or of longing for what may never be realized. Late adulthood witnesses contraction rather than expansion of the life space

137

and is usually a period in which gains are gradually outweighed by losses.

Erikson (1968) vividly described the adaptive, creative balancing that must be undertaken throughout one's life span. As he noted earlier (Erikson, 1963), the outcome reached by balancing industry over inferiority is competence, of identity over confusion is fidelity, of intimacy over isolation is love, of generativity over self-absorption is caring, and of integrity over despair is wisdom. In his own old age, Erikson expanded his psychological model of the life cycle to include the quality of humility, which he defines as a realistic appreciation of one's weaknesses and competence. Thus, the adaptive resolution of earlier life cycle tasks leads to the multifaceted wisdom of old age. The expanded Eriksonian model of the mature life cycle is shown in Table 7–1 (Goleman, 1988).

As in the Eriksonian framework, for organizational purposes, Chapters 7, 8, and 9 on adults in crisis are divided into three stages: early, middle, and late adulthood. Throughout adult life, as in the entire life span, crises related to decisions, commitment, and productivity are recurring phenomena.

TABLE 7–1   The Completed Life Cycle

Conflict and Resolution	Mature Interdependent Culmination
Old Age: Integrity vs. despair (wisdom)	Sense of integrity strong enough to cope with physical deterioration
Adulthood: Generativity vs. stagnation (caring)	Care for others, charity, and empathy
Early Adulthood: Intimacy vs. isolation (love)	Awareness of the complexity of relationships and of the value of love and tenderness
Adolescence: Identity vs. role confusion (fidelity)	Sense of the complexity of life: merging of sensory, logical, and sensory perceptions
School Age: Industry vs. inferiority: competence	Acceptance of the course of one's life and unfulfilled hopes: humility
Preschool Age: Initiative vs. guilt (purpose)	Humor, resilience, and playfulness
Toddlerhood: Autonomy vs. shame and doubt (will)	Acceptance of the whole life cycle, from integration to disintegration
Infancy: Trust vs. mistrust (hope)	Awareness of interdependence and relatedness

Source: Adapted from Goleman (1988).

DENIAL AND ILLUSIONS

In previous chapters the disequilibrium of crisis was presented in terms of cognitive, emotional, and behavioral distortions that occur. In addition to these distortions, a more subtle misperception may result from the use of denial and illusions. Some experts consider any inability to assess reality accurately as a sign of psychopathology (Taylor, 1989) but others disagree. Tendencies to interpret reality in ways that promote optimism and self-esteem may contribute to one's mental health, even when such positive feelings are unfounded (Taylor and Brown, 1988).

Inaccurate perceptions of reality are very common; they may prove adaptive or maladaptive, depending on circumstances. When such misperceptions intrude into crisis situations, they may become problematic for the counselor. The concept of denial owes much to the work of Anna Freud, who saw denial as a primitive, unconscious defense mechanism used by individuals to protect themselves against painful experiences (Freud, 1948). Weisman (1979) believed that denial is sometimes needed to deal with danger and pain until other coping mechanisms become available. Snyder (1989) proposed that short-term denial is adaptive while long-term denial may not be.

The risk factors attending illusions depend largely on who is holding the illusion. Taylor and Brown (1988) asserted that mentally healthy people often make good use of illusions even while confronting threatening situations, while individuals suffering from a psychotic process do not. Taylor (1983, p. 1161) described the concept of illusion as, "By illusion, I do not mean that beliefs are necessarily opposite to known facts. Rather, their maintenance requires looking at known facts in a particular light, because a different slant would yield a less positive picture, or the beliefs have yet to yield any factual basis of support."

It is possible for illusions to foster states of hopefulness and well being, but this may be accomplished at the expense of adaptive problem solving. Illusions may cause people to attempt the impossible or conversely, to avoid doing the possible, to take risks, or to infringe on the rights of others (Taylor & Brown, 1988).

Gross distortions found in crisis create severe distress and are incapacitating. Therefore they must be confronted rather directly before the crisis can be resolved effectively. There is less agreement about how counselors should handle misperceptions introduced by the use of denial or illusion into a clinical situation. Ersek (1992) warned that there may be hazards in asking people to give up their illusions immediately and arbitrarily. For example, the mother of a developmentally handicapped child may persuade herself that the child will eventually "catch up." Unless this illusion interferes with her willingness to offer optimum care and treatment for the child, the illusion may be all that stands between her and despair. Sometimes the same mother's use of denial may motivate her to greater efforts and increase her participation in therapeutic activities for the child.

In the absence of definitive research, Ersek (1992) found empirical evidence that client's misperceptions often are relinquished in time, even without constant reality orientation. It is not necessary to adopt a frontal, confrontational style in addressing illusions or denial. In most instances all that is required is consistent but fairly gentle reminders of social and circumstantial reality. Such data, as are available, suggest that most people do not require intensive attacks on defensive misperceptions of reality maintained through denial and illusion. In assisting individuals to readjust their misperceptions of reality, Ersek (1992) made the following suggestions.

- Reality is defined within a social context and the social reality of one person often differs from that of another.
- Some illusions and some manifestations of denial may be adaptive under certain conditions.
- Reality orientation may not always be needed, especially if reality misperceptions are not blatant, and permit problem solving to proceed.
- Experiencing a supportive rather than a confrontational relationship helps individuals to redefine reality, discard illusions, and decrease denial.
- It is usually more effective to explore specific misperceptions than to argue against them.
- In correcting misperceptions, the counselor should include suggestions on how to maintain accurate, but still optimistic, reality perceptions.
- Reality misperceptions should not be equated with gross distortions. Many healthy people resort to illusion and denial in everyday life. These widespread coping means may impede or advance problem solving.

BEHAVIOR PATTERNS

Reisman (1973) described people as being inner directed or other directed, noting that many individuals need to have their accomplishments consensually validated by other people. As adults move from early to maturing adulthood, many of them feel a mounting desire to win recognition and success. Motives and ambitions vary, so that the son of a news reporter may try to become a great writer either to surpass his father or fulfill his father's dreams. The daughter of a singer may try to emulate her parent's achievements or refuse to compete in the same field for fear of failing. Large numbers of individuals are single-minded in their striving for advancement, subordinating personal commitments to career demands. In contrast, other persons who are less avid for success may fear being outstanding and choose instead to remain in a familiar niche, not fully content, perhaps, but secure. For these individuals, safety and conformity are chosen over risk and accomplishment.

The climate in which contemporary people live and work contains many contradictions. Traditional values teach the importance of philanthropy and social conscience, but aggressiveness and competitiveness are greatly rewarded. Popular commitment to individual freedom is refuted by institutionalized repetition or the imposed monotony that thrives in educational and industrial settings. Horney (1937, 1945) described multiple conflicts originating in society that are internalized by many individuals and expressed in rigid maladaptive behavior patterns, identified as follows:

- *Dependency patterns.* This individual adopts a submissive, compliant attitude to obtain acceptance and approval. Since the overtly dependent person engages in an unending search for emotional supplies from others, there is movement toward social interaction.
- *Domination patterns.* Like the overtly dependent person, this individual is motivated by conflicted dependency needs that are denied or repressed from conscious awareness. Basic dependency needs are further distorted by adopting controlling or authoritarian behaviors.
- *Detachment patterns.* This individual uses the defenses of intellectualization and isolation to avoid emotional involvement. There is little inclination to seek domination or acceptance, for these behaviors would require closeness that the detached person cannot tolerate.

DECISION CRISES

The age at which adolescence ends and adulthood begins is subject to wide variation. Some individuals marry or become job holders and parents before reaching the age of twenty, thereby avoiding the postadolescence stage that Keniston (1974) characterized as youth. Other individuals, chronologically the same age, remain students, dependents, or rebels well into their twenties. Despite these differences, young adults, whether socially backward or precocious, confront a series of choices whose outcome will affect their whole lives.

Sexual and Reproductive Decisions

Conjugal role enactment and the sexual priorities of the spouses are affected by socioeconomic variables. In studying poverty-related problems, Rainwater (1965) found that women who became pregnant without conscious choice enjoyed sex least, felt powerless to control their reproductive processes, and were inconsistent about contraceptive precautions. This finding was an interesting contrast to the women in the study who enjoyed sexual activity and took responsibility for contraception. Except for the lowest socioeconomic group, lower-class spouses stated that marital role enactment was equitable and complementary, but that wives made more decisions for the family. Upper-class spouses also believed that marital role enactment was equitable and complementary, but said the husband made more decisions for the family.

Geographic and social mobility has isolated the nuclear family to the extent that marital partners must either turn to each other in crisis or find outside help. Because of the reluctance of many couples to solicit professional help, practitioners offering perinatal care to women or preventive health supervision to children should be sensitive to opportunities for brief marital counseling. Without intervention, many couples simply allow irritations and discontents to accumulate. Regardless of the clinical setting, troubled relationships should be assessed in terms of the respective value systems of the principals, their sociocultural orientation, and their commitment to the relationship.

Options regarding childbearing have solved some problems while creating others. The separation of sexual activity from propagation has widened vistas for women, although the desire to pursue a career while undertaking marriage and motherhood creates new dilemmas. Women who defer childbearing until they are established in a career or have contributed to the financial security of the family confront biological hazards. Even with the gynecological advances of recent years, many causes of infertility, such as endometriosis, are more common in older women.

A great deal has changed in contemporary life, but the strength of peer influence on young people persists, perhaps because recent separation from the family of origin leaves a void that must be filled. Not many decades ago, extramarital and premarital sex certainly existed but were less openly acknowledged. Many young people feel current pressures to engage in sexual activity without marriage. Self-esteem and peer approval are often based on having a live-in girlfriend or boyfriend. Ready or not, many young people engage in sexual liaisons partly from desire to be like everyone else.

In the relativistic climate of today, the values of past generations are less persuasive. Some choices were always available to young adults, but in previous years these choices were limited. The choice of whom to marry was restricted to persons who were available, and acceptable to family and community. Nowadays choices are less concerned with whom to marry than whether to marry, even though a great majority of Americans do marry at least once. With sexual expressiveness freed of involuntary procreation, there is little need to marry merely to avoid sexual frustration. Even after a decision is made to contract a legal marriage, power to control one's reproductive potential means that having children is a choice rather than an inevitable outcome of sexual intercourse. It is now possible to control reproduction with an efficiency unknown to previous generations, and even when contraception fails, parenthood can be avoided. Elective abortion is an alternative whose availability may precipitate a severe crisis of decision.

Amniocentesis is a test now available for pregnant women who fear fetal malformations. Identifying anomalies is done through the extraction, culture, and examination of fetal cells obtained through amniotic puncture. The test is usually performed in high-risk pregnancies in which either parent may be the carrier of chromosomal or metabolic abnormalities. The mother's age is also a factor, since an older mother is at greater risk of producing an abnormal child. Amniocentesis is done at three and one-half months of pregnancy, and two weeks must elapse before the results are known. Abortion, if chosen, will be performed in the fourth month of pregnancy, when simpler methods are no longer possible and the women must endure an experience akin to giving birth to a dead child.

Parents who elect amniocentesis have generally accepted the possibility of an abortion. Statistically, the odds favor a normal pregnancy but when fetal abnormalities are shown, the parents tend to elect abortion and to feel grateful that amniocentesis spared them the birth of an abnormal child. Many parents realize that the pregnancy may be aborted on the basis of test results and do not announce the pregnancy until they are assured of a normal child. When amniocentesis reveals abnormality, some parents decide never to attempt to have another child. Others are willing to try again, relying on amniocentesis to determine whether the pregnancy should be allowed to proceed. Amniocentesis gives many couples permission to try to have a child even if the mother is past forty and the couple has been intimidated by the statistical possibility of bringing a defective child into the world.

The problem of unplanned pregnancy is a serious one not only for the pregnant female, but also for her family. Any unexpected pregnancy is a crisis for a family, partly because internal family structure and control are threatened. When a young, single female becomes pregnant, additional turmoil ensues. Even if the family is resigned to the situation and supports the girl's decision, a residue of disappointment remains for a while.

Occupational Stresses

Even for individuals who work merely to subsist, there are inescapable facts about being a working member of society. Regardless of occupation, an unavoidable amount of stress is experienced, and the occupational stresses of professionals and nonprofessionals differ less than might be supposed. Whereas many professionals are autonomous and voluntarily subscribe to a code of shared values, a greater number are employed by agencies, institutions, and corporations that superimpose their own rules. For nonprofessionals, such as industrial workers, clerical workers, technical workers, and service workers, the conditions of employment are likely to be even more restrictive. Many industrial workers are now asking that their work be made relevant and fulfilling. In expecting work to offer more than financial compensation, lower-level workers are following a precedent more typical of professionals and executives.

Workers who experience occupational frustration have several alternatives available. Failing to obtain modification of working conditions, they may resort to welfare, retraining, additional education, early retirement, or passive resistance in the form of absenteeism or lowered efficiency. Occupational burnout is an existential crisis commonly experienced by conscientious workers who come to feel that their efforts are unappreciated, unrewarded, and ineffectual. There are few clear connections between specific occupations and stress reactions, although some occupations are reputed to be more stressful than others. Air traffic controllers, police officers, assembly line workers, and physicians are among those assumed to work under trying conditions, but an exhaustive study of the health records of over 20,000 workers showed that neither specific occupation nor occupational status were consistently related to stress disorders (McLean, 1980; Pender et al., 1990).

It has been suggested that the number and intensity of roles that individuals perform gradually increase until middle adulthood, and that the meaningful roles of adults revolve around work and family. The allocation of time spent enacting work and family roles is thought to cause more conflict during the middle stages of adult life than in earlier or later years, indicating that role strain is less prominent at the beginning and end of family life, and that the middle years are hazardous times for major occupational changes to be made. According to McCloskey (1990), two major requirements for job satisfaction are autonomy and social integration. *Autonomy* was defined as the degree of independence and control over one's activity; *social integration* was construed as a level of group cohesion and supportive relationships among workers.

Assembly line work is demanding for workers because of its enervating monotony, and correlation of assembly line work with coronary disease has been reported (McLean, 1980). Piecework or production work has also been shown to be stressful. One study of on-the-job stress required female office workers to perform their usual tasks for a period of four successive days. On the first and third days the women were paid on a piecework basis that increased their wages as productivity rose. The other two days were control days for which customary wages were paid.

On experimental days productivity rose 114 percent, but there were many subjective complaints of physical discomfort. On these days average adrenaline and nonadrenaline excretory levels of the workers rose 40 percent and 27 percent, respectively. In other work settings piecework has been linked to higher accident rates.

Two variables that transcend occupations and contribute to job-related stress are quantitative and qualitative overload. Quantitative overload refers to having too much to do, whereas qualitative overload refers to having tasks that are too difficult to accomplish. An investigation of quantitative overload showed this variable to be significantly related to excessive drinking, decreased self-esteem, low motivation, and high absenteeism. Qualitative stress results when there are discrepancies between what workers think the job should entail and what is being asked. Workers who are unsure of their specific assignments experience tension, dissatisfaction, and loss of confidence. Behavioral disturbance has been observed in situations in which assigned responsibilities either exceeded or did not measure up to the capacity of the worker.

Occupational stress may be a contributing factor in various psychophysiological disorders, and the crucial issue is the interaction between temperament and the work situation. Any job that is characterized by qualitative and quantitative overload, rapid change, and unrealistic performance standards will be stressful for most people, although the perception of events and the responses are individualized. Other predisposing factors include heavy responsibilities, altered responsibilities, and discrepant sociocultural expectations. Cardiac illness often develops not at the peak of a stressful situation, but after maximum pressure has subsided. This is the point at which the individual who has managed to adapt to rigorous demands becomes aware of feeling exhausted. During this time of fatigue and lassitude, blood viscosity increases and clotting time decreases, and cardiac output and oxygen consumption are reduced, all of which heighten susceptibility.

Occupational Change

Fulfillment in work can be a source of renewal and energy that facilitates the performance of intrafamily roles. There are times, however, when work is not fulfilling either because conditions of employment are unpleasant or because the individual wants additional psychological or financial compensation. The timing of occupational changes must be considered in light of their impact on the entire family. A distinction should be made between voluntary changes the individual seeks and involuntary changes thrust on the individual, since these variables influence family acceptance of occupational change. Locating the proposed change within the family life cycle may help sort out family attitudes toward occupational change.

Analysis of Risks

Judicious decision making requires examination of the amount of risk acceptable to individuals considering occupational change. Some persons are strongly attracted to risk taking while others shrink from it. Just as individual tolerance of risk varies, so do individual ideas about what constitutes risk. An actress who epitomizes poise and elegance may suffer torment when interviewed by members of the press. A corporate executive may implement policies with far-reaching effects but be unable to share his innermost feelings with anyone. Except for the rare individual who finds risks invigorating, most persons would rather deal with small risks. Individuals thinking of beginning a new venture often become unsure and seek help to resolve their doubts. For example, an ambitious young man conflicted between continuing as a junior member of a respected law firm or establishing his own practice may find himself in a state of crisis. On one hand, there is steady income, slow but predictable progress, and the prestige of belonging to an established firm. Balancing these factors, on the other hand, are autonomy and the prospect of larger earnings and greater professional recognition.

When counseling individuals who are considering occupational change, the crisis worker might begin by reviewing the risks involved. This review can be facilitated by partitioning the project into segments that can then be approached singly. If the implications of the new project are overwhelming, taking time to analyze them is essential. Gathering information from a number of reliable sources, compiling a balance sheet of advantages and disadvantages, and exploring the multiple ramifications of the project are basic methods of evaluating risks. The following relevant facts should be considered in the decision-making process:

- For some individuals lack of meaningful work may produce depression or even contribute to the onset of physical illness.
- Job satisfaction is a factor contributing to health and well-being, although overcommitment to work can be deleterious.
- Vocational advancement may be a cause for celebration but also for performance anxiety.
- Jobs that require frequent absence from home may cause marital discord or disturbed parent-child relationships, especially if the stay-at-home spouse is resentful.

The idea of success is pleasant to contemplate, but the following questions should also be asked in reviewing the possibility of failure: If the new venture fails, how far reaching and disastrous will the consequences be? What are the attitudes of other family members, especially the spouse? If progress is slow, will the spouse be an ally or a saboteur?

What criteria have been established to measure success or failure? What time frame has been agreed on? If failure does result, what options remain open? Examining risks and taking a deliberate approach is advantageous even if the result is postponement or a negative decision. Analysis of risks can be used to delineate hazards, reduce anxiety, and moderate the subjectivity that often accompany occupational change in middle adult life.

There are marked gender differences in occupational choices. Most women who enter professions become nurses or teachers, and the greater the prestige of a field, the more likely it is to be dominated by men. Women who aspire to high achievement are usually only children or oldest children without male siblings. In the absence of sons, parental ambitions tend to be implanted in daughters, especially if the mother values or models female achievement. At present, the women who fills a traditional homemaker role and the career woman are equally likely to have problems. Often the full-time homemaker suffers from low self-esteem, which causes her to have a negative image of herself, her husband, and her children. A different adjustment is made by the career woman, who resolves her doubts about her own competence by adopting a counterdependent posture. This woman exhausts herself in her attempts to be a perfect wife and mother as well as a successful career woman. The underlying cause of these behaviors lies in the inability of many contemporary women to resolve their conflict between the merger self and the seeker self.

Psychoanalytic theory views human beings as beset by two opposing drives, notably the urge to fuse or merge with another, countered by a contrary urge to remain individual and separate. In a lucid explanation of these two opposing tendencies, Sheehy (1976) labeled one the *Merger Self* and the other the *Seeker Self.* These concepts are of inestimable value in analyzing the potential for occupational crisis. It is the Merger Self that permits temporary fusion with others through love, identification, or sexual union. If uncontrolled, the Merger Self can be dysfunctional through fostering dependent attachments and relationships that preclude autonomy. If the Seeker Self is dominant, the search for personal achievement may rule out emotional commitment or involvement with others. What is productive is for neither the Merger Self nor the Seeker Self to be in sole charge, but for each to balance the other.

•CLINICAL EXAMPLE:
MARITAL CRISIS OF PRODUCTIVITY

George and Dolly Mann were professional musicians in their twenties. They were employed in an urban orchestra, had been married eight years, and were childless by choice. The orchestra was often on tour; as a result,the Manns spent considerable time traveling from city to city. One day the intake worker at the community mental health center in the neighborhood where they lived received a call from Dolly who sounded excited and desperate. "You have to do something about my husband, I can't stand living with him another minute. I must talk to someone before I kill myself." The intake worker succeeded in calming Dolly and obtained enough information to make an appointment for Mr. and Mrs. Mann to be seen that evening. Both appeared promptly to keep the appointment.

During the assessment interview, it was disclosed that the orchestra had terminated Dolly about two months earlier. She had become less and less able to play her violin because of an arthritic problem in her hands. When the orchestra manager informed her that she was not employable, Dolly was filled with despair. She accused her husband of being indifferent to her predicament and reported that life with him was intolerable. She said that he constantly found fault with her and yelled at her that she should find another job right away. In turn, George accused his wife of screaming at him, throwing things, and physically attacking him.

As the interview progressed, it was obvious that the couple agreed on only one detail—that Dolly had lost her job. They bickered over every fact, each contradicting and interrupting the other. The mental health worker realized that husband and wife were in a period of severe stress, and tried to review the chronology of their relationship in order to assess their customary interaction patterns. This approach elicited more arguments and grievances. Each reported that the other was always dissatisfied and looking for a fight. There was no indication that they had ever interacted in any other way, nor that they were distressed by their interactional pattern until Dolly lost her job. The job loss had produced a crisis, and they wanted someone to do something immediately to relieve their distress.

The couple agreed to attend five marital sessions with the agreed-upon goal of helping Dolly calm down and begin looking for some kind of job that she could do in spite of her physical impairment. In the sessions the couple examined conditions in which arguments began, and ways in which insults and accusations could be avoided. Rules were developed for discussing issues calmly and for focusing on the real cause of their disagreement. Instead of issuing ultimatums, George was instructed to use the phrase "it seems to me" when trying to explain his viewpoint to his wife. This simple phrase reduced contention because it gave Dolly an opportunity to describe how things seemed to her. At the end of the session contract George stated that there was less fighting at home and that his practice schedule did not give him time to continue the meetings. Dolly agreed that they were fighting less and could discontinue sessions even though she still had not found a job.

A week later Dolly called the clinic requesting to renew the sessions. She had a sense of unfinished business and wanted to understand her part in maintaining the conflict in her marriage.

She wanted to define and modify her own behavior in her relationships with her husband and other people. With assistance from the mental health worker, Dolly began to look at her own behavior. While she had observed and criticized her husband's actions for years, Dolly had spent no time examining her own actions. She learned that she presented herself in such a way that other people, including her husband, thought her helpless and barely competent. Due to the arthritis in her hands, she could not perform as a professional musician. In fact, she could no longer do needlework, which was a pastime she always enjoyed. Since her husband used the car, she could not go anywhere during the day. She was afraid that she could no longer drive alone and must depend on her husband to take her.

Critical Guidelines

The mental health worker did not make suggestions or give specific advice about how Dolly might solve her problems. That would have prolonged the pattern of dominance versus dependency that the client said she wanted to change. Instead of making suggestions that Dolly would probably reject, the mental health worker helped the client search for alternative behaviors. What had Dolly thought of trying? What had she done to solve her problems in the past? What had other people done in circumstances similar to hers? What sounded reasonable to attempt? There were times in the sessions when Dolly accused the counselor of being uncaring and indifferent, but within a few months she had figured out how to drive the car herself. This was her first step in realizing that she tried to get other people, especially her husband, to help her, and then resented their interference. She recognized that there were many things she could do by herself. This led to her considering what she was capable of and what she needed to achieve. Once she made some decisions, she began to put her plans into effect. She decided to teach music to children. Although she could no longer play well enough to perform, she was enough of a musician to give lessons.

During the sessions the counselor explained about family systems and how they work. As Dolly moved toward independent functioning, the mental health worker predicted some strong reactions from George, who had learned to deal with his wife's anger but not her autonomy. This helped prepare Dolly for her husband's responses to her changed behavior. He was furious when she first suggested he form a carpool to get to work so that she could have the car three days a week. She did not retreat and finally he agreed. After some months she told the mental health worker that the orchestra was going on tour. She would be traveling with her husband for a time but would continue to teach her pupils on her return. She said that she still became upset when her husband was angry with her, but instead of fighting back, she tried to avoid an argument without giving in completely.

To summarize the outcome, once the immediate situation improved the husband dropped out of treatment. His wife, who was in more distress, was not satisfied with minimal results but wanted to change the interactional pattern of her marriage. She was willing to make changes in her own behavior. Even though her husband resisted change, his wife's actions led to alterations in the marital system. Inevitably, her altered behavior influenced the interactional patterns of the couple in ways that the wife welcomed and the husband came to accept. He found disadvantages as well as advantages in having a more independent partner, but overall, family functioning improved.

After the marital crisis had subsided, the mental health counselor determined that Dolly needed further help. She seemed in control of her feelings, but undoubtedly she was very distressed at the loss of her career as a performer. She was less self-destructive in her dealings with her husband, but without additional counseling she might revert to her old patterns. Although her schedule was irregular, Dolly agreed to meet with a new therapist several times a month and to take the initiative in arranging appointments.

CAREER CHOICES

Young adults who discover their talent early in life and who have the means and motivation to develop their talent are indeed fortunate, but they probably comprise a minority. Some individuals have several gifts at their command and may have difficulty deciding which gift to develop. A number of physicians, for example, concentrated on a medical career in their youth only to forsake medicine for a literary career in midlife. For less gifted persons the search for some occupation they want to pursue is fruitless. Instead of finding something they like, many must content themselves with avoiding an occupation they really abhor.

Pressure on young people to succeed begins early in life. Greenberger and Steinberg (1986) allude to such pressure in their comment that adults no longer display the attitude that youth should be a time of protection from forces that are unnecessarily painful or stressful. Instead, the attitude of adults now is that youth is a time of preparation. Friedenberg (1987) deplored the fact that employment open to young people in the United States impoverishes their development even as it puts some money in the pockets of their jeans. In the United States there are no apprenticeships except in rare cases. After-school and spare-time employment seldom provide adolescents a taste of a career they might like to pursue. The inadequacy of employment available to most high school and college students, combined with parental admonition to "make the most of yourself," renders career decisions very difficult for conscientious (and not so conscientious) young people.

Another problem is that the duration of adolescence and youth seems to be lengthening. GAP Report no. 126 (1989, p. 51) asserted that this is "manifested by teenagers continued dependence on their parents and delay in entering the workforce. Thus, youngsters are left in an emotional no man's land between the ages of 12 and 22; they are physically mature, but emotionally and intellectually unformed."

If decisions about careers are difficult for young men, they are probably more difficult for young women. Progress has been made in removing barriers between women and advancement in business and the professions. However, the concept of working parents who share homemaking and childcare duties is more an ideal than a reality. Women choosing a career or vocation must factor parenthood and childcare into the equation. Even for traditional young women, issues of equal opportunity, equal pay, and equal education are considered when making a career choice.

Young people from affluent families headed by permissive parents can afford the luxury of a prolonged moratorium before deciding on a career, but these circumstances are exceptional, especially for young women. Since marriage and motherhood no longer spell the end of outside employment for women, career choices may be a troublesome dilemma. Gerson (1985) looked at the influence of social necessity and personal preferences in women's job options. A woman's commitment to home and children seldom advances her vocationally. Gerson observed that employer attitudes toward parenthood differ drastically, depending on whether the parent is a father or a mother.

•CLINICAL EXAMPLE:
CRISIS OF CAREER CHOICE

Katie was a twenty-three-year-old college senior who was within six weeks of graduation. She had expressed a desire to go to law school. Having worked her way through college as a legal secretary, she had become familiar with aspects of legal practice and surmised that she was intelligent enough to do that type of work. Katie was an occasional user of marijuana.

She visited a nurse practitioner due to physical complaints experienced for a few months that had recently become worse. She was anxious that her illness not interfere with her completing the semester's work and graduating.

In addition to her physical symptoms, Katie had noticed that she had become increasingly "wound up" lately. A few days prior to her visit to the health center, she had gone to Virginia to visit her boyfriend, Pete. Her agenda was to tell him that she was moving to Virginia, would get a job as a legal secretary, and that they should get married. She spoke in detail about the visit.

The relationship of this couple had been chaotic at best. Katie herself characterized it as "can't live with him and can't live without him." Pete had tended to be dependent on her as well as manipulative and exploitive. This pattern had continued despite his move south.

On arriving, Katie learned from Pete that he had just begun a casual sexual relationship with another young woman. Nonetheless, Pete claimed the other partner needed him as she was recently divorced. He asked Katie to give him time to work it all out. Katie was very upset but did not want to give him an ultimatum. She returned home, unsure of what would transpire, to face a heavy workload both at her job and at college.

The clinician she saw assessed that Katie was conflicted but not suicidal. She referred Katie to a physician in the college health services program for relief of her physical symptoms. The psychologist and Katie reviewed her options regarding work and school pressures. Katie was asked what would happen if she did not graduate soon. Katie began to realize that although she and her family would be disappointed, there would be no long-term adverse consequences. Similarly, they explored Katie's expectations of Pete. In this instance, the clinician did try to increase Katie's insight about her panicky flight to the romantic lover of her adolescence. She encouraged Katie to describe what life would be like for her if she and Pete married. Katie's response was "I'd get bored pretty fast."

Katie gradually revised her implusive plan simply to move to Virginia and work. She intended to aim for graduating in several weeks. On the last of her follow-up visits, Katie felt markedly better; her marijuana use had decreased to almost nothing, and she had graduated on time. Her plans about moving were further revised. She had acquired a full-time job and would not move to Virginia: "After all, there's more to life than the beach!" She continued to be undecided about law school but had not totally rejected that goal.

Although Katie was not sure what path she eventually wanted to follow, she was sure that graduating from college was her first goal. With the help of a few professionals, she came to realize that other decisions could be deferred until she was less conflicted. Katie had learned some significant things about who she was, and how to use her own thoughts and feelings in making decisions. The practitioners assured Katie that she could return for counseling in any situation if she considered it necessary. She also suggested that Katie take the law aptitude test in the near future. This would not prematurely commit Katie to any single course of action, but would provide useful data on which to base a later decision.

Critical Guidelines

The practitioner in the college counseling service had known Katie since her freshman year. She knew that Katie's plans for law school were realistic in terms of her ability, although her motivation was less clear. The practitioner determined that Katie was in crisis because she could not reconcile her ambitions for law school with her wish for a sustaining relationship with Pete. In effect, this was a conflict between Katie's seeker self and merger self. Even Pete's questionable actions did not cause her to break off the relationship with him. Her subsequent behavior at college placed her at risk for not completing requirements for graduation. Katie was referred to a physician and psychologist.

Wisely, the practitioner did not urge Katie to make any decision except on the advisability of finishing her course work and graduating with her class. Although Katie could not be seen at the college health facility after graduation, the practitioner assured the girl of her continued interest and of an appropriate referral in the future. Much of Katie's anxiety was attributable to the uncertainties of life after graduation and her reluctance to leave the cocoon of the campus for full membership in the working world.

PARENTHOOD ISSUES

Parenthood may occur before marriage, early in a marriage, or after a short or prolonged delay. There are advantages and disadvantages to childbearing, whatever the timing. Couples who must deal with an immediate pregnancy may have financial and relationship problems, especially if the first pregnancy is soon followed by a second. Often young husbands are uninvolved with domesticity or child care because they are struggling to earn a living, or because they want to go on feeling free and unburdened. Developmentally, new parents who are very young have a hard time moving from adolescence into adulthood. When parents have barely entered adulthood they face the task of resolving their identity as adults along with forging a new identity as parents.

Partridge (1988) saw the psychological birth of a parent as an emotional and cognitive process, not unlike a child's gradual development of identity. Benedek (1970) wrote that a mother's sense of herself as a parent is built upon her successes and failures in feeding and nurturing her child. Fathers and mothers draw upon their memories of their own childhood, and how their own parents defined and portrayed working images of parenting (Partridge, 1988). Jordon (1990) described in very sympathetic language the struggle of expectant and new fathers for "relevance."

Brunnquell et al. (1981) emphasized the essential attributes of self-awareness, insight, and self-understanding in developing positive parental identity. He found that mothers least likely to neglect or abuse their children were capable of the following behaviors:

- Understanding and tolerating normal parental feelings of ambivalence in themselves.
- Recognizing and tolerating the same ambivalence in their children.

- Balancing their own needs and the needs of others.
- Negotiating and accommodating to the complex relationship existing between mother and child.

Two external factors have been found to buffer parental stress in the childrearing domain (Koeske & Koeske, 1990). One factor is a supportive relationship with a partner that in some way conveys an intangible attitude of meaning and approval to the parent and also provides tangible assistance in child care, transportation, information, and respite. The second buffering factor was found to be higher educational levels of the mother; both of these so-called buffers are probably linked to a mother's feelings of being valued and valuable. New parents expect some restrictions in their lives but are unprepared for the enormity of change. Rubenstein (1989) described some consequences of parenthood.

- About half the couples report less overall marital satisfaction after the birth of a child.
- Many couples report frequent, bitter arguments about dividing tasks, sharing leisure time, and seeing in-laws and friends.
- Many couples report fewer expressions of affection such as kissing, hugging, praising, or complimenting each other.
- Many couples report less sexual interaction and less pleasure in making love.

Childless Couples

A new family is established when two people make a long-term commitment to each other through marriage or a less formal living arrangement. These less formal arrangements sometimes constitute families, but in this chapter family refers to the stereotypical pattern of a heterosexual couple and their offspring.

If a childless married couple live in a community or come from extended families that value procreation, they may undergo social disapproval. Many couples marry without resolving their respective attitudes toward having children. One of the partners may be reluctant to become a parent but not divulge this before marriage. The couple may have agreed not to have children but hesitate to reveal this to their own parents. Even when both partners agree to be childless, the decision may have adverse results. Their decision is usually a blow to their own parents, who had looked forward to grandparenthood. The parents' comments and questions annoy the couple, especially if one partner is more determined than the other not to have children. Having decided to be childless, a couple may need help in constructing a life style that compensates for the lack of children. Many childless couples invest greatly in the marital relationship, or devote themselves to jobs or careers. This is especially important if most of the friends in their age group are raising children. Depending on the views of the couple, childlessness may be a source of frustration or gratification. Couples who are not childless by choice suffer emotional pain that is aggravated by remarks from thoughtless friends and relatives.

Whether they are childless voluntarily or involuntarily, the childless couple looks for other interests and pursuits. They may express their parenting instincts in ways that benefit the community. Although the marital relationship becomes all-important for some partners, others detach themselves from this bond in favor of outside interests. This is more likely to happen if the couple is not childless by choice; the marital relationship may be a constant reminder of disappointed hopes, causing one or both partners to withdraw. If infertility is the cause of childlessness, practitioners need to know what, if any, steps have been taken to overcome the difficulty. Practitioners should also be familiar with community resources so that suitable referrals can be made.

It is not unusual for one partner in a childless marriage to have trouble around the issue as time passes. Tensions between the couple may originate within the relationship or be generated by people and events outside the marital system. Especially for women, the passage of time may bring regrets for a decision made earlier. When being childless brings a couple into treatment, it is essential to identify the origin of the problem and its proportions. A couple may be content in their present state, but resentful of interference from extended families. Older couples who face a now-or-never dilemma, may need counseling when deciding if they should become parents. The way couples deal with this issue depends on the nature of the marital relationship, their capacity for insight, and their willingness to accept the status quo or take measures to alter their situation.

WORKING MOTHERS

It is now acceptable for mothers to have jobs and return to work shortly after having a baby. While many mothers work from economic necessity, there is some feeling among feminists that unless a woman works gainfully, she is missing out on life. There is also a sense that staying home to rear children is unrewarding (Brazelton, 1986).

Some women, of course, find personal fulfillment in jobs and careers. However, there are vast numbers of women who hold jobs out of economic necessity, who reluctantly leave infants and children in the hands of secondary caretakers, and who would prefer to be at home with their children, especially during the early years. Childcare arrangements are often unreliable and working mothers are often uneasy about the welfare and the whereabouts of their children while they are at work.

The social and geographic mobility of recent decades has deprived families of the assistance the extended family once offered. In the absence of helpful relatives, husbands are pushed into performing untraditional tasks. While economic pressures keep many women in the workforce, the scarcest commodity in dual income families is discretionary time.

The responsibility for nurturing children and for maintaining a wholesome environment for the family is still left to mother, although men with working wives are involved to varying degrees. It is little wonder that the two-income family finds itself torn between home and work, trying to find the time and energy to do justice to both. In single-parent households the pressures are even greater, and resources of time and money are far less.

Although social disapproval has lessened, criticism of working mothers has not disappeared. Brazelton (1986) advised new mothers not to leave a child under four months old with a secondary caretaker because earlier separation from mother may impede optimal attachment between mother and child. To protect herself from the pain of leaving her baby, a mother may adopt distancing defenses. According to Brazelton (1986, p. 22), "The younger the child and the more inexperienced the mother, the stronger and more likely are these defenses. They are correlated with the earliness that mother returns to work."

The defenses outlined by Brazelton include the following:

- *Denial.* A mother is likely to deny that her leaving may have consequences for the child. She may ignore signals to the contrary in herself or the child. Thus, denial may impair the mother's ability to make wise decisions.
- *Projection.* Responsibility for both good and bad childcare issues will be projected to the substitute caretakers, thus allowing mothers to avoid involvement.
- *Detachment.* Sidestepping responsibility and discounting her strong feelings of attachment to the child eases the painful reactions to separation.

The large number of women employed outside the home has generated research into the dynamics of dual-income families, especially where there are children in the home. During the 1980s, women consistently performed more homemaking and childcare tasks than their male partners (Pleck, 1985; Kimball, 1988). When males did participate, their contributions were more in the area of childcare than in housework. Fish et al. (1992) reported that men were more likely to be involved with childcare if the firstborn is a boy. This may be because fathers are more comfortable with the physical and social needs of a boy, or because mothers encourage more father involvement in the care of a son.

In one study, Coverman and Sheley (1986) reported that husbands of working wives spent no more than twenty-six minutes per day in child-care. Hall (1992) found that couples redefined roles after the birth of their first child. Redefinition for women meant taking on multiple roles and experiencing role strain. For men redefinition produced less role strain because they monitored priorities. In general, women in dual-income marriages assume more responsibility for maintaining relationships within the marriage, and outside the marriage with relatives, friends, and religious affiliations. Household tasks are divided along gender lines, with men more involved in car and house repair and maintenance, and women more involved in cooking, laundry, sewing, and grocery shopping. Major time-consuming chores such as preparing meals, caring for sick children, and maintaining a liaison with children's schools were delegated to mother. Evidently the perception of equality is more crucial in dual-income families than is the real division of labor (Fish et al., 1992). The uneven division of family responsibility may be reinforced by the greater earnings of men. As the primary source of family income, the employment of the male receives more respect than the less remunerative job of female partner (Pruett, 1987).

•CLINICAL EXAMPLE:
CRISIS IN A DUAL-CAREER MARRIAGE

Veronica and Archie were high school sweethearts who entered the same university, studied together, lived together, and were married during their senior year. Both were outstanding students whose grade averages were rarely more than one-half point apart. Shortly before graduation, both were admitted to the same medical school, and as a minority group member Veronica received a generous grant. Archie negotiated a student loan and was partially subsidized by his parents. The couple had planned to begin medical school together, but Veronica became pregnant early in the summer. Unwilling to undergo an abortion, she requested and received permission to defer her entry until the following year. Archie entered medical school in September as originally planned.

During the time that Veronica stayed at home to care for her baby daughter, she often felt envious of Archie's progress, but she told herself that her turn would come soon. The following fall when her baby was six months old, Veronica eagerly began her medical studies. Archie by that time was a second-year student who had already proved his ability. A friend of Veronica's who was a registered nurse, divorced, and the mother of two preschoolers lived in an adjoining apartment and agreed to care for the baby during the day. The nurse was capable and attentive to children, so Veronica envisioned no problems in that area.

When Veronica functioned as a full-time housewife and mother, she did all the housework in addition to caring for the baby. Although she and Archie had not discussed in detail the mechanics of daily living after she returned to school, Veronica had assumed that she and Archie would revert to the task sharing of their undergraduate years. This was not exactly what Archie had in mind. While Veronica was at home, Archie had established the habit of studying with classmates and was reluctant to discontinue this practice. When talking to Veronica he glossed over the difficulties of the first year in medical school, assuring her that she had nothing to worry about and that the requirements of the second year were more difficult. Although Archie agreed to share shopping and cooking chores, he made no contribution to the evening care of the baby, concentrating on his studies as Veronica hurried to feed the baby in order to get to her own academic work. Sensing Veronica's impatience, the baby became increasingly fretful. The baby's fretfulness in turn annoyed Archie, who criticized Veronica and the baby and found excuses to study at the library or with a friend. Tied to the apartment every evening, Veronica cared for her cranky baby. Frequently she did not get to her books until 10 o'clock or later. Not long afterwards Archie would come home with his own assignments mastered and promptly go to bed for the night. By studying until 2 or 3 A.M., Veronica barely managed to keep up with her studies. She worried about the baby and realized she was robotlike in her interactions with the child. Discussions with Archie about her predicament degenerated into shouting matches. On one occasion Veronica accused him of deliberately making her pregnant so he could be the superachiever of the family. He responded by saying it wouldn't help them if they both flunked out of school. After several quarrels and barely passing her midterm exams, Veronica issued an ultimatum. Either both of them would visit a marriage counselor, or Veronica would leave Archie and move in with the nurse who looked after the baby during the day.

Both partners were equally committed to their careers, but only the wife was accustomed to performing parenting responsibilities. There was some sharing of household tasks, but childcare was not integrated into the pattern of family obligations. During pregnancy the wife had deferred her career ambitions, but the choice was not carefully discussed at the time. The wife made the decision by default, and the husband failed to realize that for his wife the decision was a genuine sacrifice that deserved recognition and future guarantees from him.

Although the couple had adhered to a standing pattern of egalitarianism in their relationship, parenthood had shifted the balance in favor of the husband. Inadvertently, the husband had placed his wife in the position of sacrificing too much for too long. Preoccupation with his own goals caused him to overlook the deprivation and embitterment of his wife. Oblivious of the routine demands of parenthood, the husband willingly accepted financial responsibility for his wife and child at some future point. Fear of not being able to provide for his family caused the husband to devote all his attention to his career. His excessive attention to his medical school studies was perceived by his wife as selfish but was more attributable to his wish to provide financial security. What he failed to realize was that his wife wanted to be a provider also and resented being relegated to the role of wife and mother instead of equal partner.

Critical Guidelines

Marital counseling focused on improving communication between partners. Even though Veronica and Archie knew each other as lovers, students, and spouses, their parenting roles were new. Veronica expected Archie to know intuitively when she needed help, just as he expected her to know intuitively that he appreciated her sacrifice in postponing medical school. Each needed to learn to express his or her own feelings, to ask directly, to acknowledge openly, and to compromise. The path they had chosen for themselves was difficult even without the added responsibility of a baby. The wife was unwilling to give up her dream of a medical career and unaware that her husband had reshaped the dream without her concurrence. What remained was for these two intelligent young people to begin a protracted process of negotiation and to turn their attention to rebuilding a relationship that had already proved its importance to them. With equitable and flexible role sharing the primary goal, the following issues were addressed:

1. Adequate support systems for childcare and housework needed to be arranged. Evening help was necessary so that Veronica could relax for an hour or so with her child before beginning her studies. This period of relaxation should involve Archie as well as his wife and child.
2. Archie needed to resume sharing his study time with his wife rather than with his classmates. With both partners entering the same profession, they spoke a common language. If Archie used his newly acquired knowledge to help his wife through the first competitive year of medical school, their relationship would be strengthened and their former pride in each other restored.
3. Both partners had a threefold obligation: to each other, to their child, and to their careers. A delicate balance could be maintained only if role enactment in all three areas included both partners.

COUNSELING YOUNG ADULTS

Perhaps the counselor's most important tools are observing and listening. The personal appearance of an individual may reflect his state of mind, body image, and level of functioning. How people dress usually denotes their adherence or renunciation of values consistent with their age, gender, economic status, and chosen life style. When the overall appearance of a person in crisis differs from customary patterns, the difference may be an indication of the extent of the crisis. People in crisis who are able to conform, or attempt to conform, to customary standards may be exhibiting a desire for acceptance by others, desire for relief, and willingness to participate. The debilitating effects of the crisis have not erased the individual's concern for how she appears to others. In addition to external details, the individual's posture, movements, facial expressions, and emotional expressiveness must be observed. Gait and posture can be extremely revealing, as Dixon (1979) noted

> Gait and posture are fairly easy to interpret. For example, a slow, methodical gait can show depression, fatigue, discouragement, lack of interest. On the other hand, a rapid gait could represent anxiety, fear, or agitation. Posture, like gait, very often expresses a specific mood or affect, from the person who slumps in a chair to one who perches on the edge of the seat. Also, posture may represent changes in affect during the course of the interview. An example is the client who rocks continuously in the chair until the therapist says something that is significant, and then stops. Posture can also indicate boredom and disinterest (p. 73).

Questioning and exploring are other powerful tools available to the counselor. Besides gathering information, questioning helps clarify an individual's confusion and misperceptions. Exploring consists of pursuing a subject in greater depth, and is sometimes used to facilitate emotional catharsis. Exploring should be titrated to the individual's tolerance levels. This is a therapeutic tool whose use demands some expertise. It is not the same as probing, which is an investigative technique that lacks the empathic sensitivity that should accompany exploration. Probing is concerned with obtaining information, not with the sharing of emotions.

Techniques of crisis counseling usually have one or more of the following objectives. These are: (1) to provide psychological support, (2) to promote cognitive correction, and (3) to alter relationships between the individual and the environment. Four types of intervention techniques are available to the counselor, depending on the characteristics of the individual and the crisis situation: *confrontation, persuasion, suggestion,* and *directive advice.*

Confrontation is indicated when an individual steadfastly resists the reality of a situation or problem. It should be used judiciously, beginning with mild, nonthreatening admonitions. For example, the counselor might remind the individual, "Since you must vacate your apartment in two weeks, perhaps you should begin to look for another place." Mild confrontation may be sufficient, but stronger measures may be needed, such as, "I know you want to keep your family together, but this won't happen if you are homeless. What can be done to help you find another place to live?"

Persuasion can be an effective technique for people in crisis who cannot choose between several courses of action. A man contemplating a career change should make his own decision on the matter without being directly guided by a counselor. At most, the pros and cons of any decision should be presented, and the man should draw his own conclusions. This is not true when one course of action is clearly in the best interest of the individual. Persuading a sexually promiscuous person to be tested for human immunodeficiency virus (HIV) or urging vocational testing for a person considering a career change are certainly appropriate.

In resorting to persuasion, a counselor may be rather forceful. *Suggestion* is a mild, tentative form of persuasion that leaves the individual free to follow or ignore the suggestion. Choosing suggestion over persuasion is based on the personality structure of the individual. Persuasion may evoke resistance in many individuals who may be willing to accept suggestions, after some reflection. A good rule for counselors is to begin with suggestion and move to persuasion only if the situation warrants it.

When an individual is unresponsive to less direct techniques, *directive advice* may be given on rare occasions. A counselor may utilize suggestion or even persuasion to recommend a desirable course of action; only when an individual is at risk of endangering the self or others should direct advice be given. A counselor may advise a family to hospitalize a suicidal member or tell a frightened woman to get a protection order, but such prescriptions should be given with care. The person in crisis may seem so helpless that the counselor is tempted to take charge. However, people who are assisted in drawing their own conclusions and making their own decisions tend to be more satisfied with the results.

Environmental Alterations

Environmental alteration may be defined as altering the nature of the environment or removing an individual from a harmful environment. Helping a harried mother arrange part-time day care for three preschoolers or recommending an overdue vacation for dual-income families are forms of environmental modification. Hospitalization or foster care placement are more drastic examples of altering an individual's environment. To use environmental modification effectively, a counselor must not only be knowledgeable about the individual or family, but also must be knowledgeable about personal and community resources.

Many of the counseling strategies advocated for young adults are appropriate at other stages of the life cycle. The same caveats apply regardless of when or with whom the strategies are used. Placement of counseling strategies in this chapter on crises of early adult life emphasizes their value but does not imply that their effective use is limited to young adults. Entry into adulthood presupposes some progress in cognitive and moral development, and young adults usually have the capacity to respond to the interventions described in this chapter, even during the disequilibrium of crisis.

SUMMARY

Adulthood may be divided into three stages: early, middle, and late; this chapter dealt with typical crises of the first two stages. Disequilibrium arising in early adulthood is likely to be concerned with options and decisions. Crises of productivity, crises of commitment, and crises of decision were selected to illustrate common disruptions that occur in adult life.

Crises of productivity emerge from conditions encountered in jobs or careers. This type of crisis may affect individual workers or it may affect the whole family. Lack of meaningful work and dissatisfaction with occupational advancement may cause psychological distress or contribute to psychophysiological dysfunction in workers.

Professional counseling around abortion should not be persuasive or coercive, but should be devoted to reducing emotionality and helping women make decisions compatible with their lifestyles and value systems. Once the decision is made, counseling should be directed toward helping women live with the choice they have made. Women are most receptive to contraceptive advice just after delivery or abortion, so professional counseling should not be prematurely terminated before that point.

Younger women dealing with unplanned pregnancy are more responsive to influence from others. Pregnant women who undergo amniocentesis in order to determine fetal abnormality generally regard abortion as preferable to bearing a child with a congenital disability.

The same anticipatory guidance is useful in dual-career families in which job aspirations of the wife may be construed as problems by husbands and children. In dual-career marriages the scarcest commodity is time. With time at a premium, couples may disengage or one partner may expect the other to sacrifice personal hopes and dreams.

Parenthood brings an infinite potential for stress, regardless of family structure. Single parents become overwhelmed with their responsibilities as wage earners and as the primary nurturers of children. In intact families where both mother and father work outside the home, problems may be different but no less intense. Some of the problems that young adults face can be solved on a personal or interactional level. Other problems, such as the national need for safe and effective childcare, must be solved through social, political, or legislative channels.

The chapter concluded with a discussion of specific strategies that are useful in counseling adults. The strategies may be adopted in counseling midlife and older adults as well as those in earlier adult life.

REFERENCES

Benedek, T. "The Family as a Psychological Field." In *Parenthood: Its Psychology and Psychopathology,* edited by E.J. Anthony and T. Benedek. Boston: Little Brown, 1970.

Brazelton, T. "Issues for Working Parents." *American Journal of Orthopsychiatry* 56(1986): 14–25.

Brunnquell, D., L. Crichton, and B. Egeland. "Maternal Personality and Attitude and Disturbances of Childrearing." *American Journal of Orthopsychiatry* 51(1981): 680–691.

Chess, S. "Women's Work." *Readings* 1(1986): 23–25.

Coverman, S., and J.F. Sheley. "Changes in Men's Housework and Childcare." *Journal of Marriage and the Family* 48(1986): 413–422.

Erikson, E. *Childhood and Society.* New York: Norton, 1963.

———. *Identity, Youth, and Crisis.* New York: Norton, 1968.

Ersek, M. "Examining the Process and Dilemmas of Reality Negotiation." *Image* 24(1992): 19–25.

Fish, L.S., R.S. New, and N.J. VanCleave, "Shared Parenting in Dual Income Families." *American Journal of Orthopsychiatry* 62(1992): 83–92.

Freud, A. *The Ego and Mechanisms of Defense.* London: Hogarth, 1948.

Friedenberg, E.Z. "Extracurricular Activities." *Readings* 2(1987): 4–7.

GAP Report no. 126 (Group for Advancement of Psychiatry). New York: Brunner/ Mazel, 1989.

Gerson, K. *Hard Choices: How Women Decide About Work, Career, and Motherhood.* Berkeley, California: University of California Press, 1985.

Goleman, D. "In His Own Old Age Erikson Expands His View of Life." *The New York Times,* June 14, 1988 ppC–1, 14.

Greenberger, E., and L. Steinberg. *When Teenagers Work: the Psychological and Social Costs of Adolescent Employment.* New York: Basic Books, 1986.

Hall, W.A. "Comparison of the Experience of Women and Men in Dual Earner Families Following the Birth of Their First Infant." *Image* 24(1992): 33–38.

Horney, K. *The Neurotic Personality of Our Time.* Norton, 1937.

———. *Our Inner Conflicts.* New York: Norton, 1945.

Jordon, P.L. "Laboring for Relevance: Expectant and New Fatherhood." *Nursing Research* 39(1990): 11–16.

Keniston, K. *The Uncommitted: Alienated Youth in American Society.* New York: Basic Books, 1974.

Kimball, G. *50/50 Parenting: Sharing Family Rewards and Responsibilities.* Lexington, Massachusetts: Lexington Books, 1988.

Koeske, G.F., and R.D. Koeske. "The Buffering Effects of Social Support on Parental Stress." *American Journal of Orthopsychiatry* 60(1990): 441–451.

Lidz, T. "The Life Cycle" In *Comprehensive Textbook of Psychiatry,* edited by H.I. Kaplan, A.M. Freedman, and B.J. Sadock. Baltimore, Maryland: Williams & Wilkins, 1980.

McCloskey, J.C. "Two Requirements for Job Contentment: Autonomy and Social Integration." *Image* 22(1990): 140–143.

McLean, A.A. "Occupational Psychiatry" In *Comprehensive Textbook of Psychiatry*, edited by H.I. Kaplan, A.M. Freedman, and B.J. Sadock. Baltimore, Maryland: Williams & Wilkins, 1980.

Partridge, S.E. "The Parental Self Concept: A Theoretical Explanation and Practical Application." *American Journal of Orthopsychiatry* 58(1988): 281–287.

Pender, N.J., S.N. Walker, K.R. Sechrist, and M. Frank-Stromberg. "Predicting Health Promoting Life Style in the Workplace." *Nursing Research* 39(1990): 326–332.

Pleck, J.H. *Working Wives/Working Husbands.* Beverly Hills, California: Sage, 1985.

Pruett, K. *The Nurturing Father.* New York: Warner, 1987.

Rainwater, L. *Family Design.* Chicago: Aldine, 1965.

Reisman, D. *The Lonely Crowd: A Study of the Changing American Character.* New Haven, Connecticut: Yale University Press, 1973.

Rubenstein, C. "The Baby Bomb." *The New York Times Good Health Magazine* October 8, 1989, pp. 34–41.

Sheehy, G. *Passages.* New York: Dutton, 1976.

Snyder, C.R. "Reality Negotiation: From Excuses to Hope and Beyond." *Journal of Social and Clinical Psychology* 8(1989): 130–157.

Taylor, S.E. "Adjustment to Threatening Events: A Theory of Cognitive Adaptation." *American Psychology* 38(1983): 1161–1171.

———. *Positive Illusion: Creative Self Deception and the Healthy Mind.* New York: Basic Books, 1989.

Taylor, S.E., and J. Brown. "Illusion and Wellbeing: A Social Psychological Perspective on Mental Health." *Psychological Bulletin* 103(1988): 489–502.

Weisman, A.D. *Coping with Cancer.* New York: McGraw-Hill, 1979.

8

Adults in Crisis
The Middle Years

People are always blaming their circumstances for what they are. I don't believe in circumstances. The people who get on in this world are the people who get up and look for the circumstances they want, and if they can't find them, make them.

George Bernard Shaw

Crises in the form of new decisions, new commitments, and new circumstances continue throughout adulthood. The traditional family life cycle, characterized by an early phase of expansion as children enter the family, and a later phase of contraction as they leave, is not typical of all families. Instead, many individuals experience successive stages of estrangement, separation, divorce, single parenting or co-parenting, remarriage, and stepparenting. Each of these transitional stages is likely to be a period of instability for adults and for the children who are involved. Figure 8–1 shows a model of marriage, divorce, and remarriage that is common today.

Marriages are complex relationships and failed marriages are not always marked by formal separation or divorce. However, divorce is an open acknowledgement that a marriage has failed. It represents drastic change that affects everyone involved—parents, children, and extended family members. Even under the best conditions, divorce involves a difficult legal proceeding. Although grounds for divorce vary from state to state, agreement must be reached about property, alimony, child support, and custody. Current estimates indicate that one out of every two marriages is likely to end in divorce (Brody, 1992).

Marriages end for many reasons. Couples may not know each other well when they marry, even when they have been living together for some time. Some have not separated completely from their families of origin and hope that they will resolve separation and identity issues merely by marrying. Marital partners mature and grow at different rates. One may develop socially and intellectually after marriage, while the

165

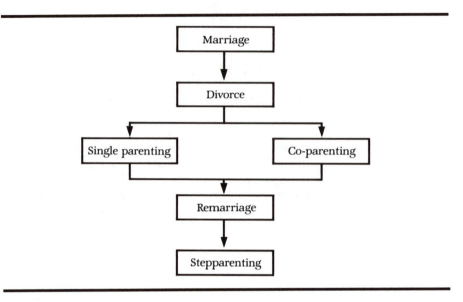

FIGURE 8–1   Life Cycle Model of Marriage, Divorce, and Remarriage

other remains transfixed at an earlier developmental stage. Incompatibility between partners is often the result of unresolved differences or of unshared goals.

Adultery is often, but not always, the cause of a dissolved marriage. When one partner finds out that the other is having an affair, the discovery may precipitate a crisis that is used in counseling to examine the marital relationship and discover what is lacking. In research supported by the National Institute of Mental Health, the husband's disappointment with the marriage was found to be the most powerful predictor of eventual divorce (Brody, 1992). Thus, the husband's feelings rather than the wife's may be the most reliable barometer of the durability of a marriage.

The final separation of the couple may eventuate only after long periods of distress, many painful encounters, mutual recrimination, and vindictiveness. Episodes of separation may be interspersed with spasmodic and temporary reconciliations. Not all separations are premeditated; some spouses desert impulsively and never return. In some marriages estrangement persists for years before separation and divorce occur. Why does it take some couples years to separate formally despite extreme dissatisfaction? Why do some divorced couples continue some kind of communication even after divorce? One explanation may be that emotional attachment persists even after divorce and marriage to someone else. Even for childless couples the marriage may be over but the relationship persists in one form or another.

EFFECTS ON CHILDREN

Considerable research has dealt with examining the effects of divorce on children in various developmental stages, such as early childhood, adolescence, and young adulthood (Hetherington et al., 1985; Aro & Palosaari, 1992). Other research has concentrated on gender differences in the reactions of offspring to parental divorce (Kalter, 1989; Southworth & Schwarz, 1987; Zaslow, 1988). In both kinds of investigation, findings tend to be inconclusive and discrepant. In studying reactions of offspring to parental divorce, little attention was paid to the family structure existing after divorce. For example, children might be living with a single-parent mother or a remarried mother. In other instances, children might be living with a single-parent father, a remarried father, or with a stepfather rather than a biological father. In support of this contention, Zaslow (1988) made the following predictions.

- In studies that deal with children living only with the mother after divorce, findings will indicate more adverse effects for sons.
- In studies that deal with children living only with father after divorce, findings will indicate more adverse effects for daughters.
- In studies that deal with children living with mother and stepfather, findings will indicate more adverse outcomes for daughters.
- In studies that do not control for custody and/or remarriage, findings will indicate no difference in outcomes for sons compared with daughters.

No exact figures are available nationally for postdivorce patterns of custody, but census data indicate that nine out of ten children in single-parent families reside with their mother. Furstenberg et al. (1983) warned that the immediate postdivorce family structure is not stable and that children of divorced parents usually experience remarriage, and sometimes a dissolved remarriage. Some 57 percent of white children and 13 percent of black children entered stepparent families within five years of their biological parents' divorce. Moreover, 37 percent of the children in stepparent families again experienced disruption when the subsequent marriage failed. Thus, the recovery of offspring from the effects of parental divorce may be complicated by remarriage and by failure of the remarriage.

Another factor in remarriage of women is the economic consequences of divorce. Sometimes it is only through a second marriage that divorced mothers can regain their predivorce standard of living. There are racial differences in patterns of marital disruption. More black women experience the end of a marriage through separation rather than divorce. The span of time between separation and divorce is longer for black women, averaging 10.6 years, as opposed to 1.8 years for white women. After divorce black women are less likely to remarry. Demographic differences by race raise questions as to the effects of divorce, custody, and step-parenting in black families where the pattern of single-parent mothers is more prevalent (Zaslow, 1988). Across the board, father custody and frequent visitation after divorce are uncommon. Zaslow reported that the Foundation for Child Development Study found that noncustodial parents rarely saw their children after divorce. Only one out of three children living with divorced mothers saw their "outside" fathers monthly; after two years, there was a marked increase in the number of outside fathers who had no contact with their children.

Contemporary research views divorce not as a single event, but as a series of changes and reorganizations that are stressful for all participants, regardless of age, race, gender, or role (Hetherington & Furstenberg, 1989). Based on a ten-year retrospective study, Wallerstein and Blakesley (1989) emphasized the profound effect of parental divorce in shaping the psychological and social experiences of the offspring as young adults. They asserted that the prevailing view in American society minimizes the trauma of parental divorce on children.

LOYALTY ISSUES

Despite their anger, confusion, and ambivalence, children may continue to harbor loving, loyal feelings for both parents for many years after the divorce. The heavy emotional burden these children carry places them under considerable stress beyond the usual developmental issues. Wallerstein (1983) presented six psychological tasks the postdivorce child faces, in addition to the usual tasks of growing up.

1. To acknowledge the reality of the marital rupture.
2. To disengage from parental conflict and resume customary pursuits.
3. To resolve the loss of the family as it was.
4. To work through feelings of anger and self-blame.
5. To accept the reality and permanence of the divorce.
6. To regain realistic hope concerning relationships.

These are very formidable tasks; years may have to elapse before they are even partially accomplished. Because failure to accomplish any or all of them may precipitate crisis, further explanation is needed.

Task one: Acknowledging the reality of the marital rupture. The child's age, developmental stage, needs, problems, and personality influence her comprehension of the parental divorce. The young child may experience frightening fantasies about being left and can be overwhelmed by intense emotions of sadness and rage. All of the children in the study had completed task one by the end of the first year of the parents' separation.

Task two: Disengaging from parental conflict and resuming customary pursuits. The child's anxiety and sadness about the parental separation needs to be put aside, but this is very difficult to accomplish since the home atmosphere may be highly chaotic, and the child may feel too unhappy and worried to invest much emotional energy outside the home. School work usually suffers, and commitments to extracurricular activities seem to wane. Some pain was eased in families where the siblings could be supportive of each other. By one to one-and-a-half years after the parental separation, most children in the study had reinvested in school and outside friendships.

Task three: Resolving the loss. Resolving the loss is perhaps the most difficult of the tasks. The nucleus of this charge is that the child must recover from his deep feelings of rejection and fears about whether he is lovable. All children feel rejected when a parent leaves. Frequent communication with the departed parent and responsible, consistent contact between the child and the departed parent help to dispel the child's fears.

Task four: Resolving anger and self-blame. Resolving children's anger and self-blame following parental divorce takes years. The experience of intense anger that parental divorce generates often goes hand in hand with school truancy and failure, and delinquent acting out behavior in adolescents. Relinquishing the anger can pave the way for forgiveness, and only then is the young person able to get rid of the feeling of helplessness and experience some sense of relief.

Task five: Accepting the permanence of the divorce. The fantasy that the divorced will remarry is prevalent among many children. This is especially true for children who were quite young when the parental divorce took place. Older children more easily give up this reconciliation wish.

Task six: Achieving realistic hope regarding relationships. This is the task that integrates all the coping abilities of the person who struggles with pain and fears about a parental divorce. Many young adults of divorced parents are afraid of intimate relationships and marriage for fear of failure. The core question of their ability to love and be loved, and to trust another person must be resolved. These young adults must find ways to establish and maintain their feelings of self-worth; they must have successfully separated themselves from the parental conflicts and found their own independent direction. Wallerstein (1983, p. 242) concluded, "It is likely that even when these tasks are successfully resolved, there will remain for the child of divorce some residue of sadness, of anger, and of anxiety about the potential unreliability of relationships which may reappear at critical times during the adult years."

During the period of separating, emotional support from relatives or close friends may be helpful. There is danger, however, that alliances will be established in which the partners perceive significant others as either allies or enemies. Moreover, dependency patterns may be established that seem useful at the time of initial impact but ultimately impede restitution. Because relatives and friends of the couple are rarely bipartisan in their attitudes, professional counseling is usually more productive than the advice of nonprofessionals, regardless of their good intentions.

The respective attorneys for the husband and wife can negotiate legal and economic issues, but they are less qualified to influence decisions of an emotional nature. Ethical counselors will not presume to influence the actual decision to divorce but can help with other controversial matters once the decision has been made. One alternative devised for mediation of disputed questions in divorce cases offered the suggestion that lawyers and counselors work together with the divorcing couple to reach decisions that are nonexploitive and mutually satisfactory.

Most contested divorces are handled by lawyers in the traditional adversarial legal system. The issues of "justice" in divorce cases are so complex, they are almost indecipherable. Mostly, the law says that the partners have to fit their difficulties into a limited structure. The law does not say, for example, that the partners should examine their relationship and give an honest statement to the court about its failure.

DIVORCE MEDIATION

As one way of trying to eliminate some destructive forces in the divorce procedure and to avoid long court delays, a process known as *divorce mediation* has developed in the last decade. By definition, it is a process in which the divorce partners agree to meet with a third person(s) to resolve differences through mutual compromise and face-to-face discussions. It is not a clinical or diagnostic procedure, nor is it considered psychotherapy. Suppressing all affect is not good, and expressing feelings on the part of both partners is encouraged, but prolonged catharsis is not recommended. It is the hope and goal of the divorce mediation that neither partner is the loser, is blamed, or is exploited. There is no coercion on the part of the mediators, who try to show the partners that everyone in the family can profit from resolving issues outside of court. The mediator(s) is nonjudgmental and, generally, encourages arbitration in a constructive emotional atmosphere. Divorce mediation requires training and skill on the part of the mediators. Lawyers and courts in some states often now suggest such services.

Not all couples seeking divorce can agree to participate in such a process, and clearly, it is not to be viewed as capable of solving all divorce problems. Although it has proven successful with a wide variety of persons, certain cautions are suggested. The problems to be settled vary considerably and are dependent upon the following factors: the resources of the couple, how long they have been married, what stage of the family life cycle they are in, and whether children are involved and at what ages. Also, such a process may not work; prolonged and intense emotional upheaval is seen as a serious threat to the rational process of negotiation.

Social uncertainty and social isolation are common during the aftermath of divorce. Divorced women complain that they are seldom included in the activities of married couples, who consider invitations to unattached females to be awkward. Although divorced men enjoy the relatively desirable status of unattached males, many of them feel uncomfortable with the unfamiliar role of bachelor. However, dissolution of a marriage seems to be a more difficult adjustment for women, perhaps because being married is more central to the identity and socialization of women.

THE DIVORCE PROCESS

During the time of emotional estrangement that precedes formal separation, a decision must be made for one parent to leave the family residence. Although parents may be reluctant to tell children about imminent separation and divorce, failure to tell the truth adds to the confusion of children. Pretending that a family breakup is inconsequential rather than cataclysmic gives children a message that they should hide their real feelings. Regardless of their feelings about one another, parents should try to separate their disillusionment with each other from their obligations as parents. The statement should be made and reiterated to children that while husbands and wives may be divorced from one another, parents and children cannot be. This reassurance is particularly important for young children who have not yet encountered peers who have survived the crisis of parental divorce.

The early period of family dissolution is extremely difficult. No longer intact, the family must undergo massive reorganization in respect to rules, roles, norms, and boundaries. Another change to which divorced couples must often adjust is what may be termed *class slippage*. The economic reality is that, after divorce, accustomed lifestyles must be sacrificed simply because they are no longer affordable. High rates of noncompliance with support and alimony decisions mean that many divorced women in middle or lower socioeconomic classes must assume a disproportionate financial burden for raising children and therefore endure downward class mobility. Divorced males who must support two households suffer financial reverses as well.

Lack of uniformity in state laws dealing with divorce settlements creates additional inequity. In some states community property laws permit divorced couples to share equally in whatever property was accumulated during the marriage. In other states the parties are not required to divest themselves of any property to which they already hold title, whereas in remaining states court decisions on what constitutes personal and community property may vary widely.

In reviewing changes in divorce legislation over the last decades, among others, Wallerstein and Blakesley (1989) asserted the new divorce legislation has resulted in the impoverishment of women and minor children. On average, divorced women suffer a 73 percent decline in their living standard in the first year after divorce, while their former husbands saw a 42 percent increase in their living standard. It is indeed ironic that the time of the woman's movement has also witnessed the erosion of the rights of divorced women and their minor children.

The reasons for this state of affairs are varied. First, there is the widespread failure of fathers to pay child support when legally ordered to do so. There is also the acknowledged reluctance of judges to order burdensome amounts, even for financially able fathers. Another explanation is found in the *no-fault* divorce legislation introduced in 1970 by California. Until that time every state required fault-based grounds for divorce. Divorce legislation also endorsed the role of husband as provider and wife as homemaker through a system of rewards and penalties. Both partners were rewarded for discharging their respective roles; each might be liable to penalties, such as denial of alimony, property, or custody, if it could be shown that rules had been broken.

A reputable study showed that no-fault divorce legislation has been almost catastrophic (Wallerstein, 1986). Support awards to women with children under age six years dropped more than other groups: 87 percent of mothers with preschool children were awarded no spousal support at all. Under the fifty-fifty property split rulings in California, many judges ordered an immediate sale of the family residence. This robbed mothers and children of familiar surroundings and social supports at the height of the family crisis.

Although no-fault divorce was expected to have only positive results, it has worked to the disadvantage of many women, especially older women who spent their lives as homemakers. With its emphasis on equality, no-fault divorce legislation assumed women to be as capable of self-support as their husbands. More than half the women married fifteen years or more received no support and were compelled, in middle age, to find jobs in a labor force they had left years before.

Research illuminates reasons for the impoverishment of women and children after divorce. The consequences of divorce are often far more severe for women. While one does not advocate a return to traditional divorce law, legislative changes have been proposed that address the unfairness of the present system and deal specifically with its deficiencies. Wallerstein (1986) has described the condition of many divorced women as follows.

> Most experienced a quality of life severely deteriorated from that which they enjoyed during the marriage. Their emotional lives had become more constricted. Their loneliness was painful and debilitating despite work and church and community involvement. Those who still had a child at home were concerned about burdening that child with their own needs for love and companionship. The impending separation of mother and child was dreaded by parents and concerned youngsters alike (p. 12).

Referral to a support group, such as Neutral Ground, may be indicated for persons moving out of marriage into new roles. Meetings of this self-help group are usually held in the homes of members, where such issues as loss, parenting, finances, and self-determination are discussed. During the meetings, group members who are at different stages of reaction to divorce attempt to raise consciousness. Individuals who have already achieved considerable readjustment are able to help members who still feel frightened and lost. Divorce is presented not as a tragedy, but as a potentially creative experience once the pain subsides and the readjustment process begins.

Later the divorced person may be ready for referral to a more socially oriented group, such as Parents without Partners, a nonprofit, self-help group organized to help divorced and widowed parents who are raising children alone. The national organization of Parents without Partners has more than 60,000 chapters, each of which tends to be independent and distinctive. Allowing for some differences of emphasis between chapters, the organization divides its activities along the following lines:

- Lecture programs or educational meetings on such issues as child development and parent-child relationships.
- Discussion or therapeutic groups, professionally led and devoted to general problems and concerns of single parents.
- Parent-child activities, such as picnics, hikes, and other appropriate outings.
- Adult activities that encourage social interaction among parents sharing similar situations and interests.

It is not only young children and adolescents who react strongly to parental divorce. Some adult children are devastated by the breakup of their parents' marriage after a union of twenty-five years or more. This may be especially true if the adult children have always idealized their parent's relationship, and if the parents have successfully concealed their problems. Secretly, the parents may have agreed to stay together until the children were grown and out of the home. For young adults engrossed in their own momentous decisions about commitment and careers, the spectacle of staid parents engaging in new, untried behaviors may be very unsettling. If the divorcing parents are in late middle age, their children may have assumed that each parent would be a companion and caretaker for the other during the years of inevitable decline. Suddenly the partnership is dissolved. Parents have turned away from their expected obligations and worried children wonder what obligations will fall upon their shoulders.

FAMILY TASKS

Just as children have certain tasks to confront after parental divorce, so do the parents. Even after the marriage ends, parents should not renounce their roles as family leaders until major reorganization is under way. The major family tasks include the following:

- Divorcing parents need to clarify their parental obligations and reach agreement on their mutual responsibilities.
- A stable living situation must be arranged for all family members. This may necessitate relocation for some or all family members.
- Economic arrangements are required in the form of child support, dual earnings, or public assistance, if required.
- New support systems may need to be found through extended families, neighborhood networks, churches, and schools; recourse to community and social agencies may be advisable.
- Requirements of the family unit should be considered, as well as the needs of any members in crisis as a result of dissolution of the previous family structure.
- Finally, there is the ongoing task of emotional healing that must take place in the midst of turmoil. Mourning is facilitated when the pain of loss can be shared with other family members. Constructive communication must be fostered between the divorcing principals. This is the only way that reorganization can proceed.
- Ideally, each divorcing partner must take some responsibility for the failure of the marriage. If the partners can manage this, they may avoid the repetition of the same mistakes in a second marriage.

The recovery period families undergo following divorce may be protracted. There are some offspring who never fully recover from the pain of parental divorce and dissolution of their original family. Initially, the post-divorce period is a time of shock and denial for the children and one or both partners. This is usually followed by a transitional period that is also accompanied by emotional distress. Finally, there is a rather lengthy recovering phase during which the pain of the past is put into perspective and a measure of emotional stability is restored. New activities and new interests are found, and the reconstructed family begins to find a new way of living and surviving.

Some families, however, do not get on with the business of building a new life, but remain in the transitional phase where recovery is always just around the corner. A divorced partner may spend years waiting and hoping for the spouse to return, unable to accept the finality of divorce. This makes it doubly hard for the children to give up their fantasies of reconciliation, since these are reinforced by the ever hopeful parent. Some partners may not conconsciously hope for reconciliation, but cannot engage in the grief work that is necessary before new attachments can be formed. They cannot mourn because they are so bitter and vindictive. They want the whole world, especially the children, to know they have been wronged. They inflict their grievances on anyone who will listen. Others may suffer in silence but their behavior attests to their unrelenting martyrdom.

Children who are subjected to such an environment suffer. They may blame themselves for a parent's pain. Their behavior may reflect their inner anguish, until they find themselves in trouble at school or with the law. When the parent who has custody becomes dysfunctional, the children in effect have lost both parents and are truly orphaned by divorce.

It is important to permit the expression of grief and disillusionment on the part of all family members when parents are divorced and a family separates. The overwhelming tasks of adjustment take a long time to complete. Support, custody, and visitation issues must be arranged in detail, but these are matters best left to the legal system rather than a crisis counselor. The counselor should not be drawn into the role of judge, adversary, or miracle worker. Instead, crisis intervention should be restricted to specific issues related to the critical needs of the moment. It is not advisable to expect every family member to react in the same way or to experience the divorce in the same way. Prolonged behavior problems in children, the deepening of depression in any family member, or the emergence of substance abuse in the post-divorce period may demand more than crisis counseling. In such circumstances, referral for traditional or ongoing evaluation and treatment may be warranted.

Divorce affects the whole interpersonal world of the couple, their children, their friends, and families of origin. Even when the decision to divorce is mutual, there is an abiding sense of failure. Relatives who have become fond of a daughter-in-law or son-in-law are conflicted; many divorced persons lose not only the partner, but significant others as well. There is some similarity between divorce and the death of a loved one, except that there are no accepted rituals to help divorced people inter their marriage. For the divorced, the dignified finality of death is not available, because they must continue to interact with former partners during and after legal proceedings, especially if children are involved. This is unfortunate because any divorce gives rise to the acute separation anxiety that irrevocable loss evokes.

There are three possible types of custody arrangements: *joint custody,* *single custody,* and *split custody,* none of which represents an ideal. In *joint custody,* children share their time between parents, and both parents continue to be involved in relevant decisions about the children. Under *single-custody* arrangements, one parent has major responsibility for the children, and the noncustodial parent has visitation rights and perhaps financial obligations. In *split-custody* decisions, some of the children become the responsibility of one parent, and the other children are consigned to the care of the other parent.

In the past, the inclination of the courts was to favor the mother in custody decisions, but joint custody is becoming more common. A child's wish to live with a preferred parent is considered in custody hearings but may not be a deciding factor. The older the child, the more likely the court is to be influenced by the child's preference, since adolescents may react to unwelcome court decisions by running away. Custody decisions are not irrevocable but may be challenged and changed in some circumstances. If the custodial parent systematically influences a child against the noncustodial parent or does not respect visitation rights of the noncustodial parent, court decisions generally take the form of warnings and orders to desist. If the custodial parent can be proved guilty of abuse or neglect, or is certifiably incompetent, the court is likely to revoke the original custody decision.

JOINT CUSTODY

If joint custody is to work, there must be a shared willingness on the part of divorced parents to cooperate for the benefit of the children. Elkin (1987) described joint custody as an arrangement that equalizes the power, authority, and responsibilities of parenting. Several advantages of joint custody come immediately to mind. The children feel less abandoned and are comforted by knowing that both parents will continue to be involved in their care. The parents enjoy the luxury of personal time and relief from twenty-four hour childcare. At the same time, parents making joint-custody arrangements must be capable of the following:

- Parents must have the capacity to separate their marital roles from their parental roles.
- Parents must be committed to the joint-custody arrangement and refrain from sabotaging it.

- Parents must give the children's needs priority over their own needs.
- Parents must engage in effective, problem-solving communication and must be able to negotiate differences.

Elkin contended that in cases of divorce, fathers have been placed in an inferior role with little authority and no responsibility except for child support. Joint custody permits fathers to remain important to the development of their children and to demonstrate their concerned caring to the children. However, he conceded that joint custody arrangements are not recommended when either parent has a record of addiction or substance abuse, or for families where neglect, violence, abuse, or psychopathology has been present. When the question of custody requires adjudication, the effect on children is likely to be severe. However, with divorced mothers working outside the home and fathers willing to discharge co-parenting obligations, more divorced partners are choosing to share custody.

Research on joint custody has revealed a new family structure called a *binuclear* family system. This new structure is the result of realignment of nuclear families in which the commitment of both parents to their children continues after divorce. In a study of urban divorced families, Ahrons (1981) found that fathers sharing joint custody were less depressed and more satisfied in their relationships with their children than fathers who did not share custody. They had a commitment to their children that transcended the issues of divorce. While recognizing their incompatibility, the parents valued each other on behalf of the children, and believed that having two parents who shared custody was better for the children than being reared by one parent. Ahron's longitudinal study produced interesting data, as shown.

- Parental commitment to joint custody produced unusual living arrangements. Some children lived one year with one parent and the following year with the other parent. Others alternated between maternal and paternal households every three months, every two weeks, every half week, and every other day. Whenever possible, and in all instances in which changeover was frequent, the children attended the same school or day care program regardless of which household they shared. Financial arrangements between the parents were diverse, but in all cases the fathers met their financial obligations regularly.
- In general, adults favored joint-custody arrangements. The mothers enjoyed being able to pursue activities outside the home without having to be full-time parents. Fathers welcomed continued involvement with their children even after they remarried. Joint custody seemed to reduce any role strain on one parent and made both parents more free to establish new relationships. From the parental viewpoint, joint custody alleviated their own feelings of guilt, lessened the deprivation of the children, and distributed the responsibilities of childrearing.

- Joint custody apparently was less successful for the children, even though they seemed to appreciate efforts their parents made to implement the arrangement. For the most part, the children were able to adapt to two residences, although some of the traveling and household changes were confusing, especially to children between four and five years old. Older children between seven and nine years voiced frustration for having to remember so many different things, such as where the utensils were kept in each household. Continuity of school life and maintaining customary friendships were important, especially for adolescents, who complained that changes of residences hampered peer relationships for them.
- Children participating in joint-custody arrangements were preoccupied with the feelings and sensitivities of their parents. If one parent seemed lonely or was less secure financially than the other parent, the children worried about this parent. Despite their awareness of the efforts of their parents, the children experienced periods of sadness and entertained thoughts of being united as a family. Although the opportunity to witness cooperative interaction between their parents reassured the children, it also encouraged fantasies of reconciliation that persisted years after the divorce. Although the children seemed able to deal with the practicalities of living in two homes, certain aspects of their existence proved difficult. For the most part, joint custody seemed to be less burdensome for parents than for the children, who seemed to suffer some disadvantage. With joint custody a current alternative to the customary practice of awarding legal custody to one parent and visitation rights to the other, there is need for careful preparation and further investigation before divorced parents routinely embark on this complicated course.

Even though the parents may have not yet worked out the dimensions of their new relationship, it is inadvisable for the children to remain isolated from the noncustodial parent. Sustained contact with the noncustodial parent reduces a child's fears of abandonment, counteracts the tendencies of single parents to construct a closed family system, and fosters a semblance of continuity between the old family and the new.

Children living with one parent lack the opportunity to witness day-to-day transactions between men and women, and tend to become possessive toward the single parent. Losing one parent intensifies the child's ties to the custodial parent and engenders resentment of new attachments the custodial parent may form with persons of the opposite sex. Clear separation of parental roles from other roles will clarify a child's distorted perception of the single parent. The female child who is encouraged to consider herself mother's confidant or daddy's "little woman" is more likely to view prospective stepparents as rivals. The male child who thinks of himself as the mother's "man of the house" or the pal of father is also likely to see potential stepparents as intruders. Maintaining distinct intrafamily boundaries is one method of avoiding undue resentment when the single parent considers remarriage.

THE SINGLE PARENT

Unless a mother is demonstrably unfit or incompetent, it is she who is usually awarded custody of the children. However, many fathers make valiant efforts to remain involved in the lives of their children, even after they become the outside parent. For either custodial parent, the burdens of single parenthood are great. Loneliness, hurt, and the struggle to put one's life back together have to be faced, as well as the ever-present financial problems. Many single-parent mothers are so overburdened that their emotional availability to the children is limited for many months past divorce. Visitation poses problems also, particularly if the separated/divorced parents have different sets of values and rules. In their own upset emotional state, children do not know what to think or believe and are at high risk of developing serious emotional and behavioral problems.

A divorced mother may need to supplement support payments, but she may be inadequately prepared to enter the job market. She must either accept a reduced living standard or find a way to obtain a marketable skill. Should she take courses or find a job, she will incur the additional childcare expense. A divorced father who pays child support or alimony has less money for his own needs. He, too, may be forced to accept a less comfortable standard of living. Divorced homeowners may have to give up the family residence and move to less-expensive quarters. Renting in a lower class neighborhood is very different from owning a home in middle class suburbia. The mother without access to support payments may have to apply for public assistance. Economic privation adds to the adjustment problems. The employed single-parent mother has little or no time for herself and has to be the sole decision maker, the sole disciplinarian, the sole "everything."

MOTHERS WITHOUT CUSTODY

Much has been written about fathers without custody; less is known about mothers without custody (Rosenthal & Keshet, 1981). United States Census Bureau data show that the number of mothers without custody tripled in the last decade. Greif (1987) noted that these mothers comprise a little known and misunderstood group, perhaps because of social disapproval toward them. Greif compared noncustodial mothers who were content with the arrangement with those who felt guilty and uncomfortable.

The mothers in the study had lived without their children for about four years. The children lived with their father rather than with relatives or in institutions. The income of the mothers, including alimony, was higher than the average income of women who lived alone and higher than the average income of single-parent mothers living with their children. Most, but not all, had given up custody without a court battle. What the study showed clearly was that mothers without custody are not a monolithic group. There was a clear division between three types of noncustodial mothers: those who were comfortable with the role, those who were uncomfortable, and those who had mixed reactions.

The mothers who expressed contentment were women who admitted some responsibility for the marital breakup, had a positive relationship with their children, and had some success in a job or career. The noncustodial mothers who were dissatisfied with the arrangement had lower self-esteem, poor job and social skills, and pervasive feelings of failure. They blamed the father for the marital problems and considered themselves to be victims, especially if they had lost custody in a court battle. They seemed to have no identity or role except through motherhood. In contrast, the satisfied noncustodial mothers had broader interests and skills. Implications for counseling of the unhappy mothers included the following goals: to mourn and work out their sense of loss; to improve vocational and social skills, and, if possible, to improve relationships with their children.

The single father, with or without custody, tends to be an overlooked figure. If he has custody and is employed, he is likely to hire a housekeeper or ask a female relative to move in. The divorced father without custody has to adjust to a different life. He no longer is head of the household and experiences feelings of anger and sadness about not being able to protect, comfort, or care for his children. He becomes an income source rather than a provider. A reduced income due to alimony payments and child support often means a lower standard of living for him, if he is conscientious about making payments.

Single-parent fathers with custody face a number of hurdles that even overburdened single-parent mothers do not confront. First, they must integrate maternal functions into their role as father. Another problem is lack of sustained support from the community at large. If he is rearing daughters in a motherless home, unique adjustments must be made. Like single-parent mothers, fathers with custody must rely on supplementary help provided by day care centers or domestic workers (Arditti, 1992).

Chang and Deinard (1982) found that fathers sought custody because they considered themselves the better parent, or because the mother was physically or psychologically unwilling or unable to cope as a single parent. Among the problems that custodial fathers reported were insufficient time, restricted opportunities for socializing, and employment inflexibility. When questioned, single-parent fathers were less likely to seek personal counseling. What they desired instead was advice in handling domestic and childcare tasks. Overall, fathers acting as single parents tend to be competent, self-confident people who were already involved in caring for their children prior to divorce. Although they may suffer periods of anxiety or depression, they are usually able to surmount the hurdles of a demanding life. Present day fathers have been encouraged to participate actively in childrearing. What seems to protect single-parent fathers is social approval and the fact that custody of the children was actively sought rather than thrust upon them, as is often true of single-parent mothers.

•CLINICAL EXAMPLE:
CRISIS IN A SINGLE-PARENT HOUSEHOLD

Bob Hughes had been divorced for two years and had sole custody of his two children, a six-year-old boy and a nine-year-old girl. He was a steadily employed machinist who worked rotating shifts in a local factory. When Bob worked the day shift, he collected his children in late afternoon from the home of the neighbor who cared for them. The children and Bob then had dinner in their own house and shared information about the activities of the day. After the children were in bed, Bob did some household chores, read the paper, and got ready for the next day.

When he worked the evening shift or night shift, Bob picked the children up from the sitter either at midnight or at 7:30 A.M. At midnight the sleeping children were carried to Bob's car and transported to their own home. Usually the children barely remembered being transferred from one house to another. If Bob was assigned to the night shift, he picked up the children in the morning after work, took them home, prepared breakfast, and helped them get ready for school. The schedule was demanding, but Bob was determined not to be separated from his children.

Bob's divorce from his wife had not been of his seeking, and the experience was still painful for him to recall. Until his wife told him she wanted a divorce, he had not been aware of any problem in the marriage. When he learned that his wife and his best friend were deeply involved, he was devastated. At first Bob refused to consider divorce and begged his wife to agree to marital counseling. However, when he learned that his wife was pregnant with her lover's child, he agreed to a divorce provided he be given full custody of his children. Months of bitterness followed, but Bob managed to conceal his anger from the children. Most of his energy was directed toward arranging his life so that he could care adequately for his children.

More than a year after the divorce, Bob attended a meeting of Parents without Partners, where he met Beth, an attractive, childless divorcee a few years younger than himself. His new woman friend was friendly and outgoing and was accepted readily by his children. As the weeks passed, Bob began to enjoy life more and to feel able to sustain a satisfying relationship with a woman.

Approximately four months after meeting Beth, Bob faced a new problem. His little boy, Paul, suffered several grand mal seizures in school and was diagnosed as having idiopathic epilepsy. During this period Beth proved to be a source of sympathy and support. Therefore, Bob was unprepared for her announcement that she could no longer see him because she had met a man without children and was planning to move in with him. Losing Beth was a loss that sent Bob into a state of disorganization. He could not function either at home or at work. Bob's two children found their father uncommunicative, absentminded, and lethargic. His little daughter, Julie, reacted by trying to help out at home. His son reacted by having seizures more frequently and by worrying about being a "bad boy."

Bob was struggling to be both mother and father to his children even though the demands upon him were excessive. His friendship with Beth briefly restored the confidence that had been shaken by his wife's infidelity. When his son developed a serious illness, Bob felt overwhelmed and looked to Beth for understanding. She was supportive for a while, but the multiplicity of Bob's responsibilities frightened her. Beth's response was to begin a new relationship with a man who had fewer commitments. Her actions reactivated the grief he felt when his wife left him for another man. In addition, Bob was having trouble dealing with his son's illness. The healthy son of whom he was so proud no longer existed. Instead, Bob was left with a sick boy whom he loved deeply, but whose illness mystified and frightened him. As a result, he felt overwhelmed. His performance at work suffered until his sympathetic foreman suggested that Bob accept professional counseling.

Critical Guidelines

The counselor at the mental health center explored with him the history of repeated losses that Bob had encountered in the previous two years. Bob had handled his divorce fairly well. For a time he had managed to function at work and as a single parent. However, the illness of his son followed by abandonment from Beth caused him to feel frightened and alone. Bob was suffering depression that was reactive to the situational and interpersonal reverses of recent months.

A contract was established in which Bob would meet individually with his counselor for eight weekly meetings. Following termination Bob agreed to accept referral to a group composed of single parents who met weekly under the leadership of a professional counselor. The group goal was to deal with feelings of loneliness and to discuss problems related to the role of the single parent. During the individual sessions Bob worked with the counselor in dealing with the following concerns.

Bob's present work schedule and childcare arrangements were burdensome for him and for the children. Since his employer was sympathetic, Bob was advised to request a day/night rotation so the children would not have to be moved from their beds at midnight.

With minor financial adjustments, Bob found the resources to hire someone to clean the house and do the laundry every week. This arrangement freed Bob and the children from housework on Saturdays.

Bob was encouraged to discuss his son's medical problems in detail with the family physician. Referral to a community health agency was made, and a nurse agreed to visit occasionally when Bob was at home in order to answer his questions and explain his son's regimen.

Church affiliation had been important to Bob and the children before the divorce. This affiliation was seen as an important aspect of their lives, and the counselor reinforced Bob's idea that he and the children begin attending church again. The counselor perceived this decision as a means of providing continuity for the children.

Since Bob had already made friends in the local chapter of Parents without Partners, he was encouraged to resume his interest in this group.

REMARRIAGE

Most divorced men and women eventually contract new marriages and establish households in which relationships are complex and intricate. A fallacious idea entertained by divorced adults beginning a new marriage is belief that a new family will spring effortlessly into existence. Every individual involved in a stepfamily has already endured a period of acute disequilibrium. Remarriage means that some turmoil must be undergone again. Among the problems that must be resolved in remarriage are the following:

- The new partner who has chosen to marry a single parent may be reluctant to accept the children as part of the package.
- Former mates may welcome the remarriage of a divorced partner but dislike the prospect of a stepparent for their children.
- Children may not easily discard fantasies that their natural parents will reconcile, in spite of the remarriage of one parent.

It is unrealistic to expect that "his" children or "her" children will enter a new family prepared for immediate compromise and harmony. Even when one spouse is not accompanied by children from a previous marriage, problems of family reintegration are inevitable. Five patterns in stepfather families were identified by Stern (1978), who discerned that remarriage usually begins with the mother in charge of her children because of their previous experience as a single-parent family. This beginning pattern gives the mother power to regulate interactions between children and stepfather and, if continued, does not lead to family integration. A second, more adaptive, pattern consists of the stepfather initially accepting existing interactions in the home and respecting prior claims of the mother. Without making arbitrary changes, the stepfather endeavors to make friends, not rivals, or the children. Every member of the new family is allowed to become a participant in developing family rules and norms. This pattern is quite likely to lead to adaptive family integration. In the third pattern, the new stepfather attempts to become family disciplinarian, and the mother is divided in her loyalty to husband and children. A fourth variation consists of the mother asking the stepfather to function as family disciplinarian, but carrying out only the decisions of the stepfather that she approves. Thus the mother establishes a quasi-traditional family in which the father is the ostensible household head but in which the mother retains actual authority. In the fifth pattern, the mother relinquishes management of the children to the stepfather, who then becomes a genuine authority figure. This situation is difficult for the children. Having lost their natural father through divorce, the children now believe that their natural mother has been lost through remarriage. Of the five divergent patterns, only the second contains the promise of adaptive integration of the stepfamily.

Stepparents

According to the latest available census reports, there were almost five million children in the United States living in stepfamilies, and this estimate is probably too low. It does not take into account the children living in households where a biological parent is living with but is not married to a new partner. Nor does it include children who have stepsiblings or half siblings living in other households. Their numbers will increase in the next decade and society will have to modify its proceedings to suit the special requirements of these families.

Every stepfamily is comprised of members who have suffered loss of one kind or another, through death or divorce. Each member may be at a different stage of becoming reconciled to the loss. This means that when a parent marries again, reactions can be intense. Stepfamilies not only begin in an atmosphere different from that surrounding first marriages; they also evolve differently. Every partner brings to marriage an unwritten contract of their expectations; in remarriage the contract may be extensive, containing ideas of childrearing, money management, and task sharing (Visher & Visher, 1989). Only recently have researchers and other professionals given stepfamilies attention. Preparatory classes are available for pregnant couples, for adopting parents, and for single parents, but programs for stepfamilies are rare, even though the difficulties these families face can be severe.

Joint custody is more common than it once was, but mother more often than father is the custodial parent. Because she has been a single parent before remarrying, the mother is usually in charge of the children at first. She tends to continue the practices she has always used. In the new family she acts as the interpreter and mediator; she explains the stepfather to the children and the children to the stepfather. This gives the mother considerable power but impedes family integration. Because he is not the biological parent, the stepfather initially asks the mother how she wants him to act toward the children. In response, the mother may suggest that they make no immediate changes and gradually get used to one another. If the stepfather is willing to move carefully and makes friends with the children, family integration is facilitated. In some cases, however, the stepfather, who, after all, is a new husband, may forcefully assert himself in a manner that makes rivals rather than friends of the children.

Occasionally, the stepfather behaves harshly toward the children, especially if they do not make him feel welcome. Unless this behavior is interrupted, the mother will be torn between the children and her new husband. In this sequence of events the family becomes disorganized. Everybody makes rules but no one adheres to them. Family members reach high levels of conflict, communicating by shouting or by not talking at all. The stepfather and mother are locked in symmetrical relationships in which both vie for control.

Mothers who are accustomed to the father being the household disciplinarian may appear to yield control. This is not a genuine gesture if the mother only enforces rules that she agrees with and sabotages the rest. For example, they may have agreed on the amounts of the children's allowances or on the chores they will do, whereupon mother will add to the allowances or excuse the children from chores without the stepfather's knowledge. Other mothers who find it hard to handle children may allow the stepfather to be totally in charge. This may also have adverse effects on stepfather-stepchildren relationships and make children idealize their intact nuclear family.

Because stepfamilies establish intimate family relationships that are not biological and have not evolved over the years, sexual boundaries may become blurred. The weakening of sexual boundaries may be exacerbated by the climate in the home during the remarried couple's early romantic interactions. Weakened sexual boundaries may lead to sexual fantasies, to anxiety expressed through quarreling, or distancing maneuvers, all of which may be used as defense against sexual arousal. Pubescent teenagers may be attracted to stepsisters or brothers, or a stepparent may be drawn to a child. Accurate data on sexual abuse in families is not readily available, but there is general belief that stepfamilies are less likely to permit or collude in the perpetuation of incest behavior than nuclear families. Sexually abused children seem less guilty or ambivalent when the abuser is not the natural parent but a stepparent. In stepfamilies the child is inclined to blame mother for bringing the abuser into the family and to want to escape from both mother and stepfather.

The disintegration of the intact nuclear family distresses the children who are involved, and they rarely have a voice in parental decisions to separate, divorce, or remarry. The adults in the picture may suffer to varying degrees, but they have control of their future in ways that children do not. Parents can do a number of things to help children accept the prospect of parental remarriage. Visher and Visher (1989) urged parents to be solicitous, but to pay more attention to building a strong marriage than to considering children's feelings. They found that many remarried couples hesitate to establish a strong alliance with the new spouse out of concern for the children. Yet a strong alliance gives children two parents on whom they can rely. Experts advise the biological parent to enact the primary parenting role with support from the stepparent. More behavior problems seem to occur when the stepparent immediately takes over major parenting functions and the biological parent abdicates.

The younger the children are, the more readily they are to accept the stepparent. Even among younger children there are differences; elementary school boys seem to have more difficulty adjusting to divorce while girls have more problems with remarriage. Younger children are inclined to express their anger, but their older siblings may withhold emotional involvement with the new family. Under the anger there is sadness about the remarriage. Children of divorced parents cherish the hope that their parents will reunite, and remarriage destroys that hope (Fassler, 1988). After a parent has remarried, children consider it important to see their biological parents together occasionally. It is reassuring for children of divorce to see their biological parents in the same place without fighting. This persuades children that they can depend on both biological parents in times of emergency.

Stepchildren

The child of biological parents who have divorced and married new partners lives in a state of flux. Even after remarriage, the biological parents must communicate from time to time about their children. Custody may be awarded to one or both of the natural parents. Even when one parent has sole custody, visitation rights mean children must adapt to two different households. The two households may have very different standards and customs. Differences become more troublesome when one parent derides the other parent and the other household. Children seem able to fit in better if the biological parents refrain from criticizing each other, and allow the child and the other parent to define the terms of their relationship, at least in the early months of remarriage.

The remarriage of a parent is undoubtedly hard on the children. Dad's relationship with his new wife reveals aspects of his personality with which children may be unfamiliar. This means that the remarried parent may seem different. The same is true of mother, whose remarriage causes her to emerge as a sexual being. At the time of divorce a son's identification with mother may be reactivated. This is strengthened when mother looks to a son for support. It is harder for a boy to suppress knowledge of her sexuality as a result of her remarriage. Based on clinical evidence, it is the relationship between stepmother and stepdaughter that is most difficult. Bohannon (1984) explained that daughters during the oedipal romance give up father so as to identify with mother. Divorce tells the girl that her father is discarding or being discarded by the mother with whom she identified. When father remarries, the girl is left with a sense of being mistaken about her parents and of confusion about the whole identification experience. It is not surprising that many stepdaughters greet a father's remarriage with doubt verging on suspicion.

Couples contemplating remarriage are already aware that marriage and parenting are exceedingly complex. If one or both have been divorced, they have been introduced to failure and dread its recurrence. As a result, many of these couples arrange for premarital counseling. The overall goal of counseling is to prepare the couple for remarriage and stepparenting, if there are children. Counseling sessions can prepare the couple for issues likely to arise. At this time it may be necessary to review custody and visitation arrangements, discuss obligations to former mates, and to custodial and noncustodial children. In stepparent families there may be several children at different developmental stages. Stepparents need information on what to expect from the children in terms of their age-related tasks. If stepparents realize that adolescents in all probability are struggling with separation and independence, they are less disappointed when adolescents are reluctant to become close to parents or stepparents.

No new family springs effortlessly into existence, and this is especially true of remarried families, where every member has already experienced much turmoil. Among the common problems faced in remarried families are the following:

- The new husband or wife who marries a single parent may be less than eager to welcome stepchildren as part of the package.
- Former mates may accept the remarriage of a former spouse but dislike being replaced as their children's parent.

• Children are reluctant to give up fantasies that their natural parents will reconcile, and therefore they see stepparents as obstacles.

Children of divorce feel that adults have let them down. Having lost one parent through divorce (or death), the children now fear that the remaining parent will abandon them after remarriage. The most adaptive behavior in stepparent families begins with the natural parent in charge of the children, provided the natural parent has functioned as the primary custodial caregiver. The stepparent initially accepts existing arrangements in the home and respects the prior authority of the natural parent. Without making immediate changes, the stepparent endeavors to make friends with the children. Changes ideally are made through consensus, with all members participating. With minor adjustments, the same adaptive patterns can be used in remarried families where some children belong to the mother and some to the father.

Competition is prominent in stepparent families. Stepsiblings are bound to have problems in living together, and must allow time to become fond of one another. The stepparent family is more open than other systems, for it must permit access to natural parents who do not live in the household. The natural parent outside the home may distrust the interest a stepparent has in the children and may need to be reassured on this score. At the same time, the natural parent may fear that the stepparent will usurp the allegiance of the children. It is necessary for parents in remarried families to remind themselves and the children that the new family will be the joint creation of parents and children. Individual and group concerns need to be negotiated, either in private or with the help of a professional counselor. Discrepant opinions of role enactment and acceptable behaviors must be resolved for the stepparent family to remain functional. Difficulties are likely to lie less in resistance to being part of a new family than to unrealistic expectations that harmony and accommodation will occur without hard work (Keshet, 1990).

•CLINICAL EXAMPLE:
THE SCAPEGOATED STEPCHILD
IN A REMARRIED FAMILY

Bruce and Amanda have been married for five years, and both have been married before. Living with the couple are Amanda's eight-year-old son, Billy, Bruce's ten-year-old daughter, June, and five-year-old Annie, who was born of the current marriage. Bruce owns a hardware store with a dozen employees. He is a generous, paternalistic employer who says proudly that he is like a father to his staff. Amanda is a few years younger than Bruce. She is a quiet, rather self-effacing woman who is a full-time housekeeper and an active worker in her church. She is conscientious about everything she does and describes herself as a worrier and a perfectionist.

Bruce married Amanda when Billy was three years old, and she had been divorced for six months. Her first husband had walked out when Billy was a baby, saying that he was too young to settle down yet. At the time of her marriage to Bruce, Amanda was having trouble dealing with Billy. When Bruce saw the temper tantrums and the struggles between Billy and his mother, Bruce asked Amanda if she wanted him to help her control Billy. Amanda welcomed the offer; she realized that she had indulged Billy after his own father left and she wanted peace restored. However, Amanda was unprepared for Bruce's idea of discipline. At first he spanked Billy, but when this had little impact he began beating Billy with a strap. Amanda protested, but Bruce told her she was too soft with the boy. His methods made sense to him because he had been beaten the same way by his parents and his grandfather.

The punishments had an effect on Billy. He became quieter and less rebellious, obeying his stepfather's rules except when he "forgot." Both Amanda and Bruce say that he forgets the rules pretty often but is improving.

Billy has not seen his natural father in four years. He knows that his father is a musician who plays in a band and travels from town to town. Billy says that he could live with his father if he did not travel so much. He likes music and his mother has told him he can join the school band as soon as he is old enough. When Billy was six, his stepsister June joined the family when her mother (Bruce's first wife) remarried. June has not seen her mother since then because the distance is great and her mother cannot afford to visit. Bruce has not allowed June to visit her mother because he feels she belongs where she is. June is never beaten because Bruce does not believe in hitting girls and anyhow "June always knows when to quit."

Amanda enforces most of Bruce's rules but is more permissive. She allows June considerable latitude and is very indulgent of Annie, "because she is still a baby." She wonders if Bruce isn't too strict with Billy but doesn't protest much because she feels that Bruce knows more about raising a boy. Testing at school had shown Billy to be exceptionally bright, but his school performance is poor. He has few friends and never brings playmates home from school. The two girls seem happy and well-adjusted. Billy is apathetic except about music; he no longer has temper outbursts but he seems listless and depressed. School personnel suggested counseling for Billy, or therapy for the family if Billy's academic and emotional status did not improve. Because school personnel impressed Amanda with the gravity of the situation, she prevailed upon Bruce to attend sessions with her and Billy. It bothered her that her son was being labeled a problem child, but she accepted Bruce's decision that the girls should not participate.

In the family meetings the practitioner observed that Billy was an alert, handsome little boy who was reserved but eager to please. Although Bruce speaks directly and firmly to Billy, the boy avoids eye contact and answers in a muffled voice. If he is slow in answering Bruce or the practitioner, Amanda answers for him. Although the two girls were not present, the practitioner was able to see that one childrearing method was being used for them and a much harsher one for Billy. Amanda stated that she was uncomfortable because corporal punishment was inflicted on Billy, but added that he had been a "handful" and she didn't want him to grow up irresponsible like his father. She praised Bruce for being a good provider and for his steadiness.

The mother in this remarried family had given her husband total authority over her son. In the sessions she admitted that before marrying Bruce, she found Billy uncontrollable. In fact, one of the reasons she married shortly after her divorce was to give Billy a father. Bruce had behaved in ways that allowed Amanda to become very close to the girls. The alliances within the household excluded Billy, who was the scapegoated child. Although Bruce was not introspective, he could acknowledge that Billy was the only child in the home who was not related to him by blood. Amanda wields little power in her own right, but she functions as an intermediary between Bruce and all the children. She protects Billy as much as possible, to the point of deceiving her husband. Once when Bruce insisted that she beat Billy, she faked a beating from behind a closed bedroom door. After Bruce has punished Billy, she provides candy and other treats to comfort him.

The signals from school personnel alarmed both parents. They persuaded Amanda to intervene more directly on behalf of her son. She knew that Billy was precocious in many ways and she blamed herself for letting the home situation harm him. Bruce was not accustomed to being confronted by Amanda and he found himself consenting when she said firmly that there would be no more beatings of anyone in the family. Although some progress was made at initial family meetings, the practitioner urged the parents to bring the two girls as well. Amanda promptly agreed and Bruce went along with her. She seemed to know that her son had not been given equal treatment and she was determined to change this.

Critical Guidelines

The family practitioner agreed to meet without the girls only to begin treatment. As soon as she realized that omitting the girls would again label Billy as the bad child, she insisted that every-one attend. In this she was joined by Amanda, who established a therapeutic alliance with the practitioner. Efforts were directed toward strengthening Amanda's parenting role. Currently Bruce was the primary parent for Billy, and Amanda was the primary parent for the girls. With encouragement from the practitioner, Amanda compared her tender parenting of Bruce's daughter with the stern measures he used on Billy. She accepted much of the responsibility for putting Bruce in charge of Billy in the early years of the remarriage. What was needed was shared parental functions, not allocation of parenting along gender lines. June and Annie needed more involvement with their father. Billy needed more involvement with his mother and a different kind of involvement with his stepfather.

The family changes made Billy feel less isolated. He drew closer to his sisters, remained wary of his stepfather but felt more protected by his mother. Amanda and Bruce were encouraged to substitute more rewards and fewer punishments to elicit positive behavior. Physical punishment of any sort was outlawed because, as Amanda said, "there has been too much of that already." Amanda became more active in school events and welcomed any friends that Billy brought home. Bruce made arrangements for June to visit her mother over summer vacation. Amanda hesitated to let Billy visit his father because he was so transient. She wrote to her former husband, telling him that Billy seemed to have inherited his father's musical talent. She invited Billy's father to visit when he was in the area and enclosed a letter from the boy. This started a friendship by mail in which Billy wrote about daily events, and his dad sent souvenirs and postcards from interesting cities. The turn of events was not wholly welcome to Bruce, but he did not resist too much. In family meetings, Bruce paid tribute to the kind of wife and mother Amanda was to all the children. Without anyone saying it directly, Amanda had become a force to be reckoned with in the household; this benefitted all the children and ultimately strengthened the remarried relationship.

ADOPTIVE PARENTS

For various reasons the number of infants available for adoption in the United States has decreased. This is attributable to dependable contraception, access to abortion, and social attitudes that encourage a single mother to keep and raise her child. Because adoptable infants are scarce, the child adopted today is likely to be well past infancy, and is often of a different race or nationality from the adoptive parents. Some of these older children have been shunted from one unsatisfactory placement to another, and may have been victims of abuse or neglect. Such factors may intensify the problems adoptive parents and the children they have taken into their home experience.

In the past, heroic efforts were made to match the child with the adoptive parents, but this is impractical today when couples cross racial and national boundaries to find an adoptable child. There is a misperception that black families seldom adopt black children. The truth is that for generations black families have accepted children in their homes with and without legal adoption. In addition, children of all races are being raised by grandmothers and other relatives who must take the place of drug-addicted biological parents. Many adoptions now result in biracial families as Caucasian parents adopt nonwhite children of American or foreign lineage. Many children that American families adopt are of Chinese, Vietnamese, or Korean ancestry; a sizeable number of these children are biracial themselves.

The practice of adopting children from another race, nationality, or ethnic group often works well, but it has the potential for problems unless parents are prepared to accept differences in the adopted child's appearance and temperament, and can deal with issues that may arise. For one thing, parents must deal with remarks from outsiders about the child. Even when parents protect the child from such comments, there will be times when the child feels different. Gibbs (1987) stated that biracial children, adopted or biological, usually have good relationships with other children in elementary school but friendships deteriorate in secondary school. At a time in their lives when peer acceptance is crucial, children in biracial families may be rejected by their adoptive parents' group and also by their own, because of discrepancies between their appearance and that of other family members.

Parents who have adopted children from other racial or ethnic groups may become overprotective, or they may try to eradicate the child's ties to the biological group. Children may respond by becoming extremely dependent on the parents or by rebelling against parental control. A support group called Rainbow Families advocates drastic change in the way adoptive parents raised their children in the past. Instead of minimizing ethnic or racial differences for the sake of family unity, many adoptive parents now believe that teaching the children about their original culture will facilitate identity resolution and forestall any future identity crisis (Nieves, 1992).

There is firm support for building bridges between the past and the present for adopted children in racially or ethnically mixed families. Gibbs (1987) reported that biracial children have fewer identity problems if they live in a racially mixed neighborhood rather than a segregated black or white area. Indo-Chinese youngsters living in American group homes or with white families were found to be significantly more depressed than were their counterparts who lived in foster care with families belonging to their own ethnic group. The youngsters in ethnic homes had less difficulty adjusting to life in the United States, were less depressed, performed better academically, and felt they had more control of their lives. Evidently, frequent contact with others of similar ethnic or racial background helps children learn who they are and how to move easily between their old culture and the new (Porte & Torney-Porte, 1987).

Adopting parents are placed in a supplicant position in that they must meet certain standards before being permitted to adopt a child. They need to pass a test of sorts undermines the confidence of a couple, who may already be dealing with their inability to have their own child. Once a couple has adopted a child, they remain under surveillance for a time. Another issue is the decision on how and when to tell a child that he has been adopted. There is always a fear that a friend or relative may disclose this information before the parents are ready to do so. There are no set rules on this matter, since much depends on the child and the situation. Some authorities believe that most adopted children can be told when they are about six years old. If the child is older at the time of adoption, or is of a different race or background, disclosures may have to be made shortly after adoption. When very young children are told of being adopted, they may become anxious. Since they lost one set of parents, they wonder if they might lose another. Some adoptive parents fear that the child will love them less after learning that they are not the biological parents. If the parents are uncertain of how and when to proceed, the matter is important enough to discuss with an expert so that parent-child relationships are not endangered.

Growing numbers of biracial and transnational adoptions mean that counselors must be sensitive to the problems of parents as well as children in these families. Participating in support groups, where common problems can be discussed, can be helpful for parents contemplating the adoption of a child who is different from themselves. If other children are already present in the family, they must be carefully prepared for the entry of the new sibling. Anticipatory planning is indicated on behalf of all family members, actual and prospective. People who adopt any child embark on a serious mission. In effect, a stranger joins the family and requires adjustment from everyone. The adopted parents, the adopted child, and any siblings already in the family need a gamut of services, including counseling education, practical assistance, and group support.

A nonthreatening approach for these families is to see troublesome issues as part of the process of becoming a family. When family members are dissatisfied with things as they are, they can be reassured by learning that a family is not a finished product and that family interactions can change for the better. In most family situations the counselor should consider the marital or parental dyad as the architects of the family, with all members participating in the construction of an adaptive and viable family system. This relabeling tactic is often effective in reducing members' perception of unfairness or injustice in family operations. It can be adapted for use with stepparent families and with single-parent families where discouragement and discontent prevail.

POST-PARENTAL ISSUES

Duvall (1977) was the first theorist to organize and define the tasks of the family. Duvall categorized eight stages of family development that encompass the entire life cycle of individual members. During the early years of establishing and expanding the family system, the marital couple either moves toward resolution of divergent loyalties and goals, or remains conflicted by failure to accomplish resolution. This means that the marital couple enters the post-parental years with an alliance which has been weakened or strengthened by past experience. If problem solving has been an endeavor in which both partners participated, this coping behavior is available to them. If the couple has not been able to acknowledge differences, or if the opinions of one partner have always prevailed, the postparental years may be quite difficult.

Some couples seem able to move tranquilly from active parenting to a life that remains rich and fulfilling. Others find that the loss of children is traumatic in terms of self-esteem and marital compatibility. Who, then, are the couples most likely to require help in adapting to the departure of children from the home? In order to understand potential problem areas for postparental couples, it may be helpful to review the developmental tasks of the family.

The developmental tasks of the middle-aged family may be summarized as follows: (1) rebuilding the marital dyad, (2) maintaining ties with older and younger generations, (3) providing security for later years, and (4) reaffirming the values of life that are meaningful. This framework emphasizes the importance of developing and maintaining interdependent relationships between the members of the marital partnership. Also regarded as essential were relationships between the postparental couple and their children, as well as between the postparental couple and their aged parents. An additional task was identified for the midlife adult, namely that of adapting self and behavior to the signals of an accelerated aging process. A couple having difficulty with any of the foregoing developmental tasks is likely to be at risk. Troubled couples may need professional intervention of a supportive nature so that the potential for renewal in the marital relationship becomes an opportunity rather than a threat.

COUNSELING ADULTS

The mature adult lives in a *prime-time* context. People at this stage of life are at the height of their powers. At the same time, their lives are complex and demanding. Usually they are deeply involved with work and family life. Their interests are rich and varied, and their obligations are wide ranging. Even though their lives are complicated, they are still young enough to be optimistic about the future. While these generalizations do not apply to every midlife adult, they emphasize the fact that most persons in this age group are embedded in some form of family life. The crises they encounter are likely to include relationship issues as well as developmental issues.

The first step in counseling an adult in crisis is to introduce oneself without trying to establish an immediate social rapport. Persons of this age respond to a professional manner that conveys dignity and respect, and implicitly states that the individual is a mature adult. It is rarely productive to dwell on abstract, esoteric definitions of emotions such as anger, hurt, or hopelessness. Well-educated persons may engage in a philosophical or semantic discussion that allows them to avoid the real problem. People who are less introspective or less verbal may be confused by in-depth exploration of their feelings. Moreover, crisis counseling is impeded when such detours are taken. Therefore, it is more helpful to ask about the circumstances that evoked the feeling. Exploring the circumstances enables the counselor to evaluate the appropriateness of the client's responses to specific situations.

Because rational cognitive processes are impaired during crisis, it is advisable to ask factual questions that elicit more than a yes or no response. Questions should be worded very carefully and should not be judgmental nor condescending. Questions such as, "What happened next?" "What did you say to that?" or "What do you think was going on?" are examples of open-ended queries that require the individual to think sequentially and rationally. These are questions to which the respondent must give some thought before answering.

Sometimes individuals have tried several approaches to problem solving without success. At this point it may be therapeutic to mention what other people have found effective. An example of this is information about an available community program or a referral to a support group. This should not be done in a manner that indicates this is the best way to go, but only as a direction that other people have taken. This avoids setting the counselor up as the person with all the answers. It also avoids having the individual say later that she followed the counselor's suggestion but it didn't help.

There are some occasions in crisis counseling when the professional sees the situation in the same hopeless way the individual views it. Counselors in touch with their own reactions soon recognize that they have become infected with the contagion of the crisis individual's negative feelings. In a situation like this the counselor should search out adequate supervision or ask for a consultation. It is not important for the counselor to have all the answers nor to offer countless alternatives. What is important is not to perceive a situation in the limited way that the person in crisis perceives it. By adopting a different, wider perspective than that of the troubled individual, the counselor can illuminate the view so that misperceptions are reduced.

Counselors must monitor their own level of anxiety during a therapeutic session. They should try to analyze what makes them anxious and how to handle their own anxiety constructively. In crisis sessions, counselors should limit themselves to working on identified, reachable goals that the individual is willing to confront. If these goals seem too restrictive, the counselor may offer the individual some options when the crisis contract has terminated.

The crises of adults in midlife, whether situational or developmental, invariably require guidance in accepting reasonable goals. Many mature adults feel that they have not realized the aspirations of their youth. When they feel disappointed in themselves or in family members, they may need to be reminded of the positive achievements in their lives. When they measure themselves against impossible standards, they may need help in setting priorities or revising their sense of themselves as inadequate. A man who was not promoted may need to be reminded of what he has already accomplished or of what he still has to offer. This approach is not the same as cheerleading if it is based on reality. Such interventions are a cognitive approach that counteracts the tendencies of some adults to cling to impossible dreams. At all times counseling should be considerate of the value system and social context of the adult, whose energies and abilities may be temporarily depleted by problems and responsibilities.

SUMMARY

Disequilibrium arising in early adulthood is likely to be concerned with options and decisions, while disequilibrium of middle adult life is apt to be family related. Role strain increases and marital satisfaction declines in middle adult life; therefore, change within this period requires careful planning and preparation. This is especially true if contemplated change introduces massive family realignment.

Crises of commitment often result from the realignments that divorce, remarriage, and stepparenting produce. Several custody options are now available to divorced parents. Custody decisions favor the mother in most instances, but joint-custody arrangements are becoming more common. Although study of the effects of joint custody is not extensive, preliminary data indicate that the arrangement may be more beneficial for parents than for children. In single-parent households in which one parent has sole custody there is danger that family boundaries will be impermeable, and that parents and children in these households will allow generational boundaries to become blurred.

The breakup of a marriage has far reaching effects on parents and children; additionally, the no-fault divorce legislation enacted in the interest of fairness, has often worked to the disadvantage of women and children. Several researchers have formulated specific tasks that children and parents must address after divorce. Unhappily, these are formidable tasks that may or may not be fully accomplished.

Mothers who have custody of their children are overburdened, physically, emotionally, and financially. The same cannot be said of fathers with custody. While fathers in this group have unique problems, they usually have sought custody and have not had it thrust upon them.

A divorced parent's remarriage establishes a stepparent family in which new norms must be developed. The parents may not agree on childrearing methods, money management, and task allocation. Children who have been living with a single parent may see the new partner as a usurper. If they have entertained fantasies that their natural parents may be reconciled, the new marriage interferes with such hopes. Stepparent families are susceptible to crisis, and the children and noncustodial divorced parent may regard the new stepparent as an intruder. In these families disciplinary questions frequently surface and must be negotiated between the natural parent, the stepparent, and the children. Families that include a stepparent cannot expect immediate reintegration, but they should expect a protracted period of reorganization.

Adoptive parents are frequently cast in the role of supplicants who must convince others that they are worthy of parenthood. Since there is a shortage of adoptable infants in the United States, children now being adopted may not be infants and may be of a different racial or ethnic group than the adoptive parents. Many people agree that children in biracial or multiethnic families benefit from ongoing contact with members of their own ethnic or racial derivation. This may dismay or even threaten the adoptive parents, but this effectively promotes understanding between the disparate groups that are involved.

REFERENCES

Ahrons, C.R. "The Continuous Coparental Relationship Between Divorced Spouses." *American Journal of Orthopsychiatry* 51(1981): 415–428.

Arditti, J.A. "Differences Between Fathers with Noncustodial Fathers." *American Journal of Orthopsychiatry* 62(1992): 86–94.

Aro, H.M., and V.K. Palosaari. "Parental Divorce, Adolescence, and Transition to Young Adulthood." *American Journal of Orthopsychiatry* 62(1992): 421–429.

Bohannon, P. "Stepparenthood: A New and Old Experience." In *Parenthood: A Psychodynamic Perspective,* edited by B.T. Cohler and S.H. Weisman. New York: Guilford Press, 1984.

Brody, J. "To Predict Divorce Ask 125 Questions." *The New York Times* August 11, 1992, CI.

Chang, P., and A.S. Deinard. "Single Father Caretakers: Demographic Characteristics and Adjustment Processes." *American Journal of Orthopsychiatry* 52(1982): 236–243.

Duvall, E.M. *Marriage and Family Development,* 5th ed. Philadelphia: Lippincott, 1977.

Elkin, M. "Joint Custody: Affirming That Parents Are Forever." *Social Work* 32(1987): 18–24.

Fassler, D. *Changing Families: A Guide for Kids and Grownups*. Burlington, Vermont: Waterfront Books, 1988.

Furstenberg, E.F., J.L. Peterson, C.W. Nord, and N. Zill. "The Course of Children of Divorce: Marital Disruption and Parental Contact." *American Sociological Review* 48(1983): 656–668.

Gibbs, J.V. "Identity and Marginality: Issues in the Treatment of Biracial Adolescents." *American Journal of Orthopsychiatry* 57(1987): 265–278.

Greif, G.L. "Mothers Without Custody." *Social Work* 32(1987): 11–16.

Hetherington, E.M., M. Cox, and R. Cox. "Long Term Effects of Divorce and Remarriage on the Adjustment of Children." *Journal of American Academy of Child Psychiatry* 24(1985): 518–530.

Hetherington, E.M., and F.F. Furstenberg "Sounding the Alarm." *Readings* 4(1989): 4–8.

Kalter, N. "Research Perspectives on Children of Divorce: Introduction." *American Journal of Orthopsychiatry* 59(1989): 557–559.

Keshet, J.K. "Cognitive Remodeling of the Family: How Remarried People View Stepfamilies." *American Journal of Orthopsychiatry* 62(1990): 196–203.

Nieves, E. "With Adoption, a Future: With Effort, a Past." *The New York Times* August 15, 1992, A25.

Porte, Z., and J. Torney-Porte. "Depression and Academic Achievement Among Indochinese Unaccompanied Minors in Ethnic and Nonethnic Placements." *American Journal of Orthopsychiatry* 57(1987): 536–547.

Rosenthal, K.M., and J.K. Keshet. *Fathers Without Partners*. Totowa, New Jersey: Rouman and Littlefield, 1981.

Southworth, S., and J.C. Schwarz. "Post Divorce Contact, Relationship with Father, and Heterosexual Trust in Female College Students." *American Journal of Orthopsychiatry* 57(1987): 371–382.

Stern, P.N. "Stepfather Families: Integration Around Child Discipline." *Issues in Mental Health Nursing* 1(1978): 50–56.

Visher, E., and L.J. Visher. *Stepfamilies: A Guide to Working with Stepparents and Stepchildren*. New York: Brunner/Mazel, 1989.

Wallerstein, J.S. "Children of Divorce: The Psychological Tasks of the Child." *American Journal of Orthopsychiatry* 53(1983): 230–243.

———. "Women After Divorce: A Preliminary Report from A Ten Year Followup." *American Journal of Orthopsychiatry* 56(1986): 65–77.

Wallerstein, J.S., and S. Blakesley. *Second Chances: Men, Women and Children a Decade After Divorce*. New York: Ticknor & Fields, 1989.

Zaslow, M.J. "Sex Differences in Children's Response to Parental Divorce: Rewards, Methodology, and Postdivorce Family Forms." *American Journal of Orthopsychiatry* 58(1988): 355–378.

9

Adults in Crisis
The Later Years

Fortunately psychoanalysis is not the only way to resolve inner conflicts. Life itself remains a very effective therapist.

Karen Horney

There is no incontrovertible answer to the question of when old age begins, but the sixty-fifth year has been arbitrarily selected as the passage from maturity into old age. Regulations regarding mandatory retirement and social security eligibility have reinforced this determination, but not only the healthy elderly are challenging it. Economists and others who fear the burdens that will be borne by future generations when growing numbers of workers retire from productive life are challenging it as well.

Although there is a tendency to make broad generalizations about people over sixty-five years of age, the fact is that they are a heterogeneous group whose ages span thirty years or more, and whose health and performance vary more than those of a random group of newborn infants. Stereotyping the elderly can be avoided, to some extent, by using additional classifications, such as age decade, gender distinctions, ethnic differences, marital status, and income levels.

There are wide discrepancies between aged persons and aging persons, although distinctions between them are sometimes blurred. The *aging* person may be described as an individual who is still trying, still competing, still planning, and still resisting the label of being old. The *aged* person has already accepted relegation to the ranks of the elderly. These are the people who have stopped competing, who struggle less, and who prefer possessions to relationships because personal artifacts remind them of the past but make fewer demands on the present. Depending on health, life stresses, support systems, and personality styles, aging and aged people cross and recross the lines of demarcation,

199

sometimes regressing, sometimes progressing, and sometimes exerting valiant efforts just to remain in place.

The emergence of *gerontology* as an area of applied study testifies to the advancing age of the general population in the United States. The census of 1820 reported that the median age was sixteen years. Subsequent census figures showed a median age rising from nineteen years in 1850 to thirty years in 1950, where it has remained for the last thirty years. Even more significant than the steadily rising median age is the proportion of elderly persons making up the general population. Since 1900, the general population has doubled, but the proportion over sixty-five years of age has increased sevenfold. The population over seventy-five years has increased ten times, and the population over eighty-five years of age has increased seventeen times since 1900 (McCluskey & Borgatta, 1980).

Longitudinal research seems to support the premise that individuals' overall self-concept fluctuates at various points over a lifetime but does not inevitably change with age. It is the challenges and crises of life, combined with the resources (personal and interpersonal) available to individuals, which largely influence their self-esteem and self-assessment (Newman & Newman, 1980; Lazarus & DeLongis, 1983). Among others, Neugarten (1973, 1975) studied personality changes in persons from ages forty to ninety years. The research results showed that after age fifty people tended to become more introspective and less outgoing. They engaged in life reviews that considered positive and negative events in their past, as if to determine the success or failure of their lives. With advanced old age, people were inclined toward disengagement and passive rather than active mastery of situations. In similar studies, Kermis (1986, p. 72) indicated that "the basic core of personality with its drives, expectancies, and coping strategies, does not change over the life span."

Table 9–1 shows the patterns of aging that Neugarten identified in her series of cross-sectional and longitudinal studies at the University of Chicago, which are widely known as the Kansas City Studies.

Loss is a recurrent experience in later years, not only loss of status and roles, but also decline of physical and mental powers. The death of old friends reminds the elderly of their own mortality and further reduces remaining relationships. The death of a spouse is a loss women face more often because of their greater longevity and the fact that many women marry men a few years older than themselves. In describing problematic situations among the elderly, the crises of retirement, relocation, and loss are prominent.

Although strength and vigor diminish in old age, a number of individuals face retirement before their capacity or zest for work lessens. Retirement means that individuals may no longer entertain dreams of future promotion or recognition. Many elderly persons welcome retirement as a reward for a lifetime of work, but others see retirement as a

TABLE 9–1 Personality Patterns of Aging and the Aged

Patterns	Subpatterns
Integrated personality	*Reorganizers.* Those who replaced each lost role with a new role.
	Focusers. Those who limited themselves to satisfying activities only.
	Disengagers. Those who willingly and consciously reduced roles and activities.
Defended personality	*Holders on.* Those who held on to roles and appearance of younger people due to aging fears.
	Constrictors. Those who were extremely fearful of the aging process.
Passive dependent personality	*Help seekers:* Those who sought help and support from others.
	Apathetic. Those who did not seek help but withdrew from all contact.
Unintegrated personality	*Disorganizers.* Those who were maladjusted and/or displayed gross personality defects.

Source: Adapted from Neugarten (1973), and Kermis (1986).

severe blow to self-esteem. Therefore, one major crisis of later life is retirement, or loss of a role as a working member of society.

Another crisis for the elderly person arises with the inability to maintain an independent household. The need to move into a relative's home is extremely difficult for older people, but placement in an institution is even more traumatic. Although the decision may be the best for all concerned, institutionalizing an elderly relative, especially a parent, is painful for the entire family. One elderly resident of a well-appointed nursing home expressed the sentiments of her peers by saying, "It's all very nice here but you still feel as if you've been thrown away." For most elderly people, independent living is preferred above all else, but residing with family members helps to give them a sense of identity and continuity. Institutionalization may erode meaningful identification with the family, which the elderly interpret as another downward step.

Changes that affect the elderly also affect their families. Kermis (1986) noted that most elderly persons are in frequent contact with their children, and participate in mutual transactions involving money, advice, visits, and services. Sometimes these transactions are based on obligation, sometimes on affection, and sometimes on choice. When the elderly person becomes frail and needy, transactions once determined by choice are now determined by obligation. The middle-aged children of elderly parents find themselves torn between obligations to their parents, to their maturing offspring, and to their own partners.

Middle-aged women, in particular, are at the mercy of these demographic trends, since women traditionally have accepted the role of family caregiver. This means that many middle-aged women must balance the tasks of parenting any children still at home, maintaining a full- or part-time job, and attending to the needs of increasingly infirm parents. Additional stresses occur as the balance of power shifts in the family system from the aged to the middle-aged members. The family performs an estimated 80 percent of all care for elderly people in the United States; as a rule, one primary person usually performs caregiving responsibilities, even when other assistance is available (Lawton et al., 1989; Lawton, 1980).

ADAPTATION TO AGING

Developmental tasks have been described as individual adjustments to the changing self (Erikson, 1963), while *adaptational tasks* have been described as adjustments to changing individual and cultural expectations (Clark & Anderson, 1967). Thus, the process of adaptation requires greater accommodation between individual capacities and cultural expectations. The critical adaptational tasks associated with aging have been identified as follows:

• Recognition of aging and its consequent limitations.
• Redefinition of physical and social life space.
• Substitution of alternative sources of satisfaction.
• Readjustment of criteria for self-evaluation.
• Reintegration of life's goals and values.

Successful adaptation does not mean that the elderly person must enjoy the limitations that age brings, but merely that limitations must not be denied. With advancing age, control over one's social environment is threatened. Personal space becomes circumscribed as certain activities and roles are no longer accessible. Searching for alternative interests is part of adaptation, and individuals who cannot give up total autonomy or accept some dependency fail to adapt well to aging. Readjustment of criteria for self-evaluation means that various criteria for self-evaluation must be modified, unrealistic standards of performance must be lowered, and self-esteem must no longer be based on autonomous functioning or the managerial ability of the elderly person. Finally, reintegration of goals and values necessitates revision of the aspirations of older people so that they can find meaning and purpose in life as it presently exists for them.

Neugarten (1975) wrote that there is no single chronology marking the transition from mature adulthood into old age, and suggested that older people be divided into the young-old, who range from (fifty-five to seventy-five years of age) and the old-old (over seventy-five years of age). Botwinick (1981) suggested five groupings: the young-old (fifty-five to sixty-five years of age); middle-old (sixty-six to seventy-seven years of age); old-old (seventy-eight to eighty-four years of age); and the very old (eighty-five years of age and over). The use of differentiated age categories reduces the margin for error inherent in sweeping generalizations of the over-sixty-five population.

Although the young-old group is likely to be healthier and more functional than the very old, it remains necessary, in many instances, to rely on data based on broad categorizations of the elderly. Among the misconceptions concerning the elderly population, the following ideas are prominent: most old people are lonely and neglected; most old people are sick and dependent; and most old people live in nursing homes or other institutions. These prevailing myths are not supported by facts. The majority of elderly people not only maintain independent lives, but have access to support systems comprised of relatives or friends.

There are, however, undeniable demographic trends that have a profound impact on elderly people and the middle-aged offspring who assume primary responsibility for their care. The U.S. Bureau of the Census reported that there were 9.1 percent more people between sixty-five to seventy-five years of age in 1985 than in 1980. There were 14.2 percent more people from seventy-five to eighty-four years of age, and 21.0 percent more people over the age of eighty-five in the same five years. Other important influences, in addition to increased life expectancy, are later marriages, decreased fertility rates, and large numbers of women in the labor force. Although family members endeavor to provide some care to elderly relatives, fewer family members are available to discharge this responsibility (Pett et al., 1988). By the year 2010, one-fourth of the U.S. population will be over age fifty-five, with 14.3 percent over age sixty-five. By the year 2050, 33 percent of the population will be over age fifty-five, with 24 percent over age sixty-five (Kermis, 1986).

RETIREMENT CRISES

The psychosocial disengagement of the elderly is not unilateral, but is a reciprocal withdrawal. Society makes fewer demands on the elderly, offers fewer outlets for self-expression and productivity, and then ponders the problem of detachment among the elderly. Throughout the life

cycle, transitions can be predicted and, therefore, made subject to anticipatory planning. This process is equally true of the transitional changes
that accompany old age. Retirement represents a precipitous change for
the elderly, which can be predicted and prepared for in advance, except in
unusual circumstances.

There are two theories related to healthy aging: the activity theory
and the disengagement theory. According to the *activity theory,* elderly
persons should try to enact the activities of middle adult life as long as
possible and search for activities to replace those that can no longer be
performed. *Disengagement theory* considers aging to be a reciprocal withdrawal by the individual and surrounding social systems. As the individual advances into old age, the disengagement process may eventuate in
disequilibrium and crisis unless adaptation to aging is maintained. Activity theory and disengagement theory both assume that lifelong work roles
are important to people and that loss of them contributes to adjustment
difficulties during retirement.

Not everyone subscribes to the notion that crisis in retirement is due
to loss of the work role. Instead of indiscriminately fostering involvement
of the elderly, it has been proposed that the regularized activities and
devotion to the work ethic that characterized midlife should be discarded
differentially according to individualized needs. Maximal involvement
may be necessary for some elderly people, but others are content with
relatively insulated lives and find no loneliness in solitude nor dissatisfaction with inactivity (Keith et al., 1990).

In a study of how various men reacted to retirement, five personality
types were identified: the "mature" type, the "rocking chair" type, the
"armored" type, the "angry" type, and the "self-haters." As might be
surmised, the mature types were well-integrated men with high self-
esteem who welcomed the chance to spend more time with family and
friends. The rocking chair types also adjusted well to retirement. These
were passive-dependent men who had never been overly ambitious and
were glad to lapse into the inertia that had been denied them during their
working years. Because of their well-constructed defenses, the armored
types of retirees managed to adjust to retirement despite their resistance to
inactivity and growing older. These men were activists who joined organizations and became busy participants, thereby avoiding thoughts of
decline or deterioration. Only the angry men and the self-haters seemed
to lack the capacity to adjust to retirement (Reichard et al., 1962).

Women who were full-time homemakers and women who worked
outside the home seemed to find retirement a less dramatic change than
did their husbands. Since women of retirement age relinquished the
important mothering role when the last child was launched, they may
have learned adaptability. A major adjustment women identified after
retirement was pressure to engage in social and domestic activities as a
couple rather than as individuals. Loss of privacy was identified as a

problem for some women married to retirees, as was a sense of reduced independence. However, most women found that the disadvantages of retirement life were offset by improvements in the marital relationship as the couple adjusted to unstructured time together (Keating & Cole, 1980).

Individual attitudes toward retirement are closely linked to status and income. People of higher occupational and educational levels have more money and less fear of retirement, but also enjoy working and are less likely to retire early. When high-status people reach their career objectives, they do not dread retirement but neither do they actively seek it. Workers at lower levels look forward to retirement, except for the consequent income loss. These people continue to work, not because they like their jobs, but because of financial worries. At middle occupational levels where money is adequate if not ample, retirement is eagerly awaited and there is no lasting devotion to work. It is the high-status workers who retire later in life, remain committed to work, and exhibit better social adjustment after retirement (George, 1980).

Retirement preparation the employer sponsored or the employee instituted can ease the shift from work to leisure, and should be an educational process wherein prospective retirees can learn what to expect of the future. Since imminent retirement introduces complex issues, preparation should include advice on how to gather and evaluate data. Relaying information to prospective retirees, and helping them compile a data base for planning and decisions are more helpful than psychological counseling, which overlooks relevant financial and social issues.

Although retirement is often thought to adversely affect health, investigation does not support this hypothesis. In a large longitudinal study, Streib and Schneider (1971) found that health reverses were associated with age but not retirement. Unskilled workers actually showed improvement in physical health after retirement. If preparation begins early enough, the prospective retiree has time to develop secondary interests beyond the work role, but it is largely the employee's responsibility to develop such interests while retirement is fairly remote. Poor health or mandated company policies may compel workers to retire before they are adequately prepared, but gradual transition and adequate guidance are desirable, although they are rarely available to all workers.

During the immediate preretirement phase, people begin to adopt a short-range view of their jobs and discern changes in the way others view them. At the same time, they engage in fantasies of what retirement will be like. When the fantasies are realistic, they can be helpful in determining issues to be faced. When the fantasies of the preretirement phase are unrealistic, the actuality of retirement may be disillusioning. The time just after formal retirement is usually satisfactory, and for some retirees it remains pleasurable. Others are unable to sustain their original satisfaction and react to disenchantment by restructuring their time in order to deal with their options. For some retirees this may mean returning to full employment or finding a part-time job. Restructuring or coming to terms with retirement is followed by a period of stability in which the retiree lives independently. Loss of stability in retirement may be due to health problems or the death of a spouse, which cause the retiree to look to others for assistance, either friends, relatives, or care providers in the health system. Here, the role of the autonomous retiree must be relinquished as the elderly person moves toward enactment of the sick role with its concomitant aspects of disability and dependency (Atchley, 1988).

Throughout family life, the biological and social differences between men and women necessitate crucial adjustments by the partners and by other members in order for the family system to survive. This remains true as couples move into the fourth and fifth decades of their lives. Frequently, the wife who sublimated her own ambitions to family needs sees the postparental years as a last chance to express herself. Some husbands are heavily involved with their work at this period, while others may want their lives to be more family-centered, and therefore may be reluctant to accept the wife's personal goals. Neugarten (1973, p. 98) aptly described the differences between middle-aged men and middle-aged women as "Important differences exist between men and women as they age. Men seem to become more receptive to affiliative and nurturant promptings, women more responsive toward and less guilty about aggressive and egocentric impulses."

Sheehy also noted disparity between the value systems of couples in their middle years. She wrote that it is essential for the second half of life to have its own significance. Menopause and separation from the last child find some women eager to pursue ambitions outside the context of family life. Other women, who gladly lived for and through their families, may feel superfluous and unwanted by husband and adult children, yet fear embarking on new ventures. In some cases, the responses of the couple are congruent, with the husband encouraging the vocational aspirations of his wife. In others, the man may resent having his wife commit herself to a developing career (Sheehy, 1976, 1992).

PLANNING FOR RETIREMENT

Some firms offer retirement planning for employees leaving their service, but this is not available to everyone. However, every person facing retirement should consider several important areas. Perhaps the first area for consideration is income. Knowing the expected level of income and predicting the purchasing power of available income is essential. Even firms that do not offer comprehensive preretirement programs usually have an available financial advisor. Where the retiree and/or the family will live is another consideration. Here, a decision may have to be made in terms of affordability and preferences. A house in which a family was raised may be too large or too expensive for a retiree to maintain. Even when a retiree is reluctant to make immediate decisions, it is helpful to consider various living arrangements. Use of leisure time is a retirement aspect that may not receive much priority, but deserves serious consideration. Hobbies, volunteering, or part-time work are possibilities for spending leisure time constructively and enjoyably. Retirement usually reduces the number of interpersonal relationships available, because many relationships depend upon shared work experiences. In spite of the best efforts of everyone concerned, work-related associations weaken in time, as shared interests and memories fade. This means that family ties may become more important, and that new sources of friendship must be found. Church affiliations, lodge membership, and community organizations may provide the interpersonal stimulation the retiree has lost.

There are certain differences in the life experiences of men and women that operate to make retirement years easier for women. For men, the prime years of career achievement occur between the ages of thirty-five and fifty, after which it seems to decline somewhat. For women, career achievement may be secondary during the childbearing, childrearing years, but become primary as the children become more independent. This means that many women are still invested in career goals when their husbands are beginning to look for gratification within the family, as career demands lessen for them.

The role of wage earner is a source of self-validation for most people; paid work gives one a sense of identity, importance, and purpose, and the onset of retirement brings an end to much of this, especially for men accustomed to define themselves only in terms of wage earner. Aber (1992) found that paid work was a critical factor in the adjustment of older women after the death of a husband. Having a paid work role identity, in addition to a wife and homemaker identity, was a positive resource for widows during the bereavement period. One possible explanation was that the role of wage earner provides individuals with confidence that they have the ability to surmount stress and challenges that come their way. The protective aspect of the wage earner role also indicates how deeply men may feel its loss as they move into retirement. Women, especially those committed to job or career, also suffer role loss. However, many women consider their wage earner role to be secondary to their roles within the family.

•CLINICAL EXAMPLE:
PANIC REACTIONS TO MANDATORY RETIREMENT

Just after his sixty-fourth birthday, Bob Jackson suffered a myocardial infarction while working in the factory where he was plant foreman. Taken by ambulance to the nearest hospital, Bob spent several weeks in intensive care before being transferred to a medical floor. After four weeks of hospitalization, he was discharged with the provision that he would return three times a week for cardiac rehabilitation.

Bob was a big, jovial, outgoing man who was emotionally shaken by his illness, but soon rallied and became his customary cheerful self. In the hospital and just after discharge, he followed his regimen faithfully, stating resolutely that he intended to be back at work in a few months. In spite of his compliance, Bob's recovery was not complete. When he filed a request to return to work, his application was rejected, partly because Bob's physician recommended only limited exertion. Bob had worked for the same company since graduation from high school and he had over forty years of service to his credit. His three children were grown and self-supporting; with his company pension and social security, Bob's income was adequate for himself and his wife. Mary, his wife, was an accomplished musician who augmented the family income by giving lessons at home.

When he was not permitted to return to work, Bob's reaction was one of outrage. He appealed the decision, but, lacking the unqualified endorsement of his physician, he was powerless to change it. Without advance warning or time to adjust, Bob found himself an involuntary retiree. Soon after his enforced retirement, he discontinued his visits to the cardiac rehabilitation center. He began to be absent from the house and spend long hours at a local tavern. He grew indifferent about his appearance and irritable with Mary when she protested about his habits. In the past, Bob had been proud of Mary's musical talent, but now he complained about students coming to the house and ridiculed the "cat calling" that Mary called singing.

Mary made some desultory attempts to reason with Bob, but in a very short time she rented rooms in a nearby dance studio and moved a piano there so that she could give lessons without disturbing Bob. The couple settled into a routine in which Mary did her housework in the morning and left for her studio about noon. Bob spent the mornings in bed and the afternoons at his favorite tavern. When the couple's oldest daughter came home for a visit, she observed the impasse of her parents and insisted that they see a family counselor. Their daughter made the appointment and drove them for their first visit to make sure they kept the appointment. Bob's response to his daughter was to say that things were never going to be any better for him and that Mary was "king of the hill" now. Mary's rejoinder was that Bob was a sick man and that she would do what she could to help him, even if he had driven her and her students from the house.

Bob's illness frightened him, and he was unprepared for his sudden retirement. Basically, Bob was a man who feared being dependent and therefore denied his feelings to himself and to others. He camouflaged his anxiety and depression by being difficult and demanding, and his wife misread his responses. While Bob struggled with loss of his work role, Mary made an impulsive move that increased the psychological distance between them. She did not consult Bob in advance nor consider the effect of her action on his fragile self-esteem. Her behavior was a reaction to Bob's displaced hostility and only increased his feelings of abandonment.

Although surface harmony had existed between Mary and Bob for many years, each of them had led separate lives. For Bob, the factory and his job formed the social center of his world. In many ways he had allowed Mary to make decisions about the house and children without expecting to be consulted. Through the years he had been proud of her musical ability and of her domestic efficiency. Her competence and self-sufficiency threatened him only when he had no external sources of satisfaction. The company's refusal to let Bob return to work robbed him of direction, since his job as foreman confirmed his self-concept. Denying his feelings prevented Bob from asking Mary directly for help. His behavior alienated her, and loneliness aggravated Bob's anxiety, which he disguised behind irritability and heavy drinking.

While Bob was a hospitalized patient, Mary was attentive and devoted, but when he was unable to resume work, she was as disappointed as her husband. She was accustomed to having her home to herself during the day and had acquired an impressive number of pupils. Once or twice a week she met with women friends for lunch or a game of bridge. With Bob at home all day, Mary found her freedom curtailed and her privacy invaded. Bob began his retirement by assuming that he and Mary would have breakfast, lunch, and dinner together every day, even though this did not fit into her routine. At no time did the couple really try to discuss their changed situation. Mary realized that her pupils annoyed Bob, but she did not consult him about rescheduling the lessons at times convenient for them both.

Mary believed that Bob's retirement had disrupted her life as well as his, and she was reluctant to compromise. Bob, in turn, thought that Mary should compensate him for the gratification that had vanished with his job. At the very time when he faced decremental losses, his wife made an incremental gain by moving her lucrative music lessons outside the home. Throughout their married life the couple had maintained different interests, each finding friendship and gratification outside marriage. Bob spent most of his spare time with pals from the factory, whereas Mary associated with a small group of women who shared her interests. Bob bowled, Mary played bridge; Bob enjoyed baseball games, Mary preferred concerts. Each accepted the other's differences and arrangements worked well until Bob's retirement upset the balance.

Critical Guidelines

The isolation unexpectedly forced on Bob meant that the couple had to reconcile some of their divergent interests. Neither could be asked to give up accustomed pursuits altogether, but some compromise was necessary. The family counselor agreed with the couple that there were favorite activities that they could continue to enjoy individually, but Mary needed to include Bob in some of her leisure activities because of the emptiness in his life. A trade-off was recommended, with Bob agreeing to learn bridge if Mary was willing to be introduced to baseball. Bob's bowling and Mary's concerts were seen as areas for future negotiation by the partners. Several of the six family sessions were devoted to effective communication techniques the couple might use in the future. Bob was advised not to depend entirely on Mary but to move out into the community in order to find companionship. He was encouraged to join the retirees' association of his company and become involved in their social and charitable activities. After attending several meetings, Bob came home and informed Mary delightedly that he had been invited to join the R.O.M.E.O. Club—Retired Old Men Eating Out Club.

The medical treatment Bob had received was excellent, but his psychological wounds were ignored, particularly by his wife. Mary had behaved much like a hostess with an unwelcome guest, forgetting that Bob had few resources currently at his disposal. Conscious of additional cooking and housekeeping tasks, she was quietly resentful of Bob's enforced retirement. Yet she was insightful enough to realize when it was pointed out to her that restoring equilibrium in the marriage depended on compromise and sharing. Self-engrossed for many years, the partners were persuaded to give more to each other. Mary was encouraged to look beyond Bob's drinking and blustering, and recognize his anxiety and depression. Theirs had been a marriage based on separateness, and the counselor respected the differences in the couple. During the retirement period, however, some readjustment was necessary for the relationship to survive. With the help of the counselor, more open communication was instituted so that neither Bob nor Mary continued to act out their conflicts but could articulate what each wanted from the other.

RELOCATION CRISES

The attempts of families to provide a home for elderly relatives incapable of living independently have received some negative attention. Present generations are inclined to forget that immigrating to the United States often meant leaving parents and grandparents behind. In those days people generally did not live as long, and there were few resources for the elderly in the form of social security benefits or long-term-care facilities. Therefore, family care was the only alternative for the disabled elderly, except for public charity.

Surroundings are extremely important for the elderly because they spend a great deal of their time at home. The quality of their residential environment in terms of convenience, safety, and comfort is an important influence on their sense of identity and well-being. Elderly people who are healthy and possess adequate resources may elect either to remain in the homes where they raised their children, to move into smaller quarters, or to relocate in retirement villages in gentle climates. Each of these alternatives is a risk of sorts, particularly when a decision to relocate means giving up family ties, old friends, or cherished possessions. Many older persons are reluctant to move their place of residence even when there are compelling reasons. Faced with undesirable conditions, on one hand, and opportunity for improved housing, on the other, many elderly persons choose to stay where they are. Resistance to mobility may be due to fear of change, income constraints, or strong attachment to familiar surroundings.

Change of residence is a stressful experience for almost everyone regardless of age, but two factors are especially significant: (1) the reason for the move, and (2) the distance involved. Moves that require massive geographic change cause higher amounts of separation anxiety. When the move is due to advancement or promotion, stress lessens, but the most important issue is whether the relocation was voluntary. Relocation of the elderly had great negative impact when the decision was involuntary. Research on the effects of relocation on the social adjustment, physical health, and mortality of the elderly is inconclusive and permits the assumption that the elderly, like other people, adjust to relocation in individualistic ways (George, 1980).

Only 5 percent of the elderly presently live in institutions, but projections indicate that 25 percent of them will be institutionalized at least temporarily. The crucial variables that determine institutionalizing an elderly parent seem to be family tolerance of the effects of retaining the elderly person at home, and commitment to the ideal of filial obligations (Atchley, 1988). Aged persons, especially after they have entered a nursing home, are generally regarded as useless and unproductive. They are assumed to be the recipients of care rather than the providers of care. There are, however, a few studies showing that a moderate proportion of nursing home residents seek opportunities to reach out to others in helpful ways, despite their own experience with loss and impairment (Hutchison & Bahr, 1991; Springer & Saylor, 1984). Nursing home residents were found to offer caring behaviors in four categories of behavior: *protecting, supporting, confirming,* and *transcending.*

Protecting behavior took the form of shielding other residents from possible injury through verbal warnings, physical support, or soliciting help from the staff on another's behalf.

Supportive behavior took the form of comforting, listening, and promoting self-esteem in others. *Confirming* behaviors consisted of recognizing and respecting the personhood of others. These actions included visiting bedridden people in their rooms or sharing food on occasion. Although limited by their own infirmity, many residents folded laundry, worked on crafts for the annual bazaar, or pushed wheelchairs.

Transcendent behaviors were exhibited in prayer rituals in which many participated. Prayer was offered in public and private ways; many residents pointed to prayer and other caring behaviors as mechanisms that kept them from being preoccupied with their own losses and disabilities. While it is true that institutionalization has negative effects on the well-being of elderly residents, allowing them some involvement in helping others may alleviate or even prevent further psychological deterioration caused by accepting the message that others have no positive expectations about them. Lack of positive expectations may contribute to the apathy and isolation that frequently descends on nursing home residents as their stay lengthens.

CAREGIVERS' DILEMMA

Families assume an estimated 80 percent of the care for elderly people in the United States. Despite the large number of women in the work force, responsibility for giving care is largely allocated to women (Kaye & Applegate, 1990). Women's nurturing activities range from the care of infants and children to the care of family members who cannot care for themselves. Thus, for many contemporary women, caregiving extends throughout their entire life span. Turner and Avison (1989), in a comparative study, found that sometimes the women's distress was related to their roles as nurturers, which they perceived as socially devalued. Turner and Avison, in the same comparative study, also noted that women were more vulnerable to the stresses of significant others, while men were more vulnerable to stresses affecting themselves. These and similar findings suggest gender differences in attitudes about taking responsibility for the care of significant others (Walker et al., 1990). Parks and Pilisuk (1991) offered the following comprehensive description of the caregiver's dilemma.

> When a parent becomes highly dependent on an adult child, for instance, an inevitable change occurs in the contours of their lives. The questions before the caregiver include these: Can I handle this situation? Am I doing enough? What does one do about incontinence or passivity or asocial behavior? The grief that the caregiver experiences over the loss of the relationship as it has been known differs from the grief over the loss of a relationship through death. Death is final and brings with it a closure to the relationship. The loss of cognitive ability is open-ended. The adult child watches his or her parent deteriorate, and gradually the relationship itself changes (p. 502).

Two-thirds of primary caregivers for the elderly are female relatives (Kaye & Applegate, 1990), but current research suggests that men are increasingly involved in the care of elderly parents and spouses. Because more women than men are victims of Alzheimer's disease, husbands are very likely to be primary caregivers for this group. This is consistent with the idea that men become more androgynous as they reach middle-age, and are therefore more willing to offer care. Although Kaye and Applegate (1990) found that male caregivers performed multiple tasks, ranging from running a household to administering personal care, the men derived least satisfaction and felt themselves least competent in the area of personal care for the dependent person. An interesting finding was that caregiving was easier for men when they or the care recipient initiated affectionate gestures. This argues against labeling men as emotionally cold and undemonstrative, and supports the notion that the androgyny of middle and later years facilitates caregiving by men. One of the most salient findings in this area, however, indicates that men tend to cope with stress by using strategies that seek to alter problems through instrumental action. Women, on the other hand, are believed to rely more on processes that regulate emotional reactions to stressful situations (Borden & Berlin, 1990).

Most couples are able to adjust to the additional role transition that follows the deterioration of aged parents. If relationships between the two generations are good, and the interdependence of the married couple is sound, this period of role reversal will be less trying. Realization of the cyclical nature of life is a factor that alleviates the turmoil of caring for aged parents. Mature couples tend to treat their own parents as they would wish to be treated in turn. According to Neugarten (1973, p. 98), one well-adjusted middle-aged woman described her awareness of her place in the parade of generations as, "It is as if there are two mirrors before me, each held at a partial angle. I see part of myself in the mother who is growing old, and part of her in me. In the other mirror I see part of myself in my daughter . . . It is a set of revelations that I suppose can only come when you are in the middle of three generations."

•CLINICAL EXAMPLE:
THREE GENERATIONAL HOUSEHOLD
INTERDEPENDENTS

Viola Briggs and her husband, Jim, are the parents of three children, two boys and a girl. When their daughter and older son were high school students and the younger boy was in fifth grade, Viola and Jim were beginning to look forward to a few years of relative freedom as the older children prepared to enter college. Their dreams were interrupted when Jim's father died after a long illness and his mother came to live in their home. Jim's mother was in relatively good health, but she was a querulous, demanding woman with whom Viola had quarreled in the past. Unfortunately, there was not enough money for Jim's mother to live independently, even if she had wished to do so. Viola was reluctant to accept Jim's mother as a permanent resident but felt she had no choice. Jim's only sister was married to an engineer whose work made it necessary to live overseas.

Always very talkative, Jim's mother constantly intruded when family members brought friends home to visit. She was critical of her daughter-in-law's housekeeping and childrearing methods. With the children of the family she was controlling and intrusive. In a short time the grandchildren stopped bringing their friends home and began socializing elsewhere. This added to Viola's resentment. She complained a great deal to Jim, who reacted by becoming distant and withdrawn. A previously happy household became contentious and discontented.

Viola had a girlhood friend, a social worker, who could see the problems objectively. When Viola confided in her, the friend suggested counseling for Viola and Jim in order to deal with a situation that seemed to grow worse every day. Counseling sessions gave the couple an opportunity to express their feelings without becoming angry and dysfunctional. Viola was surprised to learn how guilty Jim felt for placing the burden of caring for his mother on his family. Until Jim openly expressed his feelings about having sole responsibility for a parent he had never been close to, Viola believed that her husband and his mother had forged an alliance that excluded her. The positive feelings that Viola and Jim had for each other, and their wish to do what was right while regaining family harmony were hopeful signs.

Counseling sessions focused on how to integrate Jim's mother into family life so that her presence would not be disruptive. Practical arrangements were attended to first, since these were easy to solve. Jim indicated that his sister was far more affluent than he, and could contribute to the support of his mother if she chose. However, she had not volunteered to do so and Jim had not asked for help. Since this aspect of the situation was especially hard for Viola to endure, the counselor suggested that they might approach the sister and directly tell her that financial help for mother's care would be welcome. Jim and his sister negotiated the details, and it was arranged that his sister would send mother an allowance, out of which she would pay a small sum to Jim and Viola. This arrangement was extremely valuable. It removed some pressure from the son and daughter-in-law, and it gave the mother a sense of independence that alleviated her tendency toward self-pity and martyrdom.

Viola had been planning to take a job as a salesclerk to help with the older children's college expenses. When her mother-in-law came to live with her, Viola no longer felt free to do this, yet Jim's mother was in fairly good health and did not require full-time care. Jim, with the counselor's encouragement, assured Viola that she could carry out her plan. Viola was ambivalent because she feared that if she took a job, her mother-in-law would take complete charge of the household. Acknowledging that this was a possibility, the counselor suggested that family meetings be held to establish ground rules for everyone when Viola started her job.

The meetings were surprisingly effective. With Jim as family spokesperson, Viola's role as mother, homemaker, and decision-maker was reinforced. The older children could see advantages in having more money available and promised their cooperation. The younger boy, who rather liked his grandmother, said that it would be nice to have someone in the house to greet him after school. The person who was most receptive to the idea was Jim's mother, who saw that the family reorganization would give her a place where her contributions would be needed.

Of course, there were times when Jim's mother was difficult. Viola and Jim had to remain united as household heads in order to prevent the older woman from taking over. The reorganization worked because the self-esteem of the members was no longer jeopardized by the grandmother's presence in the home. Receiving a regular allowance from her daughter allowed Jim's mother to be independent and even generous, at times, to her grandchildren. Together, Viola and her mother-in-law prepared the week's menus; because she prepared the evening meal, Jim's mother received a small sum from Viola. The older woman continued to pay for room and board because, as she explained, "I can have more to say about planning the meals."

Critical Guidelines

Because Jim and Viola had a functional marriage, they were able to use the limited counseling sessions to their advantage. After talking with each other, they found the courage to impose rules for all family members and to set limits for Jim's mother that benefited everyone involved. This was a caring family, but they were not accustomed to sharing feelings, nor to attacking problems directly. In changing their behaviors, Viola and Jim modeled a new way of dealing with each other that eventually modified the behaviors of other family members, including the grandmother.

One of the basic needs of all persons is recognition of their human dignity, and this need does not disappear with age. One way that human dignity finds expression is through the maintenance of activity and independence. Therefore, it is important to permit the elderly to feel useful and in control as much as possible. All too frequently, people live in progressively restrictive environments as they age. Although some restrictions may be necessary, the elderly should be allowed control over their possessions and should be given choices as long as they are able to make reasonable decisions. Until the moment of death, people need to feel that their wishes and preferences will be respected whenever possible. Although the aging person values independence, interdependence is also a human need. To be interdependent means to be involved in a mutually rewarding exchange with one or more people. Interdependence means giving and taking, and sharing. Forming interdependent relationships is one way of preserving human dignity and maintaining the quality of life in old age.

The decision to place an elderly relative in a long-term care facility is not easy for families. Most nursing home residents are old, female, and white. The degree of disability is not the major influence on institutionalizing the elderly; more reliable predictors are the lack of reliable support systems and filial commitment. Regardless of the extent of disability, older people from black families or traditional ethnic groups are more likely to remain with their families (George, 1980).

The implications of institutionalization are painful for most elderly persons. Placement is a clear statement that the elderly person is no longer considered fully competent. Personal preferences must be left behind on entering an institution. Privacy is curtailed, possessions relinquished, and choices about food or dress become subject to institutional control. One cannot choose one's neighbors; propinquity is thrust on the elderly, even to the extent of sharing a bedroom with a stranger.

The average age of persons entering nursing homes is eighty-four years, and four out of ten are over eighty-five. An average stay in nursing homes lasts eighteen months; for residents in the lower age range, institutionalization is not necessarily permanent. Through rehabilitation, more than half the residents eventually leave to resume more independent lives. It is essential, therefore, that the type of facility be appropriate to the individual's needs. Professionals involved in crisis or long-term work with the elderly should be familiar with the services offered by different types of facilities.

TYPES OF FACILITIES

Residential

Residential facilities offer minimal supervision, room, board, and planned activities. They are appropriate placements for persons who need some help with activities of daily living, but do not require nursing or medical care. Such facilities are not usually covered by Medicare or Medicaid.

Intermediate Care

Intermediate care facilities constitute the majority of nursing homes and are eligible for Medicaid reimbursement. Some form of nursing care is available for persons under the supervision of a physician, but the care may range from admirable to deplorable.

Skilled Nursing

Skilled nursing facilities are recognized for Medicare and Medicaid coverage, and may be accredited by the Joint Commission on Accreditation of Hospitals. Nursing service is provided on a twenty-four-hour basis, and preventive, rehabilitative, social, and psychological programs are offered as needed.

Extended Care

Extended care facilities are an extension of hospital care and are available on a long-term, but not always permanent, basis. Round-the-clock nursing and medical supervision are available. Medicare and private insurance plans cover extended care facilities, most of which receive accreditation from the Joint Commission on Accreditation of Hospitals. Auxiliary services similar or superior to those available in skilled nursing facilities are also provided.

Whenever possible, the elderly person should participate in the selection of the facility, and accessibility is important if family and friends are to visit. A physician, clergyperson, the local medical society, welfare department, social security office, or councils for the aging are valuable sources of information in choosing a facility. The American Health Care Association can give information about proprietary facilities; the American Association of Homes for the Aging can provide information about nonprofit facilities.

Two potential crises surround institutionalizing the elderly. One is the disequilibrium of the family that leads to a decision to place an elderly member and is likely to become more acute just as the elderly person leaves the household. The second potential crisis concerns the adjustment of the elderly person who must enter the facility. Both potential crises are interdependent, because the adjustment of the elderly person to the facility can do much to mitigate family disquiet.

Residents placed in nursing homes initially manifest signs of confusion and disorientation that may be slight or reach psychotic proportions. Some persons exhibit behavioral problems on entry, and the attitudes of the staff greatly affect the adjustment of the elderly resident. The following are five general behavioral categories into which nursing home residents can be placed. There are, of course, some residents who remain generally cheerful and compliant; they are rewarded by being staff favorites.

1. *Depressed patients.* These individuals are compliant but show psychomotor retardation, somatic preoccupation, and sleep disturbances. Behavior is often ritualistic.
2. *Passive, uncooperative patients.* These individuals are quiet but negativistic and seclusive. They resist routines, are inclined to wander off, and sometimes refuse to eat. In extreme cases, they become mute, immobile, and stuporous.
3. *Disturbed, aggressive patients.* These individuals are overactive, assaultive, boisterous, suspicious, and unpredictable.

4. *Agitated patients.* These individuals are tense, anxious, self-blaming, and fearful. They fear being left alone and seek constant reassurance.
5. *Deteriorated patients.* These individuals suffer severe impairment to the point of incontinence and extreme disorientation. Behavior is inappropriate and unpredictable. Usually these individuals do not survive long after placement.

The critical period in the adjustment of individuals to nursing homes seems to be the first month after placement. Two factors can be used to ascertain chances for successful adjustment. One is the individual's attitude toward the transition. Elderly persons who do not become excessively anxious, angry, demanding, withdrawn, or regressed are likely to adjust fairly well. The second factor is the staff's ability to deal effectively with the problems of new residents. If the staff tries to help the new arrival feel at home and copes with deviant behavior, the possibility of good adjustment increases. Excessive tolerance of unacceptable behavior by the staff is rarely therapeutic. When staff members wait too long before setting limits, residents continue to engage in maladaptive behavior that then causes rejection by the staff. Among the significant variables affecting adjustment, the following were noted: compatible relationships with other residents, especially roommates; adequate preadmission preparation; and active participation in activities after entry.

Medicare and Medicaid are partly responsible for the growing institutionalization of the elderly, since access to these programs has reduced the financial burden of placement. It must be admitted that the nursing home industry is less regulated than might be wished. In contrast to hospitals, 80 percent of which are nonprofit, over 75 percent of nursing homes are proprietary or profit-making ventures. Some proprietary homes provide excellent care, but the range of quality is considerable. The decision to send a parent to a nursing home is not easily reached and incites strong feelings. One way to reduce feelings of guilt and grief is to investigate facilities carefully before making a choice.

Medicare and Medicaid are federal programs, but their administration varies from state to state. The following briefly describes the dimensions of these programs and other sources of assistance for elderly persons who are sick or disabled.

- *Medicaid.* This is a state-administered program designed to help people with low incomes and few resources; it pays for most medical expenses, including nursing home costs
- *Medicare.* This program enrolls anyone over sixty-five years of age; it is a two-part program that covers hospital and medical costs up to certain limits. Persons under age sixty-five who receive social security disability are also covered. Medicare does not cover long-term nursing home

care, routine dental care, routine checkups, immunizations, prescription drugs, eye tests, glasses, or intermediate or custodial care. *Intermediate* or *custodial care* is defined as help with activities of daily life, such as bathing, dressing, and feeding.

Figure 9–1 shows the financing of long-term nursing home costs for the elderly.

Broad knowledge of available resources is essential. Access to such information is available to crisis counselors and should be shared with any families trying to deal with the declining health of an elderly relative. These situations can overwhelm such families and they need guidance in locating appropriate sources of aid, and in fulfilling the requirements of various agencies. Provided here is a brief list of well-known programs; counselors will find it advantageous to compile a more comprehensive list for their own use and to benefit the people they serve.

AARP
1909 K Street, N.W.
Washington, D.C. 20049

Alzheimer's Disease & Related
Disorders Association
70 East Lake Street
Suite 600
Chicago, IL 60601
800-621-0379 (in Illinois
800-572-6037)

American Association of Homes
for the Aging
1129 20th Street, N.W.
Suite 400
Washington, D.C. 20036

Foundation for Hospice and
Homecare
519 C Street, N.E.
Stanton Park
Washington, D.C. 20002

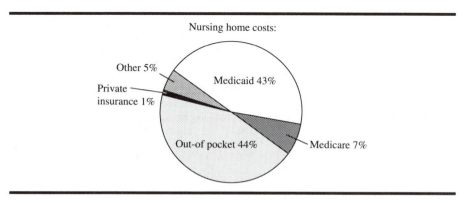

FIGURE 9–1   Financing of Long-Term Care for the Aged. *Source:* U.S. Health Care Financing Administration (1989 data), Washington, D.C.

Gray Panthers Project Fund
311 S. Juniper Street
Philadelphia, PA 19107

Hospice Association of America
519 C Street, N.E.
Washington, D.C. 20002

Make Today Count
National Office
514 Tama Building
Burlington, ID 52601

The National Association of Area
Agencies on Aging (N4A)
600 Maryland Avenue, S.W.
Suite 208-W
Washington, D.C. 20024

National Association for Home
Care
519 C Street, N.E.
Stanton Park
Washington, D.C. 20002
(202) 547-7424

National Cancer Institute
NIH Publications List
Office of Cancer Communications
Building 31, Room 10A-18
Bethesda, MD 20892

National Institute on Aging
Federal Building, 6C12
7550 Wisconsin Avenue
Bethesda, MD 20814

The National Self-Help
Clearinghouse
c/o City University of New York
33 W. 42nd Street
New York, NY 10036

The Self-Help Center
1600 Dodge Avenue
Suite S-122
Evanston, IL 60201

National Support Center for
Families of the Aging
P.O. Box 245
Swarthmore, PA 19081

•CLINICAL EXAMPLE:
NURSING HOME PLACEMENT OF AN ELDERLY PARENT

The Grady family consisted of the parents, Jim and Jean Grady, five adolescent youngsters, one of whom was in college, and the grandfather, who had moved in after the death of his wife eight years previously. Until the last two years, the grandfather had been a resourceful, self-sufficient family member, always willing to stay with the children when his daughter and son-in-law wanted a night out. Shortly after his eightieth birthday, the grandfather began to change in ways that were subtle at first, but became blatant. Although he was a diabetic, he became a habitual refrigerator raider, especially at night when the family was asleep. He was forgetful, confused, and amnesic concerning his nocturnal raids. Always a reticent, quiet man, he was now very garrulous. When other family members entertained friends, he was intrusive and repetitive. In a short while the grandchildren stopped bringing their friends home and began socializing elsewhere.

Because the grandfather was her father, Jean Grady was inclined to be rather tolerant of his idiosyncrasies. More and more often she found herself in the position of trying to restrain her father while apologizing to her husband and children for his behavior. As time passed, the grandfather became increasingly unmanageable. He began wandering through the neighborhood, getting lost several times, and neighbors or the police returning him. Occasionally he was incontinent, especially after he had generously helped himself to forbidden alcohol. One morning when Jean was working in the garden, the grandfather accidentally started a kitchen fire, which firefighters had to extinguish. Jim Brady was an easygoing man, but as the grandfather began to need constant supervision, Jim issued an ultimatum to his wife, "Either your father leaves this house within the next month, or the kids and I will."

The Grady family loved the grandfather and felt guilty because they resented the tension his deterioration brought into the home. They had always been a family with a tradition of taking care of its members. Jim's mother had moved in with them in the last months of her life, as she battled cancer. For most of their married life, Jean and Jim had devoted their energies to the family, working and sacrificing to fulfill paternal and filial obligations. Even though they still had five children to send through college, they were beginning to anticipate the years when their obligations lessened and they would have more time for themselves.

Jim's ultimatum regarding Grandpa was partly selfish, but he was also worried about the strain on his wife and his children's estrangement. Having taken a firm stand, Jim then became very supportive of Jean, and promptly began to investigate facilities where the grandfather might be placed. There were times when Jean felt angry with Jim as they visited various facilities, but inwardly she was a little relieved that a difficult decision had been eased.

Jean had a close friend who was a social worker and who was willing to accompany the couple on their observational tours. Following the advice of her friend, Jean compiled a checklist of things to look for on her visits. The checklist included the following considerations (Kayser-Jones, 1989):

- *Environmental factors.* Are the rooms cheerful, spacious, and clean?
- *Costs and accreditation.* Are expenses manageable, given the grandfather's income and resources; is the facility currently accredited, on probation, or unaccredited?
- *Nursing care.* What is the ratio of nursing staff to patient population; how many registered nurses are on duty per shift; are nursing attendants certified?
- *Medical supervision.* Is an institutional physician in charge of medical care for all residents or may their private physician continue to monitor their care?
- *Dietary considerations.* Is a trained dietition in charge of meal planning and preparation; are residents' preferences given sufficient consideration?

- *Programs and activities.* Are the programs and activities appropriate, and based on the skills and interests of the residents; do qualified personnel plan and administer the activities' program?
- *Social amenities.* What laundry facilities are available; are residents permitted to hang pictures or have favorite objects in their rooms?
- *Philosophy and policies.* What is the staff's attitude towards visitors or to suggestions from family members; are there provisions for church services or visits from the clergy; do all staff members treat residents with dignity and respect?

Critical Guidelines

The facility the family eventually chose was a skilled nursing home that the county health department supervised. It was located two miles from the Grady residence. The family took the grandfather to see his new quarters a week before placement. The family told him of the impending change and reassured him that they would be very near. The grandfather seemed to understand that he was leaving the family home, but he talked vaguely of just going on a visit. Jean was very upset during the week that her father was due to leave. Because she became tearful every time she thought about the prospect, Jim prevailed upon her not to go with them to the nursing home on the day her father was admitted. Therefore, Jim, Jean's friend, and two grandchildren accompanied the grandfather to the nursing home. When the time for departure came, Jean clung to her father, and the family members were glad she had been spared the ordeal of escorting her father to the facility. At the suggestion of the nursing staff, Jean agreed to wait a day or two before visiting so that the staff could help her father accept his new surroundings.

The Grady family regained equilibrium shortly after the grandfather was placed in a long-term-care facility, but his long-term adjustment remained an unknown. There was no doubt that his physical and behavioral deterioration had increased the tensions within the family system. Even a daughter as loving and conscientious as Jean was unable to supervise his regimen, and the grandfather's regressive actions were hastening his own decline. The grandfather embarrassed the children and Jim was impatient with the sacrifices being asked of his wife and himself. In her more honest moments, Jean admitted to feeling a sense of relief after her father left the household. The care facility had been carefully chosen and was near enough for all family members to visit frequently. There was no doubt that the nursing staff could monitor the grandfather's physical problems more efficiently than Jean. Reality orientation and resocialization techniques seemed, for the present, to have arrested further cognitive deterioration for Grandpa. His general condition was stable, and there were no signs that the placement adversely affected him. The relationship between Jim and Jean was more harmonious, and the Grady home was again being used for teenage gatherings.

LOSS CRISES

A realistic fear of elderly persons is loss of a husband or wife through death. Older couples inevitably entertain thoughts of what life might be like without the partner, and the thoughts stir feelings of fear and anxiety. Females over seventy-five years of age more often experience the state of widowhood, since women usually live longer and marry men a few years older than themselves.

When family dissolution occurs because of the death of a spouse, there is an end to the marital life cycle and the emergence of a new role for the surviving spouse, that of widow or widower. The survivor, most often the wife, suffers multiple role loss as companion, lover, confidant, and partner. Beyond role loss, the survivor also must endure the reality of no longer sharing, belonging, nurturing, or being needed. Death of a spouse causes extreme disruption in the survivor's lifestyle. Even in the best of circumstances, painful adjustment must be accomplished. Sometimes the grief of the surviving spouse is denied or avoided to the extent that feelings of depression and ideas of suicide become dominant (Botwinick, 1981).

Attachment between elderly couples with a shared life history tends to be very strong. When a spouse dies, a highly cathected object is lost and the survivor must redistribute the cathexis. In less psychoanalytic terms, this means that the emotional attachment invested in the deceased must eventually be withdrawn and the energy reinvested in other attachments. This process can be difficult and protracted for many individuals. Older widows often view the death of the husband as the end of their status as a wife and partner, with resultant lowering of self-esteem and self-identity. With widowhood, most women must relinquish a role central to their existence and adjust to the absence of the one individual who could best validate their self-image in terms of personal attributes. Furthermore, the social status of women, especially older women, is largely dependent on the occupational success of the husband. With the onset of widowhood, this derivative identity is dissipated; new social roles with new demands and expectations are thrust on the widow. After years of interdependence, she must learn how to live independently and how to enact a solo role in the social environment.

Widowhood contains the potential for an identity crisis, especially for elderly women, but fortunately, this potential can be alleviated in many cases. Memories and material possessions accumulated during the years of a marriage can help wifehood retain significant meaning for widows. Children and grandchildren can be powerful reinforcers to the identity and self-esteem of the widowed elderly. Adjustment to widowhood is not the same for everyone. Not every woman gives equal value to the role of wife and mother. For many women, the role of mother overshadowed that of wife, and when the children left home, both roles were discarded, and considered inconsequential. Among such women the role of wife may have been considered subordinate, and a warm, intimate marital relationship may never have existed. Despite this state, the final severance of the marital relationship by death may engender profound grief, intensified by feelings of guilt and regret on the part of the survivor. At the same time, for these women a sense of autonomy and independence may eventually facilitate adjustment to the state of widowhood.

The degree of marital attachment, therefore, is an issue in the crisis of widowhood. If attachment bonds were strong, the death of a spouse has a more adverse impact on the survivor. The antithesis is that in marriages in which separate friends, separate interests, or separate careers were the norm, the surviving spouse may be grief-stricken but be less subject to crisis. Thus, the quality of the marital relationship and the intensity of attachment between the couple are factors that may impede or ease adjustment to widowhood.

Widowhood affects the role enactment not only of the surviving spouse, but also of the immediate family, the extended family, and friends. A mother's widowhood modifies mutual patterns between parents and children. Older widows and their adult daughters frequently draw closer and support each other in various emotional and practical ways. In contrast, widows tend to grow more distant from adult sons because the son may have conflicting feelings of responsibility for his widowed mother and for his wife. After the death of a spouse, communication with in-laws usually declines gradually. Although communication increases with members of the extended family just after the death, it too subsides, and contact is maintained in the manner that existed previously.

A variable that greatly influences the adjustment of a widow is the number of women in her circle of friends who are also widows. When a woman is the first in her social group to be widowed, her friends with living husbands may be uncomfortable with a situation that reminds them of what their own future may hold. If others in the group have already been widowed, they can become a source of support and comfort. Indeed, as the group of women becomes older, it may be the still-married member who feels isolated, particularly since she may be less free to leave her husband in order to participate in group activities.

Comparatively, little attention has been given to conditions of widowerhood for older men. It is only after reaching seventy-five years of age that substantial numbers of men are widowed, and even then, men are less likely to face an identity crisis due to loss of the husband role. There are problems, however, that are uniquely masculine during widowerhood. Widowerhood drastically alters conditions of retirement for elderly men, and they experience more difficulty managing daily routines during the early grief period. Widowers seem to be more distant from their families than widows, so that loneliness and loss of an important confidant is a serious problem for widowers. Since they are less prepared to assume housekeeping tasks, widowers are more likely to give up their own residences.

The surplus of widows over widowers poses both a problem and a solution for men. Some men are inhibited in their socializing and in their participating in community affairs because women so outnumber them. In many respects, such as their health and general adjustment, men find widowerhood more difficult than their female counterparts do. Redeeming features of widowerhood include the facts that men are likely to have higher incomes, enjoy more opportunities to develop friendships, and are more apt to remarry.

Atypical grief reactions exhibited by the elderly may be classified as *delayed, distorted, inhibited,* and *chronic.* A *delayed grief* reaction is shown in situations in which grieving has been delayed until the anniversary of the loss or until a significant experience activates realization of the loss. *Distorted grief* reactions take the form of psychotic depressive or schizophrenic states. A less pathological, but still distorted, reaction manifests itself when the survivor identifies with the deceased and assumes behavior and mannerisms of the lost one. Grieving in a passive fashion over a very long period is termed *inhibited grief.* *Chronic grief* takes the form of long-term disbelief and shock that resembles the temporary reaction observable in the normal initial stage of grieving. The elderly most often display inhibited and chronic forms of grief. Since these forms of grief customarily prevent open expression of mourning, somatization through physical symptoms becomes a substitute way of venting feelings.

The most common mental disability among the elderly is depression, a not-surprising finding in view of the many losses they sustain. Death of a significant person is the most common cause of depression in the elderly, but other losses can be crucial. Children moving away, giving up an accustomed residence, and separating from friends or relatives are all forms of loss that may precipitate crisis. Repeated losses may cause elderly persons to become reluctant to make additional investments in people or events. Loss of vigor, productivity, or sexual function are additional factors leading to depression and a sense that life is no longer rewarding. When elderly persons withdraw emotionally from others, they often project their own feelings of anger and disengagement to people in the immediate vicinity. This projection contributes to a process of mutual withdrawal in which disengagement of the elderly person progresses alarmingly.

Elderly persons comprise only 10 percent of the total population, but 25 percent of all suicides occur in the over-sixty-five group. Females over sixty-five years of age have a suicide rate twice the national average, while males in the same age group have a suicide rate four times the national average. The married elderly have a lower suicide rate than the unmarried elderly; 60 percent of the elderly who commit suicide have severe physical disorders (Crandale, 1980; Goleman, 1985).

When the elderly attempt suicide, it is likely to be successful since the action is rarely an attention-seeking tactic or a gesture to attract sympathy. The wish for death is apt to be strong, and the elderly are people whose physical conditions are rather fragile. Therefore, self-injury is more likely to have fatal consequences for an elderly person than for a younger one. The social disengagement and isolation of the elderly are additional factors that preclude timely intervention in response to cues. Among elderly people, a single overt act, such as shooting or hanging may accomplish suicide. Failure to take needed medication, intemperate drinking, exertion, or other behaviors that are fatal to individuals with known vulnerabilities may achieve covert or passive suicide over time.

SUICIDE AS A GRIEF REACTION

Death involves leaving and being left, and who is to say which causes greater suffering. Acute and profound grief can play havoc with the mourner's reason and sense of reality. In the case of a terminal illness, the task of the dying person is clear, whereas the tasks of the survivors are less so. As Elizabeth Kubler-Ross (1970, p. 142), a Chicago psychiatrist, observed, "The dying patient's problems come to an end, but the family's problems go on." Kubler-Ross encourages practitioners to interact deeply and extensively with the dying person and the family, pointing out that professionals often view death as an adversary whose arrival is met with denial and detachment.

After the death of a spouse, there are many psychological tasks for the rest of the family to perform. The surviving parent may become overly preoccupied with her own distress, and be unable to give much to the children, whose grief around the loss may be equally intense. Frequently, the persistent needs and demands of the children help the surviving parent to become less self-engrossed and to deal with pressing realities. People who suffer a loss eventually learn that the passage of time considerably diminishes the acute feelings of sorrow and loss.

The work of mourning the loss is the first order of psychological business for the family, and is a complex, but necessary, process. Immediately following the death of a spouse, there may be a period of disorganization in family life, but this is to be expected, and most families eventually settle back into familiar routines of daily life in the weeks following the funeral.

The goals of caring for the suicidal client are directed toward providing protection from self-destruction until the client is able to assume that responsibility himself. It will be necessary to assist the client to express feelings of aggression and hostility constructively and outwardly rather than focusing them destructively and inwardly. During this time, the client must be assisted to meet her physical needs, as she may be so preoccupied with self-destructive thoughts that she neglects other necessities. The long-range goal is to help the client achieve a more realistic and positive self-concept so that her feelings of self-esteem, self-respect, acceptance by others, and belonging are enhanced.

Clients with high suicidal potential who appear out of control will require hospitalization. In addition, clients without external support systems may need short-term hospitalization until supports can be established.

Most clients, however, can be treated on an outpatient basis, either by establishing a trusting relationship with close monitoring of the client's status or by referral to another suitable agency, depending on the need.

Several resources can be used in planning the client's care. The client should be encouraged to discuss his problems with the family, if possible. If it is considered desirable for someone to be with the client during the crisis, a family member should be called and apprised of the situation, even if the client is reluctant to have this done. The family must accept responsibility for the emergency and help the client get the recommended treatment. Close friends can often be used in the same way. If the client belongs to a church group, the clergyperson may be of assistance. The police should be used only in cases of clear and immediate emergency, such as when a suicide attempt is about to occur or has occurred. The client may need prompt medical attention, and the police are the ones who can procure that treatment most quickly.

Because death is no easy escape from misery, the suicidal person approaches this finality with ambivalence. Even in deep despair and hopelessness, the depressed person longs to be rescued from his deadly inclination and usually communicates this longing to those around him. Suicide prevention consists of knowing the potential signs and responding when they appear.

•CLINICAL EXAMPLE:
SUICIDE IN RESPONSE TO LOSS OF A SPOUSE

Bill Bennett and his wife, Laura, had raised two sons on a farm that had been in the Bennett family for three generations. As youngsters, the boys had joined 4-H clubs and enjoyed entering their animals in state fair competitions. Because Laura and Bill had always assumed that the sons would eventually take over the farm, they were surprised when the sons announced that they would not attend an agricultural college. The older boy wanted a career as a chemist, whereas the younger was interested in pursuing a career in music. Reluctantly, the parents acceded to the boys' request that they be allowed to attend the colleges of their choice.

After the boys left for college, Bill and Laura hired farm hands and tried to keep things going, even though their hard work exacted a toll. Laura, in particular, began to show signs of strain. When she suffered strep throat that first winter, an antibiotic was injected to which Laura proved allergic. She suffered a severe anaphylactic reaction at home; in spite of her physician's heroic measures and the local rescue squad's arrival, Laura died without regaining speech or consciousness. The boys came home for the funeral, were contrite and miserable, but did not offer to stay on the farm permanently. After the funeral they returned to their respective colleges.

For a while friends and neighbors were quite attentive. Bill was invited out for meals, the minister called, and church women brought over homemade soups and casseroles. Even with this attention, Bill became more and more morose. He described himself as an old horse who had reached the time to be put out to pasture. Bill missed Laura, with whom he could discuss signs of changing weather and make decisions about when to plow or plant. It was a different existence for a man who loved the earth and the changing seasons, but had always shared his thoughts and questions with Laura. The winter was slow in passing, but Bill hoped he would feel less discouraged in the spring. The boys were due to come home for a few weeks, and Bill anticipated their visit.

While his sons were home, the three of them worked together on the farm. As they went about accustomed tasks, things seemed almost as they had always been. Only at mealtime was Laura's absence painful for the boys, but out of consideration for their father they did not mention their grief to him. During the evenings, the boys were restless, talking animatedly to each other about subjects that were unintelligible to Bill. Only when Bill was not present did they discuss their mother.

After the boys returned to school, the farm seemed lonelier than ever. Bill kept busy but it seemed harder for him to concentrate on what had to be done. For years Bill had risen with the birds, but now it was difficult to get out of bed in the morning. Following Bill's example, the hired men became more lax in their work, and as weeks passed the farm began to take on a neglected look. Bill became so irritable and taciturn that his two helpers turned resentful, packed their gear, and left the farm without giving notice. Finding himself completely alone, Bill became more despondent. One early morning after feeding the animals and cleaning the barn, Bill took out his rifle and shot himself in the head. A few days later the minister found him in the barn. He had missed Bill at church services. A note was discovered saying that the farm was to be sold and the proceeds divided between his two sons, whom he wished well in their chosen occupations. "The farm was only important to my wife and to me," he wrote. "Without her the farm is nothing and I am nothing."

Bill was in a state of crisis as a result of the death of his wife and separation from his boys. Even though his minister, his sons, and his neighbors tried to be helpful, no one realized the acute distress Bill was experiencing. Isolated on the farm, showing little outward emotion, unwilling to burden his sons or confide in anyone, Bill sent to clear warning messages. For a while the prospect of seeing his sons again sustained him, but when the reunion ended, Bill's wish to join Laura in death was far stronger than his wish to live. In his suicide, as in most matters, Bill discussed his plan with no one; and as usual, he completed his plan.

Critical Guidelines

The Bennett's were a family who seldom expressed their feelings. The sons did not share their own legitimate ambitions with their parents, nor did the parents try to discuss their fears and disappointments with their sons. As a result, no one in the family understood or reached out to other members. Too much emphasis was placed upon independence and self-sufficiency. Bill and his sons all felt guilty about Laura's death. The two sons did talk to one another on occasion and found some solace in sharing, but they did not include their father. Bill, on his part, was all too willing to turn away from his sons, as he had turned away from helpful neighbors in the church and community.

The sons' indifference to the family tradition of farming was a blow to Laura and Bill that they concealed from them. When Laura became ill, Bill blamed himself and his devotion to the farm for her untimely death. An inarticulate man, he shared little of his feelings with others, but was devoted to Laura. After her death, he began to hate the farm and believe that the farm had robbed him of his wife and his sons. When Laura died, Bill experienced an inhibited grief reaction. He shared his deep sorrow and self-recrimination with no one, and his sons lacked the insight to help their father express his feelings. Feeling guilty, they protected themselves by avoiding open discussion of their mother's death and their own pain. As a result of mutual avoidance, Bill's feelings found no outlet. He held his emotions within, and as time passed, the inhibited grief reaction became a chronic depressive state.

Bill's suicide added to the guilt that the sons undoubtedly felt. Unlike Bill, they did have one another and probably were less socially isolated than their father had been. It is possible that their failure to resolve earlier issues with their parents would complicate their mourning and grief work. Their prolonged failure to see that their father was in crisis is a potential source of great pain and guilt. The circumstances surrounding the death have much to do with the nature of the grieving process. The process is also affected by the relationships within the family before the death, which have the power to mitigate or exacerbate feelings of loss. A conflictual and highly ambivalent relationship with the deceased family member can complicate and prolong the mourning process for an individual or for the whole family. Family members who never had the chance to resolve a hostile and guilt-ridden relationship when the relative was alive are likely to experience a painfully prolonged mourning process that may last for years, unless the person seeks therapeutic intervention.

Both public and private mourning are necessary in the working-through process. Sharing the painful feelings of the grief and allowing friends to comfort relieves feelings of isolation. A person also needs to grieve privately; the pain of the loss needs to be experienced, and felt, since, when painful feelings are denied, or pushed aside, emotional complications may follow.

Significant others may not be helpful or may even be injurious. If they reject involvement and deny the suicidal behavior, the desolate person may withdraw physically and psychologically from continued communication. Sometimes significant others resent the client's increased demands and insistence on gratifying dependency needs. In other cases, they may act helpless and indecisive, giving the suicidal person the feeling that help is not available, thereby increasing her feelings of despair. To help the situation, treatment for the significant others may be indicated as well.

SUICIDE MYTHS: FACT AND FICTION

- *Myth 1.* People who talk about suicide don't do it. *Fact:* Eight out of ten clients who kill themselves have given warnings about their intentions.
- *Myth 2.* Suicide happens without warning. *Fact:* The suicidal person gives many clues—they are just unrecognized or disregarded.
- *Myth 3.* Suicidal people wish to die. *Fact:* Most are ambivalent about dying and are gambling with death, hoping others will save them.
- *Myth 4.* Once a person is suicidal, he is always suicidal. *Fact:* Persons are suicidal only for short periods of time.
- *Myth 5.* Improvement after crisis means the risk is over. *Fact:* Suicides commonly occur about three months after improvement, when people have the energy to put thoughts into actions.
- *Myth 6.* Suicide is inherited and runs in families. *Fact:* Suicide is an individual experience.
- *Myth 7.* Suicidal persons are mentally ill. *Fact:* Although suicidal persons are extremely unhappy, they are not necessarily mentally ill.

WORKING WITH THE ELDERLY

More and more people are living well into their seventies, eighties, and even nineties. More importantly, they are enjoying life. Many conditions once attributed to aging have been found to result from poor nutrition, lack of exercise, social isolation, and treatable physical ailments. There are some attributes—such as reasoning ability, spatial ability, and verbal comprehension—that do seem to decline with age, but the extent of decline may be overstated. Researchers have found that when the same subjects were followed from adulthood into old age, the amount of decline was far less than that found in studies that compared two different population groups, one in middle adulthood and the other in old age. As Tavris (1987, p. 24) wrote, "The greatest difference in sexual activity—or any other aspect of aging—is not between the young and the old, but between individuals."

The way society regards old age intensifies the maturation crises of the elderly. Youthfulness is highly valued in American society, and fear of aging is reinforced. Many individuals see in the elderly the prediction of their own future, fear their own aging, and try to avoid accepting the later stages of the life cycle until they must. This is unfortunate, because planning for the final life cycle stage can help avoid or ameliorate some of the problems.

Adjustment to recurrent loss is a prevailing theme in the lives of older people. In addition to the loss of youthful strength and vigor, and of friends and loved ones, the elderly suffer role losses as their children become independent, and as retirement arrives.

One of the most painful encounters with death is the demise of a spouse, for this means the loss of a companion, confidant, friend, and lover. Because women tend to live longer than men and to marry men who are somewhat older, they are more likely than men to face widowhood. Of course, not all marriages are happy and not all partners find the role of husband or wife congenial or central to existence. Allowing for these variations, a marriage dissolved by death still brings strong feelings of grief and regret. Some widows and widowers may idealize the deceased, forgetting her faults and weaknesses. This may be disconcerting for those who have a more accurate recollection of the deceased, but idealization is part of the grief process, and distortion need not be corrected. When the mourner accurately perceives the strengths and weaknesses of the deceased, it is likely that his grieving has been completed.

While the federal government tries to deal with the problem of how to bear the cost of caring for the elderly, family members continue to assume the burden, especially the women. An important precept to remember is that caretakers need relief, and the relief should be periodic, frequent, and available. Support services should be used throughout the caretaking process, not merely in times of crisis or when the primary caretaker is on the verge of collapse. Many families lack information about support services and respite care.

Sometimes the caretaker feels guilty about spending time away from the relative or blames herself for not being able to halt the inroads of time. Here, nurses can assure the caretaker that caring for herself is an important aspect of caring for the relative. As long as family members continue to provide most of the care the elderly relatives need there is little incentive for government or other agencies to become very involved. There is a strong case for voters to exert pressure on elected officials to integrate long-term health care, in the home or in institutions, into the reimbursement system (Quist, 1989). In these days of expanded opportunities for women, many of them looked forward to living in an empty nest that would finally allow them time to develop interests and talents, either as volunteers or late-blooming careerists. Instead, many women have found themselves caught between the demands of a job and the arduous task of caring for a parent who is less than competent (Wood, 1987).

Successful adaptation does not mean that the elderly person must enjoy the limitations that age brings, but merely that limitations must not be denied. With advancing age, control over one's social environment is threatened. Personal space becomes circumscribed as certain activities and roles are no longer accessible. Searching for alternative interests is part of adaptation, and individuals who cannot give up total autonomy or accept some dependency fail to adapt well to aging. Readjustment of criteria for self-evaluation means that various criteria for self-evaluation must be modified, unrealistic standards of performance must be lowered, and self-esteem must no longer be based on autonomous functioning or the managerial ability of the elderly person. Finally, reintegration of goals and values necessitates revising the aspirations of older people so that they can find meaning and purpose in life as it presently exists for them.

Old age is a time of loss—of self-worth, of role performance, and of significant others. The perception that life is no longer meaningful becomes a reason for ending that life. Displacement from job-related roles and family roles may produce a feeling of hopelessness and uselessness. Widows and widowers are particularly vulnerable, especially in the first year following the death of a spouse.

Many suicide victims have feelings of loneliness, helplessness, and hopelessness that a loss often aggravates. Suicides occur more frequently among divorced people than among single people, and among single people more frequently than among married persons. For the survivors, suicide is a highly personal tragedy that produces feelings of pain, guilt, remorse, and bitterness. Social isolation is another contributing factor. Women tend to have a greater chance for survival because of the contact with friends and the responsibility for integrating kinship groups.

There are sex differences in the methods chosen: men are more likely to commit suicide with a gun, while women usually resort to barbiturates and other less violent methods. Some experts feel that women use these methods because they fear disfigurement or because society does not sanction violence on the part of females. The clearest example of direct behavioral communication is a suicide attempt, or "practice run."

Although it is commonly believed that clients who frequently attempt suicide will never actually complete the act, a previous attempt is actually one of the strongest indicators of potential suicide. For some, the aborted attempt is but another example of failure, increasing feelings of hopelessness and worthlessness.

Interest in the field of suicide and suicide prevention has shown a dramatic upsurge in recent times. The number of community suicide prevention centers has grown, and suicide research has expanded in new directions. Statistics concerning suicide are not totally reliable since it is impossible to tell whether many "accidental" deaths, especially those by car accidents, may have been intentional. Also, because of persistent cultural taboos and financial pressures, some families and communities refuse to admit that a suicide has occurred.

SUMMARY

Progressive changes for the elderly person and the family occur in the later years of life. Some of the changes are welcome, but most of them are not. Few changes in later life consist of triumph or accomplishment. All too often, changes take the form of declines and losses, which result in lowered autonomy and self-esteem.

Retirement is a significant change for the mature adult. Its meaning depends on the retiree's feeling about work and willingness to develop other interests. Programs already offered by some employers can circumvent the adverse effects of retirement. Such programs are not always available, and the employee must prepare for retirement without much institutional help. When work-related associations are lost because of retirement, family relationships become even more crucial. If a retiree develops a problem that requires counseling, family intervention may be needed. The retiree may respond to crisis counseling, but sometimes long-term measures may be needed. Once the acute phase of a retirement crisis has abated, referral to support or community interest groups may prove helpful. For a number of reasons, retirement seems to be more difficult for men to accept than for women.

Relocation is another critical change that imposes stress on elderly people, since it is usually a decision not chosen, but thrust upon them. Whenever an elderly person moves into the home of an adult son or daughter, massive readjustments are required of everyone. As the health and vigor of the elderly person declines, one family member, usually female, becomes the primary caregiver. This gives rise to a host of new problems, any one of which may precipitate a marital or family crisis.

Even more difficult than bringing an elderly relative to live in the family household is the decision to place a feeble relative in a nursing home. Feelings of guilt, anger, and regret are almost unavoidable, but searching for acceptable solutions and making careful choices may somewhat alleviate these feelings. Financial considerations certainly influence decisions, but such factors as geographic location, level of care, and the elderly person's well-being deserve the utmost consideration as well.

Losing cherished friends and loved ones is a recurrent experience for elderly people. In responding to any loss, grief and sorrow should neither be denied nor avoided. Failure to engage in, or acknowledge grief, after any significant loss, may prolong, intensify, or inhibit the adaptive effects of the painful, but adaptive, mourning process. The inability or refusal to grieve often leads to depressive reactions, which may generate suicidal thoughts and feelings. Such ideation sometimes results in suicide attempts that succeed.

A number of experts have formulated frameworks depicting sequential stages of grief. More important than these is the counselor's ability to recognize grief in all its forms. It is essential to realize that bravado, withdrawal, or apparent indifference may camouflage grief and mourning. It is important for crisis workers to be aware of the many masks that grief may wear (Archer and Smith, 1988).

When death is untimely or unexpected, or when the mourner feels responsible in some way, the grief reaction may be more intense because guilt is added. The age of the mourner also influences how grief is expressed and its extent. Older people whose personal worlds have narrowed to a few cherished persons or objects may feel especially desolate. Adolescents mourn much as adults do, but younger children, whose cognitive and language development are incomplete, have difficulty comprehending or expressing feelings of grief.

The younger a child, the more difficult the grieving process is. Since grieving is a form of primary prevention against later depression, children need help from family members. When children want to talk about a relative who has died, they should be permitted to do so without being diverted. Adults who listen ease the child's pain and may even find their own grief lightened. Denial of loss and avoidance of grieving are defenses that are not helpful.

As in so many aspects of counseling, therapeutic intervention in response to the crisis of loss consists of listening, observing, accepting, and validating the experience of the troubled individual. A counselor can accomplish this when she encourages reminiscing, reinforces the elderly person's sense of self, and conveys honest respect for lifetime accomplishments, even if they took place fifty years ago.

REFERENCES

Aber, C.S. "Spousal Death, A Threat to Women's Health: Paid Work As a Resistance Resource." *Image* 24(1992): 95–98.

Archer, D.N., and A.C. Smith. "Sorrow Has Many Faces: Helping Families Cope with Grief." *Nursing 88* 18(1988): 43–45.

Atchley, R.C. *Social Forces and Aging.* Belmont, California: 1988

Borden, W., and S. Berlin. "Gender, Coping, and Psychological Wellbeing in Spouses of Older Adults with Chronic Dementia." *American Journal of Orthopsychiatry* 60(1990): 603–610.

Botwinick, J. *We Are Aging.* New York: Springer, 1981.

Clark, M., and B. Anderson. *Culture and Aging.* Springfield, Illinois: Charles C. Thomas, 1967.

Crandale, R.C. *Gerontology: A Behavioral Science.* Menlo Park, California: Addison-Wesley, 1980.

Engel, G. "Grief and Grieving." *American Journal of Nursing* 64(1964): 93–96.

Erikson, E. *Childhood and Society.* New York: Norton, 1963.

George, L.K. *Role Transitions in Later Life.* Monterey, California: Brooks Cole, 1980.

Goleman, D. "Clues to Suicide: A Brain Chemical is Implicated." *The New York Times* October 8, 1985.

Griffin, J.Q. "Physical Illness in the Family." In Family-focused Care, edited by J.R. Miller and E.H. Janosik. New York: McGraw-Hill, 1980.

Hutchison, C.P., and R.T. Bahr. "Types and Meaning of Caring Behaviors Among Elderly Nursing Home Residents." *Image* 23(1991): 81–85.

Justice, B. *Who Gets Sick.* Houston: Tarcher, 1988.

Kaye, L.N., and J.S. Applegate. "Men as Elder Caregivers: A Response to Changing Families." *American Journal of Orthopsychiatry* 60(1990): 86–95.

Kayser-Jones, J. "The Environment and Quality of Life in Long Term Care Institutions." *Nursing and Health Care* 10(1989): 124–130.

Keating, N.C., and P. Cole. "What Shall I Do with Him 24 Hours a Day: Changes in the Housewife Role After Retirement." *Gerontologist* 2(1980): 84–89.

Keith, P.M., R. Braito, and M. Breci. "Rethinking Isolation Among the Married and Unmarried." *American Journal of Orthopsychiatry* 60(1990): 289–297.

Kermis, M.D. *Mental Health in Late Life: The Adaptive Process.* Boston: Jones and Bartlett, 1986.

Kubler-Ross, E. *On Death and Dying.* New York: Macmillan, 1970.

Lawton, M.P. "Psychosocial and Environmental Approaches to the Care of Senile Dementia Patients." In *Handbook of Psychology of Aging,* edited by J. Cole and J. Barrett. New York: Van Nostrand Reinhold, 1980.

Lawton, M.P., E.M. Brody, and A.R. Saperstein. "A Controlled Study of Respite Service for Caregivers of Alzheimer's Patients." *Gerontologist* 29(1989): 8–16.

Lazarus, R.S., and A. DeLongis. "Psychological Stress and Coping in Aging." *American Psychologist* 38(1983): 245–254.

McCluskey, N.G., and E.F. Borgatta. *Aging and Society: Current Research and Policy Perspectives.* Beverly Hills, California: Sage Publications, 1980.

Neugarten, B.L. (ed.) *Middle Age and Aging.* Chicago: University of Chicago Press, 1973.

_____. "The Future and the Young-Old" *Gerontologist* 15(1975) 345–349.

Newman, B.M., and P.R. Newman *Personality Development Through the Life Span.* Monterey, California: Brooks Cole, 1980.

Parks, S.H., and M. Pilisuk. "Caregiver Burden: Gender and the Psychological Costs of Caregiving." *American Journal of Orthopsychiatry* 61(1991): 501–509.

Pett, M.A., M.S. Caserta, A.P. Hutton, and D.A. Lund. "Intergenerational Conflict: Middleaged Women Caring for Demented Older Relatives." *American Journal of Orthopsychiatry* 58(1988): 405–417.

Quist, J.C. "Helping a Caregiver Keep Up the Good Work." *RN* 4(1989): 88–91.

Reichard, S., F. Livson, and P.G. Peterson. *Aging and Personality.* New York: Wiley, 1962.

Sheehy, G. *Passages.* New York: Dutton, 1976.

_____. *The Silent Passage.* New York: Random House, 1992.

Springer, F., and H. Saylor. "People Need to Give As Well As Receive." *American Health Care Association Journal* 10(1984): 8–11.

Streib, G.F., and C.J. Schneider. *Retirement in American Society.* New York: Cornell University Press, 1971.

Tavris, C. "Old Age Is Not What It Used to Be." *The New York Times Good Health Magazine* September 27 (1987): 24–25, 91–92.

Walker, A.J., C.C. Pratt, H.Y. Shin, and L.L. Jones. "Motives for Parental Caregiving and Relationship Quality." *Family Relations* 39(1990): 51–56.

Wood, J. "Labors of Love." *Modern Maturity* 30(1987): 28–34, 90–94.

PART
THREE

FAMILIES
IN CRISIS

10

Marginal Families in Crisis
Illness and Disability

There is a tide in the affairs of men which taken at the flood leads to fortune. Omitted, all the voyage of their life is bound in shallows and in miseries.

William Shakespeare

The limited nature and scope of crisis counseling sometimes pose a problem that is compounded when a family rather than an individual is the focus of intervention. One solution is to formulate short-term goals that give direction to immediate problem solving, so that other issues can be dealt with later. Short-term objectives can be formulated around the most urgent needs of a family as it confronts illness, accidents, decisions, or conflicts that are unlikely to be resolved quickly. With this restriction in mind, a family-oriented approach to crisis work is appropriate. For example, a family dealing with the progressive illness of one of its members may displace anger and bitterness toward the patient's health care professionals. If caregivers respond in a defensive style, the resentment that the family and staff express may impair optimum care of the patient. In such a situation, crisis intervention could be used to explain essential procedures to frightened family members and to assure them of the staff's commitment to the patient. In addition, negative family behaviors should be interpreted by caregivers as human reactions to a frightening situation rather than a personal attack on hardworking staff members.

Fleck (1980) classified family functions into six groupings: marital, nurturant, relational, communicative, emancipational, and recuperative functions. In everyday life these functions overlap, although at various times one or another function may be dominant.

1. *Marital functions.* Families begin as marital dyads within which each partner hopes to receive gratification from the other. Accepting and

sharing family leadership tasks are essential aspects of the marital function.

2. *Nurturant functions.* Nurture includes all basic care of children and encompasses their security, protection, socialization, and sensory stimulation.

3. *Relational functions.* Accepting the critical tasks of family members requires continuous adaptation so that parents and children can interact comfortably with each other and with their respective extrafamilial peer groups.

4. *Communicative functions.* Communicative competence is essential for human adjustment, and includes verbal and nonverbal messages. Family communication must be congruent and consistent so that messages are clearly understood. In addition, family communication should be compatible with the linguistic customs of the surrounding community.

5. *Emancipational functions.* Emancipation of children from a family must accompany the attainment of adult status, but the departure of each child requires the parents and remaining siblings to adjust. Thus, every family must deal with recurrent issues of individuation and separation as children grow up and leave home.

6. *Recuperative functions.* Families provide a milieu in which members may safely relax, regress, and recuperate from the demands and rigors of life outside the home.

Friedman (1981) described the contemporary family as a unit whose major function is mediation. Within its borders, the family mediates between the individual and collective needs of its members. The family also mediates between the needs of its members and pressures emanating from the supra-systems of society. For example, society imposes restrictions on when young people may leave school to enter the work force, and defines parental responsibilities by means of legal and community sanctions. Society also monitors many aspects of health care delivery through professional licensing and regulating certain treatment modes.

Whenever the total physical and emotional resources of a family are insufficient, critical tasks and family functions are threatened. Disproportion between family needs and family resources endangers group functionality. Families who attempt to overcome disproportion by appropriate, but inadequate, role enactment are called *marginal*. Families who attempt to relieve disproportion by inappropriate or distorted role enactment are termed *disorganized*.

MARGINALITY IN FAMILIES

When family resources and family needs become disproportionate because of illness or disability, marginality is a more frequent result than disorganization. In general, disorganized families are more pathological and more deviant than marginal families, although both types of families are likely to experience disequilibrium. Marginal families are those in which suitable role enactment is attempted and barely maintained. Disorganized families are those in which suitable role enactment is rarely attempted and never maintained. In disorganized families, dysfunction is more obvious; in marginal families, functionality seems to be present but is tenuous. As a result, marginal families are extremely vulnerable to change despite their efforts to cope.

For purposes of this chapter, *marginality* is not a pejorative term but is largely descriptive. A change of any kind makes new demands on individuals and families. When the family's resources are adequate to deal with change, equilibrium is preserved. Because marginal families have limited discretionary resources in the form of energy and adaptability, their equilibrium is always precarious. Whenever the balance between resources and demands is upset and crisis follows, the experience is more painful because marginal families entertain hopes of remaining functional.

One factor contributing to the marginality of families in modern life is industrialization, which transformed extended families into separate nuclear households in which the working unit is the solitary individual. Even in dual-career marriages, the partners tend to be single units of production, each pursuing an occupation independent of the other. Small nuclear families lack the capacities of extended families for deflecting or absorbing hostility between members, or for dealing with the hazards of illness or disability. When adverse conditions are extended or severe, few relatives are at hand to provide help, and nuclear households have no peripheral members to neutralize intrafamily conflicts or assist with responsibilities.

Disorganized families usually live from crisis to crisis; this pattern is less true of marginal families, although they are crisis-prone. Adding to the problems of marginal families is the inverse correlation between the prevalence of illness and high socioeconomic status. This inverse correlation may be partly caused by the susceptibility of lower socioeconomic families to physical and mental illness, and to their slowness in responding to early signs of malfunctioning. There is no doubt that family perceptions of events influence their recognition of conditions that merit attention and their subsequent actions. Families who interpret all events as threatening, who magnify or minimize reality, and who devalue or exaggerate their coping abilities are more likely to suffer crisis. Intervention is often difficult with these families because their problem-solving skills are limited and they cling to accustomed methods, even when these have already failed.

The effort of marginal families to enact roles appropriately limits their access to community resources. All families differ in their willingness to accept help from outside sources, but marginal families who outwardly conform to community values often hesitate to let outsiders examine internal family operations. These relatively closed families discourage intrusion, and therefore respond to crisis situations by making excessive demands on their own members, and by exacting self-sacrifice and self-discipline in order to safeguard privacy. This pattern is particularly unfortunate in families whose inner resources are already meager, because external input in the form of information, guidance, and services facilitates crisis resolution. Caplan (1974) described some forms of input that are important for families in crisis and offered the following guidelines for providing external supplies:

- Active processing and utilization of relevant information.
- Prolonged association between families and community networks.
- Extensive referrals and reliance on the following resources:

  Informal community supports, such as friends and neighbors.
  Formal, nonprofessional supports, such as self-help groups.
  Formal, professional supports, such as clinics and agencies.

Several factors prevent marginal families from looking beyond their own borders for help. First, any request for help is an admission that the family is deficient. Second, marginal families may be unaware of potential sources of assistance. Disorganized families are less inclined to be sensitive about seeking help, partly because their crises take more dramatic forms. Moreover, disorganized families may already have come to the attention of community agencies either through receiving aid or being subject to supervision of one sort or another. Marginal families are likely to reject growth-producing behaviors during times of crisis and rely on defensive tactics that alleviate anxiety, but do not resolve crisis adaptively.

Families in crisis may adopt a variety of defensive strategies. Friedman (1981) identified some of these as follows:

- Denying the problem and its implications.
- Exploiting selected family members.
- Some family members exhibiting authoritarian behaviors.
- Other family members exhibiting submissive behaviors.
- Inculcating guilt in certain family members.
- Establishing alliances and coalitions.
- Emotionally withdrawing through detachment and indifference.
- Physically withdrawing through abandonment or prolonged absence.

Other defensive reactions include continuing to have fixed attitudes and refusing to modify behavior, even when family circumstances have undergone drastic alteration. Resistance to modifying behavioral responses can be a family as well as an individual trait, and has the effect of exacerbating crises and reducing the family's coping ability.

A distinction exists between marginal and disorganized families who face illness. In marginal families, the parents attempt appropriate role enactment, even though they are living at a subsistence level. In disorganized families, there is virtually no attempt at appropriate role enactment, and addiction, violence, impulsivity, and low stress tolerance may further strain meager resources. It is the disorganized family whose dramatic episodes bring the family to the attention of professional agencies. The marginal family is less visible, even in times of illness. Yet the marginal family, with little money and few connections to community or extended family, is subject to the greatest stress. Solving the everyday problems of buying food, paying rent, and just surviving consumes all its resources. When acute illness strikes the marginal family, there is pressure on the patient to recover quickly so as to relieve the family of the burden of the illness. Since the marginal family, unlike the disorganized family, may have little knowledge of community resources, referrals must be prominent in the work of the health professional.

Families can be alerted to potential problems when professionals discuss some of the problems the families probably will face. It is helpful for families to know what behaviors and attitudes frequently precede or follow various problems. Teaching families merely to comprehend the overall risks associated with illness or death is insufficient, since this information may increase rather than decrease anxiety. Families need to be warned of specific problems they will face and told how these problems may be handled. Families also need assistance in evaluating information so that effective decisions can be made as problem situations arise.

There are three general categories of physical illness: acute, chronic, and terminal. One way of distinguishing between the three types is the way in which the illness is resolved. *Acute illness* usually disables individuals for a temporary period, after which they recover to all or most of their previous level of wellness. *Chronic illness* has no such hopeful resolution. There may be periods of relapse or remission, but the individual suffers or is disabled to some extent until the end of his life. Chronic illness may be progressively debilitating or it may have a prolonged, but stable, course. In some instances, chronic illness restricts activity but does not shorten the life expectancy of the sufferer. *Terminal illness* is the phase of acute or chronic illness that ends in death, usually after a fairly predictable course. The onset of all three types of illness may be either sudden or gradual. Often the onset may appear to be sudden, but the disease process has, in fact, been insidious and hidden. The family must then deal with an advanced stage of illness of which there was no previous knowledge.

The intrinsic features of these three categories of illness influence the interventions of professionals helping the family to cope. In contemporary times, acute illness depends primarily on the physician for cure. For maximum recovery, chronic illness depends on the patient and family. While chronic illness needs sound medical treatment, the responsibility for the necessary dietary regimen, activity adjustments, and life modifications falls on the patient and the family, rather than on the doctor.

Terminal illness may be the outcome of acute or chronic disability, and the characteristics of the onset often affect the response of the family. The transformation of chronic illness into terminal illness may find the family somewhat prepared. On the other hand, preceding conditions of chronicity may have already depleted the physical, psychological, and economic resources of the family.

Every family reacts to physical illness in its own way, exhibiting different strengths and weaknesses, and using different methods of coping with stress the illness has caused. The family's ability to use adaptive coping measures depends, in part, on attitudes and interactions that are already present in the home, on socioeconomic factors, and on the life stages of the patient and other family members. The ages of family members and the time in the family life cycle at which a member becomes ill greatly affect the system and the problems the family must face.

How an illness is discovered or recognized can affect the family's ability to cope. Sometimes an illness that begins without warning, converting an apparently healthy person into a sick one, is easier for the family to accept. Often the crisis nature of the event causes the family to mobilize its energies and respond adaptively. In the case of an individual who suffers a myocardial infarction, the life-threatening crisis is obvious. Regardless of ultimate economic and social consequences, the illness can neither be ignored nor immediately denied. At first there is no time for feelings of guilt or anger. In a sense, the urgency of the problem defines the priorities: (1) obtain immediate medical care; (2) rearrange family functioning in order to maintain essential family services; and (3) reassure, support, and serve the sick member.

An illness, known or unknown to the family, which slowly and imperceptibly becomes acute, presents different problems. The family still faces the need to make all the adjustments described previously, but a sense of urgency and priority may be lacking. If the family has known that the illness was present for weeks, months, or years before becoming acute, there may be feelings of anger or guilt. If the illness has already caused role restriction for the patient, negative feelings accumulated during earlier stages of the illness may complicate an acute phase. A wife may feel that her husband knew he was sick, but did not care enough for his family to take proper care of himself. The ill husband may feel that family demands were excessive or that his wife should have insisted that he seek medical care earlier. Each may displace feelings on the other that something should have been done to prevent the development of acute illness. Meanwhile, the children may react with fear and confusion to the realization that the family provider is mortal and is in peril.

The family's ability to recognize and respond to early signs of poor health can influence the course of the illness. A family's willingness to do this is a function of personal, ethnic, and social variables. Families who enjoy an adequate income are more able to pay for health maintenance, and to seek professional help at the first indication of illness. Such families are generally sensitive to changes in the health status of their members, and of adverse effects of failing to act on early warning signals. At the other extreme are many marginal families who define health only as the ability to work, and ignore signs of illness until they are incapable of working.

THE SICK ROLE

Individuals in the family, their internal relationships, and their willingness to receive external aid influence their response to the crisis of illness or disability. In more traditional times, life and death, health and illness were considered to be one continuous process. All outcomes were attributed to the will of God, and the promise of eventual reunion with the deceased somewhat relieved the grief of survivors. In contemporary life, such comfort is less widespread. Furthermore, for marginal families who already have little control over their existence, the onset of illness or disability constitutes another reminder of their limitations. Failure to deal well with stress or crisis then becomes part of a familiar experience of feeling overwhelmed.

Marginal families are sometimes slow to recognize serious disturbance in a member, but after acknowledging the symptoms, they make an effort to respond (Minuchin, 1974; Minuchin et al., 1967). Many of these families first try random solutions and intrafamily consultation before searching for professional help. After accepting care from health professionals, an ailing family member is expected to enact the sick role with its accompanying exemptions and obligations. Depending on the identity of the family member and the life cycle stage of the family, obligations of the sick role occupant may outweigh exemptions. This pattern is especially true when it is the wife and mother who becomes ill. Because the mother is crucial to carrying out daily family routines, immediate readjustment is necessary when she is the ailing member. When it is the husband and primary provider who falls ill, economic deprivation may be an early consequence. In two-parent households, reallocation of tasks is feasible, but role flexibility is a luxury unavailable in single-parent homes, which comprise about 16% of all households in the United States (Bjornsten & Stewart, 1985).

Observing the ways that families respond to serious illness or disability reveals interesting variations. When a family member becomes chronically or terminally ill without hope of recovery, other persons in the family are unlikely to look for help with their own emotional problems, either because they do not relate their problems to the illness, or because they hesitate to involve a person who is ill. When illness continues without remission for a protracted period, families become enmeshed in the schedules the illness necessitates and are unwilling to delegate tasks. At the same time, there may be deep resentment for having to be so attentive at the expense of individual fulfillment. Occasionally, a family member will withdraw from those in the family who are well, existing only to protect and nurture the ill member, ultimately becoming dependent on enacting the caretaker role. When families are preoccupied with illness or disability, life cycle tasks, such as separation, which are chronologically suitable for younger family members, may be delayed due to the burden of caring for the ill member (Collings, 1981).

Noting how families responded to ailing members, Parsons (1951) described characteristics of the "sick role" and outlined the obligations and freedom from obligations that accompanied enactment of the sick role. Society-at-large generally shares the family perspectives of sick role exemptions and obligations.

Exemptions of the Sick Role Occupant in Physical Disorders:
• Exemption from responsibility for being ill.
• Exemption from customary role obligations.

Obligations of the Sick Role Occupant in Physical Disorders:
• Obligation to accept competent assistance.
• Obligation to cooperate in the recovery process.
• Obligation to be dependent, submissive, and compliant.

When Parsonsian concepts of the sick role are applied to mental illness, other discrepancies become apparent. In effect, enactment of physical and psychiatric sick roles are contradictory in the exemptions and obligations extended to the occupants. It may be stated that sick role concepts are more readily applied to physical illness than to psychological or psychophysiological disorders. In other words, viewing individuals as suitable occupants of the sick role is unlikely when the illness is not considered fully somatic in origin and expression. Whenever a purely somatic disorder is present, the patient is not held responsible for being ill. When the disorder has overt psychological overtones or is thought to be the result of deviant social behavior, such as alcoholism, the sick role occupant may be held accountable for causing, as well as coping, with the disorder.

Exemptions of the Sick Role Occupant in Psychiatric Disorders:
• Partial responsibility for being ill.
• Partial exemption from customary role obligations.

Obligations of the Sick Role Occupant in Psychiatric Disorders:
• Obligation to accept competent assistance.
• Obligation to cooperate in the recovery process.
• Obligation to be adaptive, interactive, and self-directed.
• Obligation to accept the stigma of a psychiatric label.

It is evident from this discussion that enactment of the sick role is not consistent or unidimensional. The nature of an illness, the identity of the ailing family member, and the context in which the illness develops are factors that determine how the sick role is enacted and how other family members relate to the role enactment of the afflicted member.

Factors other than the prognosis of the illness affect the enactment of the sick role. Insufficient attention has been given to variations of sick role behavior among different populations and families. This neglect may be due, in part, to the ethnocentricity of practitioners, who represent the mainstream of society, or to a sincere, but misguided, wish to avoid stereotypical judgments.

Risk Factors

Indications of effective family functioning are fairly easy to recognize. Open communication, nonexploitive attachments, and willingness to compromise are essential to performing the core tasks of family life. Dysfunctional families do not engage in open communication, are unwilling to negotiate, and are more committed to the status quo than to growth. The arrival of crisis unmasks family fragility and discloses multiple signs of dysfunction, although the family may be aware of only one overriding complaint and look for help solely in that area. This complaint then becomes the presenting problem brought to the practitioner. An experienced practitioner will realize that the most conspicuous problem represents only one aspect of a process perpetuated by the relationships, behaviors, and attitudes used when the family was operating in a state of equilibrium.

Even in brief crisis intervention, a comprehensive family assessment should precede planning and implementing. Family members may insist that only symptoms of the presenting problem should receive attention, but assessment must include family process as well as family symptomatology. Following the assessment, a practitioner must determine whether to confine intervention to the presenting problem or endeavor to alter the family process. Much will depend on the motivation of the family and the practitioner's contractual restrictions. In crisis work, a decision may be made to give priority to the presenting problem, while calling some attention to the family process. When distress from the immediate problem has moderated, families often become receptive to suggestions and referrals for more extensive help.

Physical or psychological disruptions affecting all the family members are indications of family dysfunction. Not every family member will exhibit equal symptomatology, or show the same amount of disturbance. If family assessment concentrates only on the presenting problem and on the identified patient, the effects of dysfunction on other family members will be overlooked. Only by including every family member in the assessment can the full impact of the crisis be ascertained. Since family-centered crisis work must be concerned with the presenting problem and with the family process, an assessment guide that considers both should be adopted.

Dimensions of the Family

Usually the presenting problem is the major issue identified by the family searching for help. Family members rarely understand objectively the family process and the practitioner must analyze it carefully. Process includes the whole fabric of family life, its emotional texture, the nuances of interactional patterns, and the preferred interactional styles of all family members. When attempting a comprehensive assessment, a useful strategy is to follow the five dimensions of the family outlined that Howells (1975) outlined. Although Howells applied the word *dimensions* to the assessment of families, the term *resources* would be equally accurate. The suggested dimensions are listed as follows:

1. Dimensions of individuals in the family.
2. Dimensions of internal family communication.
3. Dimensions of external family communication.
4. Dimensions of family psychological properties.
5. Dimensions of family physical circumstances.

The composition of the family influences the total experience of other members. Each family member interacts individually and collectively with other members, thereby generating the dimensions of internal family communication. Even though the composition of the family may change as members enter or leave, prevailing interactional characteristics tend to be maintained. Prevailing family characteristics of optimism, pessimism, openness, or secretiveness affect all the internal relationships.

As interacting groups, families have borders or boundaries within which internal communication takes place and across which external communication is exchanged with larger institutions in society. Although families possess many communicational and interpersonal features typical of all small groups, they establish a configuration of dimensions unique to each family.

Family boundaries are more or less permeable so that individual members and the family as a group can react to and interact with suprasystems, such as schools, churches, and government. These interactions and reactions constitute the dimensions of external family communication, and it is the permeability of family boundaries that determines the relative openness of each family to outside input. In addition to the foregoing dimensions, families exist in a physical environment that includes a place of residence in a neighborhood and the material circumstances of the family. All five dimensions of the family have a historical past, a shared present, and an undiscovered future. By endorsing the consideration of family dimensions in the three time frames, a clinician should be able to make a comprehensive assessment of family strengths and weaknesses, and mobilize the family to help resolve the presenting problem in an adaptive way.

The family dimensions have a bearing on how families behave during the crisis of physical illness, especially when there is little hope of recovery. When feelings between family members are warm and caring, and one member is gravely ill, the sense of impending loss will be great. The very ill person may wish to conceal the extent of suffering in order to protect loved ones and to be as undemanding as possible. When family members have angry feelings that preceded illness, the ill person may make excessive demands of those who are well. They, in turn, are likely to perform necessary services in a detached or hostile manner. Family members who have never communicated effectively will find that serious illness multiplies these difficulties. Whatever the antecedent circumstances, chronic or terminal illness places stress on all dimensions of family life. Among the factors influencing disequilibrium are the timing of the illness in the family life cycle, the receptiveness of the family to outside help, and the identity of the afflicted member.

Learning that one member is stricken with cancer is a crisis for the most functional of families. In the period following diagnosis, the family becomes joined with the ill member in a common struggle and should be regarded as a single, suffering unit (Giacquinta, 1977). The imminence of crisis begins when the disease is suspected and arrives with the diagnosis; stress within the family increases as treatment and the side effects of antineoplastic therapy begin. Every family member is fearful of what lies ahead and questions his or her ability to endure the future. The patient fears pain, death, and losing control. Family members fear being witnesses or participants in the ordeal. Life may never again be as it was before, for family members must meet formidable challenges with a member facing a disease with a questionable prognosis. One challenge is the necessity of adapting to the illness and its associated symptoms. Another is the challenge of adjusting to the altered conditions of everyday life. The diagnosis of a chronic or terminal illness will test to the utmost whatever emotional and behavioral resources the family has developed over time.

To illustrate the usefulness of family dimensions as a basis for crisis assessment and intervention, two clinical examples are presented, one analyzing family dimensions in psychiatric disorder and the other analyzing family dimensions in physical disability. In both clinical examples, marginality of family resources is a complicating factor. Figure 10–1 shows the tools of family dimensions.

•CLINICAL EXAMPLE:
FAMILY DIMENSIONS IN A PSYCHIATRIC DISORDER

The DeLuca family was of Italian derivation, although all members were born in the United States. The nuclear family consisted of the mother, the father, and two children; there were no extended family members living within a radius of one hundred miles. The present problem brought to a child guidance center was that Mark had school phobia and encopresis. The six-year-old son had been absent from school forty-five out of the last sixty days.

Individual Dimensions. Tony DeLuca, the husband and father, was a car salesperson whose business was in a prolonged period of economic decline. A hardworking man, he was committed to traditional role enactment in his family and had difficulty reducing his hopes of providing well for his wife and children. Reluctant to talk about his concerns, he had become aloof and morose during the last year. Marie DeLuca, the wife and mother, had been looking forward eagerly to returning to work as a secretary as soon as both her children were in school. Working had always been a source of contention between Tony and Marie, but Tony reluctantly withdrew his obligations when his wife pointed out that the family could certainly use her supplementary salary for a while. Angela DeLuca, the twelve-year-old daughter in the family, at first had no complaints about her mother working, but within a few weeks she became disillusioned. Her freedom was severely curtailed when she found herself responsible for her brother every afternoon until mother came home from work.

Dimensions of Internal Communication. Angela resented having to sacrifice her free time and was bitterly disappointed because she had anticipated fewer restrictions as a result of her mother

	Antecedent past	Here and now	Anticipated future
Dimensions or Characteristics of Individual Members			
1. What members comprise the nuclear family?			
2. What members comprise the families of origin?			
3. Which member is the identified patient or patients?			
4. What signs of equilibrium or disequilibrium are apparent in the indentified patient?			
5. What signs of equilibrium or disequilibrium are apparent in other members?			
6. What signs of equilibrium or disequilibrium are apparent in the family system?			
Dimensions or Characteristics of Internal Family Communicaton			
1. How does each family member communicate and interact with other members of the nuclear family?			
2. How does each family member communicate and interact with members of the families of origin?			
3. How are decisions made in the family?			
4. How is conflict handled in the family?			
5. Who is the socioemotional leader in the family?			
6. Is leadership invested in both parents, one parent, or neither parent?			
7. Are family alliances based on natural distinctions of age, gender, and generational roles?			

FIGURE 10–1 Assessment of Family Dimensions or Characteristics. *Source:* Adapted from Howells (1975).

	Antecedent past	Here and now	Anticipated future
Socioeconomic Dimensions or Characteristics of the Family			
1. Are family and socio-economic resources sufficient for basic needs?			
2. Is there harmony between material resources and family expectations?			
3. Are the hopes and expectations of family members realistic?			
4. Are the hopes and expectations of the family members unrealistic?			
5. Are conditions present that are likely to promote class advancement?			
6. Are conditions present that are apt to promote class slippage?			
7. Are external socioeconomic resources available to the family?			
8. Are external socioeconomic resources acceptable to the family?			
9. What are the prevailing communication patterns in the family? Specific? Consistent? Ambiguous? Tangential? Contradictory? Placating? Blaming? Confusing?			
Dimensions or Characteristics of External Family Communication			
1. Are family boundaries open or closed to external influence?			
2. Is the family integrated into the social mainstream?			

FIGURE 10–1 *Continued*

	Antecedent past	Here and now	Anticipated future
3. Is the family isolated from the social mainstream?			
4. How does the family relate to larger systems, such as school, church, or community?			
5. How do individual family members relate to external systems?			
Psychological Dimensions or Characteristics of the Family			
1. Whose needs are being met in the family?			
2. Whose needs are being ignored in the family?			
3. Where is the locus of power in the family?			
4. Who is the task leader in the family?			

FIGURE 10–1 *Continued*

working. Afraid to tell her parents about her feelings, Angela became impatient and dictatorial with her brother, Mark. All the changes in his close-knit family puzzled Mark and he disliked most of them. He reacted behaviorally like the rest of his family, saying little but developing somatic complaints that enabled him to stay home from school most of the time. When his mother insisted that he attend school, Mark would soil himself in the classroom so that his mother would have to leave the office and bring Mark home for a change of clothing. Knowing that she would probably be called to school anyway, Marie became more and more hesitant about insisting that Mark attend. This meant that when Mark complained at breakfast of feeling ill, his mother did not go into the office, but stayed at home with him. Angela was then released from taking care of Mark, and could spend more time with her friends. Tony was worried about Mark and always felt better when Marie stayed at home with the boy. Even though Marie was only paid when she worked, her husband felt that his wife really belonged at home and in being with Mark she was merely accepting her proper place in the family.

Dimensions of External Communication. When she was unable to participate in peer group activities, Angela felt isolated. Many mothers of her classmates worked outside the home, and Angela noted that these girls seemed to have more freedom than she was allowed. She could not understand why her little brother was giving everybody so much trouble. Mark had enjoyed school until his mother went to work, but now he saw her job as a threat to his security. He hated the way Angela treated him, and honestly felt too sick to go to school. Even though Mark's "accidents" annoyed his teacher and the other children teased him, Mark preferred this embarrassment to staying in school all the time. His erratic attendance caused Mark's teacher to warn the parents that the boy was not making satisfactory progress. No one in the family informed the teacher that Mark's altered behavior coincided with his mother's return to work outside the home. The family did not discuss Tony's business worries with outsiders, nor had the parents told Angela that her mother's job was financially important. The office manager where Marie worked was impatient about her unreliability. Since the office manager was unaware of the family's financial problems and of Mark's school phobia, she told Marie that her job was in jeopardy unless things changed. Marie was an intelligent, competent secretary, but her boss was under the impression that the job meant very little to Marie and therefore she considered Marie irresponsible.

Dimensions of Psychological Properties. Mark's symptomatology accomplished several purposes. For Mark and Angela, the school phobia offered many rewards, whereas the events simultaneously rewarded and deprived their father. Only Marie felt completely trapped by the situation. By means of the school phobia, Angela regained her after-school leisure and Mark was able to regress to age-inappropriate dependence on his beloved mother. Their father was reinstated in his cherished role of family provider, even though Marie's salary was sacrificed. Marie was the person most exploited by her son's somatic complaints and his inability to attend school regularly. She was angry with Mark and resented her family obligations, but felt guilty about her anger and resentment. Her guilt was relieved when the family physician confirmed her suspicion that Mark's complaints had no medical basis, but were being used to keep her at home with him. Mark's father found it hard to believe that his bright little boy would go to such lengths to stay home from school and thought the child must be ill. It was inconceivable to the father that Mark would soil himself in school just to return to his mother, even though father secretly felt better when Marie was not working at the office.

Dimensions of Physical Circumstances. Although Tony had not disclosed this fact to Marie, his business was so poor that he had missed several mortgage payments on their home. Marie surmised that Tony was under pressure, but she had no idea of the extent. Tony was too proud to admit his concerns to Marie, but he was aware that her salary was necessary to keep the family solvent. With Mark at home so much, Marie's financial contribution diminished and sometimes Tony felt desperate. If his brothers or father had lived closer, Tony might have confided in them. Most of the time, though, he was glad that there were no relatives around to witness the family's predicament.

Critical Guidelines

Although Mark's school phobia was the presenting complaint, most of the problems of the DeLuca family lay within the dimensions of internal communication. The parents never shared their feelings or resolved their discrepant perceptions of family obligations. Even though Marie DeLuca eagerly welcomed a chance to work outside the home, her employment threatened her husband's self-image. Financial worries were very real for the family, but both parents avoided the subject. In their well-intentioned zeal to protect their children, the parents had not told Angela or Mark about the importance of their mother's job. Extra duties were imposed on Angela without soliciting her understanding or rewarding her cooperation. In many ways she was as puzzled as her little brother. Since she could not engage in reprisals against her parents, she was as unpleasant as possible in her dealings with Mark.

Mark's school phobia produced a family crisis that brought the boy and his mother to a child guidance clinic. A family dimensional assessment was used to clarify the problem, which was actually one of deficient internal and external communication. It was not only Mark, but all the other family members who were using primitive, nonverbal communication techniques. Several meetings were arranged so that parents and children could discuss the family's temporary financial problems. Poor communication was due to the father's pride and to the overprotectiveness of both parents. A short-term goal was set to improve verbal communication. In one family meeting, Mark indicated that a boy in his class had become very unhappy when his parents were recently divorced. Both of the divorcing parents had worked outside the home, and Mark connected the two facts. When the boy was placed into his father's custody, Mark leaped to the conclusion that working mothers did not keep their little boys. The family communication avoidance patterns prevented Mark from obtaining the reassurance he needed.

After meeting with all family members, the counselor met with the husband and wife. In these meetings, the focus was less on the family crisis that Mark's school phobia (presenting complaint) had created than on poor communication (family process). The parents were advised to arrange with school personnel that Mark would arrive late on the days he complained of feeling ill, but that he would not spend the whole day at home with his mother. When Mark had an accident at school, his mother would bring a change of clothing, but she would not take Mark home with her. Mark's teacher and Marie's boss were to be told of the plan and their cooperation was sought. Her parents were to give Angela recognition for taking good care of Mark in the form of free time during weekends and the parents expressing their appreciation.

With the immediate problem eased, the parents became willing to admit their own disagreement. The counselor pointed out that reticence between the couple was contributing to the children's dysfunctional, imitative behavior. Fear of abandonment was the cause of Mark's behavior, and inadequate communication among family members had nourished this fear. Tony's pride and his traditional views of family role enactment were interpreted as functional, except when he resorted to controlling tactics that made Marie feel like one of the children.

Resolving Mark's school phobia was successful as a result of the meetings, and the dimensions of internal and external family communication improved. No characterological changes were produced in either Tony or Marie, but both proved capable of some insight. Moreover, a state of trustfulness was established between the family and a professional counselor as a result of Mark's improvement. Subsequent issues in the family would find them more receptive to adaptive problem solving.

REACHING VULNERABLE POPULATIONS

Many bereaved persons do not consider themselves in need of counseling and do not seek professional help after the death of a child or a spouse. Although friends and neighbors help to relieve anxiety and grief, there is a wide difference between social support and emotional support. Sable (1989) found two fears that persons who suffered the recent loss of a spouse shared: fear of being alone and fear of strange situations. Sable attributed such fears to anxiety about attachment, not only attachment to the deceased, but attachment to other significant figures. Women expressing these fears should not be regarded as childish or overly dependent when they cling to others or become afraid of being alone. These responses can be expected in bereavement and people trying to comfort the bereaved need to understand this. In addition, the bereaved individuals can be assured that their reactions are typical rather than pathological.

Germain (1991) conceptualized a helping continuum in which diverse programs, formal and informal, can be made available to hard-to-reach families. Such programs include family networks, self-help groups, informational groups, support groups, and community groups, as well as health professionals. Interest in connecting formal and informal sources of assistance grew in the 1970's and 1980's. Gottlieb (1981) described "natural caregivers" in the community; McLennan and Greenwood (1987) included among natural caregivers: police, teachers, clergy, lawyers, and family physicians. They also proposed structured programs to educate natural caregivers so as to respond therapeutically to troubled persons they encounter through their work roles.

Many bereaved persons reject the well-meant consolation that friends and family offer. Some of the bereaved hesitate to engage in individual counseling, but they are willing to accept group intervention. In many localities, reliance on self-help and/or support groups has increased as people have become aware of the value of sharing grief with others who have endured similar experiences. In Oregon, Masterman and Reams (1988) advocated the WICS model (Widowed Information and Consultation Services), composed of groups offering support, grief education, individual counseling, and advice on settling an estate. Separate groups were organized for persons widowed at younger ages, whose concerns centered on being single parents and helping children adjust to loss.

In families where a parent has died, children feel many emotions beyond grief. They are angry at the disruption in their lives and are fearful of their own death or the death of the surviving parent. A wish to join the deceased parent may be reflected in suicide ideation, which is expressed as separation anxiety or in reckless, death-defying actions (Masterman & Reams, 1988).

•CLINICAL EXAMPLE:
FAMILY DIMENSIONS IN PHYSICAL DISABILITY

The Goodmans owned and operated a "mom and pop" grocery store in a midwestern town. Though small, the store was prosperous enough to support Dora, Ben, and their five children. The grocery store was open for business fourteen hours a day, six days a week. The hours demanded a great deal of Ben and Dora's time, but they liked working together and were accustomed to hard work. The family had lived above the store for years. Dora would steal a few hours from the business to fix meals and take care of the home. Ben was a diabetic who required a special diet, which Dora carefully prepared.

Individual Dimensions. Ben and Dora were in their late forties. The children were Jim, Dave, Sara, George, and Benjie, whose ages ranged from ten to eighteen years. Jim was a student at a community college, Dave and Sara were in high school, George attended junior high school, and Benjie was in elementary school. The children were bright and attractive. When the children were younger, they enjoyed spending time in the store, waiting on customers and putting stock away. In the evenings they would do their homework upstairs while Dora and Ben worked in the store. Some years earlier, when Ben was forty, a large crate had fallen on his foot, crushing it severely. Because of his diabetes and because he returned to work too soon, an infection set in, and Ben's leg was amputated just below the knee.

During Ben's convalescence, the family mobilized to keep the store open. The three older children got up early to open the store, and arranged shifts after school to help Dora in the afternoons and evenings. The emergency period lasted six months, after which Ben returned to work in the store.

Dimensions of Internal Communication. The disengagement of the children from the business was so gradual that, for a time, Dora and Ben were not aware of the change. At first they were only conscious of being more tired at night; then Ben began to complain of his throbbing stump. Because the Goodman children were handsome and popular, they were much in demand. School activities became all-engrossing for the older three, and the store seemed dull by comparison. Before long Dora and Ben were getting little help, except from Benjie, who was willing to help out now and then. Ben, who had to endure the discomfort of a prosthesis, alternated between anger and bitterness. He had always been the decision maker in the family, proud of being bigger and stronger than his sons. Dora was the family placater, pleading the case for Ben when he was too hard on the children and making excuses for them when he was angry.

Dimensions of External Communication. Ben was angry most of the time. He raged at Dora when none of the children came into the store to help, although he refused to admit to anyone that he could not do as much as he used to. When Dora suggested hiring outside help for the store, Ben angrily refused. After one of Ben's outbursts, Dora would ask the children at dinner to come into the store to help the next day. This request always caused an argument among the three older children about who was busiest and who should help. The argument never failed to enrage Ben, who would shout that he did not need anyone, whereupon Dora would explain that the store was not so busy right now and maybe she and Ben could manage on their own.

Ben had little faith in physicians or outsiders. He followed his diabetic diet that Dora prepared and he depended on her to take care of his leg. In time, however, even her faithful ministrations proved insufficient. The flesh of the stump broke down, becoming dark and odoriferous. Only then did Ben agree to see a physician. He was hospitalized for several weeks and, for a time, physicians contemplated amputating more of his leg.

Dimensions of Psychological Properties. Things continued to go badly within the family. The only discernible change was that Ben berated the children less, perhaps because he did not have the energy. He remained angry, but turned surly and taciturn. Dora's agitation increased as she moved between her busy, popular children and her ill, bitter husband. Attending to Ben's bad leg was now a nightly ritual of bathing, massaging, and dressing the stump. She suggested shortening their business hours, but this set Ben off on a tirade against his lazy children and against Dora for spoiling them.

After their parents retired for the night, the older children would vent their guilty feelings on one another and on the "damn" store, which they were tired of hearing about. The two youngest boys would huddle near the television set, feeling miserable and resolving inwardly never to be as selfish as their older brothers and sister.

Dimensions of Physical Circumstances. Dora and Ben had begun their married life with few financial resources and had been quite poor at first. Through the years, their hard work in the store had made the family prosperous. The contributions of the three older children, who had worked willingly beside their parents, had benefited the business. Now, however, the older children were involved in their appropriate tasks of individuation and separation from the family. The youngest boys still helped their parents, but their efforts were not enough to compensate for Ben's disability and Dora's waning energy.

Even though the family had no financial worries, Ben continued to behave as if the family was very poor. To Ben, the store was a symbol of his effectiveness as a provider and decision maker. For him, reducing the work week meant the erosion of his manhood. Even though he could afford to hire outside help, Ben wanted his children to work beside him on a daily basis. He regarded their failure to do this as a personal betrayal. Seeing his children mature made Ben feel old and abandoned. Because he had been a generous father, he felt he had earned the right to lean on his children. He also believed they should help him without being asked. The children, engrossed in their own lives, resented the excessive demands of the business and their father's unwillingness to hire a paid worker, which he could easily afford. They also resented Ben's demands on Dora and were aware of Dora's fatigue. As a result of their conflicted feelings, the older children, in particular, manipulated in order to escape working in the store. Observing the turmoil, a visiting nurse referred the family to a mental health facility.

Critical Guidelines

Despite the problems in the family, strong bonds of affection existed. Poor communication patterns, existing among all the members, impaired the family function. Ben wanted and needed help, but he never discussed his needs rationally. Dora, who could not tolerate recriminations or quarrels, passively accepted the behavior of her husband and children. The parents had not clearly requested the children to work in the store for a specific number of hours, nor had they allocated working hours equitably so that no one was seriously inconvenienced. It was apparent that, as the children matured and the parents aged, old rules were outgrown but new rules were never formulated.

Because of the obvious strengths in this family, a crisis approach proved effective. Ben needed to realize that it was no longer necessary to work himself and Dora into exhaustion. The first goal in the family meetings was to reduce the business hours to some extent. Both parents and all the children were involved in these negotiations. It was hard for Ben to agree to this reduction, but eventually he became willing to participate. Ben's reward for reducing store hours was a written commitment from the three older children that each would work eight hours a week in the store. The younger boys agreed to each work four hours a week. In addition, a paid helper would be employed on Saturdays, so that all the children would be free on weekends.

Since schedule conflicts were bound to arise, the family was given the task of solving a simulated problem. The role play resulted in the following procedures:

- When a child could not work a designated time in the store, that child was responsible for arranging a substitute. Whenever a sibling substituted, the time given was a debt that must be repaid as soon as possible.
- The right of each family member to engage in outside activities was acknowledged, and individual priorities deserved respect. However, the hours promised to Ben constituted a primary obligation that could not be avoided or changed without preliminary discussion. Dora was not to be called upon to work extra hours in the store to make up for the absence of a son or daughter. When dissatisfied with the children, Ben was to deal directly with them, and not discharge his resentment on Dora.

The brief family counseling sessions focused on the changing needs of every family member. Communication patterns were encouraged in which messages were clearly transmitted and rules were clearly stated. Change was presented as a universal process, which could be handled constructively if communication lines were open and direct. Many positive feelings existed in this family, but they were rarely expressed. As a result, negativism and frustration characterized most family interactions. Members were encouraged to demonstrate the pride and affection they felt for each other, and to be less self-centered and withholding.

WORKING WITH MARGINAL FAMILIES

Because their resources are already stretched, marginal families are predisposed to crisis when change in the form of illness, accident, or disability occurs. In addition, programs designed to augment their meager resources already underserve disadvantaged families. The greatest need is for programs capable of early responses to troubled families and for counselors sensitive to family values and lifestyles (Paster, 1986).

Hollister and Rae-Grant (1972) advised counselors to use "principles of effective parsimony," which state that whatever care is offered should cause the least disturbance in a recipient's life. The same source also suggests that help should be provided at various community locales, such as home, school, or work. Most marginal families are committed to appropriate role enactment. Therefore, available programs should not be unduly intrusive or extensive, in terms of goals acceptable to the family. This means that crisis intervention may be the most effective, least expensive modality in meeting the needs of disadvantaged families.

The onset of serious illness or disability increases stress in the family, regardless of the identity of the patient. When the parent of young children is afflicted, the healthy spouse wonders how to manage dual roles and responsibilities. Added burdens that the well parent assumes reduces energy once available for child-parent interactions. Children in the home witness frightening changes in both parents. As the ill parent's condition worsens, the well parent becomes preoccupied with imminent loss. Often this makes children feel that both parents have abandoned them. Investment in parenting activities declines, at least temporarily. The well parent has less ability to be emotionally responsive toward the children, to set limits, and to provide reassurance.

A child who is seriously ill or disabled also disrupts lifestyle patterns of the family, but in different ways. Marginal families have few discretionary resources, even in ordinary situations. For many of them, lack of social support, lack of transportation, and lack of money add to their distress (Agosta et al., 1987). When a family wants more involvement in the care of their child, it often feels that busy professionals have excluded it. Unless the family has some background in the health care profession, terminology and invasive procedures are mystifying and intimidating (Green & Wilson, 1989). Professionals may give double messages, that the family should be involved, but not too much.

Although one family member actually suffers the illness or disability, the entire family is affected. Needs change as the illness progresses; programs must offer support for family members that "match" the current demands of the situation. Distinctions are drawn between informational support, emotional support, and practical support. It is futile to offer one kind of support when another is more needed. All three kinds of support are indicated at different points and to different degrees.

Parents have described to investigators the type of relationship they would like to have with the health care professionals who are caring for a family member. They strongly objected to interactions in which the health care professional acted as an all-knowing expert, and denigrated the family's contributions. Above all, the parents wanted to know that their emotional investment and day-to-day contributions were recognized. Based on research, Kalyanpur and Rao (1991) formulated two categories of parent-professional relationships. The first category was more traditional, with the professional obviously in charge of transactions. This relationship was considered to be *unempowering* or belittling of the family. The second category was collaborative, supportive, and participatory. This relationship was considered *empowering* or enhancing of the family's self-esteem.

Three facets of professional behavior characterize unempowering relationships: (1) disrespect, (2) emphasis on family deficits, and (3) intolerance of differences in family life style. Empowering relationships were established by professionals who engaged in two specific activities: (1) providing emotional support to families, and (2) providing specific services. Emotional support took the form of informing families of their rights and translating professional jargon into everyday language. Professionals performed no tasks *for* the families, but shared in the planning and resolution of problems they faced.

In offering specific services, consideration was given to the expressed needs of the families. For example, mothers were asked to state the most convenient times for clinic appointments and for home visitation. Based on family needs, no appointments were made for the days when welfare checks arrived and groceries were purchased. If school children were in the home, visits were never made until late morning, when the rush had subsided. When family needs were overlooked, the mother of an educationally handicapped child described her dilemma as follows (Kalyanpur & Rao, 1991):

> The other woman (the home visitor) came in at 10 in the morning when I have to give John a bath, make his lunch, put on his clothes for him, put his Pampers in. They don't understand that. She comes in at 10 a.m. and then wants me to talk to her. How can I? My son John has to be ready for school. And then because I don't have time to talk to her, she goes and says I am not cooperating (p. 526).

Sometimes the exchanges between professionals and marginal families become a power struggle in which the interests of the patient are forgotten. Empowerment is not a list of strategies that help professionals provide care to needy families. As Kalyanpur and Rao (1991) describe, empowerment of families requires shared knowledge, mutual respect, and acceptance of family values. Crisis theory, with its insistence on time limits, problem solving, and collaboration between client and counselor, can be very effective for marginal families where the potential for crisis is ever present.

One in every twenty-seven children under eighteen years of age will lose a parent to death. For children suffering parental loss, outside intervention in the form of age-related group intervention has been found to facilitate adaptive grieving. Appropriate locations for these groups include schools, churches, hospitals, mental health centers, and other community settings. Evidence has accumulated that support groups for children are very effective before and after the loss of an ill parent (Masterman & Reams, 1988). Often, a referral to a support group can make the difference between adaptive grief reactions and prolonged depression (Sable, 1989).

SUMMARY

Even though crisis counseling is short term and addresses limited goals, it is useful in helping marginal families facing a crisis of illness or loss. Marginal families strive for adequate role enactment, but become dysfunctional when demands outweigh the family's physical and psychological resources. These are vulnerable families, whose urgent needs often go unrecognized. Unlike disorganized families, where role enactment is inappropriate, marginal families rarely come to the attention of organized sources of help. Whenever the total resources of a family are limited and the demands on the family become excessive, the result is disequilibrium and family crisis.

When a family member falls ill, that person is expected to fulfill the obligations and exemptions that are considered part of being sick. The attributes of sick role enactment, as Parsons conceptualized, have been widely accepted despite some inconsistencies. Individuals who suffer psychiatric disorders enact the sick role differently from persons suffering physical disorders. Those physical disorders that are acute and curable adhere most closely to the Parsonsian model. When a physical disorder is chronic or terminal, there are substantial departures from the Parsons's formulation.

There are clinical obstacles in crisis work with families. The practitioner engaged in crisis work must decide whether to confine intervention to the presenting problem or to expand intervention to include modification of family process. Even when family process is not given direct attention through interventions, it is part of family assessment in crisis work. In working with most families, a middle-of-the-road approach is advisable. Short-term goals can be constructed that respond to the immediate problem, after which the family may be receptive to more extensive measures.

Comprehensive assessment is required for families in crisis, even when interventions are time limited. Applying the paradigm of family dimensions is an excellent way of organizing family assessment data.

Even under the best circumstances, marginal families constitute a vulnerable population. Group programs offered in the community may be more acceptable to these families than programs that imply a deficiency or disability. Another factor important to marginal families is the feeling that health care professionals respect them. The concept of empowerment has been applied to tactics used by caring professionals to acknowledge and include the contributions families have made on behalf of sick or disabled family members.

This chapter contains two comprehensive clinical examples illustrating the use of the family dimensions assessment tool. One example depicted the psychiatric disturbance in the form of school phobia; the second example described the impact of chronic illness and disability on a family that had previously functioned well.

REFERENCES

Agosta, J., M. O'Neal, and J. Toubbeh (eds.). *A Path to Peace of Mind: Providing Exemplary Services to Navajo Children with Developmental Disabilities.* Window Rock, Arizona: Save the Children Federation, 1987.

Bjornsten, O.J. and T.J. Stewart. "Marital Status & Health" (ed) *New Clinical Concepts in Marital Therapy* Washington, DC American Psychiatric Association 1985.

Caplan, G. *Support Systems and Community Mental Health.* New York: Behavioral Publications, 1974.

Collings, G. "Families Deal with Chronic Illness." *The New York Times* October 12, 1981, C1.

Fleck, S. "The Family and Psychiatry." In *Comprehensive Textbook of Psychiatry,* 3rd. ed., edited by H.I. Kaplan, A. Freedman, and B.J. Sadock. Baltimore: Williams & Wilkins, 1980.

Friedman, M.M. *Family Nursing: Theory and Assessment.* New York: Appleton-Century-Crofts, 1981.

Germain, C. *Human Behavior in the Social Environment.* New York: Columbia University Press, 1991.

Giacquinta, B. "Helping Families Face the Crisis of Cancer." *American Journal of Nursing* 77(1977): 1585–1588.

Gottlieb, B.H. *Social Networks and Social Support.* Beverly Hills, California: Sage Publications, 1981.

Green, C., and B. Wilson. *The Struggle for Black Empowerment in New York City: Beyond the Politics of Pigmentation.* New York: Praeger, 1989.

Hollister, W., and Q. Rae-Grant. "Effective Parsimony: Principles of Effective Parsimony." *Canadian Mental Health* 20(1972): 1.

Howells, J.G. *Principles of Family Psychiatry.* New York: Brunner/Mazel, 1975.

Kalyanpur, M., and S.S. Rao. "Empowering Low Income Black Families of Handicapped Children." *American Journal of Orthopsychiatry* 61(1991): 523–532.

Masterman, S.H., and R. Reams. "Support Groups for Bereaved Preschool and School-Age Children." *American Journal of Orthopsychiatry* 58(1988): 562–570.

McLennan, J., and J. Greenwood. "Informal Counseling in the Community: A Study of Members of Five Natural Helping Occupations." *Australian Social Work* 40(1987): 17–22.

Minuchin, S. *Families and Family Therapy.* Cambridge, Massachusetts: Harvard University Press, 1974.

Minuchin, S., B. Montalvo, B. Guerney, B. Rosman, and F. Shumer. *Families of the Slums.* New York: Basic Books, 1967.

Parsons, T. *The Social System.* New York: Free Press, 1951.

Paster, V.S. "A Social Action Model of Intervention for Difficult to Reach Populations." *American Journal of Orthopsychiatry* 56(1986): 625–629.

Sable, P. "Attachment, Anxiety, and the Loss of a Husband." *American Journal of Orthopsychiatry* 59(1989): 550–556.

11

Disorganized Families in Crisis
Child Abuse

Children begin by loving their parents; as they grow older they judge them; sometimes they forgive them.

Oscar Wilde

Many functional families endorse physical punishment as a necessary component of childrearing, and there is a popular viewpoint that physical expressions of disapproval from parent to child are sometimes quite acceptable. Certain localities permit school personnel to function in loco parentis and to impose physical punishment for misbehavior. Only in extreme situations does society consider the punishment of children by parents or by individuals with delegated authority to be illegal or even reprehensible.

Socially defined *aggression* consists of behavior that results in personal injury or property destruction, if an external evaluator rather than the perpetrator has judged the situation. It may be stated that inflicting physical pain on children is widely condoned as a socializing influence, and that criticism arises only when actions against the child produce obvious damage or exceed community norms. Parents are rarely criticized for physically punishing children, but only for using extraordinary disciplinary measures that cause bruises, scars, fractures, or other adverse consequences.

Child abuse, physical or sexual, is not a new or modern phenomenon. Extensive accounts of childrearing have described the harsh treatment of children and traced chronological patterns of infanticide, abandonment, intrusiveness, and socialization as prevailing modes of parental behavior over the centuries (deMause, 1974). A society to protect animals from cruelty preceded the American Society for the Protection of Children, which was established in 1847 after a battered, starving child was discovered chained to a bed, and the abusers could only be charged under statutes forbidding cruelty to animals.

Definitions of *child abuse* change from one decade to another and from one culture to another. For centuries, harsh treatment of children was justified on religious and economic grounds. Patriarchal family systems enforced control measures that relied upon severe physical punishment. Mutilation in the form of castration, clitoridectomy, and scarring are still practiced in some societies. These are ritualized rather than punitive practices, but they constitute abuse in the broad sense of the term. Children have been mistreated in the workplace throughout the world. They have been enslaved, recruited as forced laborers, abandoned to starvation, sold into sexual bondage, and deliberately killed.

Child neglect and abuse has been acknowledged as social problems in the United States only in recent years. Henry Kempe (1961) introduced the term *battered children syndrome* and chaired a symposium on the issue at the American Academy of Pediatrics. This well-attended meeting became the impetus for wide public interest in child abuse as a national problem.

The true incidence of child neglect and abuse is greatly underestimated because there is undoubted disparity between incidence rates and reported cases. Statistics indicate that about three million children are abused every year. Reports on the sexual abuse of children indicate that one-third to two-fifths of such incidents involve other family members, and one of every twelve involves a father or step-father (Kissel, 1986).

Child neglect and abuse ranges from indifference to a child's physical needs for food, clothing, and shelter, to physical mistreatment resulting in severe injury and sometimes death. Culp et al. (1991, p. 116) defined *physical abuse* as "any physical injury inflicted on a child other than by accidental means." They defined *neglect* as "failure to provide the proper or necessary support, education required by law, medical, surgical, or any other care necessary for the child's well being."

Mandated reporting of child neglect and abuse is required by all 50 states. Certain professionals, such as medical and nursing personnel, social workers, teachers, and counselors, must not only report any case of abuse, but they also must report any suspicion of abuse. In addition to mandated reporting, most states offer immunity from civil and criminal action to any person reporting in good faith, even if the report proves to be erroneous. Some states provide possible civil penalties against those who fail to report child neglect or abuse. Although officialdom is committed to mandated reporting, there is evidence of substantial underreporting. In their study, Hampton and Newberger (1985) disclosed bias in the reporting of child abuse. In a national sample they found that hospitals underreported white families to child protective agencies. Ninety-one percent of Hispanic and 74 percent of black families were reported, compared to

61 percent of white families. Aber (1981) found that family history of substance abuse and police involvement influenced court decisions to remove children.

ABUSE TARGETS

Frequently, a single child in a family is the target for especially severe abuse. Unwanted infants may be targets because they do not fulfill the parent's fantasy of what a child should be like. An irritable, demanding infant frustrates parents, who then take their feelings out on the child. Any child who is different or special may be at risk, especially if the child's needs deplete family resources of energy and time.

Parental mistreatment of children may occur at any age; in confirmed reports, about 32 percent of these children are under five years of age. Twenty-seven percent are between five and nine years old, 27 percent are between ten and fourteen years old, and 14 percent are between fourteen and eighteen years old. The children who receive the most severe injuries are among the younger groups (Fontana, 1985). A relatively low incidence of adolescent mistreatment may be attributed to such behaviors as running away, teenage pregnancy, delinquency, and suicide, any of which the teenagers may see as escape mechanisms.

Occasionally, the abused child manifests a strong sense of loyalty and affection for the parent, and there are several explanations for this. Some abusing parents can be kind and caring at times, and the child searches repeatedly for this aspect of the parent. On the other hand, the abused child may have learned how to "manage" the parent. To protect against recurrence of abuse or neglect, the child takes a protective role toward the parent.

Family isolation and other social and environmental factors may be present that are inherently undesirable, but these may be the result rather than the cause of abuse. Ideally, an intervention plan should be based on identifying the causes of the abuse, the degree and extent of the abuser's dysfunction, and most importantly, the risk to any children of ongoing mistreatment if they are permitted to remain in the home.

Based on information regarding the abuser, the abused child, and the home, several options are available, all of which involve the efforts of several professionals and paraprofessionals. Usually, a selected counselor who serves as surrogate mother to an abusing mother is chosen. Since many abusers have never experienced a nurturing parenting relationship, the surrogate mother attempts to remedy this deficiency. Through this relationship the abusing mother is given an outlet for her previously unmet needs. Here she can express her anger, fear, and anxiety instead of wreaking them on the child.

Other interventions include reducing demands on the mother to a manageable level. This can be accomplished through partial day care for a young child or housekeeping assistance. Eliminating social and environmental stress as much as possible not only improves a mother's ability to function, but also convinces her that people consider her worthy of help. One young mother at risk for abuse was more motivated to change when the health care team was able to obtain a telephone for her. The phone became a link to the outside world and a lifeline to the counselor who had become her surrogate mother.

Learning about an abuser's early life helps counselors to develop better understanding for the perpetrator. Abusing parents may learn how to parent by being parented themselves, and they may respond readily when their pain and neediness are recognized. This does not mean that abuse should ever be condoned on the basis that "he is mentally disturbed" or "she has had a tough life." If abusers are to be helped, they must want to change and take responsibility for their own acts. It is possible to reject behavior without rejecting the perpetrator.

In child abuse cases, it is discovering and reporting abuse that constitutes the original crisis. Immediate intervention is limited to enlisting an expert team composed of protective workers and health care professionals and paraprofessionals. It is the team that devises and allocates various aspects of the plan for treatment and prevention of abuse. The designated plan is usually long-term and ongoing. Various modalities are used, including home visits, childrearing classes, nurseries and day care facilities, support groups, and twenty-four-hour hot lines. Any prevention and treatment in child abuse programs should contain the following objectives:

- Prevent further abuse and neglect.
- Avoid separating child and parent whenever possible.
- Prevent institutional placement of child if possible.
- Promote and maintain family stability and self-sufficiency.
- Teach parents the developmental levels and capacities of children.
- Interpret and model parental roles and responsibilities.
- Remove child from parents who can not or will not respond positively to intervention.

ABUSERS' TRAITS

Many experts believe that abusing parents are recreating their own upbringing, but Kaufman and Zigler (1987) examined the accuracy of this belief, citing methodological deficiencies in various studies. Although a history of abuse is more common among parents who mistreat their children, other parents with no childhood history of abuse may be abusers. Significantly, many parents who were mistreated as children do not abuse. Hunter and Kilstrom (1979), in a prospective research design, were able to identify forty parents (82 percent of the sample) who broke the intergenerational cycle of abuse. The effects of a history of abuse upon subsequent parenting cannot be separated from other influences such as poverty, stress, and isolation. Mitigating factors in the intergenerational transmission of abuse were the following: (1) the presence of a supportive spouse or partner, (2) less stressful environments and current life events; and (3) a greater awareness of their own history of being abused as children. These nonabusive parents were consciously resolved not to repeat abusive behaviors with their own children.

Many abusing parents have expectations that are far beyond the child's capabilities. For abusing parents, children exist primarily to satisfy parental needs. They tend to project their own problems onto the children and gradually believe that the children are the problem. Rather than trying to solve their problems, they relieve anxious feelings by attacking the children.

Despite tributes to mother love, the perpetrator of child abuse is more often the woman; this may be due to the fact that women are with children for extended periods of time. Usually one parent consistently mistreats the child, but the other parent may contribute by openly accepting and encouraging the behavior, or by silently tolerating it. If the nonabuser is protective or attentive toward the child, envy and resentment may generate greater abuse from the other parent. In some families abuse is directed either at the wife or the children. In other families the spouse and the children are targets of abuse. Sometimes the child is a scapegoat for conflict between the parents. Almost always, the abusing parent has unrealistic demands that the child can not meet. These demands may consist of performance levels or in parental needs for affection and comfort that the child can not and should not be asked to satisfy.

According to Fontana (1985, p. 1820), battering parents are usually "immature, narcissistic, egocentric, and demanding, and show impulsive, aggressive behavior." Isolation, substance abuse, financial problems, mental illness, or teenage parenthood all may play a role in child neglect and abuse. Regardless of specific circumstances, three components are present: (1) a potentially abusive parent, (2) a relatively helpless child, (3) and a sudden or ongoing life crisis.

For many reasons, single parents may be at risk for child abuse or neglect. The mother may transfer her anger at her husband to a son, who then becomes the object of mother's rage. Sometimes a parent's inadequacies or fantasies are projected to a target child. A father may punish a son brutally for imagined signs of weakness or effeminacy that the father fears in himself. A mother may project her own coping style by accusing her four-year-old daughter of being seductive and manipulative. In families where the children have different fathers, the alleged shortcomings of one father may be attributed to his child so that the child is punished for the sins of that father (Gelles, 1989).

COUNSELING ABUSING FAMILIES

Professionals who can control their own emotional responses and realize that helping the child includes helping the parents are more likely to be effective. When all attention is directed to the unacceptable behavior of the parents and no attention is paid to their human needs, the parents become defensive and less open to change. Professionals must avoid emotionality when dealing with abusive parents and should be reminded that the parents are probably replicating the patterns of their own childhood because they have no other way of interacting with their children. In general, abusive parents expect their children to act like adults, and they establish unrealistic standards of behavior for the child. Parents who beat or burn their children frequently recall similar acts their own parents performed and point, with pride, to the efficiency of such methods in teaching children a lesson.

Abusive parents become suspicious and guarded when professionals begin to investigate suspected child abuse. Expressing concern for the parent as well as the child is an intervention that helps reduce defensiveness and elicit the truth. It is productive to acknowledge that parenting is a difficult task, especially when superimposed on holding a job or maintaining a single-parent household. Certain nonthreatening questions may be used advantageously in interviews with parents suspected of child abuse:

- Is there anyone available to help when your child is very demanding?
- When you are disappointed with your child's behavior, how do you feel?
- When your child cries or refuses to obey, what do you do?
- Do the eating, sleeping, or toilet habits of your child upset you?
- What is your first reaction when you become angry with your child?

Pregnancy and childbirth may be natural processes, but parenting is not. Parenting is a behavior that must be learned, either through childhood exposure to good nurturing or through attitudinal changes achieved in later life. Relationships established between abusive parents and concerned professionals can go far toward producing attitudinal and behavioral change if a message of understanding is conveyed. This attitude does not imply acceptance for abusive practices, but rather belief that the abusing parent can alter maladaptive patterns with the help of skilled professionals. Some interventions are more productive than others. Among the unproductive interventions are the following:

Unproductive Interventions with Abusive Parents:
• Criticizing, confronting, and castigating the parents.
• Imposing personal values and standards.
• Expecting immediate changes in the behavior of the parents.
• Identifying either with the abused child or with the abusive parents.

Productive Interventions with Abusive Parents:
• Discuss childrearing and child discipline in general.
• Modifying unrealistic parental standards.
• Cooperating with the parents rather than retaliating.
• Tolerating anger the parents express.
• Modeling and teaching good parenting behavior.
• Consultation to reduce overinvolvement and validate progress.

It is extremely difficult for caregivers to monitor their personal reactions to child abuse or neglect. Identifying with the child and having negative feelings toward the abuser will inhibit establishing a therapeutic alliance. For this reason, it may be inadvisable for the same counselor to work with the abused child and the abusing parent, although a collaborative relationship is essential.

In some communities, interdisciplinary teams have been brought together to help families in which actual or potential abuse has been discerned. One urban prototype for child abuse prevention is organized around a nursery that admits babies and children from homes that may be unsafe for them. The crisis nursery accepts abused children and children who may not have been mistreated, but whose parents verge on losing control.

For other parents who are undergoing stress but are struggling to function, a day care facility for the children is available. Supportive and psychotherapeutic group work is offered to parents whose children are in the crisis nursery or the day care center. Community nurses and social workers make frequent home visits that are an indispensable part of the crisis prevention program. A twenty-four-hour hotline is also available for families being served or needing to be served by the staff.

Whenever possible, families are kept intact, and parents are encouraged to seek help whenever family tensions increase. Caretakers involved in the crisis program retain the right to take families to court and remove children from homes when necessary. At the same time, interdisciplinary team members function as spokespersons and advocates for the parents as well as the children. They coordinate support services, visit homes at night or on weekends, offer referrals for marital counseling and alcohol or drug rehabilitation, and make crucial decisions to remove children from homes or allow them to return. Workers involved in effective child abuse programs move beyond the point of regarding abusing parents as incorrigible. Most abusing parents are neither psychotic, wholly unloving, nor unteachable. As products of dysfunctional family systems, they must be included in preventive programs if permanent foster care or institutionalization of the children is to be avoided (Aber, 1981).

Working with child-abusing parents requires a multifactorial approach. An abusive parent can often be helped by psychodynamic concepts that accept the underlying dependency needs of the abuser and facilitate parental movement through psychosocial developmental stages. Inherent in this approach is building the trust between the parent and the care provider. Psychotherapeutic individual therapy for an abusive parent is a valuable adjunct to the comprehensive social and environmental measures the interdisciplinary teams working collaboratively with the family use.

Group work with abusive parents can be useful, as the support network made available through Parents Anonymous shows. For those parents who are unwilling to affiliate with an organization clearly identified with child abuse, alternative groups are available. Bowers (1986) suggested that groups organized for abusing parents first allow ventilation for members' frustrations and then move into the realities of child development and parenting. Issues need not be restricted to current parenting problems but may include the childhood experiences of the parents in their families of origin, their interpersonal relationships, and their social milieu. Group work with abusive parents should be augmented with interdisciplinary measures that ensure that the children are protected and that the abusive practices do not continue. Frequent contact with community nurses, social workers, pediatricians, and protective agencies is not only therapeutic for parents, but maintains ongoing family surveillance.

Some clinicians, who fear that reporting will impair the therapeutic alliance, perceive the mandate to report any form of child abuse or neglect as a burden. Harper and Irvin (1985) saw the mandate to report as a therapeutic tool that cuts through denial and contributes to the task at hand. It is obvious that being labeled *abusers* pushes parents into greater awareness of reality. The counselor should establish a relationship with the family that combines empathy with consistent limit setting. It is essential that all professionals and paraprofessionals maintain similar attitudes and present a united front. The following precepts in mandated reporting of child mistreatment, adapted from Harper and Irvin (1985), should be followed in clinical dealings with abusing families.

- Counselors and clinicians in possession of data *must* report. Do not collude in the denial of a nonreporting colleague. Consider reporting *with* a colleague who also has data.
- Report *any* child suspected of being at risk, no matter what else is known. There really are no mitigating circumstances when children are being abused or neglected.
- *Inform parents* candidly when a report is made. Tell them that you dislike doing this, but believe it necessary, which conveys your commitment to the child and concern for the parents.
- *Use the clinical team* to consult with, to share data, and to discuss your course of action.
- Attend to any physical damage the child may suffer. *Record the extent of injuries* and *all* physical findings.
- After reporting the problem to a protective agency, follow up to ascertain official decisions.

•CLINICAL EXAMPLE:
A MULTIFACETED APPROACH TO CHILD ABUSE

Mona was a twenty-year-old mother who was raising her two children in a single-parent household. Betsy was an active, energetic three year old; her sister, Daisy, was a placid but responsive six-month-old baby. The two children had different fathers. Daisy was the child of a legal marriage between Mona and Joe, who was a part-time member of the household. Many of Joe's activities were illegal; periodically he had to drop from sight to avoid arrest, and he had already served two prison terms for burglary. Although violent at times and unreliable in contributing financially to the household, Mona had high regards for Joe because he had married her. Mona gave Daisy adequate care, due partly to the baby's pleasant disposition and partly to the fact that Daisy's father, though unreliable, was Mona's husband. To be a married woman in Mona's social circles was a positive social indicator. Betsy, on the other hand, had characteristics that predisposed her to be selected as a target child. Alert and energetic, Betsy was restless and inquisitive. As a baby, she had been a poor sleeper who cried a great deal. Once she started to walk, she tested her mother's patience and the limits of her environment.

Historically, the relationship between Mona and Gus, Betsy's father, had been stormy. Mona remembered Gus as being an uncaring man who seduced her when she was sixteen years old. Their life together included alcohol and drug abuse, and bitter fights followed by brief reconciliations. When Mona was with Gus, she yielded to his insistence that she allow men to pay her for having sexual relations with them, and she walked the streets looking for partners when other assignations were unavailable. When Mona became pregnant with Betsy, Gus left, saying that he was not going to support any kid that might not be his. Mona was convinced that Gus had fathered her child and she saw in Betsy many resemblances to Gus.

Mona's behavior to her daughters reflected her attitude toward their respective fathers. Daisy was fed regularly, hugged, and rocked to sleep occasionally. With Betsy, Mona behaved like another child rather than a mother. She yelled at Betsy constantly, and slapped her often. When Betsy cried, Mona would pinch her arms or legs to make her stop. Mona bought toys for both children, but Betsy's were placed on a high shelf so that the child could only gaze longingly at them. Mona's explanation was that she could not afford two sets of toys, that Betsy was such a terror she would break everything and there would be no toys left for Daisy when she was ready for them.

Once in a while Mona tried to hug Betsy, but the child pulled away. When Mona was depressed or lonely she would turn to Betsy and ask, "You do love your mommy, don't you, honey?" Betsy would giggle nervously or else stare round-eyed and silent at her mother. Mona would then lose her temper and berate and strike her unloving child. When Mona completely lost control, she would drag Betsy across the room and lock her in a closet. Betsy's frightened cries enraged her mother even more. Mona would scream at Betsy not to wake the baby and threaten to throw Betsy off the fire escape if her sister awakened. Eventually, Betsy would cry herself to sleep. More often than not, Mona let the child go without supper and kept her in the closet all night. In the morning, a remorseful Mona would unlock the closet, insist that Betsy eat a big breakfast, and then put the bewildered child in bed in order to make up for spending the night in the closet. Even though Betsy was not particularly sleepy, she learned quickly that it was better to stay in bed, for the alternative was another isolation period in the closet.

Betsy was a typical target child in many respects. Brighter and more active than her sister, she made demands that her mother considered excessive. Moreover, the treatment Mona received from Betsy's father left a residue of anger and hostility that was displaced to Betsy. As a child, Mona received abuse from an alcoholic father and an indifferent mother. She left school in the tenth grade to live with Gus, and her knowledge of child development and child care was rudimentary and distorted. Because Daisy was a calm, cuddly baby, Mona loved her and felt that the child loved her in return. In contrast, her feelings about Betsy were conflicted. Mona insisted on behavior that was inappropriate in terms of Betsy's age and temperament. Mona expected both children to meet her deep needs for affection. In addition, self-control, obedience, and maturity were expected of Betsy. Mona did not understand that she wanted the impossible from her three year old. When the child failed to conform or achieve, Mona interpreted this failure as "badness" and punished Betsy wildly and irrationally. Because Betsy had a vitality that was not easily quelled, Mona saw Betsy as the embodiment of the man who had mistreated her. Since he was beyond her reach, she vented her anger on his child.

Except for a few girlfriends, Mona led an isolated existence. It was a welfare worker visiting the home who first became aware of the bruises and welts on Betsy's small face and body. After the child pointed out the narrow closet as "Betsy's bed room," the worker began a systematic inquiry into Mona's mothering practices. The result was a referral to the children's protective association, to a community health nurse, and to a local mental health center for an evaluation of Mona.

Critical Guidelines

After Mona was evaluated at the mental health clinic and no diagnosable psychiatric disorder found, she was assigned to a psychiatric nurse clinician for help with problems of immaturity, impulse control, and poor self-esteem. The visitor from the children's protection association considered the family to be at risk. Ongoing supervision was advised and a protective worker began to visit the household regularly. The community health nurse used her concern for the health of the children in order to win Mona's trust. Once she was accepted in the home, the nurse began to teach Mona what to expect from her children as they moved from one stage of growth to the next. The welfare worker functioned as case coordinator and arranged several meetings at which all the professionals involved with the family met together.

Discussion at the first meeting dealt with the possibility of removing Betsy and perhaps Daisy from the household. Because there was agreement that removing the children would probably cause Mona to have a replacement child or children, the care providers considered how to make the home a safe place for the children. The multiple problems in the family were apparent to all the care providers, but their emphasis differed according to their discipline.

Problems the Community Health Nurse Identified:
• Mona had no understanding of the developmental capacities and limitations of preschool children. An essential goal was to teach her about normal growth and development. In addition, Mona needed to acquire some understanding of temperamental differences among children, especially between Betsy and Daisy.
• Since Daisy would inevitably become a mobile toddler, knowledge of normal behavioral patterns would prevent this child from sharing her sister's fate.
• Although the children had different fathers, both belonged to Mona. Her fondness for Daisy was obvious, but she needed to accept Betsy as a child equally deserving of care. The community health nurse began to relabel Betsy's behavior so that Mona could appreciate the precocity and intelligence that now provoked her anger. Some similarities between Mona and Betsy were evident. These resemblances could be pointed out to discount Betsy's paternity and foster closeness between mother and daughter.

Problems the Protective Worker Identified:
- Mona had public assistance support because the whereabouts of her husband was unknown. Although Mona managed her money fairly well, she could afford few luxuries. For example, she could not save enough money to cover the security deposit necessary to install a telephone. This meant that she was isolated in her small apartment, especially during the winter when she and her girlfriends were unable to visit with their children. The protective worker believed that a telephone was essential so that Mona could maintain communication with the outside world, and prevailed on the welfare worker to arrange telephone service.
- Although the protective worker was unsure about leaving Betsy in her mother's care, it was thought that with close supervision Betsy might be allowed to remain. Arrangements were made for Betsy to attend day care at the home of a welfare-approved mother. Since other preschoolers would be present, the socialization would be beneficial for Betsy. The day care mother would also be in a position to observe any evidence of abuse and monitor Betsy's progress.

Problems the Psychiatric Clinician Identified:
- Mona was deficient not only in her knowledge of child development, but also in her early experience with a mother figure. She described her own mother as cold and neglectful rather than abusive. According to Mona, her mother never praised or punished, but allowed her children to fend for themselves. A succession of men lived with Mona's mother after her natural father died. Some of these men were violent with Mona and her three brothers. Betsy's father had been living with Mona's mother when his sexual relationship with Mona began.
- Feelings of competition and rivalry characterized the relationship between Mona and her mother. Indeed there was reason to suspect that Mona had entered the relationship with Betsy's father primarily to annoy her mother. Therefore, Betsy represented a transgression against the mother whose love Mona still wanted. Since many of Betsy's personality traits were like Mona's, there was a tendency for Mona to project her old rivalrous feelings toward her mother onto Betsy. Thus, she saw in Betsy a rival rather than a tiny girl. These unconscious conflicts were reinforced when Mona's pregnancy caused Gus to abandon her.
- The attention of the community health nurse and the protective worker was appropriately directly to the children. However, Mona had suffered nurturing deficits that prevented her from being a good mother. So far, her care of Daisy was exemplary, but Mona was likely to become abusive toward both her children unless her own psychological needs were met. Mona needed to be shown how to be tender and caring with her children, but she first had to experience tenderness. The psychiatric clinician proposed that Mona be permitted a period of dependency so as to develop trust, self-worth, and control of her impulsive reactions.

- Besides meeting Mona's dependency needs in their therapeutic sessions, the psychiatric clinician used a behavior modification approach. When Betsy's behavior aroused anger, Mona was told to leave the room immediately without responding to the behavior. She was to call one of her care providers on the phone and discuss what had happened. If none was available, Mona was to leave a message and then call the twenty-four-hour crisis line to discuss the situation and plan her response to Betsy. Only then would she begin to deal with Betsy's problematic behavior.
- A prompt referral to Parents Anonymous, a self-help group formed to prevent child abuse, was recommended for Mona, and arrangements were made for members of the group to take Mona to the meetings.

The plan for the family was multifaceted and required collaborating with the representatives of several agencies. Three levels of prevention were operating as the plan for Mona was made. There was primary prevention of abuse toward Daisy as she moved toward the active negativism of the average toddler. Betsy was the beneficiary of interventions in the category of secondary prevention. Therapeutic modification of Mona's attitudes toward herself and alteration of her behaviors toward the children constituted a form of tertiary prevention.

CHILD SEXUAL ABUSE

Child sexual abuse is another term whose meaning changes over time and from one society to another. What does not change is the fact that children are fairly helpless and uninformed, and the very people responsible for their care often exploit their helplessness and ignorance. In a national study of known sexual abuse, the exploitation of children was estimated at 44,700 cases annually. Every year from 1976 to 1980, the number of reported cases of child sexual abuse increased substantially, after which it seemed to stabilize. However, figures for prevalence and incidence are very unreliable. According to various population surveys, between one-fifth to one-third of all adult women in the United States have had a childhood sexual encounter with an adult male. Father-daughter incest is the least likely to be reported, but it has been estimated that approximately one million women in this country have been involved in an incestuous relationship with their father, and that 16,000 new cases occur annually. It is not known whether child sexual abuse has increased over the last few decades, but it is clear that it continues to be a problem of enormous proportion (Parker & Parker, 1986).

Despite investigative efforts, the etiology of child sexual abuse is obscure. Certain family systems such as stepparent families and broken families seem to be vulnerable, but other reports show that sexual abuse takes place in many intact families where both natural parents are present in the home. Lower socioeconomic class has been linked to sexual abuse, but other data indicate that, unlike physical abuse, the sexual abuse of children is not connected to class. Alcohol abuse is sometimes thought to be a factor, but a study by the American Humane Association showed that sexual abusers of children had consumed low amounts of alcohol (Parker & Parker, 1986).

Despite research contradictions, there is agreement on some points. In reviewing the literature in the field, Parker and Parker (1986) found that:

- Perpetrators are overwhelmingly male and victims are female.
- Deprivation in the perpetrator's family of origin has induced low self-esteem and social inadequacy.
- Perpetrators are not mentally retarded, nor characterized by psycho-pathology or criminality.
- Sexual abuse of children in the family is rarely accompanied by physical abuse.
- Stepfathers or other father surrogates, such as the mother's "boyfriend," are overrepresented among abusers.

Female children living with stepfathers are at high risk for sexual abuse. In describing the antecedents of abuse, Finkelhor (1980) wrote that:

> One of the strongest risk factors, having a stepfather, more than doubled a child's vulnerability. Moreover, this risk factor remained the strongest correlate of victimization, even when all other variables were statistically controlled . . . Apparently there is substance to the notion that stepfathers are more sexually predatory toward their daughters than are fathers (p. 269).

The same investigator found that stepfathers who were not present in the home during a daughter's early years were more prone to sexual abuse; those present in the home in a daughter's early years were no more likely than a biological father to engage in sexual abuse of the girl. Evidently, physical and psychological distance between a girl and a father or step-father produces a low threshold stimulus for sexual arousal. The combi-nation of a man's psychosocial deficits and his lack of involvement in the early years of a daughter's life seems to increase the probability of sexual abuse. For men who cannot meet the demands of a mature sexual rela-tionship, a child becomes a perfect object of gratification. Incest between an adult male and a child resembles other immature activities, such as voyeurism or exhibitionism, although these modes of gratification are somewhat less exploitive of others. Consistent with later findings, Storr (1964, p. 101) described,

> It is not from superfluity of lust, but rather because of a timid inability to make contact with contemporaries that a man generally finds that children form the focus of sexual interest.

A father who sexually abuses a daughter seldom needs to use physical force because of the helplessness of the girl and the strength of the emotional bond. Added to the father's power as provider and authority figure is the threat of reprisal or a family breakup unless she submits. The feared punishment need not be specific, for the greatest fear of children is that their parents will withhold love and approval if the child disobeys or rebels. It is usually the threatened loss of love that persuades children into colluding in their own sexual victimization.

If the incestuous relationship brings attention or pleasure to the victim, there may be some gratification. However, many young girls are psychologically traumatized, not gratified as victims, and also experience great physical pain and damage. Physical, emotional, and behavioral consequences of child sexual abuse, adapted from Janosik and Davies (1989), are summarized as follows:

Physical Consequences:
Rectal fissures and rectal sphincter damage
Anal and vaginal lacerations
Gonorrheal infections of genitals, tonsils, larynx, and pharynx
Pain and physical discomfort

Emotional Consequences:
Sense of betrayal
Feelings of guilt and shame
Need for secrecy and concealment
Loss of trust in significant others
Anger toward both parents and generalized hostility
Feelings of helplessness and powerlessness
Confusion and mystification

Behavioral Consequences:
Reclusiveness and withdrawal into a fantasy world
Promiscuous sexual behavior
Phobic avoidance of sex and sexuality
Poor school performance and delinquency
Inability to set limits for self or others
Running away from home

Even when discovered, the man involved in an incestuous relationship is inclined to externalize responsibility. He may blame his wife for being cold and unresponsive; he may accuse the child victim of being the seducer or a willing participant. Alleging that incestuous acts were performed when the man was drunk or under the influence of drugs is an excuse offered to avoid responsibility. Even when wives claim that they were not aware of incestuous acts, some professionals suspect that the wife had repressed her knowledge of what was happening and colluded in a pretense that nothing untoward was taking place. A common rationalization of incestuous males is that they really derived no pleasure from the sexual encounters, but were merely teaching the victim the facts of life in order to prepare her for her future as an adult.

Although most incestuous relationships involve a female child, the practice of older males sexually exploiting boys is not uncommon. Not all males who engage in sexual acts with boys are homosexuals, and a significant variable is the age of the young partner. The younger the male partner of the sex offender, the greater the probability that the offender is bisexual rather than exclusively homosexual. Sex offenders who engage in relationships with boys under twelve years of age also have a predilection for sexual intercourse with girls under the age of sixteen years. Thus, for most child molesters, arousal comes from contact with an immature young body regardless of gender.

Current estimates show that ten girls are molested for every boy, but projected estimates show that if present trends continue, 25 percent of all female children will be molested before reaching age thirteen, and an adult will molest 10 percent of all boys in childhood. Most offenders against male children are not strangers, but are relatives or family friends; mother-daughter incest and mother-son incest are thought to be less common than father-son incest (Singer, 1989).

Boys involved in sexual encounters with adult males tend to react in various ways, ranging from pleasure and pride to ambivalence and shame. When the boy feels helpless and emasculated by the experience, he is ashamed. However, when the boy identifies with the aggressor and feels no loss of masculinity, he views the experience as either unimportant or pleasurable. As boys grow older and become more confident of their male identity, many are able to recall the experience without emotion. Thus, the responses of the male victims of sexual abuse seem to be less uniformly negative than the responses of female victims. Once the powerlessness of immaturity gives way to vigorous sexual prowess, the feelings of humiliation experienced at the time of sexual exploitation are attenuated in males. Boys who have been introduced to sexual intercourse by older women are more likely to feel excited than exploited by the initiation. When ambivalence or shame is present, the reaction seems to

be associated with fears of seeming unmanly because of the aggressiveness of the older woman (Rush, 1980).

The sexual molester of male and female children is likely to be male,
and may be either homosexual, bisexual, or heterosexual. Comparatively
few heterosexual women make advances to children, and many lesbian
groups have issued official statements opposing the sexual exploitation of
children by any individual, whether heterosexual or homosexual.

Children who have been sexually abused reveal behavioral signs of
internal turmoil. The reaction of very young children is one of pain and
mystification. Later, the child may realize that the actions are forbidden,
but may be reluctant to confide in anyone because of intimidation or fear
of being blamed. Confused by the actions of the molesting adult, the
young child may withdraw into a fantasy world to avoid dealing with
unpredictable reality. During late childhood or the early teen years, sexually abused children often exhibit aggression or hostility outside the
home. Sexual promiscuity is another response that molested adolescents
engage in, perhaps in an effort to demonstrate that sexual acts are unimportant. Some adolescents feel helpless and bitter, but others come to
enjoy the sexual experience even though they are guilty and conflicted
about the relationship. A significant number of sexually abused children
run away from home and turn to prostitution, justifying this action by
saying that prostitutes have some choice in sexual partners whereas at
home the molested child had none.

Sibling incest is thought to be rather frequent but is largely unreported. Body exploration and exhibition is common among young siblings; it is generally harmless and usually the result of natural curiosity.
The greater the age difference between siblings, the stronger is the likelihood that the older sibling will impose sexual behavior on the younger
sibling. Older siblings are usually aware of prohibitions against this kind
of activity. If it continues, professional help is indicated for both children.
Sibling incest, like other forms of incest, constitutes a serious problem for
the entire family, and the victimized child is endangered when there is no
one to turn to for help. Many variations of sibling incest are possible:
older brother-younger sister; older sister-younger brother, and homosexual sibling incest.

Studies of males molested as children and comparable females
showed few gender differences, except that females suffered more extensive abuse. Both male and female victims had an equally high likelihood of
reactive suicide attempts. One hypothesis, as yet unproven, is that sexual
abuse may be more traumatic for males, since less severe abuse of males is
associated with residual effects equal to that of females. It has also been
suggested that male victims of sexual abuse are more inclined to act out
their trauma through violence toward others, whereas females tend to

express their trauma internally by self-destructive behaviors, including repeated victimization (Briere et al., 1988). It is quite possible for women to commit sexual offenses against male and female children, but the social conditioning of women over the years has encouraged sublimation of female sexuality.

While acknowledging that incest is a family problem, practitioners must emphasize that the responsibility for the incestuous behavior belongs solely to the offender. If marital counseling follows or accompanies family therapy, there are times when shared responsibility for conflict may be attributed to the husband and wife, but marital friction or incompatibility cannot be considered justification for the sexual abuse of children.

COUNSELING INCESTUOUS FAMILIES

The discovery of an intra-family incestuous relationship produces a family crisis. The wife's immediate reaction is usually anger, often followed by feelings of personal rejection. When the victim has confided in someone so that the relationship is discovered, the child has a sense of having brought trouble to the family. This response is inevitable since the partner has repeatedly warned the child not to tell so that "we" won't get into trouble. The inclination of professionals who discover an incestuous affair is to remove the child immediately from the home, but this decision should be reviewed carefully. In some instances it is better for the child to remain in the home and the father to be removed. The child who is quite young may feel responsible for causing daddy so much trouble, but if permitted to remain in familiar surroundings, the child will feel less distress. When the victim of sexual abuse is removed from the home, there is danger that the child will have a sense of being punished and believe that the warning of the molester has come true. Such misgivings may arise even when the child remains in the home, but having to adjust to a new environment will not become part of the child's distress.

In the crisis following the discovery of an incestuous relationship, the needs of all family members must be considered. Psychological evaluation is mandatory for the molesting adult and the molested child. Following evaluation, individual therapy is indicated for the offender. The entire family should be offered conjoint therapy, along with marital counseling for the couple if they are motivated to continue their relationship. Siblings who have been living in an atmosphere of forbidden sexuality have formed their own impressions of what was going on. In many families, the adult offender has already subjected the younger children to sexual caressing as they await their own eventual victimization.

The practitioner engaged in conjoint work with an incestuous family must endeavor to reduce the high level of emotion, particularly if the parents wish to remain together. A constructive way to reduce blaming and mobilize the family is to employ role theory. The incestuous adult can be reminded firmly of the disruption that always follows inappropriate role enactment. The joint responsibility of parents is to protect all their children and to confine sexuality to their own relationship. These are principles that can be simply and strongly expressed through role theory terminology. Even fairly young children can understand the basic concepts of role theory, and the appropriate role performance of all family members can be described to them. An incestuous relationship between an adult and a child fragments sibling loyalties, even when there is pity rather than envy for the chosen child. Strengthening relationships among siblings reduces the power of the molesting adult and the children's silent acceptance of victimization. Secrecy is the ally of the incestuous adult; children benefit from strengthening sibling bonds through clarification of family role enactment. An example of the value of a strong sibling subsystem may be found in the account of a divorced mother who brought criminal charges against her former husband for the sexual abuse of their eleven-year-old daughter during weekends spent with the father. The mother credited the girl's teenage brother for reporting the situation to the mother as soon as he became aware of it.

Apprehended child molesters usually enter treatment as a condition of probation or as an alternative to prison. If family work is considered the treatment of choice, it is incumbent on practitioners to avoid blaming the victims of incest, namely the child and the mother. Behavior modification that attempts to extinguish sexual responsiveness to children and substitute responsiveness to heterosexual adults is one form of treatment for child molesters. Aversion therapy may combine visual images of prepubescent children with unpleasant stimuli, such as electric shocks. Another form of behavioral conditioning consists of using visual images of children combined with derogatory comments on the sexual immaturity and unattractiveness of children. When visual images of attractive adults are shown, the commentary describes the advantages and pleasures to be found in mature sexual relationships.

Treatment of the child victim may be required for many years. Sometimes psychological evaluation of the child leads to a decision to defer treatment until adolescence, when maturing sexuality reactivates previous memories and conflicts. If the child has learned to enjoy the incestuous relationship and feels guilty, treatment may be required immediately, last for an extensive period, and be reinstituted intermittently. The practitioner may use the child's guilty feelings to demonstrate that free choice was absent, and that victims are not accomplices even when the child had accepted the relationship.

•CLINICAL EXAMPLE:
ROLE STRATEGY IN AN INCESTUOUS FAMILY

The Colt family appeared in the emergency department of a medical center one evening. Vera Colt, a disheveled, tearful woman in her early thirties; her husband, Jeff; two girls, aged eight and ten; three younger boys; a one-year-old baby; and Vera's mother made up the family group. The reason for the visit was that the grandmother had discovered that her son-in-law, Jeff, had sexually molested the two girls. Marie, the older girl, confided in her grandmother that her father had been "doing things" with her and her sister for over a year. The irate grandmother confronted Vera and Jeff. When Jeff admitted to the allegation, the grandmother insisted that all the children be examined to see whether they were being used to satisfy Jeff's "lust."

A pediatrician was called to examine the children. Marie was found to have been penetrated by an adult male but her younger sister had not. Careful questioning indicated that the boys were not involved and this fact was confirmed on examination. When the girls were asked how and when the sexual encounters occurred, they explained that their father got the children ready for school each morning while their mother stayed in bed with the baby. The boys rode the school bus, but their father chauffeured the girls to school. En route, they often stopped at the apartment of an uncle who was already at work. Here the trio engaged in sex play, which began with genital caressing and ultimately progressed to intercourse with Marie. It was Marie's complaints of discomfort that alerted her grandmother to the situation. After interviewing the adults and examining the children, the hospital personnel requested consultation from a member of the department of psychiatry.

After talking collectively and individually with the family, the consulting psychiatrist suggested that the grandmother take the three boys and the baby home in a taxi. This left Vera, Jeff, Marie, and her younger sister, Caroline, to be interviewed at length before further referrals were made. The psychiatrist stressed the fact that Jeff's actions were illegal and that any disposition would include a report to the police.

Jeff was obviously embarrassed and ashamed at being discovered. His eyes were downcast, and he clenched and unclenched his hand as he talked. Questioned at length in an individual interview, Jeff revealed a boyhood spent with a dominating, overprotective mother. As a high school student he was socially inept, and his mother's insistence that he spend most of his time at home aggravated his ineptness. Even at the age of seventeen he was not allowed to go out at night, except with one of his parents. Frustrated but unable to shake his mother's domination, Jeff joined the Navy as soon as he became eighteen years of age.

Vera was a plump, rather pretty young woman who was more assertive than her husband. She expressed surprise and disgust at Jeff's behavior. At the time, Vera seemed more angry at the insult to herself than the injuries her daughters suffered. "This whole mess makes me feel awful," she said. "I must not be enough of a woman to satisfy my husband." She was mollified when the psychiatrist responded, "Perhaps you are too much of a woman for your husband right now. Dealing with grown-up women may be part of his problem."

Marie and Caroline looked scared and uncomfortable. They clung to each other and Marie said softly that everything was her fault, not her father's. The psychiatrist and the pediatric nurse, who was sitting with the girls, went to some lengths to reassure the girls that they had not been at fault in any way.

Critical Guidelines

After reporting the incident to the police and notifying the Children's Protective Association, the staff, the pediatrician, the consulting psychiatrist, and the pediatric nurse made the following decisions. The children were not to be removed from the home provided the grandmother remained with the family until treatment was instituted. Because this was a police matter, the recommendations were mandatory for the family.

- Psychological evaluation and followup for Marie and Caroline.
- Psychiatric evaluation and individual psychotherapy for Jeff.
- Marital counseling for the couple.
- Long-term supervision by the Children's Protective Association.
- Crisis intervention for the entire family unit.

Family crisis intervention involved every member, including the grandmother, who wielded considerable influence. A nurse and a social worker, functioning as a family crisis team, provided this aspect of treatment. At the start, family feelings were high. Jeff was guilty and anxious, Vera was depressed and self-engrossed, and the grandmother was angry with her daughter for not knowing what was happening. The two girls were worried because there was so much trouble in the family, and the boys were bewildered by events.

In order to reduce tension and recrimination in the family, the crisis team chose to use role theory to explain family disorganization. This tactic enabled the crisis workers to point out that the family was in trouble because role enactment was inappropriate, particularly the role performance of the parents. Vera was told that it was part of her role as mother to get up and help get the children ready for school. Jeff was told that his role performance was the most destructive of all. His role in the family was to be a husband to Vera and a father to his children. This role did not include making love to his daughters or exploiting them in any way. When marital and sibling roles in the family were performed properly, every member was protected. When role enactment was selfish and exploitive, every member suffered and the family became disorganized and dysfunctional.

Using role theory enabled family members to understand and accept the interventions of the crisis workers, thereby reinforcing the idea that role confusion had created a great deal of pain for this family. Jeff remained the victimizer, but the family problem was defined and clarified in role theory terms, which invited everyone to change family behavior. Crisis intervention merely prepared family members for the comprehensive treatment that lay ahead. During the time-limited contract, the crisis team taught the family that behavior that is not role appropriate threatens the rights of all family members and creates chaos in the system. With this preparation, the family members were more amenable to long-term therapy.

SUMMARY

Battered children, like battered women, are all too common in contemporary life. The intergenerational transmission of family violence and respect for parental rights have operated to victimize countless children. Since children cannot extricate themselves from abusive situations, the responsibility of professionals to report suspected abuse is ethically and legally mandatory. Preventive programs for families at risk have been instituted with significant results. Educating parents about child development and correcting the nurturing deficits of abusive parents are tandem approaches that have been successful in many instances. Support groups, such as Parents Anonymous, are widely used by parents who need help with impulse control and related childrearing problems.

Sexual molestation of children occurs in disorganized families in which role enactment is blatantly inappropriate. The crisis that follows the discovery of an incestuous relationship affects every family member. Psychological evaluation is indicated for the molesting adult and the molested child. Following evaluation, individual counseling is needed for the offender and often for the child. If the parents are motivated to keep the family intact, conjoint family therapy, in addition to marital and individual therapy, is necessary. Since incest demonstrates abdication of appropriate role enactment, the use of role theory early in treatment reduces anger, fear, and recrimination in the family members who are not the principals, but who have become aware of the incestuous relationship. The decision to remove the victim or the aggressor from the home is best made on an individual basis, but ongoing supervision of the family and the involvement of various voluntary and official agencies must be maintained over time.

REFERENCES

Aber, L.A. "The Involuntary Child Placement Decision: Solomon's Dilemma Revisited." In *Child Abuse: An Agenda for Action,* edited by G. Gerbner, C. Ross, and E. Zigler. New York: Oxford University Press, 1981.

Bowers, J.E. "Group Work with Couples and Families." In *Life Cycle Group Work in Nursing*, edited by E. Janosik and L. Phipps. Boston: Jones and Bartlett, 1986.

Briere, J., D. Evans, M. Runtz, and T. Wall. "Symptomatology in Men Molested as Children: A Comparison Study." *American Journal of Orthopsychiatry* 58(1988): 447–461.

Culp, R.E., V. Little, D. Letts, and H. Lawrence. "Maltreated Children's Self Concept: Effects of a Comprehensive Treatment Program." *American Journal of Orthopsychiatry* 61(1991): 114–121.

deMause, L. *History of Childhood*. New York: Harper & Row, 1974.

Finkelhor, D. "Risk Factors in Sexual Victimization of Children." *Child Abuse and Neglect* 4(1980): 265–273.

Fontana, V. "Children Maltreatment and Battered Child Syndromes." In *Comprehensive Textbook of Psychiatry*, 4th ed., edited by H.I. Kaplan and B.J. Sadock. Baltimore: Williams & Wilkins, 1985.

Gelles, R.J. "Child Abuse and Violence in Single Parent Families: Parent Absence and Economic Deprivation." *American Journal of Orthopsychiatry* 59(1989): 492–501.

Hampton, R., and E. Newberger. "Child Abuse Incidence and Reporting by Hospitals: Significance of Severity, Class, and Race." *American Journal of Public Health* 75(1985): 56–60.

Harper, G., and E. Irvin. "Alliance Formation with Parents: Limit Setting and the Effect of Mandated Reporting." *American Journal of Orthopsychiatry* 55(1985): 550–560.

Hunter, R., and N. Kilstrom. "Breaking the Cycle in Abusive Families." *American Journal of Psychiatry* 136(1979): 1320–1322.

Janosik, E.H., and J.L. Davies. "Situational Alterations: The Crises of Suicide and Violence." In *Psychiatric Mental Health Nursing*, 2nd ed., Boston: Jones and Bartlett, 1989.

Kaufman, J., and E. Zigler. "Do Abused Children Become Abusive Parents?" *American Journal of Orthopsychiatry* 57(1987): 186–192.

Kempe, H. "The Battered Child Syndrome." *JAMA* 181(1961): 17–24.

Kissel, S.J. "Violence in America: An Emerging Public Health Problem." *Health and Social Work* 11(1986): 153–155.

Parker, H., and S. Parker. "Father-Daughter Sexual Abuse: An Emerging Perspective." *American Journal of Orthopsychiatry* 56(1986): 531–549.

Rush, F. *The Best Kept Secret: Sexual Abuse of Children*. Englewood Cliffs, New Jersey: Prentice-Hall, 1980.

Singer, K.I. "Group Work with Men Who Experienced Incest in Childhood." *American Journal of Orthopsychiatry* 59(1989): 468–471.

Storr, A. *Sexual Deviation*. New York: Penguin Books, 1964.

12

Disorganized Families in Crisis
Spouse Abuse

*If men and women are to understand each other, to
enter into each other's nature with mutual sympathy, and to become capable of genuine comradeship,
the foundation must be laid in youth.*

Havelock Ellis

In the United States, violence is sanctioned under certain conditions, such
as defending national interests or protecting one's life and property.
Purposeless, irrational violence is not condoned, but violence used for
social control is usually considered acceptable. One factor perpetuating
violence against wives is the notion that aggression between marital
partners is a private matter. This alleged right of privacy has permitted
concealment of family violence and therefore outsiders hesitate to interfere in domestic matters. In addition, the historical implication that a wife
is the husband's chattel permits men to treat or mistreat their property as
they see fit. There are no statutes mandating observers to report instances
of wife beating. The beaten wife's reactions to would-be rescuers are
often unpredictable, so much so that police officers may hesitate to intervene, except on a superficial level. A bruised, frightened women may
indicate willingness to charge her husband with abuse, but for complicated reasons, may change her mind a few hours later.

It is difficult to exaggerate the prevalence of domestic violence in
contemporary life. About one out of every eight adults in the United
States has been involved in a violent episode, either as a victim or a
victimizer. Lamb (1991) wrote that, in any single year in the United
States, almost two million husbands abuse their wives. For decades,
family violence was considered to be more common in lower socioeconomic groups and between disturbed partners. Violence between a
husband and wife was often attributed to masochistic tendencies on the
wife's part. Behaviorists attribute the woman's actions to "learned helplessness." When people receive negative reinforcement unrelated to their

289

actions, they soon learn that their voluntary behavior has no way of controlling what happens to them. Therefore, they learn to be helpless and their survival instincts are extinguished.

The organized movement against wife beating began in England in 1971 when a woman named Erin Pizzey opened a modest home where local women and their children could flee from violent husbands and fathers. Within a few years, a network of such refuges was organized in the United Kingdom, and a parliamentary investigation of domestic violence was instituted. A group calling itself Women's Advocates, Inc., began a telephone information and referral service in St. Paul, Minnesota, in 1972, and two years later opened a shelter for battered women. About the same time systematic research on violence in the home began to appear in professional journals. In 1976, the National Organization for Women made available to the public a landmark publication entitled *Battered Wives.*

Many studies show that family violence in the form of wife beating transcends ethnic and social groups. One study of women in a shelter for battered women found that the population was 62 percent white, 13 percent Chicano, 3 percent Asian, and 2 percent other. The abusing husbands of these women represented almost every profession and occupation. It is highly likely that protective and law enforcement agencies noticed the families at the lower-end of the social scale more often. When upper- or middle-class husbands abuse their wives, the behavior is hidden from public view because wives are too ashamed to tell others (DeLorto & LaViolette, 1980).

Until the advent of the women's movement, responsibility for men battering women did not altogether focus on the men. Instead, research centered on understanding *why* men beat women and why women *continue to stay* with men who beat them. The problem was intellectualized and conceptualized in various ways. Instead of emphasizing choice and responsibility on the men's part, researchers viewed violence as a family problem and a social problem. This allowed responsibility to be allocated to both husband and wife, and to blame adverse social forces that permitted men to act violently toward women.

Lamb (1991, p. 250) stated that "language both reflects and shapes our understanding." She calls for a new linguistic style that does not diffuse the responsibility for beating women. She also dismisses suggestions that men behave violently toward women because they witnessed or suffered abuse from their fathers, and discounts cultural standards that equate manliness with wife beating. Family counseling is rooted in *systems theory,* which states that any element of a system is related to and influenced by other elements within the system. What Lamb states is that apparent collusion in a family may be the result of coercion and intimidation. When an abusing husband's violence toward his wife is interpreted only as the result of interaction between them, the victim may be perceived as being no different than the victimizer. It may be true that some men beat their wives out of their own terrible despair, but the following description vividly states the grim case without excusing anyone. Even here, however, husbands are not identified as the agents in the battering of women. According to Straus et al. (1980, p. 10), "Wives in America have been raped, choked, stabbed, shot, beaten, had their jaws and limbs broken, and have been struck with horse whips, pokers, bats, and bicycle chains."

When reports of wife beating are couched in ambiguous language, it is hard for outsiders to accept the cruel reality in which battered women live. Moreover, the depiction of wife beating as a function of the family system makes it harder for wives to defend themselves or protect themselves through legal safeguards. There are women who have met violence by defending themselves violently, and the courts have not always been sympathetic. Men, who have declared that the women "provoked" their violence, have absolved themselves of considerable responsibility. They also allege that their actions were beyond their control, and that they were not "themselves" during the violent encounter. Feminists and activists in the movement to protect battered women call for reframing the language of writers, clinicians, and researchers so as to place responsibility fully on any husband who beat his wives, for whatever reason (Schechter, 1989). Feminists and activists introduced the term *battered women* to bring the problem into public awareness. Some in the women's movement even decried this accurate expression. Their contention is that the phrase does promote an urge to protect women and to hold violent men responsible. At the same time, the phrase conjures a picture of helpless and isolated women, brutalized, but by whom? (Kurz, 1987).

HUSBANDS WHO BATTER WIVES

Clinicians and research investigators have noted the characteristics of men who batter their wives or intimate partners. Much of this work has resulted in generalizations about all men who batter, without differentiating the types of abusers. Treatment programs tend to use the same approaches with all men who batter, although certain types of abusers may respond to certain types of intervention (Saunders, 1992). Clinicians formulated early typologies, which were not validated empirically. One of these was the following typology of men who batter women, derived from clinical observation (adapted from Elbow, 1977):

- *Controller.* This man uses the partner as an object that he can control.
- *Defender.* This man mingles hate and love; he depends on his partner to accept and forgive him.

- *Validator (approval seeker).* This man is subject to self-doubt; he looks for ways to reinforce his self-image as a man.
- *Incorporator.* This man sees no separateness between himself and his partner; he sees the partner as an extension of himself.

The typology that Elbow (1977) formulated has interesting implications. The four personality patterns of abusers are characterized by specific actions and behaviors that can be identified. The *controller* gets his way by persuasion, threats, or use of force. People are important to him only in terms of what they can do for him; they are seen as objects and there is no emotional reciprocity. Violence occurs when the controller feels unable to dominate the wife. He opposes ending the relationship because of his anxiety about losing control of his wife, who is considered a possession. Granting her any autonomy is equated with her controlling him.

The *defender* is not afraid of being controlled, but of being harmed. He is able to feel strong only if his mate continues to cling to and depend on him. Because he anticipates that his mate may punish him for being sexual and aggressive, he believes that he must render her powerless so that he will not be vulnerable to attack from her.

The *validator* has high expectations of himself. His self-esteem is contingent on the acceptance and approval of others. Since his self-esteem is low, he expects rejection and behaves in a manner that elicits rejection from others. The prospect of losing his mate is extremely threatening, for this loss would confirm his low regard for himself. He tries to avoid the loss of his mate through intimidation, followed by remorse.

The *incorporator* is desperate because he cannot experience himself as a whole person without incorporating his mate. Possession and incorporation of the mate permits a degree of self-esteem, fear of losing her leads to ego deterioration and self-doubt.

Some investigators have proposed a dichotomy of batterers, many of whom are violent only at home and many who are violent both at home and outside the home. The latter group engage in more severe violence and are more likely to abuse alcohol. Men who are violent only within the home are more dependent and more remorseful after being abusive (Shields et al., 1988; Brisson, 1983). Men who are aggressive at home and outside the home are less inclined to accept help and are more traditional in their ideas of what women should be. To summarize, there is consensual evidence that there are two major types of batterers, the *dependent abuser* and the *dominating abuser.* It is the dominant abuser who seems to have more antisocial traits and engages in the most severe forms of violence.

In a carefully designed research study, Saunders (1992) presented a typology that differentiated three groups of men who batter women.

- *Type 1:*
  Family-only batterers. These men reported lower levels of anger, depression, and jealousy; they also reported higher values placed on social desirability. Their violence was alcohol-related about half the time.
- *Type 2:*
  Generalized batterers. These men were the most likely to be violent inside and outside the home; many suffered abuse as children, yet they reported low levels of anger or depression. Their attitudes on sex role enactment were very rigid. Their reports of a high use of alcohol and severe battering were reflected in frequent arrests for drunk driving and for violent behavior.
- *Type 3:*
  Emotionally volatile batterers. These men were violent less often than the other types, but were the most abusive psychologically. They were least satisfied in their relationship with their partner. Their use of alcohol was less than that of types 1 and 2. They tended to be the least defensive and the most accepting of treatment.

An alternative explanation of this typology and others is that types or categories of batterers represent different phases of the abuser's behavior. Neidig et al. (1986) noted that most batterers "explode" into violent behavior. Over time they realize that negative consequences rarely follow the explosion, and they soon learn to employ violence as a means of controlling or coercing their wives. The work of Walker (1984) showed that batterers showed "loving contrition" after the first violent episodes, but with time the remorse disappeared.

Treatment Based on Typology

The family-only abuser (type 1) is probably most responsive to intervention. He can profit from assertiveness training, which helps him to express negative emotions verbally. Batterers of this type are suitable candidates for marital counseling, if both partners are willing to participate.

The man who is globally aggressive is type 2. A generally violent batterer usually needs help in dealing with his memories of childhood abuse and in dealing with his alcohol abuse. Cognitive restructuring can help him modify his rigid ideas about sex role performance. Emotional exploration will put him in touch with his feelings. Once he is able to recognize what he is feeling, work on communication and impulse control can be undertaken. The batterer who demonstrates generalized aggressiveness requires more than short-term, crisis-limited intervention.

The emotionally volatile batterer (type 3) needs help in dealing with inner turmoil without resorting to violence. He needs a cognitive approach that will help him realize the destructive consequences of prolonged psychological abuse of his partner. Cognitive restructuring will help with impulse control and with learning to express emotions in more constructive ways.

ALCOHOL AND VIOLENCE

A significant influence in the manifold disturbances present in disorganized families is excessive drinking by one or more members. Alcoholism is not only a problem in itself, but complicates other crises in disorganized families, notably spouse abuse and child abuse. Therefore, in such families, alcoholism may be considered a crisis in its own right and a factor intensifying recurring crises of family violence.

Three competing theoretical positions have been proposed to explain the relationship between alcohol and aggression, particularly interpersonal aggression. The first of these is predicated on the assumption that alcohol affects aggressive behavior by the "energizing" influence of alcohol on general activity level and aggressive fantasies. Another explanation is that alcohol does not directly elicit aggression, but instead reduces inhibition and facilitates expression of aggression by reducing fear of the social and physical consequences of aggression. A third explanation of the relationship between alcohol ingestion and aggression is that it is mediated by a psychological acceptance set regarding the behavioral effects of alcohol consumption based upon the popular tendency to attribute antisocial acts to the alcohol rather than the alcoholic. One reward of heavy drinking is that it offers an acceptable excuse for engaging in aggressive behavior without suffering great social disapproval.

If the connection between alcohol and violence is based on reduced inhibition via physiological channels, violence would presumably be greater among individuals who drink most often. However, the most severe alcoholics seemed to be anaesthetized rather than uninhibited, using alcohol to erase a world too painful to contemplate. Persons who were inebriated from time to time were more likely to use alcohol to engage in behaviors otherwise unacceptable to themselves or others.

Even though there is an association between alcohol and violence, many researchers are not sure that alcohol is a cause of wife beating. It is unclear whether people become violent because they are drunk or get drunk to obtain implicit freedom to be violent. Adding to the ambiguity is the fact that violence often occurs in families who abstain from alcohol because of religious or other convictions (Helfer & Kempe, 1976). Whatever the sequence, the need for clinical intervention is obvious.

According to Hanks and Rosenbaum (1977), women who continue to live with violent, alcoholic men seem to come from three types of family structures: subtly controlling mother, figurehead father; submissive mother, dictatorial father; and disturbed mother, multiple fathers. Most of the women professed warm feelings toward their parents and saw relationships with their original families as excellent. They were sympathetic toward their husbands, rarely sought help, and were overprotective of their children. The investigators concluded that involvement with a violent, drinking man was psychologically necessary to these women, regardless of the family structure of their original family. It was thought that violence made the women feel superior and needed when they rescued their husbands. The interactional pattern gave meaning to their otherwise directionless lives.

THEORETICAL EXPLANATIONS

Intrapsychic Formulations

Traditional explanations of wife beating have relied on Freud's concepts of feminine masochism. In this formulation, the masochistic woman is described as wishing to be treated like a helpless, dependent, naughty child. For the masochist it is the suffering that is important, not the person who imposes punishment. The maintenance of suffering is essential because punishment relieves feelings of guilt. Freud (1959) saw this self-destructive behavior as a result of failure to resolve the oedipal conflict. The female child is competitive with her mother, but fears loss of the mother's love. In order to renounce the father, the girl unconsciously provokes his aggression. This causes her to forsake the male and mitigates the guilt associated with her earlier desires for the father. This paradigm implies that women submit because of unconscious beliefs that they deserve to suffer.

Shainness (1979) presented masochism as a process that involves certain sociocultural features. Violent men tend to use violence as an ego-enhancing mechanism because their repertoire of nonviolent behavior is limited. Often this is the type of man to whom masochistic women are attracted. In this explanation, masochism is not considered an instinct subject to libidinous forces, but a behavior that developmental and cultural events influence. Masochistic women have experienced and incorporated significant persons who were harsh or cruel. Other factors, such as superior masculine strength and lack of control over their reproductive processes, reinforce the submissiveness of women. Thus, the tacit acceptance of abuse by women is a social and biological heritage causing them to act in ways that perpetuate abuse.

In violent families, attacking others may deflect anger toward the self. Men who feel inadequate or frustrated displace their negative feelings on their wives and children. A vicious cycle of disappointment and resentment activates feelings of guilt in some women, which are reduced when they are beaten. This welter of confusing feelings leads to more anger in the women and ultimately to more beatings. Furthermore, the violent behavior defends the male from dependency urges to merge with, surrender, or submit to the female.

Sociological Formulations

The social organization of family life that contributes to intimacy also predisposes to a high rate of violence, despite the image of the family as a place of love and gentleness. Age and gender discrepancies, conflicting activities and interests, and role dissonance and inflexibility are only a few of the variables that add to family tension. Another important variable is the violence of the society in which contemporary families are imbedded. There is evidence of a circular pattern in which violence generated within families leads to a violent society. At the same time, a society that accepts violence in public spheres of life aggravates violent tendencies within families. In some segments of society, violent behaviors may be legitimized and regarded as appropriate responses.

Pursuit of rewards and avoidance of punishment guide human behavior and interaction. Violence within a family will continue until the costs of violence outweigh the rewards, and norms surrounding violence undergo change. There are no strong indications that this process of change has begun.

Stressful life experiences are associated with assault between husbands and wives; people under the least stress have the lowest assault rates. Men under stress are more likely to assault their wives if the marriage is not important to them or if they believe that a husband should be the dominant member of the marital dyad. Exploring status relationships in cases of spouse abuse showed that status inconsistency and status incompatibility were associated with risk of psychological abuse, greater risk of physical abuse, and still greater risk of life-threatening violence. Status inconsistency was characterized by occupational underachievement of the husband, while status incompatibility was characterized by the higher occupational achievement of the wife. Interestingly, status inconsistency in the form of occupational overachievement by the husband seemed to be a safeguard against outbreaks of violence (Hornung et al., 1980).

The Feminist Formulation

In the feminist position, wife battering must be examined against the background of a patriarchal society. Patriarchal rules and regulations reinforce the subordinate position of women and the authority of men. Social emphasis on obedience from subordinates indirectly permits the superior male to subjugate women through violence or other tactics.

A contrasting stance is that society is not patriarchal, but is matriarchal in nature (Lesse, 1979). Since women are the primary enforcers of moral values and the dispensers of discipline in the home, they are dominant in the lives of children. The psychosocially dependent male reared in a matriarchal environment interacts with his mother in a dependent fashion. In marrying, he transfers his dependency needs, but retains latent hostility and ambivalence toward women. Hostility is more readily expressed against the wife because of cultural inhibitions against hitting a mother. If men are persuaded or coerced into relinquishing rights they have enjoyed in the past without receiving any return benefits, there is a possibility that violence toward women may increase as a result of the women's movement.

Maria Roy, founder and director of the Abused Women's Aid in Crisis, New York City, provided a historical, contemporary, and future view of the problem (Roy, 1977). According to Roy, wife beating is cyclic and is transmitted intergenerationally. Therefore, a gestalt approach is needed that includes societal, educational, and legislative changes. In a violent society, anyone can become an aggressor or a victim. When violence is tolerated and victims blamed, men, women, and children learn that physical aggression can be useful. Roy called on units of government, organized religion, and the media to introduce legislation, programming, and new interpretations of the marriage contract in order to forestall violence. A comprehensive approach is advocated because violence is a way of life that begins in the home, extends to the streets, and affects the lives of everyone.

The economic victimization of women is a crucial issue when a battered woman tries to remove herself and her children from the arena of domestic violence. When a woman separates from an abusive husband, she is, in effect, homeless. Many women who lack education, skills, and money remain in abusive situations because they cannot afford to leave. Even when women manage to achieve a measure of economic independence, many believe that men victimize them in authority positions outside the home. Sexual assault, sexual harassment, medical exploitation, pornography, and prostitution are among the methods society uses to victimize women.

Martin (1977) has stated that men beat their wives simply because nobody stops them, alleging that women are beaten because they are conditioned to be dependent. Marriage is an institution through which women are routinely cast in the roles of victims. They are taught from birth that marriage and motherhood represent fulfillment. To reach this goal, women must be feminine, permissive, and submissive, submerging their inclinations to be free and assertive. The patriarchal family structure legitimizes the inequality of the sexes. If women assert themselves, they are abused for their temerity. If they remain passive, they still provoke the husband's displeasure. According to Martin, women are in "no win" positions.

It is important for practitioners to be familiar with the feminist viewpoint. Such writings are useful in outlining necessary changes in society, in the legal system, and in family structure. However, they do not provide guidelines for assessing and helping individual families in which violence is a problem. Their major contribution may be to raise the consciousness of care providers and the public-at-large.

Response to Violence

The concept of learned helplessness states that noncontingent negative reinforcement leads to belief that no voluntary actions can control the consequences that follow. This concept may be applied to the behavior of battered women whose motivation to act is diminished by repeated beatings. Believing that no response she makes will result in a favorable outcome, the woman generalizes her feelings of helplessness and becomes passive. Therefore, she does nothing, and her emotional state is one of helplessness and ultimately hopelessness.

A stress-response syndrome was observed in battered wives that consisted of a paralyzing terror similar to that of women who had been raped, except that the stress was unending and the threat of assault was ever present (Hilberman, 1980). Agitation and anxiety bordering on panic, combined with chronic dread of impending doom, were found in the women studied. Their nightmares and dreams were violent, but passivity, inertia, and an inability to act dominated these women's waking lives. The women were emotionally drained, fatigued, and numbed. They believed themselves unworthy, unlovable, and unable to make changes. Their psychological configuration reflected not only the fear of another assault, but a constant struggle to contain their aggressive impulses. Passivity and denial seemed to be their last refuge against pent-up rage and homicidal urges.

Beatings produce observable responses of anxiety, fear, depression, guilt, and shame that are similar to the effects of brainwashing. The brainwashing technique essentially consists of isolating individuals from the supports and rewards of their previous milieu. Enforced isolation results in hypersuggestibility and receptivity to new values and behaviors. The captors offer the only validation of the victim's worth. Inconsistent, contradictory, and threatening treatment, interspersed with kindness, produce the effect known as *brainwashing*. Many features of this technique are present in the lives of battered women, notably, loneliness, constant fear, and lack of support from friends, relatives, and community agencies, which inadvertently reinforce the negative self-image of the battered woman.

Children who witness spouse abuse may be affected in diverse ways. Bandura (1986) noted that children and young adults were inclined to identify with aggressors, and clinical observation supports the statement that male children of battered women often behave aggressively toward the mother. The assumption is that the father provides a role model of violence for the sons, while the mother provides a role model of ineffectuality for the daughters.

One reason that battered women give for not seeking help is that their husbands are likely to retaliate. Retaliation may occur at times, but a study of New York City programs for battered women indicated that they were less likely to be victimized if they sought help (Barden, 1982). In this three-year study, over one hundred abused wives who had received assistance from voluntary and official agencies were interviewed. The investigators found that most husbands who had been arrested or served an order of protection were unlikely to continue their abuse, even when the wives did not follow through on legal action. Clinicians working with battered women can truthfully assert that filing complaints is helpful, even when women drop the charges rather than see their husbands imprisoned. The report stated that 47 percent of the women said that they were not beaten again once charges were filed. One woman noted that reporting her husband to the police convinced him that any future violence would bring reprisals.

The most effective form of assistance for battered women in the study was crisis counseling, even though this form of aid did not directly reduce violence. Crisis counseling helped the women explore their options, provided support, and promoted decision making. Whether offered through hot lines, shelters, or consciousness-raising centers, crisis counseling was considered to be very helpful. About one-third of the women obtained professional individual counseling in addition to crisis intervention; one-fifth of the group found this counseling helpful.

VIOLENT WIVES

Although it is posited that there is little difference in the overall rates of violence that husbands and wives enact, men tend to escalate levels of violence, and most of the violence from wives constitutes self-defense. In examining police calls for "domestic disturbances," there is little support for a battered husband syndrome (Lamb, 1991). Generally, it was the women who were found battered in these incidents, and in most domestic disturbances, the men inflicted harm. The existence of a kin network system may act as a deterrent to violence and also may play a decisive part in determining the intensity and direction of family violence.

Family violence accounts for one-quarter of all homicides in the United States, according to Federal Bureau of Investigation (FBI) Uniform

Crime Reports. Meyers (1980) found that 52 percent of women killed in California within a one-year period died at the hands of a husband or lover. The same study noted that police officers often ignore the beating of a woman by her husband, and persons in the criminal justice system tend to blame the victim for actions that elicited violence. Angela Browne's book entitled *When Battered Women Kill* is a study of 250 battered women, forty-two of whom murdered their husband or lover. From her data, it is possible to predict, to some extent, which women are at risk of murdering their partners. Browne (1987) cited a series of determining factors as follows:

• Frequency of violent acts by the man.
• Abuse of alcohol and other substances by the man.
• Severity of injuries inflicted on the woman.
• Sexual assaults against the woman (real or threatened).
• Threats by the man to kill the woman and/or the children.
• Suicide thoughts and tendencies on the part of the woman.

There were no other differences between abused women who killed and abused women who did not kill; differences lay in the pattern of abuse and in the actions of the men.

SEXUAL ABUSE AND THE BATTERED WOMAN

Wife rape has aroused the interest of many investigators, who report that forced sexual intercourse is more traumatic for the wife than battering alone. As a research issue, the problem is just beginning to be explored. Until recently, stranger rape was considered to be the prototype of rape; it is very likely that date rape is a frequent occurrence and that sexual assault within a marriage may be the most common form of rape (Pagelow, 1982). State legislatures in eleven out of the fifty states have enacted protective legislation, thus acknowledging that wife rape is a serious social and legal issue (Griffin, 1989).

In Boston, Finkelhor and Yilo (1982) conducted in-depth interviews with women whose husbands used physical force or threats to have sexual relations with them. They found that 45 percent of the women suffered battering rapes, 45 percent suffered nonbattering rapes, and 10 percent endured rapes that had a sadistic component. Frieze (1983) studied wife rape in a group of 137 battered wives; one-third of these women reported being raped by their husbands and two-thirds reported being "pressured" into having sexual relations. Pressuring was characterized by threats of violence unless the wife submitted. In this study, the raped and battered women demonstrated more extreme reactions than did women who had been battered but not raped (Frieze, 1983). Reactions of wives who suffered marital rape included outrage, fear, depression, anger, shame, self-blame, pervasive sadness, and unhappiness. The intimate aspect of marital rape makes disclosure difficult.

Alcohol seems to play a significant role in the perpetration of wife rape. Finkelhor and Yilo (1985) found that out of forty-seven women in their sample, 70 percent stated that their husband had been drinking before an episode of forced intercourse. In her study, Frieze (1983) found that 63 percent battered women's spouses were either sometimes, usually, or always drinking during violent episodes. Weingourt (1985, 1990) stated that the mental health community has overlooked the marital rape issue. She also alleges that women tend not to report marital rape or forced intercourse unless sensitive questioning concerning the issue was encouraged.

The physical coercion that husbands inflicted included pinning or arm twisting, hitting, slapping, and choking. Some women experienced no physical abuse other than incidents of rape, many of which were accompanied by threats of force. These wives emphasized their global feelings of shame and worthlessness, anxiety, helplessness, and depression. Women who were raped but not battered were more likely to remain in the marriage, but their psychological reactions were remarkably like those of women who were battered and raped. Many battered women are reluctant to publicly admit the abuse, and women subjected to marital rape are even more reluctant. Since wife rape is one of the most damaging forms of abuse that husbands inflict, the assessment of battered women should consider this possibility. Weingourt (1990) declared that wife rape is a factor in the lives of many clinically depressed, anxious women in the absence of overt battering. Marital rape is a complex, hidden problem. More research is needed to discover the parameters of the problem. More clinical attention is needed so that reticent women are encouraged to disclose the existence and extent of this form of abuse.

COUNSELING BATTERED WOMEN

For battered women crisis does not exist only in the abuse itself, but in the turmoil that surrounds the decision to stay with the husbands or separate. Unlike the child who is abused, the battered wife who does not leave her husband, or who leaves and returns, does not receive much sympathy from the public or even from caregivers. The suffering of many battered women is unreported because the women have no hope of rescue. When a woman does leave the abusing husband, she needs to be convinced that she is a worthwhile person, and that responsibility for the abuse is the husband's, not hers. The ambivalence and indecision of battered women is reflected in their pattern of repeated reconciliations with the husbands, most of which turn out disastrously.

In counseling a battered woman, discussion of the family's social and financial resources are in order. What stressors are currently affecting the family? Is the husband out of work? Are religious differences being used to justify the beatings? Were the children planned or unplanned? Is there evidence of drinking, gambling, or infidelity by either partner? Exploring behavior patterns in the families of origin can be helpful. Was violence prevalent in the original families of either partner? If original families were a training ground for violence, can these ingrained behaviors be overcome?

The norms and values the partners hold are important. If violence is an ingrained trait in the husband, should intervention deal with preserving the relationship by working toward change, or should intervention deal only with the battered wife's predicament? Only the main participants in the domestic drama can answer this question, and the children's well being must be considered, particularly if they, too, are being abused. The battered woman merits a great deal of attention, especially when she has separated from her husband and is trying to establish a new life for herself and her children.

Depending on the circumstances and the motivation of the principals, individual, couple, or group therapy may be appropriate for battered women in crisis. If the couple wishes to stay together, marital counseling may be the treatment of choice. Through this modality, their dysfunctional communication and interaction can be identified and hopefully corrected. Behavioral modification can augment marital counseling, not only to induce change, but to measure change. Substitute actions and conditioning can be used to modify negative behaviors that produce violent outcomes.

When working with battered women, the clinician should avoid advising anyone either to leave or remain with a partner. Many abused women continue for years in the abusive relationship and cannot separate until they have confidence in their own powers. For most battered women, the decision to leave is a protracted process, characterized by repeated separations and reunions. Because the battered woman is ambivalent and confused, it is essential that clinicians not deride or criticize the husband. Frequently, the response of the woman is to defend the abuser and blame herself. If workers do not accept her confusion and ambivalence, the battered woman will feel belittled and misunderstood.

Prevention Levels

Interventions based on assessment and planning can be implemented at all three levels of prevention. Primary prevention involves early recognition of family violence and identification of couples at risk. Communication problems between couples, predisposing family backgrounds, and the presence of current stressors are among the early indicators of family violence. Premarital counseling and prenatal counseling can be used to help couples compare their expectations of marriage and parenthood, and perhaps circumvent certain problems. Genetic counseling is an aspect of primary prevention that receives less attention than it deserves. Exploring the risks and difficulties attendant on bringing a congenitally damaged child into the world can reduce the introduction of additional stress into the family system.

Secondary prevention can be equated with crisis intervention for the violent family or any members thereof. The battered woman is encouraged to look at her marriage and decide whether to separate, even temporarily. Within the crisis framework, the woman's readiness for change can be noted, and she can observe adaptive behaviors that other women have modeled in dealing with similar problems.

Shelters for battered women are now available in most localities, and group work is usually the basis of therapeutic programs at shelters. Group work with battered women provides a support system in which the women realize, perhaps for the first time, that they are not unique in their predicament. Workers in the shelters are excellent resource persons to help with such problems as child support, protection orders, housing, or vocational guidance.

Groups organized for battered wives provide a support system by which the woman can, perhaps for the first time, realize that she is not alone. She realizes that not only do many women share her problem, but some of them have found the courage to separate from the abuser and begin new lives. She feels less isolated as she begins to share her experiences with understanding listeners. Within the group network, she learns how other women have dealt with problems about housing, jobs, money, and legal rights.

Access to the group is open ended, with new members accepted through professional or self-initiated referrals. In this way, older group members who have made decisions to separate can function in advisory, almost co-leadership roles. Newcomers may require orientation and special consideration if they are to continue in the group long enough to benefit from it.

It is futile to encourage separation or to urge the woman to leave her partner. Other people in the woman's life have probably attempted to do this in the past, but to no avail. Initially, the woman needs help in restoring her confidence and advice in meeting basic survival needs. Only then can she decide whether to separate or to resume her marriage. Elbow (1977) listed these alternatives for battered women: (1) she can leave, (2) she can continue in the relationship hoping that her husband will change, or (3) she can continue in the relationship while giving up hope that he will change. When women opt for the second or third alternative; they are encouraged to recognize that this is a conscious, deliberate choice. Often the decision-making process is lengthy and difficult for the woman.

Since the battered women's group is ongoing and open ended, members will be at different stages. Because of the vacillation and hesitation the women experience, the group itself goes through cycles of progression and regression. Sometimes the group is task-oriented; at other times the group climate is stormy and emotional. Experiencing these recurring phases gives group members an opportunity to see others face temporary setbacks, give up for a time, and then find the resolve to take charge of their own lives.

Shelters and programs for battered women and their children have proliferated in recent years, but less is being done for men who batter. Edelson and Brygger (1986) described one group program for men. The program offers cognitive restructuring, interpersonal skills training, and relaxation exercises, using a small group format with male leaders. Early in the program of twelve two-hour sessions, members analyze events that generate anger in themselves. They are asked to record incidents and subsequent feelings of anger, using a chart. Specific situations that evoked anger are called *critical moments* and these are brought to the group for discussion. Reactions to critical moments are presented and alternative behaviors are suggested to replace violent behaviors. Good results have been reported for groups using this format. The program is three-dimensional, meaning that it combines cognitive, emotional, and behavioral repatterning.

•CLINICAL EXAMPLE: POSITIVE OUTCOMES FOR TWO BATTERED WOMEN

A shelter for battered women offered a sixty-day residential program for abused women and their children. Shirley and Juliet came to the shelter within a few days of each other and soon became friends and confidants. Shirley was eighteen years old, the mother of a ten-month-old boy, and five months pregnant. She was a pretty, young woman with pleasant features and dark eyes that reflected her sadness. Juliet was in her mid-twenties. She was a fast-talking, brash young woman who was an attentive mother to her eight-year-old son and six-year-old daughter. The two women seemed to have little in common except motherhood and a history of being battered. Despite apparent differences, they seemed drawn together; Juliet behaved like an older sister to Shirley and sometimes managed to make Shirley laugh.

Shirley was a shy, dependent young woman whose religious faith opposed divorce. She had married just a few months before the birth of her first child and became pregnant again shortly afterwards. Until the second pregnancy, her husband had been neglectful but not abusive. He went out a great deal with male friends and lavished more attention on his motorcycle than on his family. The second pregnancy embittered Shirley's husband, and the battering began almost as soon as he learned that another child was expected. The violence quickly escalated and nothing Shirley could do appeased him. She fled to the shelter after her husband pushed her down a flight of stairs. Fearing for her son and her unborn child, Shirley gathered a few belongings while her husband was out with his friends and came to the shelter. When she called her parents to tell them where she was, they told her that she should return to her husband "where she belonged."

Juliet worked as a waitress while her children attended school or a babysitter watched them. Her relationship with her husband had always been stormy, even before they were married. He drank excessively and resented Juliet's willingness to laugh and joke with other men. Her explanation, that she flirted with male customers in order to obtain larger tips, did not satisfy him. Many of the quarrels between the couple were brawls rather than beatings. Juliet used any available weapon to defend herself and attack her husband. Once she cut him with a broken bottle, causing a laceration that required sutures. The recurring battles and reconciliations did not upset Juliet greatly until her son, in trying to protect her, received the blow intended for his mother and was knocked unconscious. The boy was hospitalized for a week and expressed fears of returning home. A children's protective agency investigated the entire incident and made Juliet realize for the first time that she and her children could be seriously hurt. She came to the shelter to think over her situation and deal with her son's fear of his father.

Both women were in the early stages of defining the problems in their marriages, and neither was ready to divorce the abusive partner. Shirley's situation was more difficult. With one small baby and another expected, she was unable to look for work. Neither her husband nor her parents was willing to offer financial or emotional support.

Critical Guidelines

The workers in the shelter watched with interest the growing friendship between the two women. Juliet obtained a restraining order against her husband and through a lawyer negotiated for child support and sole access to the apartment she had shared with her husband. Although he begged for reconciliation, Juliet insisted that her husband had to enter treatment for alcoholism and remain sober for at least a year before she would discuss reunion. Shirley's husband had made no gestures toward reconciliation, and despite pressure from her parents, she was afraid to return to him. It was a great relief to her when Juliet asked Shirley to share her apartment. In return for free housing, Shirley would care for Juliet's children when they were not in school. This would relieve Juliet's mind and save the cost of after-school care.

When the shelter workers learned of the plan, they began to help with the logistics of the move. Shirley applied for a support order and supplementary welfare. Some nursery furniture was provided from donations made to the shelter. Together, the two women met with a worker and were encouraged to work out specific aspects of the living arrangement. Anticipatory guidance was used to avert potential problems and clarify each woman's expectations of the other. They were encouraged to commit themselves to the living arrangement only for a period of one year and to review their situation at that point.

Sudden friendships are not uncommon among residents of shelters for battered women. Some of these friendships are durable, but others are short lived. Because of the temperaments of Shirley and Juliet, shelter workers believed this friendship had a good chance of lasting. Juliet was the executive of this newly created household, and Shirley respected this arrangement. Each woman was able to give and receive something from the other. Because Shirley could help with child care, she felt valuable and worthwhile. Her worries about her confinement were minimized by Juliet, whose pseudosophistication concealed kindness and a strong maternal drive. There was a chance that Juliet would return to her husband after a year if he controlled his drinking problem. Shirley's marriage was less likely to be resumed, but living with Juliet solved her most urgent problems and gave her time to plan for the future. With independent Juliet as a role model, there was some possibility that Shirley would eventually become more autonomous. Both women were encouraged as ex-residents to participate in the support groups the shelter staff offered.

Crisis intervention is necessary and appropriate in the first weeks after a battered woman leaves her partner. Many women, however, are so demoralized by their experience that long-term help is indicated. Curry et al. (1988) provided the following guidelines for crisis counselors and for other health care providers working with these woman:

- Counseling a battered woman may be a lengthy process. These women respond to a caring, empathic approach.
- Although battered women feel inadequate and worthless, they need to begin to help themselves. A counselor may help a woman discover alternatives, but the woman herself should make the choices.
- A battered woman feels that her whole life is out of control; she needs to learn that she is capable of taking charge of her own life.
- Help the woman sort out her confusion and conflicted feelings; assure her that her terrible experiences can be used to avoid making the same mistakes in the future.
- Encourage the woman to look at her situation realistically; support her during the decision-making process.

Curry et al. (1988, p. 1190) wrote that battered women may "deny the past, rationalize the present, and ignore the future." It may require persistent counseling for battered women to realize that they cannot change the batterer very much. Only he has the power to change himself. The woman, with adequate assistance and motivation, can find the courage to take charge of her own future. Many battered women use community programs and shelters to their advantage, but many others sentence themselves to a lifetime of beatings, reconciliations, and shattered hopes. The following clinical example illustrates an adverse outcome for one battered woman.

•CLINICAL EXAMPLE:
NEGATIVE OUTCOME FOR A BATTERED WOMAN

The police took Meg to a shelter for battered women when they found her huddled in the doorway of a downtown store. It was a bitterly cold night in a Northeastern city. Meg refused to tell the police very much about herself, except to ask them to take her to the shelter. She explained that she knew people there and they would take her in as they had done in the past. The night staff at the shelter was willing to admit Meg, but added that she should not continue to use the facility as a short-term refuge from her problems.

Meg was nineteen years old, unmarried, and a high school dropout. She had been living with the same man since she was sixteen, and insisted that "underneath it all, he really loves me." Meg was a runaway from a small town. She had met Ollie shortly after coming to the city. She was penniless and when Ollie asked her to move in with him, she jumped at the chance. Sexually inexperienced, Meg was initiated into acts that included anal sex, bondage, vaginal insertion of objects, and other variations, which Meg found frightening and ugly. Whenever she objected or tried to substitute more conventional sexual behavior, Ollie became enraged. He either knocked her around or threatened to toss her out of the house. As time went on, Ollie became more impatient and more abusive toward Meg. His drinking increased and he began to combine alcohol and cocaine usage. Meg often drank with him, but rarely used cocaine because she saw how frightening Ollie became after using it. Meg found that the alcohol was helpful in overcoming her aversion to Ollie's sexual tastes.

Meg had come to the shelter on her own several times before the police brought her. On each admission she made an effort to be helpful and agreeable toward the staff and other residents. In group meetings, she recounted horrendous stories of physical and sexual abuse by Ollie, and tearfully asked for help in leaving him. Yet, when appointments were made for her to apply for welfare benefits or look for an apartment, she did not follow through. Within a week or two she had renewed her association with Ollie and began defending him as vehemently as she had criticized him.

Each time Meg returned to Ollie, his treatment of her grew worse. Beatings became more frequent and his sexual demands became crueler and more perverse. His craving for cocaine escalated so that there was no money left for food. When this happened, Ollie insisted that Meg prostitute herself. At first she did well walking the streets, but with the arrival of winter, customers were few. Ollie reacted by giving Meg a quota that she had to meet. Until she fulfilled the quota, she was not allowed to come home. The night the police found her, she had not met Ollie's quota and was afraid to go home.

Because of Meg's pattern of returning to Ollie, the staff at the shelter was not hopeful that she would extricate herself from her miserable situation. Nevertheless, they were committed to helping her and again placed the resources of the program at her disposal. The telephone at the shelter was unlisted, and security personnel prevented the entry of unwelcome spouses or boyfriends. Since no restrictions were placed on outgoing calls or on the whereabouts of shelter residents during the day, it was easy for any of them to contact old friends or to resume relationships with the men they had just left. This was what Meg had done on her previous admissions, and this is what she did during the most recent admission. As winter gave way to spring, Meg evidently forgot about being forced to walk all night, freezing in a skimpy outfit, and being unable to return home until she had made enough money. On previous occasions she had told staff members when she was going back to Ollie, always assuring them that things would be different this time. On the last occasion of leaving, she left the shelter without a word of explanation. Other residents told the staff that Meg had been seeing Ollie, that he was entering a drug treatment program and needed Meg to help him. Meg had been too embarrassed to inform the staff of her decision.

No one heard of Meg until the following winter when a news item appeared that she had been found frozen in an unheated car where she had crawled for shelter, and had fallen asleep. Her body showed signs of recent beatings by an unknown assailant. When the police went to the address in her wallet, there were no signs of the occupant with whom she had lived. Efforts were made to reach Meg's parents to make decisions about a funeral. Her father told the city police to do whatever they liked, because Meg "had made her own bed and now she could lie in it."

Critical Guidelines

The news of Meg's death upset residents and staff members who had known her. For battered women, this was a reminder of how precarious life with an abuser could be. For staff members, Meg's death caused them to ask questions about their effectiveness as counselors. Her records were reviewed in their entirety; in essence, a psychological post-mortem was held.

Judging by the attitude of Meg's father, low self-esteem and lack of self-confidence had been instilled in Meg as a child. Although she was young and pretty, she lacked other social resources. She was poorly educated, even illiterate. Her knowledge of the world was limited until she met Ollie. What he gave her was a dark world in which the strong overpowered the weak, and in which a girl like her would never survive. Ollie was able to convince Meg that she needed him because she could never take care of herself. Prostitution was not something Meg engaged in willingly, because no love was involved between the girl and the customer. What made it bearable for Meg was awareness that she was a professional whore only because she loved Ollie so much. With his sociopathic tendencies, Ollie was able to talk Meg into anything. She wanted to believe in him and wanted to believe that eventually they would have a fine life together as long as she did whatever he asked.

Counselors at the shelter knew that Meg lived in a fantasy world and hoped to make her more realistic. Even so, they did not quite realize how frightened she was at the prospect of being alone. Any contact with the welfare department or the housing authority made Meg tremble with fear, although she concealed this under youthful exuberance.

Almost all battered women have trouble accepting autonomy and independence, but Meg's conflict was greater than most. In trying to learn something from Meg's death, the staff concluded that they might have been more sensitive to her dependency needs. One staff member, in particular, had considered Meg's distress less overwhelming than that of resident mothers who had been abused. This counselor told Meg more than once that she would very likely go back to Ollie, just as she had in the past. Although it was too late for Meg, the counselor openly regretted her remarks. She received some support from her colleagues, all of whom learned something from their failure to help Meg.

SUMMARY

The disorganized family is characterized by inappropriate role enactment and recurring crises. For many of these families, alcoholism is not only a problem in its own right, but is a condition that exacerbates the crises of spouse abuse and child abuse. In modern life, domestic violence has reached epidemic proportions, but has received public attention only within recent decades. Wife battering is a practice that transcends ethnic and socioeconomic boundaries, although it is more likely to be apprehended in lower-class families. Psychoanalytic explanations of wife beating as a reciprocal sadomasochistic interaction is not an adequate formulation, nor are sociological theories of the etiology of spouse abuse.

The feminist viewpoint is useful for consciousness raising, but does not present clear guidelines for clinical intervention. The reality is that family violence and spouse abuse are complex problems that require an eclectic approach. Crisis counseling has proved its effectiveness as a treatment modality, whether offered in women's shelters, through crisis hot lines, or in supportive group programs. A battered woman's decision to leave an abusive spouse is often a lengthy process characterized by repeated separations and reunions. Periods of separation are likely to be times of crisis for the battered woman, her children, and also for the abusive spouse. Clinicians engaged in work with battered women should avoid directive advice and derisive statements about the abusive spouse. Such interventions by workers may cause the battered woman to become defensive and to feel personally belittled by this approach.

The battered women is an individual whose problems are psychological, physiological, situational, and interpersonal. In a crisis as complex as this, the simplistic explanations of female masochism are interesting but hardly adequate. The same might be said of sociological formulations and the feminist position. In working with battered women, an eclectic approach that synthesizes several theoretical formulations is more apt to be effective.

REFERENCES

Bandura, A. *Social Foundations of Thought and Action.* Englewood Cliffs, New Jersey: Prentice-Hall, 1986.

Barden, J.C. "Battered Wives: How Law Can Help." *The New York Times* February 27, 1982.

Brisson, N. "Battering Husbands: A Survey of Abusive Men." *Victimology* 6(1983): 338–344.

Browne, A. *When Battered Women Kill.* New York: Free Press, 1987.

Curry, L., L. Colvin, and J. Lancaster. "Breaking the Cycle of Family Abuse." *American Journal of Nursing* 88(1988): 1188–1190.

DeLorto, D., and A. LaViolette. "Spouse Abuse." *Occupational Health Nursing* 1(1980): 17–19.

Edelson, J.L., and M.P. Brygger. "Gender Differences in Self-reporting of Battering Incidences." *Family Relations* 35(1986): 377–382.

Elbow, M. "Theoretical Considerations in Violent Marriages." *Social Casework* 31(1977): 515–523.

Fagan, J.A., D.K. Stewart, and K.V. Hansen. "Violent Men or Violent Husbands? Background Factors and Situational Correlates." In *The Dark Side of Families Current Family Violence Research,* edited by D. Finkelhor, R.J. Gelles, G.T. Hotaling, and M.A. Straus. Beverly Hills, California: Sage Publications, 1983.

Finkelhor, D., and K. Yilo. "Forced Sex in Marriage: Preliminary Research Report." *Crime and Delinquency* 7(1982): 459–479.

──── . *License to Rape.* New York: Holt, Rinehart and Winston, 1985.

Freud, S. "The Economic Problem of Masochism." In *Collected Papers of Sigmund Freud.* New York: Basic Books, 1959.

Frieze, I.H. "Investigating Causes and Consequences of Marital Rape." *Journal of Women in Culture and Society* 8(1983): 532–533.

Griffin, M. "In Forty-four States It's Legal to Rape Your Wife." *British Journal of Law and Society* 9(1989): 21–23.

Hanks, S., and P. Rosenbaum. "Battered Women: A Study of Women Who Live with Violent, Alcohol Abusing Men." *American Journal of Orthopsychiatry* 47(1977): 291–306.

Helfer, R.E., and C.E. Kempe. *Child Abuse and Neglect: The Family and the Community.* Cambridge, Massachusetts: Ballinger, 1976.

Hilberman, E. "Overview: The Wifebeater's Wife Reconsidered." *American Journal of Psychiatry* 37(1980): 1036–1037.

Hornung, C., B. McCullough, B. Clove, and F. Sugimoto. "Status Relationships in Marriage: Risk Factors in Spouse Abuse." Paper presented at annual meeting of American Sociological Association, New York, August 1980.

Kurz, D. "Emergency Department Responses to Battered Women: Resistance to Medicalization." *Social Problems* 34(1987): 69–81.

Lamb, S. "Acts as Agents: An Analysis of Linguistic Avoidance in Journal Articles on Men Who Batter Women." *American Journal of Orthopsychiatry* 61(1991): 250–257.

Lesse, S. "The Status of Violence Against Women: Past, Present, and Future Factors." *American Journal of Psychotherapy* 33(1979): 190–200.

Martin, D. "Society's Vindication of the Wifebeater." *Bulletin of American Academy of Psychiatry and the Law* 5(1977): 391–410.

Meyers, L. "Battered Wives: Dead Husbands." In *Family in Transition,* 3rd ed., edited by A. Skolnick and J.H. Skilnick. Boston: Little, Brown, 1980.

Neidig, P.H., B.S. Collins, and D.H. Friedman. "Attitudinal Characteristics of Males Who have Engaged in Spouse Abuse." *Journal of Family Violence* 1(1986): 222–233.

Pagelow, M.D. *Women Batterings: Victims and Their Experiences.* Beverly Hills, California: Sage Publications, 1982.

Roy, M. *Battered Women.* New York: Van Nostrand Reinhold, 1977.

Saunders, D.G. "A Typology of Men Who Batter: Three Types Derived from Cluster Analysis." *American Journal of Orthopsychiatry* 62(1992): 264–275.

Schechter, S. "Treatment and Advocacy of Battered Women: Principles and Distinctions." Paper presented at Harvard Medical School Conference on Abuse and Victimization. Boston: March 1989.

Shainness, N. "Vulnerability of Violence: Masochism as a Process." *American Journal of Psychotherapy* 33(1979): 322–334.

Shields, N.M., G.J. McCall, and C.R. Hanneke. "Patterns of Family and Nonfamily Violence: Violent Husbands and Violent Men." *Violence and Victims* 3(1988): 83–98.

Straus, M.A., R.J. Gelles, and S.K. Steinmetz. *Behind Closed Doors: Violence in the American Family* New York: Doubleday/Anchor, 1980.

Walker, L.E. *The Battered Woman Syndrome* New York: Springer-Verlag, 1984.

Weingourt, R. "Wife Rape: Barriers to Identification and Treatment." *American Journal of Psychotherapy* 39(1985): 187–192.

———. "Wife Rape in a Sample of Psychiatric Patients." *Image* 22(1990): 144–147.

PART
FOUR

GROUPS IN CRISIS

13

Communities in Crisis
Disasters and Unemployment

If you have built castles in the air, your work need not be lost; that is where they should be. Now put the foundations under them.

Henry David Thoreau

When communities rather than separate individuals or families confront crises, the terms *disaster* or *catastrophe* are applied. *Community* may be defined as an aggregate of people engaged in reciprocal interdependent transactions within a shared environment. Common needs, interests, values, and expectations connect communities. Community may mean different things to different people. A community may be a specific place or neighborhood contained within geographic limits.

A community may be a group whose members share certain values regardless of whether members reside close to one another. Any group organized around the same mission or concerns may constitute a community. Religious orders are communities created around similar beliefs. Any ethnic or racial group possessing a common culture may be regarded as a community, even when members are widely dispersed. Belonging to the black community in the United States is based on shared experiences, historical and contemporary. Hispanics living anywhere in a city are apt to consider themselves part of the Spanish American community when issues such as education or employment are raised. When the influence of a group on its members is pervasive and encompassing, the definition of community can be expanded to denote culture, rather than group or place.

Cultural ideology includes racial and ethnic beliefs about the nature of health, accidents, and illnesses. Many cultural beliefs are durable and persistent, and tend to last beyond the immigrant generation. During periods of disaster and catastrophe, behaviors of survivors may reflect cultural attitudes and biases. Whenever survivors and would-be rescuers represent different cultures, building trust between them may be a

315

prolonged process. Frequently, those who have lived through a cataclysmic event form a new community to which only other survivors are admitted. While this phenomenon may be beneficial for survivors, it may not ease the tasks of rescuers or caregivers.

Many smaller communities, organized formally or informally, exist within larger communities. Such communities are formed for special reasons and members' commitments will vary. Students may be part of a school community for only a few years, while teachers may belong for their entire working lives. Not only does membership have different time frames, it also carries different role expectations. One kind of role enactment is expected from students and another kind from teachers. During times of disaster or catastrophe, it is generally assumed that police officers, firefighters, nurses, and physicians will function as protectors and rescuers, since those are their expected roles in normal times.

The equilibrium of any community is important to its members because disequilibrium creates conditions that have far-reaching effects. This is true whether community is regarded as a place, a group, or a shared culture. For our purposes, the definition of a community is based on geography, since the idea of a shared place conveys a sense of collective experience based upon being at a particular place at a particular time. Disasters usually originate in forces external to individuals and families that are affected and are rarely subject to control. During times immediately preceding or following a disaster, the physical and social resources of a community will be tested to the utmost. The community's support systems and the population's problem-solving capacity largely determine whether crisis is averted, solved adequately, or resolved minimally.

EPIDEMIOLOGY OF COMMUNITY CRISIS

Epidemiology, with its interactive components of agent, host, and environment, provides a framework for understanding the development of community crisis. Equilibrium represents a balance between host factors and agent factors operating in a dynamic environment. When environmental conditions shift the balance in favor of the host, the likelihood of disequilibrium and ensuing crisis decreases. If environmental conditions favor agent factors, the result is a shift toward increased probability of disequilibrium and crisis. Host factors that influence the relative susceptibility of individuals include such variables as age, sex, race, occupation, and marital status. The response of individuals to agent factors depends on their levels of functioning, previous experiences, present needs, and future goals. Agent factors include any stressors of sufficient intensity and duration to produce disequilibrium in the host. An epidemiological model of community crisis is depicted in Figure 13–1.

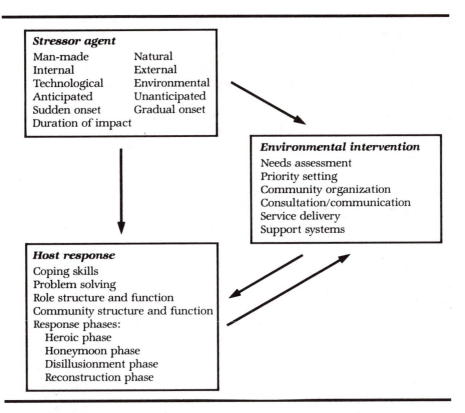

FIGURE 13–1 Epidemiological Model of Communities in Crisis.

HOST RESPONSES TO CRISIS

As communities advance technologically, they become more distant from their environment and more dependent on the organization of complex systems. In a disaster situation, this dependence can aggravate problems. Disasters cause individual disorganization, family disorganization, and community disorganization in the form of confusion and fragmentation. Each form of disorganization intensifies the others, for individuals and families find restoration of equilibrium more difficult in the face of community breakdown. The emergence of a crisis after disaster follows the sequence of other crises. There is a hazardous event or stressor, failure of usual coping behavior and disorganization, followed by recovery or reorganization.

In disaster situations there are threats of separation, injury, abandonment, or death. Panic reactions to disaster have received dramatic treatment in the media. Officials have used the alleged propensity of people resorting to panic behavior as an excuse for withholding information from the residents of disaster areas. Observation and research have refuted the belief that panic behavior is a customary response to disaster. The reality is that in the period before disaster strikes, people may be frightened, but tend not to engage in flight behavior. Even when given official instructions, people are reluctant to obey orders to evacuate their homes. Perceptions of impending disaster are subject to individual interpretation. For example, families are inclined to base their decisions on information gathered from relatives and neighbors, rather than official reports. The life cycle stage of a family may determine whether a disaster is seen as a crisis or merely a matter of some concern. The possibility of nuclear contamination is an urgent issue for pregnant women, mothers of young children, and for most persons in the childbearing or childrearing years. An older couple, less worried about genetic mutation or the welfare of children, might have no compelling reason to avoid danger and decide to remain in their own home regardless of official warnings. Some families choose to ignore official reassurances that they are in no danger, and leave the scene of the impending disaster for reasons of their own (Kinsinger, 1980).

During the period preceding the impact of disaster, the defense mechanism of denial may operate to the extent that people consider themselves invulnerable. Despite warnings, they remain convinced that disaster will occur elsewhere, and that they will be untouched. Disbelief may be due to optimism, fatalism, or religious faith. Once disaster strikes, their sense of personal invulnerability is shaken. Behavioral responses then depend on the gravity of the situation, the duration of adverse conditions, and the accessibility of relief measures. Many individuals who have lived through a major disaster comment later on their reordering of priorities and reshaping of values as a consequence of the experience. Cohen and Ahearn (1980) have argued that the term *survivor* is more appropriate than the term *victim,* because the latter carries overtones of passivity and helplessness, which discredits the tenacity of survivors. Camus (1948) emphasized that, for survivors, the importance of performing routine tasks during a time of catastrophe stems not from actual heroism, but simply from a need to continue daily existence.

DISASTER CLASSIFICATIONS

Various typologies may be used to differentiate disasters. Human beings have encountered various forms of disaster throughout their history, recorded and unrecorded. Each year thousands of lives are lost because of disasters in underdeveloped and in highly developed societies. Two disasters of equal magnitude will have significantly different consequences, depending on population density in the affected area and the support systems available to stricken communities. Highly industrialized societies with dense populations and complex technology are prone to greater impact, but have more resources to alleviate suffering and disruption (Berren, 1980).

Human-derived disasters are more likely to be generated by events within the community, whereas natural disasters originate outside the community and may be less amenable to control. Strikes, riots, economic decline, and urban decay are examples of human-derived, internally derived disasters. It must be acknowledged that distinctions between natural and human-derived disasters may be blurred in cases in which human ineptitude has aggravated natural environmental hazards.

Another classification of disasters considers the expected or unexpected nature of the disaster. Disasters that have occurred before or that give warning signals allow for a degree of preparedness. People living in a valley that is periodically flooded are more prepared to cope with flood control, just as people living in the vicinity of a volcano have learned evacuation procedures based on careful estimates of potential danger. Whenever the onset of disaster is gradual rather than precipitous, those who are threatened have time for anticipatory planning. Other factors that warrant consideration are the duration of the disaster's impact and the broad distribution of consequences throughout the population. When disasters are sudden, unprecedented, and nondiscriminatory in their effects, there is greater likelihood of severe community disruption.

Regardless of classification, disasters disturb community equilibrium and create conditions of crisis. Natural and human-derived environmental disasters differ in etiology, since the latter are a consequence of human decisions and actions. Even so, the effects of natural and environmental disasters possess certain similarities. This is not true of economic disasters, which have a uniqueness that justifies separate classification. In this chapter, natural and environmental disasters are discussed as similar phenomena, whereas economic disasters are discussed separately because of their particular characteristics.

NATURAL AND ENVIRONMENTAL DISASTERS

Siporin (1976, p. 216) described *disaster* as "an extreme social crisis situation in which individuals and social systems become dysfunctional and disorganized, sustain personal, collective, and public hardships, and also become a community of sufferers." Because disasters are more severe than previous events, alterations of individual, family, and community behaviors occur. Ambiguity concerning the outcome of disaster causes anxiety, which is exacerbated when customary behaviors prove inadequate. The unexpectedness of a disaster and the inexperience of the inhabitants in coping with disaster can drastically alter the outcomes. People who live where landslides are common become practiced in preventive and restorative measures. The same is true of inhabitants of arid regions where a brush fire can become a conflagration of terrifying proportions. Relatively isolated communities often suffer undue hardship because of their inaccessibility to rescue workers. An example of unexpectedness, unpreparedness, and relative inaccessibility may be found in the accounts of a severe earthquake that occurred early in this century in the northeastern part of the United States and Canada, where such events are rare. When a severe earthquake did occur in this region, the tremors annihilated three farming communities and caused damage from Portland, Maine, to Halifax, Nova Scotia. All along the coastline, small communities lost contact with the outside world for forty hours. Houses were flattened, and water, gas, and electric lines were severed. A forty-eight-car Canadian Pacific train plunged into a river, creating more havoc when sixteen railroad cars loaded with propane gas exploded with the fiery intensity of an atomic explosion. Additional injuries were suffered when flying debris landed on a busy highway, igniting buildings and vehicles in the suburbs of Fredericton, New Brunswick, which was located at the center of the earthquake.

Natural and environmental disasters can take many forms, and many uncontrolled variables influence their impact. Natural disasters are usually attributed to God, fate, or bad luck. Thus, no one is really held responsible. When a disaster results from action taken by other people, time and energy are devoted to assigning blame. The question of compensation is not easily resolved and litigation, if pursued, adds to the stress of the disaster. Table 13–1 depicts representational forms of community disasters and the global range of their occurrence.

In dealing with the consequences of disaster, an important rule is to keep families together, if possible. Research in clinical settings and in the laboratory indicate that stress is tolerated more easily if significant persons are present. Separation from families and evacuation from London in World War II seemed to be more harmful for children than remaining and enduring air raids in the company of their families. Studies of combat soldiers have indicated that membership in a supportive group, such as a platoon, does much to reduce battle stress (Bovard, 1959).

Separation anxiety is a universal human experience; loss of loved ones, loss of possessions, and loss of comforting routines are examples of separation that produces feelings of helplessness and hopelessness. In these circumstances, community workers can reduce anxiety wherever possible by providing information about other family members and missing possessions. For many survivors, uncertainty is harder to tolerate than the actual knowledge of what has happened.

TABLE 13-1   Location, Type, and Extent of Representative
Disasters, 1963–1991

Date	Location	Type	Extent
1963	U.S.S. Thresher	Submarine lost	129 lives
1964	Alaska	Earthquake	117 lives
1970	Bay of Bengal, East Pakistan	Tidal Wave	200,000 lives
1974	Zagreb, Yugoslavia	Train Wreck	153 lives
1974	Darwin, Australia	Cyclone	67 lives 35,000 evacuated
1977	Canary Islands	Airplane crash	582 lives
1979	Chicago, Illinois	Airplane crash	272 lives
1980	St. Petersburg, Florida	Ship and bridge collision	36 lives
1981	Las Vegas, Nevada	Hotel fires	92 lives
1983	Victoria, South Australia	Bush fires	72 lives 2000 homes lost
1985	Dallas-Fort Worth Airport	Airplane crash	137 lives 30 injured
1985	Armero, Colombia	Volcano erupted	22,000 lives
1991	Philippines	Volcano erupted	341 lives

Source: Adapted from Janosik and Green (1992), Cohen (1987), and Gavalya (1987).

Young children are apt to regress and cling to parents or favorite possessions that have been rescued. Such regressive behaviors should be tolerated and understood. Adolescents may display uncharacteristic behavior by becoming withdrawn or belligerent. Either manifestation should be met with consideration coupled with limit setting. Encouraging adolescents to assume responsibilities that are constructive but not unduly demanding may help restore age-appropriate behavior. For adults in the family, loss of home and possessions is a bitter blow. Realization that the rewards of a lifetime of hard work have been swept away may cause depressive reactions with accompanying somatic complaints.

Many variables influence the readiness of victims to accept assistance. People in lower socioeconomic groups are usually more willing to accept physical treatment than psychological counseling. This is a compelling argument for including mental health services in comprehensive disaster programs. Members of ethnic or racial minorities, who do not accept the customs of the dominant culture, may misinterpret, and therefore reject, help that is being offered. This problem can be dealt with by enlisting the help of racial and ethnic representatives or religious leaders whom the minority segment of the population trust. In meeting the total needs of communities beset by disaster, coordinating the relief program is a major undertaking on which successful recovery depends. Human and material resources are too scarce to be wasted on duplicated efforts or uncoordinated missions.

Role Reorganization

Disaster conditions disrupt patterns of role performance established over the years. Under ordinary circumstances, role performance is distributed between family, job, and social responsibilities. In times of disaster, additional demands are made at all three levels of role performance. When individuals must choose between meeting the responsibilities of one role at the expense of other roles, the result is ambivalence and role conflict. For example, an ambulance attendant working round the clock in the aftermath of a disaster must decide whether to remain on the job or look for the well-being of his own family. It is natural at such moments for personal considerations to intrude on the decision. Members of police and fire departments usually continue in their occupational roles and endeavor to meet community demands that, for them, supercede personal obligations. Balancing family tasks against community needs is less a choice of one over the other than a need to maintain communication between family members and the community worker. If a firefighter knows that his own family is relatively safe, reluctance to fulfill community responsibilities is erased and external role performance is facilitated. Losses are handled better when borne in the context of the suffering of others. Even though families must live in crowded temporary quarters, propinquity with other victims seems to have some mitigating effects by reducing feelings of isolation.

There is some evidence that personal commitments may take precedence over community duties in times of disaster. One dedicated director of a children's home did not participate in community rescue efforts following a flood until she loaded the children in her charge on a bus and drove them to another area. This evacuation was accomplished even though the children were in no immediate danger and she had never before driven a bus. Once the children were transported, their protector was able to participate in rescue operations.

Disasters impose internal strains on family role enactment because members are not sure what is expected of them nor what the future will bring. When central family members, such as parents, cannot meet their own role expectations in protecting and caring for the family, the result is role strain accompanied by feelings of personal inadequacy.

During disasters, roles are organized around priorities; irrelevant tasks and responsibilities are temporarily discarded. Lowering community and family role expectations increases efficiency in performing essential core roles. At this point, communication networks between individuals, families, community workers, and community service facilities are of great importance. Any disaster disrupts collective behavior, and people involved in the disaster must know whom to interact with, what should be done, and for what purpose. Always there are problems of imbalance between resources and needs, but equitable laws of supply and demand tend to prevail and are invoked to maintain balance between needs and resources.

In analyzing human responses to disaster, economic, physical, and psychological effects should be evaluated. At present, there is a tendency to measure the severity of a disaster in quantifiable terms, such as financial losses or number of fatalities. Comparatively, little attention has been directed to social or psychological impairment following disasters. Lately, there has been some recognition of the need to include mental health counseling in relief programs organized for disaster victims, and judgments have been made that on-site crisis intervention is probably the most efficacious approach. Data accumulated thus far indicate that relatively few disaster victims experience long-term emotional damage, even though substantial numbers report transitory difficulties around problems of everyday living. The value of traditional psychotherapeutic intervention offered in clinical settings is questionable for crisis victims who were functioning adequately before the disaster experience.

In the aftermath of natural and environmental disasters, physical needs are dominant, and providing food, clothing, and shelter for victims is probably the most therapeutic initial intervention. Basic survival needs, such as care of the injured, followed by search and rescue missions, have the highest priority. Since professionals may be in short supply, a considerable amount of work must be delegated to uninjured victims and concerned outsiders. Such assignments do much to eradicate feelings of powerlessness. The rationale for advocating crisis intervention in the postdisaster period is that during this time of acute distress, many individuals simultaneously experience the same feelings and reactions. There is irrefutable evidence that disasters provoke great distress in the victims, but the permanence of psychological impairment has not been extensively studied. The current belief is that psychological effects are temporary and that crisis intervention is all that may be required. Researchers willing to pursue on-site and longitudinal investigation need to verify this further.

Phases of Disaster Reactions

Victims of disasters frequently undergo the following sequence of emotional reactions: heroic phase, honeymoon phase, disillusionment phase, and a reconstruction phase (Burgess & Baldwin, 1980).

The *heroic phase* appears at the time of the disaster and is characterized by excitement and by people working together to survive the event. During the heroic phase, panic behaviors are infrequent and maladaptive responses are quite low. Fight-flight behavior is rarely evident and irrationality is notably absent. Dynes and Quarantelli (1978, p. 235) wrote that "solo or collective panic is so rare as to be an insignificant practical problem." At this time, victims adapt by assessing immediate exigencies and cooperating with others to alleviate conditions. In the infrequent cases in which panic was evidenced, there was urgent, severe danger arising within seconds, a limited number of escape routes, and inadequate information, especially in regard to escape routes. Three phases of disaster reactions appear in Table 13–2.

The period following the heroic phase has been labeled the *honeymoon phase*. This interval is of fairly short duration, generally lasting from two weeks to two months after the first impact of the disaster. During this time, optimism runs high, and plans for rebuilding and restoring are formulated. In normal times, a community attends to the production and distribution of goods, social control, social protection, and social needs. During the honeymoon phase, community priorities change; production of goods is reduced in importance because the objective is to meet basic needs rather than maintain economic productivity. Schools may be closed temporarily, and the media may become a means of communication rather

TABLE 13–2 Theoretical Phases of Disaster Reactions

Phase	Time Frame	Reactive Behaviors
Initial, or honeymoon phase	Occurs within two weeks to two months after impact.	Plans are made to rebuild and restore. Optimistic and energetic moods. Services regulated and allocated. Social control is high.
Middle, or disillusionment phase	Appears after a few months; may last a year or so.	Awareness of a new reality. Feelings of grief, anger, and despair. Feeling of guilt for surviving. Irrational fears; sleep disorders. Erosion of confidence and trust. Rebuilding and restoring begins.
Final, or reconstruction phase	May last several years or more.	Cooperative efforts to rebuild. Periods of discouragement. Impatience with slow progress. Modification of values and expectations.

Source: Adapted from Burgess and Baldwin (1980).

than a source of entertainment. Social activities assume a low profile, but social control and social protection receive high priority. Mutual support among the victims takes the form of regulating and distributing services in an equitable manner unknown in the community before the disaster occurred.

Following these phases of work and optimism comes a period of *disillusionment,* characterized by grief, despair, sleep disturbance, haunting visual memories, and anger at the destruction of life and property. Burgess and Baldwin (1980) suggested that this disillusionment phase might be compared to a second disaster, whereby victims must cope with a new social reality replete with losses, destruction, unemployment, and other problems. Occasionally, the victims of disaster present depressive reactions, recurrent fears, nightmares, and guilt for surviving when loved ones died. The disillusionment phase may last from several months to a year or more. During this phase, rebuilding is begun, but survivors may experience frustration and failure. A sense of alienation, loss of confidence, and erosion of basic trust compound these negative reactions.

The *reconstruction phase* can be identified by collaborative efforts designed to restore predisaster levels of functioning to the community. Depending on the magnitude of the disaster, this phase may last a number of years. During this lengthy period, discouragement and apathy may surface if favorable results are slow to appear. At other times, cooperation during the reconstruction period causes people to draw closer to each other and perhaps modify their values. According to Zeigler (1981, p. 9), in an interview with a flood victim seven years after the disaster, the victim said, "A house is a very important part of our lives—but it's not the most important part. Let me put it this way . . . a home could never be washed away . . . but a house could." The following post-disaster reactions are adapted from Cohen (1987):

- Ambivalence about learning details of the disaster.
- Unwillingness to accept the reality of losses.
- Painful emotions expressed through somatic complaints.
- Use of primitive defenses such as denial, withdrawal, and magical thinking.
- Verbalizing painful emotions as the extent of losses are comprehended.

Burnout

During the period just after impact, disaster workers extend themselves heroically. Professionals and paraprofessionals, and volunteers work side by side to meet essential community needs. The unprecedented suffering that surrounds the workers causes them to be unsparing in their attention to survivors. An essential consideration for leaders of relief work following disaster is knowledge that everyone is operating under adverse conditions and must be protected against overextending themselves. Desperate conditions may last for days, weeks, or months, and helpers gradually exhaust themselves without realizing it. At first, others do not notice their accumulated fatigue, which is later revealed in cognitive, emotional, and behavioral deficits that are beyond the conscious awareness of the helper. Black (1987), who worked closely with the families of passengers killed in a plane crash, found that the noise of airplanes and newspaper accounts of other disasters would reactivate his anguish and empathy for victims and survivors. Cohen (1987) reported that the ongoing demands of survivors annoyed many helpers, and the helpers avoided contact with the survivors to control their reactions.

Burnout alters judgment, influences moods, and alters the power to see situations objectively. Indecisiveness, irritability, excitability, and somatic symptoms are part of the burnout syndrome. Burnout may appear early in the postimpact period, or may be delayed until the crisis is over and a semblance of normalcy is restored. Burnout may also be characterized by feelings of having failed or being unappreciated. Irrespective of the underlying feelings, burnout represents a depletion of physical and psychological energy that must be identified for those workers who are unable to recognize their own exhaustion. Burnout can be averted by reducing demands made on workers, by offering support and encouragement, and by acknowledging their contributions to disaster relief. The following list of services for rescuers and other workers is adapted from Cohen (1987):

- Consultation and education to help workers understand conflicting and inconsistent messages from survivors.
- Relief for front-line workers to overcome burnout after long hours of rescue work.
- Coordination and linkage of services to prevent isolation of workers and promote open communication between service groups.
- Cooperative arrangements between on-site workers and personnel in hospitals, community agencies, and emergency shelters.
- Access to support groups and mental health facilities for workers suffering psychological distress.

Counseling Disaster Survivors

In recent years, mental health workers have become part of crisis intervention teams responding to catastrophic events. Their experiences have clarified the psychological and behavioral responses of survivors. Clinical observations of workers have been augmented by research tools to assess reactions. Eth and Pynoos (1985) differentiated grief and mourning that accompanies loss from the psychic numbing that follows trauma. Cohen

(1987, p. 1317) wrote, "In a disaster, the suddenness of death and the catastrophic impact on individual lives produce both trauma and grief which are sequential responses to the traumatic event." A disaster elicits conflicting thoughts and feelings. Almost always, the survivors are flooded with anxiety that impairs reality testing and alters the grief and mourning process. Cohen and Ahearn (1980) stated that attention to survivors' anxiety should be the first form of intervention.

According to Cohen (1987), survivors show a need to be active and an inability to relax in the aftermath of a disaster. Their drive for action is often coupled with indecision and social unresponsiveness. Although they wanted to be active, survivors performed tasks in an automatic, blunted fashion. Crisis workers need to be accepting of prolonged apathy; this reaction may be related to trauma, but it also may indicate that grief work has begun. A related issue is the importance of allowing survivors to express anger at helping efforts without retaliation from care providers. It is quite usual for survivors to become bitter and explosive as denial gives way to realization of what has been lost. When survivors are irritable or uncooperative, it may precipitate similar behavior in workers, some of whom risked a great deal in order to help. Mutual withdrawal by care givers and survivors worsens the social isolation of survivors.

The psychological distress of survivors is frequently expressed through physiological channels. Many survivors have reported altered sensory perceptions in the form of illusions, hallucinations, and delusions. Some have described feelings of being out of touch with reality. This, at times, took the form of refusing to believe that loved ones had died, and insisting that the absent one would be found despite all evidence to the contrary.

Comparatively, little research has centered on children's reactions to disasters, but some investigators (Galante & Foa, 1986; Terr, 1983) asserted that children exposed to disaster are twice as likely to develop stress-related problems later in life than children who were not similarly exposed. These researchers found that traumatized children have fears that increase over time, they cannot control their thoughts, they experience sleep disturbances, and they have difficulty concentrating. Parents reported disobedience and tearfulness; teachers reported inattentiveness and distractability. Parents and teachers alike found that the children were restless and sought attention. McFarlane (1986) indicated that immediately after a disaster, children seemed to be very "good" but adverse effects developed later, up to the second year afterward. Morbidity in children correlated with parental preoccupation with their own disaster experiences.

A comprehensive assessment of needs and analysis of resources available to the stricken community are essential to understanding the gravity of the situation. Delivery of services to survivors and rescue of persons still in danger are major areas of concern. Other pressing issues are the identification of community leaders and utilization of persons with special skills and abilities.

Mental health services during times of disaster have received less attention than they merit, although there is growing recognition of their importance. The importance of mental health counseling through the pre-impact, impact, and post-impact stages of disaster can be regarded as a form of psychological intervention that combines primary, secondary, and tertiary prevention. Burgess and Baldwin (1980) wrote that mental health services in the aftermath of disaster are an essential aspect of relief and reconstructive programs. Mental health counseling can be offered in evacuation centers as soon as people are relocated. Groups and group leaders recruited from outside or from within the community can be used to inform people about what is being done and to encourage participation in rescue and salvage work. Supportive group counseling during times of disaster has been very successful with survivors, young and old, regardless of whether family support was available to them.

The help provided to crisis victims should not be withdrawn prematurely. It must be remembered that high levels of anxiety during and immediately after a disaster impede communication and cognitive understanding. Victims of disaster need to tell their story more than once; repetition of details should receive the careful attention that emotional catharsis deserves. People living in a disaster situation cannot comprehend immediate instructions very well because of the cognitive distortion that anxiety brings. Three months after a flood, one elderly person was discovered living alone in a trailer, incapable of understanding the financial aid forms a community worker had left. She had received instructions at the time of the disaster, but was not, at that point, able to comprehend nor to remember what she had been told to do with the papers.

Every disaster produces sequelae that require specific planning and intervention, even though there are commonalities to be found in disasters. Many interventions used in disasters are extensions of generic approaches used for any crisis. One of the most important elements of crisis counseling is acknowledgment that people in crisis are not ill; rather, they are simply people in need for whom the community has a responsibility. Community crisis intervention does not adhere to the traditional methods of taking the client's history and scheduling appointments in a clinical setting, but professionals and paraprofessionals can work wherever disaster conditions exist.

The Nature of Unseen Disasters

Many disasters are considered "acts of God"; they result from uncontrolled forces of nature for which no one can be held responsible. While the severity and the duration of the disaster are important considerations, even more important is the essential nature of the event. Environmental contamination is a human-derived threat that people all over the world face. It is estimated that, in the United States alone, over one million people have been exposed to ionizing radiation through nuclear accidents, contaminated waste, or industrial or scientific work (Murphy et al., 1990). Mounting evidence of environmental contamination has spurred interest in the physical and psychological effects of human exposure to unseen toxins (Edelstein, 1988). A case in point is the plight of American servicepersons exposed to nuclear radiation.

Between 1946 and 1963, 250,000 members of the armed forces were subjected to nuclear exposure as part of a testing program. More than 340 nuclear bombs were detonated in the Pacific area and in western parts of the United States. These veterans and those who served in Hiroshima and Nagasaki compose the community now known as "atomic veterans." It must be acknowledged that little was known of the long-term effects of radiation in the 1940s and 1950s. Even so, many American service personnel were deliberately exposed to testing. Their distance from the explosions varied, with some servicepersons placed within two miles of the epicenter. As a result of their exposure, in 1979, the affected veterans formed the National Association of Atomic Veterans (NAAV). A study in which NAAV cooperated undertook in-depth interviewing of atomic veterans and their families. There was considerable variation in the views expressed, but focal themes emerged.

The first theme was that persons in authority had invalidated or repudiated the veterans' experiences. Invalidation occurred in several ways. First, the government had not informed the veterans of the potential hazards of exposure. Later, the Defense Department and the Veterans Administration reinforced invalidation. They were reluctant to admit any connection between radiation exposure and the multiple physical problems of veterans.

Because radiation is an unseen menace, validation of its effects may be difficult. The same can be said of environmental contamination of one kind or another. Vyner (1988) noted that exposure to invisible contaminants disrupts the usual process of identifying and responding to a disaster. Vyner further maintained that the psychological effects of invisible contaminants include heightened fear and anxiety, adaptational dilemmas about coping, hypervigilance, altered views of the world, and traumatic neurosis. Interestingly, Murphy et al. (1990) reported that the veterans' experiences had not made them less patriotic, and had increased their altruism.

The second theme the atomic veterans expressed was worry about the intergenerational transmission of genetic defects. They worried about children they already had and about their unborn grandchildren. The third theme was protectiveness toward their children. Their wives also joined in this theme. Silence about radiation was invoked within the family so the children would not be upset. In most instances, the children disclosed to interviewers that they were well-aware of their parents' fears. The fourth theme dealt with the legacy atomic veterans hoped to leave behind them. They wanted public recognition of their experience so that future generations would benefit. Some veterans found positive meaning in their illnesses and disabilities, expressing a deeper appreciation of joys in the present. They clung to hope that good might arise from their misfortune.

Counseling Victims of Unseen Disasters

Human-derived disasters are very hard for the families of victims because, in many cases, the disaster was preventable. As atomic veterans have shown, their reactions and those of their families are confused and labile. Often their responses would alter drastically within a single interview. Their changeable views ranged from wishing to be left alone, wishing to join with others, outrage at their predicament, and altruistic concern for other people within and outside the family. This complex range of responses has practical implications for clinical intervention. Being exposed to toxic contamination of any sort evokes images of futility and betrayal that repeatedly seek an outlet. In this context, Heron (1981, p. 19) recommended that clinicians use "cooperative inquiry." This would allow all participants to "contribute directly to hypothesis making, to formulating the final conclusions, and to what goes on in-between." In light of the atomic veterans' bitter criticism of the "certain" assurances the authorities made amidst uncertain conditions, their participation in building hypotheses and reaching conclusions seems essential. The same can be said of any situation where a group or community must deal with unknown forces. The use of cooperative inquiry can apply to any community looking for answers and solutions to human-derived disasters. Edelstein (1988) described how governmental agencies with jurisdiction over decisions are frustrating residents of contaminated communities, especially when little is known of the ultimate consequences. Atomic veterans, for example, claim that they were reassured about safety limits for exposure, only to find that safety limits were revised upwards when it was shown that the exposure levels of the veterans were higher than safety levels previously set.

ECONOMIC DISASTERS

For people old enough to remember the Great Depression of the 1930s, massive economic decline and unemployment constituted a disaster that has not been forgotten even after years of relative affluence. Those were days of humiliating economies for some families and of great suffering for many more. The American dream of prosperity and upward mobility was tarnished. Men blamed themselves for their inability to provide for their families, and housewives existed at less-than-subsistence levels in order to offer more food to their children. Whenever there are more workers than jobs, the concept of equal opportunity receives minimal attention. During the Great Depression, people lucky enough to be employed allowed themselves to be exploited in order to retain their precarious jobs.

According to a Johns Hopkins University study, a New York community experiencing a 1 percent rise in unemployment may expect 5 percent more suicides, 3 to 4 percent more hospitalizations for mental illness, 4 to 6 percent more homicides, 6 to 7 percent more prison incarcerations, and a 2 percent increase in the overall death rate (Bird, 1982). Some economic disasters are national in scope and have a rippling effect that carries economic consequences beyond national borders. The Great Depression was a worldwide phenomenon and probably contributed to upheaval that led to the outbreak of World War II. Lesser economic disasters are more circumscribed, and their impact is felt only in one region or by one segment of workers. A single-industry town may become a disaster area as a result of a corporate decision to relocate a factory. Technological changes or reduced demand for certain products may cause large-scale layoffs of workers, some of whom must retrain or relocate in order to become employable.

Being laid off, even temporarily, is an awesome experience for contemporary workers, for it is a dramatic reminder that the individual is expendable. Even the fortunate workers who retain their jobs when others are laid off fear that their luck will not last forever. Economic disaster in the form of massive unemployment makes everyone anxious—families, friends, and business people who must depend on the purchasing power of working men and women.

Whenever there is widespread economic adversity, mental health facilities report an increase in the number of people seeking help. Massive unemployment can precipitate community disruption in the form of vandalism, riots, and looting. Family conflict is a by-product of troublesome economic conditions. Not only is marital maladjustment more prevalent, but parents and children seem to have more difficulty with each other. In Hartford, Connecticut, one out of eight workers laid off by an aircraft factory reported that their marriage deteriorated as a result, and 15 percent reported more quarrels with their children (Pines, 1982). The same source observed that every notice of job furlough or termination should be accompanied by a Surgeon General's warning that the notification may be hazardous to your health.

Demographic Data

In 1986, the unemployment rate in the United States was between 6 and 7 percent, and this attracted little public attention. Unemployment seems to worry politicians and others only when it reaches 8 or 9 percent, as it has in some regions early in the 1990s. Because jobless people are family members, the number of persons unemployment affects is two or three times the official rate. Joblessness disproportionately victimizes ethnic and racial minorities, young people, and older workers. Unemployment in such groups may be twice that of the general population (Briar, 1983).

The advances of modern technology have reduced demand for unskilled and semiskilled labor. In the United States, technological changes in agriculture have reduced the farm work force massively. At one time, the agrarian work force constituted 90 percent of all workers; at present, it amounts to 3 percent of all workers. Employment in industry accounts for 20 percent of all jobs; by the year 2000, it is predicted that this figure will decrease to between 3 and 5 percent. In studying the consequences of unemployment on low-income women who had lost their jobs, Donovan et al. (1987) identified five crucial areas: (1) loss of needed income, (2) loss of self-esteem and sense of fulfillment, (3) loss of social support and associations in the workplace, (4) internal stress and strain within the family, and (5) loss of structure and purpose.

For men, and for many women, feelings of confidence and self-worth are linked to paid employment. If the wife does not work outside the home, the husband is perceived as the primary provider. In these more traditional families, the husband's joblessness erodes his status in the family. His feelings of competence are further impaired when his wife enters the work force to earn food and shelter for the family.

Like natural and environmental disasters, economic adversity is likely to be evaluated primarily in financial terms. It is possible to challenge the use of income as an indicator of the deprivation individuals and families suffer during economic decline. This evaluative measure perpetuates Victorian thinking that restricted basic human needs to food, shelter, and clothing. Since human beings are social as well as biological entities, deprivation should be measured in relationship rather than monetary terms. A deprivation index was compiled that included social indices of economic decline, such as not inviting people to the house, not having birthday parties for the children, not taking vacations, and not having money for recreation or other amenities. The premise is that the accumulated deprivation that accompanies lowered income eventually reaches a level at which people can no longer function as social beings. When, for example, parents must keep their children home from school because there is no money for athletic equipment or school outings, neither the parents nor the children are able to perform their socially accustomed roles. Communities have definite expectations of family in various socioeconomic strata, and the families have certain expectations of themselves. These expectations cannot be fulfilled in periods of severe economic decline, and the result is family disequilibrium expressed in discord between spouses, between parents and children, and between families and community institutions, such as school, business, and the legal system.

Several investigators have found a relationship between unemployment and health. In Canada, the United States, and other developed countries, researchers have found increased mortality rates for unemployed people, even when rates consider socioeconomic factors. Health risks of unemployed workers extend to all family members, from infants to adults to the elderly. Although Zuravin (1988) found no association between child abuse and parental unemployment, other studies suggested the contrary (Zlotnick & Cassanego, 1992).

Unemployment insurance is based on previous earnings. This means that families unlikely to have a financial cushion receive less in the way of benefits. Without steady employment, the worker finds himself and his family without health or medical coverage. Nutritional standards are abandoned, as adequate diets become unaffordable. As Zlotnick and Cassanego (1992) bluntly stated,

> The literature is very clear: Unemployment is associated with increased stress and morbidity for the worker and spouse, and this stress may eventually have an impact on the workers' children. The clear indication for the public health sector is that unemployed workers and their entire families need . . . intervention, particularly preventive health care (p. 80).

The household of an unemployed worker is a stressful place, where worried parents become frightened and angry. Almost all layoffs or job dismissals disrupt established family patterns, and have the potential for crisis.

Bearers of Bad News

Many industrial executives and union officials assigned the task of deciding who will be laid off feel that they are expected to be executioners. Ramirez (1992) predicted that people losing their jobs would become angry or numb. Some try to persuade the overseer to retract the decision, using persuasion and threats. Several effective responses were suggested to deal with blandishment and with attacks. It is not a good idea to say "I know how you feel" unless you too are being dismissed. Otherwise, your comment sounds trite and dishonest. Do not protest that the decision was out of your hands unless you really had no input. Above all, do not say that the dismissal is a "blessing in disguise"; this statement is patronizing and infuriating to the person who has just lost a job. Remember that being laid off is an affront and a body blow to a conscientious worker. The best way to handle the situation, whether the jobless person is a friend or an underling, is to empathize and offer practical suggestions on career counseling and planning for the future. Rimer (1992) found that uncertainty about the future compounded the troubles of jobless workers. When layoffs are under way, there are no guarantees about existing or future employment. According to Rimer (1992, p. D5), one union official, who had no more information than rank and file members, was quoted as saying, "All I can do is listen and tell them to get together with their spouse and their children and talk it through. Some people I try to get into therapy. Families are in turmoil here. They don't know what's going to happen. They're worried about money. And when there's problems with money, love goes away."

There is no doubt that plant closings and large-scale layoffs are demoralizing for entire communities. Some workers are able to relocate easily but many cannot. There is a trend today toward governmental and corporate involvement in the retraining of workers whose skills have become redundant in today's marketplace. Two conditions, if present, can go far toward protecting workers and their families against the physical and emotional deteriorations that follow joblessness. The safeguards consist of financial benefits sufficient to ease the transition from one job to another, and the reliable support of family and friends. Many negative effects of unemployment would be reduced if workers were informed of what was going on, to the fullest possible extent. Sharing information with workers would reduce their feelings of powerlessness and negate the effects of wild rumors. Employers would alleviate the effects of unemployment if they gave longer notice to workers before closing a plant or engaging in massive layoffs. One proposal that has been considered, but not passed in most states, is legislation requiring companies to give advance warning to workers of any intent to close a plant.

Counseling the Unemployed

The furloughed worker with no assurance of being called back to work exists in limbo, for there is reluctance to accept a less satisfactory job if there is any hope of being rehired. It is not only the unemployed worker, but the entire family who endure the unemployment crisis. Losing one's job frequently causes workers to blame themselves for decisions they had taken earlier. They begin to wish they had chosen another occupation, pursued more education, or moved to another part of the country. The self-recrimination of unemployed workers means that worried wives must deal with the depression and guilt of their husbands in addition to managing financial retrenchment. Sometimes a wife who had preferred being a homemaker becomes a reluctant wage earner, or a wife whose job provided small luxuries for the family finds herself the major breadwinner. This role shift is difficult for couples, even in families in which there is little emphasis on gender-differentiated role enactment.

When the parents are feeling uncomfortable with the role changes in the family, the children are invariably affected. A child who was fairly well adjusted at home and at school may begin to fail academically, withdraw, or become obstreperous. Well-meaning parents may try to shield children from the facts by glossing over or not explaining the problem. This avoidance makes it difficult for children to understand the reason for family tension. The result is that they may engage in fantasies of separation or family dissolution that are more frightening than the reality from which they are being protected. Even when this fantasizing does not happen, the children feel excluded rather than part of a family system in which every member must adapt to new conditions.

Role enactment tends to be stabilized in functional families, with varying degrees of role flexibility. Economic disaster can dramatically change role enactment and role distribution in families when the primary provider becomes unemployed. This shift is particularly difficult in traditional families in which role changes are not easily accepted. If individuals in the family are externally, rather than internally, directed and ascribed roles are highly valued, the loss of conventional role enactment may lead to feelings of depersonalization or nihilism. Other individuals prove able to adapt to new role dimensions in productive ways that eventually enhance self-esteem and family perception of itself as a working, functional system.

Loss of morale and deprived feelings characterize families faced with indefinite periods of employment. Crisis counseling cannot produce jobs, but can help make the period of unemployment less bleak. Group counseling programs for unemployed workers, for their spouses, and children are perhaps the best form of supportive work. These programs can range from vocational retraining for workers whose skills are obsolete to emotional support for workers who blame themselves for being unemployed. Shared unemployment in a community tends to reduce the guilt and self-blame of the workers but perhaps intensifies their feelings of powerlessness. Unemployed men usually feel a loss of role and status within the family, particularly if authority was dependent upon the man's economic contribution. Abandoning the meaningful family role of provider adds to the frustration of the unemployed worker, even when family affection is strong and role flexibility can be accomplished within the system.

Even though there is comparatively little loss of life attached to economic disasters, there is loss of roles and family stability. When unemployment affects large numbers of workers in the community, there is a collective interpretation of the situation that may help affected families. Usually, families of unemployed workers tend to externalize blame,

and this externalization is less destructive than the self-blame of workers
or the scapegoating of a family member. However, anger should not be
allowed to continue to the extent of immobilizing the problem-solving
potential of the family. General precepts of crisis intervention that permit
catharsis before moving on to productive problem solving can reduce
confusion and depression. Assessment of family resources in terms of
marketable skills and willingness to relocate can help the members focus
on strengths rather than weaknesses. Jobless people see themselves as
victims of economic disasters. They deserve to be helped in ways that
avoid any hint of blame or stigma. There is genuine need for retraining,
social action programs, and self-help groups operating on behalf of the
unemployed. Referrals for mental health counseling are imperative when
there is emotional distress in the wage earner and turmoil in the family.

•CLINICAL EXAMPLE:
FAMILY CONSTRUCTION OF A LIBIDINAL COCOON

At 5:04 P.M. (Pacific daylight saving time), an earthquake mea-
suring 7.1 on the Richter scale struck the area of northern California surrounding San Francisco. The epicenter was about sixty
miles south of the city in the Santa Cruz Mountains. There were
damage, deaths, and injuries from Santa Cruz to the San Francisco marina, and the city of Oakland. The economic costs of the
disaster were estimated at more than $8 billion. Sixty-two peo-
ple died and 3,000 were injured. About 116,882 buildings were
damaged; 14,000 people were made homeless (Laube-Morgan,
1992).

When they felt the first tremors, Vincent and Maria Garcia
were at home preparing dinner. The couple were in their middle
fifties and the parents of five children, all of whom were married
and lived in their own homes. The Garcias owned and operated a
shoe repair shop in a business section of San Francisco, a short
distance from the house they owned. As a young, married couple, Vincent and Maria had come to California from Mexico.
They joined relatives in the states, were sponsored legitimately,
and adjusted well to American life. Their children were natural
born Americans. Vincent and Maria were proud of that fact and
of the hard won prosperity they now enjoyed.

When the house began to shake and dishes flew off the
shelves, Vincent knew at once what was happening. He grabbed
his wife by the waist and pulled her under the kitchen table.
Huddled together, arms round one another, they listened to the
sounds of glass breaking and doors banging open and shut. A
heavy bureau fell over in a bedroom and Maria screamed that the
ceiling was caving in. She moaned and said prayers for the safety
of her children and grandchildren who were somewhere in the
city. Between prayers, she wept at the destruction of her cherished possessions. This drew no sympathy from Vincent, who

told her fiercely that this was no time to cry about dishes. He added that Maria already had too many dishes and they could get along on whatever was left. When the kitchen clock fell off the wall and crashed onto the floor Maria screamed again; Vincent told her to get hold of herself. He said he would get her a new clock, but only if she stopped crying and praying. All this made Maria cry and pray more than ever, but it had the expected effect of making her angry with Vincent rather than afraid.

It seemed like a lifetime before the tremors stopped. After a time, the Garcias crept out from under the table to examine the damage to their home. Within an hour their daughter Rita arrived to make sure her parents were safe. Her husband was a police officer who came with her, bringing along their six-year-old son. The son-in-law stayed only a few minutes because he had to report on duty. Rita, who was a nurse, wanted to go to the nearest hospital to help but decided she would stay with her parents until hearing from the rest of the family.

Maria was worried about her four sons and their families, and Rita tried to reassure her. Because the earthquake occurred near the end of the day, most of the children were home from school. Substantial numbers of workers whose day ended at 5:00 or 6:00 P.M. were still trapped in the city, inside buildings or on the streets. The Bay Bridge had collapsed with the first tremors, hurtling cars and people into the bay. Public transportation was at a standstill and most phone lines were down. To help commuters get home, sight-seeing ferries were pressed into service. Most of these people were able to get to their homes by midnight. Until then, worried families waited without news.

Vincent found it intolerable to wait at home. Maria and Rita protested, but he insisted on leaving the house to go to his store. Instructions were being broadcast that empty houses, offices, schools, and other buildings the earthquake had damaged were off limits until inspectors certified them as being safe. Maria thought they all should leave the house, but Vincent told them to stay where they were. Restless and anxious, he found inactivity unbearable. He was, in fact, more worried about looters than about collapsed buildings. After he arrived at the store, he found neighbors assessing the damage to their business places, talking about what they were doing when the earthquake struck, and wondering what to do next. Vincent was not a patient man, and he quickly tired of his neighbors' idle talk. He was more impressed with the work of police officers, firefighters, and a few volunteers searching for people who might be trapped under debris. Explaining to one police officer that he had a son on the force, he offered his assistance. For the next four hours he was kept busy cleaning up streets and erecting barricades around perilous buildings. Tired and hungry, he finally decided it was time to go home, but promised to be back the next day.

On arriving home, he found that his wife was very worried about him. Rita's husband had stopped by to say that he had located all four brothers and their families. Two of them had been evacuated from their homes and were in a school being used as a shelter, but planned to come to their parents' home the next day. With her daughter's help, Maria had managed to prepare an evening meal. Vincent's share was warmed up. He ate his supper and persuaded the other family members to get some sleep. Maria again warned that the house was probably unsafe, but she had no idea where else they should go. The block where the store was located had been cordoned off but the blocks around the house were still accessible. This helped convince Maria that they could go to sleep.

A second earthquake struck at 7:30 A.M. This time the four members of the Garcia family left their house for several hours and were allowed back because their area suffered minimal damage. Elsewhere they saw buckled sidewalks, uprooted trees, overturned cars, and demolished or barely standing buildings. During the day, the rest of the family joined the group, bringing food and blankets. They had decided to accept Maria's invitation and Vincent's command that they all stay together until the city was back to normal. With her sisters-in-law available to care for her son, and with cousins as playmates, Rita decided to go to the nearest hospital where she knew she was needed. One sister-in-law, who had spent the previous night in a shelter, decided to return to the shelter to help with the cooking. Vincent and his sons felt that able-bodied men were absolutely essential for cleaning up the area around the marina and left to see what they could do. With her daughters-in-law and grandchildren around her, Maria was able to push her worries aside. It was always a treat for her to have everyone near. During the next few days, mealtime at the Garcia's household became almost festive. In the secure domestic atmosphere, lost cars and damaged homes did not seem so overwhelming. Members who were working with less fortunate survivors, recounted some tragic stories. This made them much more resigned to their losses, and grateful for being alive and together.

Critical Guidelines

The combined property damage the extended Garcia family suffered was considerable. In an ordinary situation, this would have been very distressing, but after the earthquake they saw property loss as inconsequential. Except for the children, some of whom suffered night terrors about the earthquake, the other family members showed no negative effects. Vincent Garcia reacted in his customary style. He took charge of his wife and his household, and used purposeful activity to deal with his anxiety. Once he learned that all the family members were safe, he minimized the importance of property damage. He was gratified that his home had been used as a haven for the whole family. Moreover, he was proud that he, his daughter, all his sons, and a daughter-in-law had extended themselves to help others during the emergency.

Maria was a religious woman who believed that her prayers were answered when family members were unhurt. Her life was more home centered than that of her husband; in caring for her family, she was able to suppress her knowledge of possible danger. Even though her husband often infuriated her, his firm way of dealing with events made her feel safe. To avoid adding to her emotional distress, Maria stayed at home when the rest of the family went outside to help or simply to view the damage. Most of the time, everyone stayed quietly together.

In forming a tightly knit family group, the Garcias unknowingly replicated the "libidinal cocoon" that Black (1987) described. In 1985, the families of 137 passengers killed in a Delta plane crash were placed in a secluded hotel while waiting for bodies to be recovered and identified. In this protected environment, known as a *libidinal cocoon,* a mental health team composed of a psychiatrist, nurses, clergy, and hotel and airline agents cared for and nurtured the families. The bereaved families gradually interacted on an intimate basis and responded to each other's pain. Inside a warm environment, families were allowed to regress as they wished, secure in the knowledge that every physical or emotional symptom they experienced would be ministered to. Survivors of the plane crash were placed in the same secluded environment and received the same tender care. As Black (1987, p. 1324) described, "Soon they were able to laugh and cry at the same time and to accept nurturing from a variety of helpers. Before long they could reach out to others." Family members and survivors who chose not to stay in the protective, cocoon-like environment that was made available exhibited more signs of psychiatric disturbance than did those who allowed themselves to be cared for.

In many ways, the Garcia family formed its own libidinal cocoon. Their behavior followed most of the recommendations made in operationalizing this form of treatment. The recommendations are as follows:

- The presence of a strong caretaker or caretakers is needed.
- Interactions with the outside world are limited or controlled.
- The people who have experienced disaster or loss are encouraged to regress.
- Physical, emotional, and behavioral needs are met to the fullest possible extent.
- Denial is permitted as long as it is adaptive and necessary to maintain individual and family equilibrium.
- The entire process of offering nurture, care, solicitude, seclusion, and understanding continues without interruption and as long as necessary (for example, for hours or days).

Since this airline crash, the libidinal cocoon has been used several times, with good results. The United States Army used this approach after an air crash in Newfoundland that killed two hundred servicepersons; officials also used it in Texas after the Guadalupe River flooded, killing ten children who attended a religious school. Here, regression and the religious implications

of untimely death were used to comfort families. In both instances, families were secluded and protected from the demands
of the outside world.

SUMMARY

Community crises may result from disasters that affect segments of the
population rather than single families or groups. Disasters are diversified
in nature, and several typologies can be used to differentiate forms of
disaster, even though distinctions are sometimes blurred. Disasters may
be expected or unexpected, recurrent or unprecedented. They may be
natural occurrences or the result of human-derived decisions about the
environment. Some disasters are generated by forces external to the community; others are the result of internal forces.

By using an epidemiological model, most responses to disaster can be
discussed in community terms. Despite popular beliefs, imminent disaster does not usually cause panic, although the actual impact may precipitate varying degrees of disorganization. Victims can depend upon the
durability of roles among police officers and firefighters, although the
work of all rescuers is enhanced if they remain in communication with
their own families. The possibility of burnout among rescue workers
must not be discounted, and leaders of rescue operations should assume
responsibility for identifying burnout. Some experts have formulated
three stages of response to disaster, but others see greater variation in
survivors' reactions. Most survivors require only crisis intervention,
which is most effective if integrated into comprehensive relief programs.
There are some vulnerable individuals who suffer long-term effects that
require sustained intervention.

Economic disasters possess a uniqueness that warranted their discussion as separate phenomena. As in all disasters, massive economic adversity affects role enactment. Families in which role flexibility can be
maintained are more likely to adapt successfully to conditions of severe
economic deprivation. A recommended form of primary prevention
would require employers to give advance warning of layoffs or shut-
downs so that workers can adjust, relocate, or retrain during periods of
economic decline. The importance of supportive family counseling and
problem-solving approaches to the alleviation of economic disaster cannot be overemphasized.

A relatively recent approach to helping people cope after disaster is
the construction of a libidinal cocoon. In this approach, survivors and
bereaved relatives are housed in a secluded, protected environment
where their physical and psychological needs are tenderly met. Regression is not only permitted, but it is fostered. Although research on the
results of this approach is mostly anecdotal, it has been very helpful in

some instances. The clinical example described a family who survived a severe earthquake in California. Without any previous knowledge, this family virtually created for its members a libidinal cocoon that reduced the earthquake's psychological impact. The libidinal cocoon offers a contrast to reality-based crisis intervention, but it has powerful implications for crisis workers in shelters and dining halls where people come for help after a disaster has displaced them from their homes.

REFERENCES

Berren, M.R. "A Typology for the Classification of Disasters." *Community Mental Health Journal* 16(1980): 103–110.

Bird, C. "Joblessness Scars Deeper than Simple Totals Tell." *The Plain Dealer* April 10, 1982.

Black, J.W. "The Libidinal Cocoon: A Nurturing Retreat for Families of Plane Crash Victims." *Hospital and Community Psychiatry* 38(1987): 1322–1336.

Bovard, E.W. "The Effects of Social Stimuli in Response to Stress." *Psychological Review* 66(1959): 267–277.

Briar, K.H. "Unemployment: Toward a Social Work Agenda." *Social Work* 28(1983): 211–223.

Burgess, A.W., and B. Baldwin. *Crisis Intervention Theory and Practice: A Clinical Handbook.* Englewood Cliffs, New Jersey: Prentice-Hall, 1980.

Camus, A. *The Plague,* Translated by Gilbert Stuart. New York: Random House, 1948.

Cohen, R.E. "The Armero Tragedy: Lessons for Mental Health Professionals." *Hospital and Community Psychiatry* 38(1987): 1316–1321.

Cohen, R.E., and F.L. Ahearn. *Handbook for the Mental Health Care of Disaster Victims.* Baltimore: Johns Hopkins University Press, 1980.

Donovan, R., N. Jaffe, and V.M. Pirie. "Unemployment Among Low Income Women." *Social Work* 32(1987): 301–305.

Dynes, R., and E.L. Quarantelli. "The Family and Community Context of Individual Reactions to Disaster." In *Emergency and Disaster Management: A Mental Health Source Book,* edited by H.J. Parad, H.L.P. Resnik, and L. Parad. Bowie, Maryland: Charles, 1978.

Edelstein, M. *Contaminated Communities: The Social and Psychological Impact of Residential Toxic Waste Exposure.* Boulder, Colorado: Westview, 1988.

Eth, S., and S.R. Pynoos. *Post Traumatic Stress Disorder in Children.* Washington, D.C.: American Psychiatric Press, 1985.

Galante, R., and D. Foa. "An Epidemiological Study of Psychic Trauma and Treatment Effectiveness for Children After a Natural Disaster." *Journal of American Academy of Child Psychiatry* 25(1986): 357–363.

Gavalya, A.S. "Reactions to the 1985 Mexican Earthquake: Case Vignettes." *Hospital and Community Psychiatry* 38(1987): 1327–1330.

Heron, J. "Philosophical Basis for a New Paradigm." In *Human Inquiry: A Sourcebook of New Paradigm Research,* edited by P. Reason and J. Rowan. New York: Wiley, 1981.

Janosik, E., and E. Green. *Family Life: Process and Practice.* Boston: Jones and Bartlett, 1992.

Kinsinger, B.J. "Consequences of Disaster and Unemployment." In *Family-focused Care,* edited by J.R. Miller and E.H. Janosik. New York: McGraw-Hill, 1980.

Laube-Morgan, J. "The Professional's Psychological Response in Disaster: Implications for Practice." *Journal of Psychosocial Nursing* 30(1992): 17–22.

McFarlane, A.C. "Posttraumatic Morbidity of a Disaster: A Study of Cases Presented for Psychiatric Treatment." *Journal of Nervous and Mental Diseases* 74(1986): 4–14.

Murphy, B.C., P. Ellis, and S. Greenberg. "Atomic Veterans and Their Families: Responses to Radiation Exposure." *American Journal of Orthopsychiatry* 60(1990): 418–427.

Pines, M. "Recession is Linked to Far Reaching Psychological Harm." *The New York Times* April 6, 1982.

Ramirez, A. "Those Giving the Word Suffer in Lay Offs." *The New York Times* January 26, 1992.

Rimer, S. "Hearing the Fears with No Answers." *The New York Times* September 24, 1992.

Siporin, M. "Altruism, Disaster, and Crisis Intervention." In *Emergency Disaster Management: A Mental Health Source Book,* edited by H.J. Parad, H.L.P. Resnik, and L. Parad. Bowie, Maryland: Charles, 1976.

Terr, L.C. "Chowchilla Revisited: The Effects of Psychic Trauma Four Years after a School Bus Kidnapping." *American Journal of Psychiatry* 140(1983): 1543–1550.

Vyner, H. *Invisible Trauma: The Psychosocial Effects of Invisible Environmental Contamination.* Lexington, Massachusetts: Heath, 1988.

Zeigler, M. "After the Flood." *Upstate* 1(1981): 9–13.

Zlotnick, C., and Cassanego, M. "Unemployment and Health." *Nursing and Health Care* 13(1992): 78–83.

Zuravin, S.J. "Child Maltreatment and Teenage First Births." *American Journal of Orthopsychiatry* 58(1988): 91–103.

14

Society in Crisis
AIDS and HIV

The mutual confidence on which all else depends can be maintained only by an open mind and a brave reliance upon free discussion.

Learned Hand

AIDS (acquired immune deficiency syndrome) and its rapid proliferation within a short period of time have created a pattern of crisis for many individuals, families, communities, and nations. In this chapter, the AIDS parameters are discussed, beginning with the crisis that ensues when individuals first discover that they are HIV (human immunodeficiency virus) positive, indicating that they harbor the virus that causes AIDS. As HIV infection progresses, the depressed immune system of seropositive individuals renders them susceptible to recurring infections that resist treatment. While some of these infections can be overcome, others continue to develop. For HIV-positive individuals, every serious illness may precipitate another crisis. Because the course of HIV infection and AIDS is unpredictable, and the general prognosis is poor, ways must be found to prevent further contagion, to help infected persons maintain a satisfying life as long as possible, and to care adequately for them during the advanced stages of their illnesses.

Not only individual, but also the families of HIV-positive individuals and AIDS patients face critical challenges. Discussion of AIDS-related family crises is included in this chapter. Demands made on health professionals caring for AIDS patients are very heavy and are compounded by fears of contagion. Like infected individuals and their families, people taking care of AIDS patients benefit from supportive counseling that enables them to avoid crisis by meeting their own physical and emotional needs. Therefore, this chapter offers a realistic view of HIV and AIDS in the context of crisis prevention and intervention.

In the 1960s and 1970s, people were vaguely aware that disrupting the balance of nature could have far reaching implications on world health. They were unprepared, however, for the rapid transmission of HIV and AIDS throughout the globe. The reason for this global transmission is neither obvious nor simple. Perhaps Richard H. Krouse, former director of the National Institute of Allergy and Infectious Diseases that is part of the National Institutes of Health (Henig, 1992), gave the most convincing explanation.

> A major dislocation in the social structure—love, hate, peace, war, urbanization, overpopulation, economic depression, people having so much leisure that they sleep with five different people a night—whatever it is that puts stress on the ecological system, can alter the equilibrium between man and microbes. Such great dislocations can lead to plagues and epidemics, more often than not caused by microbes that already reside on our doorstep (p. 55).

Through the systematic study of various infectious diseases, scientists have been able to develop vaccines that virtually eliminated poliomyelitis, smallpox, and many childhood diseases. Wonder drugs in the form of antibiotics proved to be very effective against those infectious diseases that did not respond to vaccines. In 1962, the Nobel prizewinner, Macfarlane Burnet, wrote that infectious disease was no longer important in the twentieth century except in a historical sense. William H. Stewart, the U.S. surgeon general, declared in 1969 that the war against infectious diseases had been won (Henig, 1992).

Scientists knew that viruses had the ability to alter their genetic structures in ways that made them resistant to therapeutic weapons. They were less knowledgeable about the possibility of new viruses that did not result from mutation, but from ecological disruptions and from patterns of human behavior. Unhappily, they discovered that new or "emerging" viruses were not uncommon, and could be triggered by apparently unrelated decisions of political, environmental, or economic nature. The most lethal of emerging viruses is the one that causes AIDS.

The worldwide prevalence of AIDS has demonstrated that the battle against infectious disease has not yet been won. Moreover, the failure to control one disease may lead to a resurgence of other maladies once thought to be vanquished. For example, in the wake of AIDS, strains of drug-resistant tuberculosis have developed and claimed new victims. Even though its mortality rate is high, HIV continues to thrive and multiply. Because the virus has a latency period of up to ten years, many persons who harbor the virus look and feel well. The long latency period gives the carriers ample opportunity to infect others before they themselves become ill. Given the extended latency period of the virus and the propensity of many individuals for sexual risk taking, it is not surprising that an estimated ten million people around the world are HIV positive. Within the United States, more than one million Americans (1 out of 250) are estimated to be HIV positive. The majority of HIV-positive Americans are between twenty-five and forty-four years of age, usually a time of greatest productivity (Noble, 1992). In 1993, more than 365,000 Americans will have been diagnosed with AIDS, with the annual death toll in excess of 170,000 (Leukefeld, 1989).

Within the last ten years, AIDS has assumed the proportions of a medieval plague. Initially, its prevalence within the homosexual community and in underdeveloped countries allowed many people to feel uninvolved. Moralists attributed the spread of AIDS to perverted or promiscuous sexual practices, going so far as to call AIDS a form of divine retribution. Very soon, though, the AIDS virus proved not to discriminate against race, age, nationality, gender, or sexual preference. This is no longer a minor epidemic confined to a particular community, eventually abating. Already the disease has decimated communities of people in the creative arts, in inner-city neighborhoods, and in developing countries. The virus has crossed national boundaries, contaminated blood supplies, intruded into heterosexual and homosexual encounters, and doomed hapless children—all within the space of a few years.

AIDS PARAMETERS

AIDS is an infectious disease characterized by a latency period, acute episodes, chronicity, and ultimately death. AIDS was first identified in the United States in 1981 when two men died from a type of pneumonia that was seldom fatal. These men succumbed because their immune systems were depressed. It is now known that AIDS is an infection caused by a retrovirus, i.e., human T-cell lymphotropic virus type III (Human TLV-III Lav). There are three stages of the infection. At first an individual may be seropositive but have no symptoms. In the second stage, known as AIDS-related complex (ARC), the individual may experience swollen glands, fever, night sweats, and weight loss. The third stage is characterized by severe immunodeficiency and such complications as Kaposi's sarcoma or pneumocystis carinii pneumonia (Perry & Markowitz, 1988).

No illness arouses more dread than AIDS nor carries more stigma. Although AIDS is no longer confined to any one group, there is a tendency to categorize the sufferers. There are the "innocent" victims who were infected by a legal spouse or a contaminated blood transfusion. Then there are the "guilty" victims—homosexuals, drug addicts, and prostitutes—who deserved to get sick.

Ours is a society that looks for connections between cause and effect. We have solved so many mysteries already that we continue to search for answers no matter how elusive. Our wish to understand and alter events makes us impatient with illnesses that do not respond to available resources. Thus, when a chronic or incurable illness develops, we tend to blame the victim.

It is true that many behaviors do contribute to ailments and disabilities. Smoking, alcohol abuse, and indiscriminate sexual habits certainly constitute risk factors. However, the time to call attention to reckless, self-defeating behavior is when the behavior is exhibited, not after serious illness has appeared. Once an illness has developed, it is cruel to remind the victim of her own contribution. The sick person will not benefit from self-recrimination and will be less able to cope if energy is wasted in guilt. Matter-of-fact acknowledgment of contributing factors is permissible, but should be laid aside so as to deal with more pressing matters (Wechsler, 1990).

Flaskerud and Thompson (1991) called attention to a valuable message that *behaviors* spread AIDS, not any single group. This message is essential, since it is white, heterosexual persons who are more likely to deny their vulnerability, and more than any other population segment have not changed their sexual behaviors.

Activist groups have accused the U.S. government of mounting an inadequate campaign to combat the AIDS epidemic. Without taking sides in the debate, it is possible to state that further efforts are needed to finance research; establish additional programs; formulate practical, effective legislation; educate the public; and encourage community involvement. As Figure 14-1 indicates, worldwide, the number of reported AIDS cases is dramatically lower than the estimates. This is due to underreporting, delays in reporting, and underdiagnosis.

At present, the most effective way of preventing the spread of AIDS is to use preventive measures. Family members and health care professionals should understand the following recommendations of the U.S. Public Health Service regarding AIDS transmission, and impress these upon clients at risk (U.S. Public Health Reports, 1988).

- Avoid sexual relations with persons having AIDS or persons belonging to any group at risk for contracting AIDS.
- Avoid sexual relations with multiple partners or with anyone who has multiple partners.
- Do not give blood if you have AIDS or are at risk of contracting AIDS, i.e., HIV positive.
- Exercise extreme care in handling, using, or disposing of hypodermic needles and syringes in all health facilities.
- Do not use intravenous drugs. If you persist in this unsafe practice, do not share intravenous equipment with others.

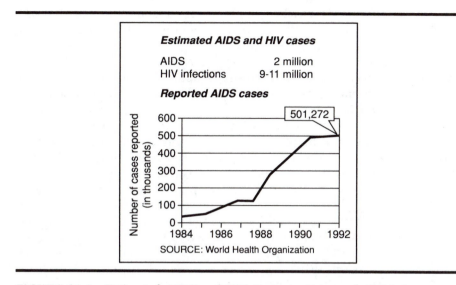

FIGURE 14–1 Estimated AIDS and HIV Cases vs. Reported AIDS Cases (Cumulative Number Reported to the World Health Organization as of March 1992).

- Any woman using intravenous drugs or having sexual relations with a high-risk partner should practice contraception. If she becomes pregnant, she is likely to transmit AIDS to the unborn child.

HIV-POSITIVE INDIVIDUALS

Many researchers oppose compulsory or mass HIV testing because of imprecise results. It may take six to twelve weeks for an HIV-infected person to develop enough antibodies for a positive result. Within this interval, results are liable to be falsely negative. Mass screening for HIV often produces false positive results, as do home testing kits. A seronegative person who has engaged in high-risk behavior should be retested at two-month intervals. Perry and Markowitz (1988) reported that, in the United States, roughly 35 percent of seropositive persons will develop AIDS within the next seven and a half years; 40 to 45 percent will develop ARC with its accompanying symptoms. About 20 percent of HIV-positive persons will remain symptom-free. Advisors and counselors should realize that these statistics are frequently revised and therefore should review *Morbidity and Mortality Weekly Reports,* which the Centers for Disease Control publish.

For many individuals, AIDS becomes a threat only when they learn that they are HIV positive. For many, this represents a crisis that is met with denial and refusal to accept the full implications of positive testing.

Since these individuals may be symptom-free for some time, denial may be relatively easy to maintain. This is a dangerous state of affairs unless the individuals are willing to act responsibly toward sex partners.

It is true that the AIDS epidemic has led to changes among some segments of society. The gay community is mobilized and unified as never before. Even among homosexual people, the behavioral responses of people who are HIV positive are not very encouraging. Perry and Markowitz (1988) reported that, after testing HIV positive, homosexual men do reduce the frequency of high-risk sexual encounters, but over 30 percent of seropositive homosexual men continue to engage in unprotected insertive anal intercourse with multiple partners. Gay men who were found to be seropositive had an average of 5.8 sexual partners in a year and only 46 percent in the sample consistently used condoms after being told of their status. Based on fifty studies conducted in twenty-three cities, the Centers for Disease Control (1987) estimated that, overall, about 20 to 25 percent of homosexual men are HIV positive, but in some localities, about 68 percent may be seropositive.

The Centers for Disease Control estimates that, in New York City and in Puerto Rico, 50 to 65 percent of intravenous drug users are seropositive; elsewhere in the United States, less than 5 percent of intravenous drug users are HIV positive. For persons with hemophilia, the Centers for Disease Control estimates of HIV prevalence range from 65 to 70 percent. These rates are moderately lower than earlier statistics. For bisexual men, seropositive rates are about 5 percent, provided their homosexual encounters are infrequent. Heterosexual partners of persons who are HIV positive or are in high-risk groups show great variation in seropositive rates; the range of HIV positive readings among this group is between 10 and 60 percent. In the general population without identified risks, seropositive rates are about 0.02 percent (Curran et al., 1988; Booth, 1988).

COUNSELING THE HIV-POSITIVE INDIVIDUAL

When an individual is HIV positive, every unprotected sexual transaction, especially if the partner is HIV negative, is a violation of the partner's rights. Upon discovering that they are seropositive, some individuals are so angry that they want others to share their misfortune and knowingly choose to put others at risk. Others want to warn their previous partners and urge them to obtain testing and treatment, if necessary. Regardless of their reactions, most HIV-positive individuals find that life is a never-ending round of Russian roulette.

At present, most HIV testing tends to be voluntary, but this continues to be a problem as medical and legal experts grapple with the issue of balancing the rights of the individual against the spread of the epidemic.

Anyone counseling a seropositive individual must know the existing regulations and inform the client of circumstances in which confidentiality may be broken. The American Medical Association (1987) and the American Psychiatric Association (1988) have stated that counselors have an ethical obligation to warn partners about an HIV-positive person, if the individual refuses to disclose the information. In most instances, HIV testing is voluntary.

Many states have ruled that HIV-positive results may not be a basis for discrimination in housing or education, but the results may affect insurance coverage and job placement when positive test results are made part of the medical record. Therefore, many persons use anonymous testing sites where code numbers are used to protect individuals' identity.

Counseling at HIV testing centers is often divided into pre- and post-test sessions, each of which contains certain components, adapted from Perry and Markowitz (1988) as follows:

Pre-Test Counseling Sessions:
• Assessment
• HIV and AIDS information

Post-Test Counseling Sessions:
• Notification of results
• Reduction of immediate distress
• Transmission prevention
• Clarification of instructions
• Follow-up advice and planning

The individual's strengths and liabilities should be assessed prior to testing. At this point, the counselor ascertains why an individual has come for testing and asks what the individual will do if the results are positive. If appropriate, the counselor may suggest that a significant person attend the notification session. Additional inquiry should deal with the life style of the individual and with any physical symptoms that may be present. Even before results are known, the counselor should provide time to answer an individual's questions. Information about transmission may begin at the time pre-test counseling is offered. Regardless of test results, individuals should be warned of their obligations to engage in safe sex practices. Until test results are available, the individual should be advised to refrain from all sex activity.

Post-test counseling requires at least one two-hour session or two one-hour sessions. Notification of results is the first order of business. When the results are positive, considerable clarification is needed. Some of the information covered in post-test counseling may have to be repeated. In such cases, the individual may respond first with disbelief and shock; followed by fear, despair, and anger. Although counselors should correct misperceptions and distortions, they should not give false reassurance. Empathetic understanding is needed as the individual begins to sort out his feelings. Sufficient time must be allowed for emotional expression before the individual can begin to attend to instruction about viral transmission. Some counselors fear that an individual who has received word that the test was positive would not care to hear about preventing the spread of the infection. Perry and Markowitz (1988) found the opposite to be true. Talking about preventive measures gives seropositive individuals a greater sense of control of their lives. Information regarding prevention is crucial; the counselor should allow as much time as is needed to deal with this component. Additional time should be allocated to answering questions. Pamphlets and written notes may be used to reinforce verbal instructions. These can be studied later when the individual is less upset.

The individual who is seropositive, but symptom-free, lives with uncertainty. This uncertainty continues even after physical signs indicate that the infection has progressed. The specific course of the illness depends on the individual's response to treatment and whether new, relatively effective modalities are available. Whenever uncertainty extends over a period of time, the individual experiences an increased sense of danger and a lessened sense of control (Mishel & Sorenson, 1991). Regan-Kubinski and Sharts-Engel (1992) noted that for some individuals this leads to confusion and instability, as well as to cognitive disorganization. The following list, adapted from Mishel (1981) and Mishel and Braden (1988), presents major factors contributing to prolonged uncertainty in illness. Such uncertainty impedes action and reliable information gathering, and encourages wariness and avoidance tactics.

- Ambiguous information from disparate sources.
- Lack of definitive information.
- Failure to understand complex information.
- Disappointment with the treatment process.
- Unpredictability regarding prognosis.

Even in lengthy post-test sessions, all of the individual's concerns cannot be addressed. Seropositive individuals should be strongly urged to tell their lovers, personal physicians, dentists, and nurses of the test results. At the same time, they may be permitted to be selective in telling employers, landlords, and casual acquaintances, who are not being placed at risk. The counselor should ask where the seropositive individual plans to obtain further treatment and advice. It is appropriate to make referrals or even set up appointments for follow-up care when the individual is too distressed to do this. Even when essential information has been covered fully, continuity of care is essential for the individual and for other people. When condoms, for example, are advocated to prevent viral transmission, explicit instructions are needed. The sexual encounter can be considered safe only when the individual uses latex (not sheepskin) condoms, applies a virucidal contraceptive jelly, and follows detailed instructions for wearing and discarding the sheath. Directions may be given during post-test counseling, but ongoing clarification is almost always needed (Hicks et al., 1985).

THE INDIVIDUAL AND AIDS

The onset of weight loss, intransigent infections, atypical pneumonia, the lesions of Kaposi's sarcoma points to the presence of an AIDS-related illness and introduces a new period of crisis. The individual's watchfulness and careful living are no longer sufficient, and the individual must face a new situation. Friends and family usually must be told, if they do not already know. Some will rally to help the person who is ill, but others will turn away.

In addition to being ravaged by illness, AIDS patients face a frightening future. Moreover, if they are homosexual or are drug addicted, social and emotional problems with lovers, spouses, or parents may add to the stress of the situation. Persons suffering from AIDS need a wide range of services, not all of which are available across the country (Chaches, 1987).

- *Housing.* Misconceptions about contagion and transmission modes make it difficult for persons with AIDS to obtain and keep adequate housing.
- *Finances.* Costs of treatment for AIDS are staggering. Even when hospitalization is avoided, medications are extremely expensive. Jobs are lost; insurance is canceled or benefits are exhausted. Impoverishment is added to the indignities of the disease.
- *Home care.* Persons with advanced AIDS are likely to be hospitalized three or more times within the span of a year. Between hospitalizations, home care services are essential, especially if no hospice or voluntary caretaker is available.
- *Childcare and foster care.* Mothers with AIDS and mothers of children with AIDS need childcare in order to keep appointments for treatment. Temporary foster care may be needed when the mother is hospitalized; permanent foster care may be needed when the mother dies.
- *Legal counsel.* Decisions about child custody, power of attorney, wills, and bequests require legal assistance.
- *Medical care.* Different kinds of treatment are indicated at different stages of illness. In addition to medical treatment, nursing care and mental health counseling may be needed. A health care professional should act

as case manager and coordinate various aspects of care. The coordinator, who may be a member of any major health care discipline, should assume responsibility for teaching, explaining, and humanizing procedures as much as possible.
• *Public education.* The person suffering from AIDS, along with concerned friends and relatives, deserve accurate, up to date information about AIDS, with emphasis on prevention measures.

Denial is often considered an indication that an individual is not responding realistically to a life situation, but denial can be an intricate mechanism. Some individuals who are seropositive deny some aspects of AIDS but accept other aspects. Frequently, denial is expressed verbally but not behaviorally. Saunders and Buckingham (1988) cited an example of one infected person who claimed that he could not have AIDS because he felt so well. At the same time, his actions showed considerable awareness of his circumstances. This person was a male homosexual who asked his lover to move out of the house they shared so that the lover would not become infected. He also arranged with his employer to work at home in order to protect his associates at the office. Thus, even though he did not acknowledge all aspects of his infection, his denial was not complete.

Partial denial may be functional if it motivates the individual to feel optimistic and autonomous. Instead of opposing denial, it is better to build on what the individual is able to accept. Despite his insistence that he would not fall ill, this individual realized the hazards that were present and tried to protect others. His decision to live apart from his lover can be supported without suggesting that the relationship should be terminated altogether. There are many ways of encouraging AIDS patients to stay in control. One way to accomplish this is to provide accurate data on which to base their decisions and to encourage them to explore options and alternatives. The following, adapted from Saunders and Buckingham (1988), lists guidelines for counseling AIDS patients:

• Include biopsychosocial assessment in every interaction.
• Observe and listen without overreacting. Overreacting may elicit negative responses, such as fear or resistance.
• Understand and follow local legal standards, agency policy, and ethical obligations.
• Develop professional links to at-risk populations, such as gay community groups and substance-abuse treatment facilities.
• Know and use available crisis resources, such as hot lines, suicide prevention centers, and AIDS hot lines.
• Consult colleagues and supervisors to augment your skills and validate your work.
• Recognize your own limitations. Working with an AIDS-infected person is very demanding; do not allow your energy to become depleted.

• Do not ignore the strong emotions that working with an AIDS-infected person can arouse. If you are to be therapeutic, you must stay in touch with these emotions. Suppressing them will reduce your effectiveness.

MANAGEMENT STYLES OF AIDS PATIENTS

Ragsdale et al. (1992) explored the quality of life from the viewpoint of AIDS patients. The investigators identified six management styles these patients used to solve aspects of their illnesses. Because the authors suggest that quality of life for AIDS patients can be improved if others recognize and accept their chosen management style, descriptions of the various styles is appropriate here. Care providers soon learned there were significant differences in the ways patients responded to their illnesses. As care providers became aware of distinctive styles, they shaped their interventions accordingly. The six types of management styles were as follows: loner, activist, mystic, victim, timekeeper, and medic. Neither the staff nor the caregivers applied these terms pejoratively, but they used the terms descriptively to develop helpful interactions between staff and patient.

The Loner

The *loner* is a patient who tends to avoid social interaction whenever possible. The loner spends as much time as she can either sleeping or reading. Although the loner resists attempts others make to talk about AIDS or its implications, she does not avoid all social interaction. She likes some care providers more than others and recognizes efforts staff members make on her behalf. She discourages support groups and communication with other AIDS sufferers. Neither friendly nor hostile, the loner simply does not want intimate communication with anyone.

The Activist

Unlike the loner, the *activist* does not avoid interaction with others. This individual manages his situation by immersing himself in the larger issue of AIDS. His personal dilemma is seen as a collective problem, and he derives satisfaction by trying to help others within the structure of a support group in which he is an active member. Activities in various support and political organizations help him feel he is contributing to his own well-being and that of other AIDS victims.

The Victim

The *victim* makes excessive demands on other people and seems to be extremely dependent. Control is relinquished to other people, who then are expected to share the anxiety and take charge. Even though she appears to be compliant and appreciative, there may be underlying anger that often bursts through. Ragsdale et al. (1992, p. 262) cited a self-description of an AIDS patient who employed the victim management style. She presents herself as ". . . disgusted, mad. I'm mad that I don't have my independence anymore. I'm mad that I had to go on social security disability. I'm mad that I have to sleep more . . . I'm mad because I have to worry about what sickness I am going to have next. I'm mad, I am just mad."

The Timekeeper

The *timekeeper* is a managerial type who organizes his life by waiting for things to happen. He describes his typical day by means of a schedule that lists his activities in chronological order. Specific events or activities that occupy time but fail to convey a full sense of involvement mark the routine of his typical day.

The Mystic

The *mystic* management style approaches her condition spiritually rather than medically. For her, AIDS is not merely a disease, but the embodiment of a contest between good and evil forces. The mystic spends a considerable amount of time reading inspirational literature, praying, and receiving religious instruction and consolation. She may regard AIDS as a sign that the human race is in need of physical and spiritual cleansing. Many consider death to be neither frightening nor ominous, but a transition or passage from one life to the next.

The Medic

The *medic* employs a management style that uses medical concepts in handling AIDS-related events. He tries to gather as much data as possible on treatment developments, medications, and research advances. He attends lectures and seminars on HIV and AIDS whenever possible. When visiting a physician or when hospitalized, the medic asks many questions about procedures. Over time, the medic achieves a degree of expertise, which is then used to monitor personal physical and medical status. Communication networks are important sources of information, especially if medical information is disseminated.

    The implications of the foregoing management styles are meaningful for health care workers and for family members. If a patient's style of dealing with AIDS is respected, it can enhance patient care in several ways. By permitting the patient some autonomy and control over how therapy is administered, cooperation between patient and concerned others is facilitated. This may operate to improve treatment outcomes. It should be noted that a patient's management style may shift in response to the course of the disease. As the physical condition of a patient deteriorates, an activist may become a loner or a medic may begin to act like a victim. When physical powers are depleted, those management styles that require substantial outputs of energy may be impossible to maintain.

COUNSELING THE AIDS PATIENT

Ragsdale et al. (1992) reported positive results when nurse caregivers recognized that a patient's preferred management style could be mobilized in productive ways. Because the loner wants to be left alone as much as possible, care should be offered in a nonintrusive manner. Since the loner resists moral or political persuasion, few attempts should be made to influence her thoughts or feelings about her illness. The loner resists exploration and interference, but accepts caring overtures designed only to heal.

The needs of the activist are quite different. Many of these patients welcome visitors; they want to read newspapers and periodicals that report health programs. A stream of daily visitors may prove upsetting to staff or family members worried about excessive demands on the patient. When the number of visitors must be regulated, writing material may be provided so that the activist can remain in touch with the political- and group-oriented programs that are so meaningful.

The action of AIDS patients who elect the victim style is perhaps the most problematic for health care providers and for family members. Manipulation is always difficult to handle, especially when the perpetrator is seriously ill. Here, clear communication is needed so that the victim's behavior does not split the staff or engender family rifts. The victim is often skilled at getting other people to do what she wants and does not hesitate to use flattery, threats, or persuasion to obtain what she wants. It is not unusual for the victim to behave like a saint in the presence of one care provider and a virago in the presence of another. Staff dissension may result unless divergent interpretations of the patient's behavior are objectively compared, and the evidence weighed.

Introducing pleasant activities to fill the day will improve the quality of life for the timekeeper. This kind of patient welcomes any congenial distraction, such as conversation, musical interludes, art classes, or group discussions. When physically or emotionally able, the timekeeper derives satisfaction from performing small tasks at home or in the health care facility.

For the mystic, the quality of life benefits from a tranquil, peaceful environment. Mystics may crave the counsel of spiritual advisors who are outside traditional religious denominations. Family members and professional care providers must be accepting of the esoteric doctrines that bring comfort to some AIDS sufferers. When the belief system of health care providers coincides with that of the patient, compatible discussion may be helpful, but this is no time for spiritual or theological debate.

The patient who has chosen the medic's management style is usually rational and practical in many ways. These patients do not want to be dependent, physically, intellectually, or emotionally. They are often well-informed about many aspects of their illness. If they have questions, they want honest, careful answers, and they are offended when their questions are not handled seriously.

In short, there is a two-pronged approach to meeting the manifold needs of persons who have AIDS. First, health care providers should endeavor to recognize and accept the management style the patients have adopted to deal with their illness, intervening only when the preferred style becomes an impediment to progress. Second, health care providers must be alert to changes of management style as the disease progresses. This means that caregivers must do more than institute approved regimens. Observation of the AIDS patient's management style is an important aspect of understanding his inner values and reactions.

The high level of uncertainty and anxiety AIDS-infected individuals experience contributes to depression and negativism. Regan-Kubinski and Sharts-Engel (1992) noted that memory loss, difficulty concentrating, agitation, delirium, or mood changes may be related to disease progression, opportunistic infections, medications, or may be a cognitive response to uncertainty the illness engenders. Their research involved HIV-infected women; their data can also apply to men. A comprehensive, nonpunitive attitude is essential in counseling individuals who are infected with AIDS. Knowledge of available services, advice in obtaining them, planning for dependent family members, and referrals to social support networks should be incorporated into counseling whenever a need is recognized. Regan-Kubinski and Sharts-Engel (1992, p. 15) wrote, "The more the focus is on problem solving, the more certain the woman may feel about herself and her family in the future, with an accompanying reduction in anxiety and other negative emotions that impede action to solve problems."

AIDS AND THE FAMILY

When AIDS afflicts a family member or a loved one, people must stand by and watch the inroads of the illness. Their support is crucial, even though they may feel quite helpless. In the absence of effective cures, social and family help is all-important. It is the homosexual with AIDS, however, who is most frequently beset with family problems. Some families may have become reconciled to the sexual orientation of a homosexual relative, but the diagnosis of AIDS seems to open old scars.

The deterioration, physical and emotional, that AIDS causes may lead to regressive behaviors on the part of the patient and the family. A frequent consequence of AIDS is the reemergence of parents as caregivers to their ill adult child. In their pain, parents may search for something or someone to blame. They may blame the sick person for choosing a life that entailed so much risk. If drug use, promiscuity, or prostitution are involved, family members may feel angry and humiliated. They may blame themselves for being poor parents who somehow contributed to the habits that caused the illness. AIDS differs from other illnesses in that it activates problems that were once pushed aside. Relationships between homosexual persons and their families may have been troubled for years before the onset of AIDS (O'Donnell & Bernier, 1990). Even when parents did their best to be accepting, there may have been little contact between them and a homosexual son or a drug-addicted daughter.

The AIDS diagnosis may prove to be a catalyst that does not greatly change ingrained parental attitudes, but may change parental behavior. Parental reactions to an adult child with AIDS are varied. Kubler-Ross (1987) stated that between 1984 and 1986 about half the mothers of AIDS-stricken sons actively cared for them and a third of the fathers in her study were involved to some degree.

Fathers seem to have more difficulty adjusting to homosexuality in a son than mothers do. Difficulties may arise between parents of a homosexual son or daughter when the father and the mother do not react in the same way. Difficulties develop between the parents when one is more accepting than the other, or when one expresses opinion that the other parent does not wish to hear. It is not uncommon for parents to become estranged from each other upon learning of their child's homosexuality. Parents who had looked forward to welcoming grandchildren are dismayed to realize that this is unlikely to happen. A proper therapeutic stance is to help these distraught parents realize that each experiences stress in different ways and uses different coping methods. Parents may have managed to reach a state of equilibrium after finding out about a son or daughter's homosexuality, only to be propelled into crisis when an AIDS diagnosis is made. The parents may need counseling so that they do not turn away from each other and from their ill child.

There are several community support groups to which parents, relatives, and close friends may be referred, many of which can be reached through local phone directories or health agencies. Another source is the Federation of Parents and Friends of Lesbians and Gays, Inc., P.O. Box 27605, Washington D.C. 20038. Federation has branches across the country. For advice, phone: (202) 638-4200 or hot line: (800) 4-FAMILY.

In many cases, the mothers relocate to distant cities to be more available. Fathers are less involved than mothers in giving direct care, but they too suffer grief and ambivalence. In the natural order of things, parents do not expect their children to die first, and the untimely death of a son or daughter is terrible to contemplate.

The predicament of women with AIDS differs from that of men in several ways. Lesbian women are less likely than men to become infected as a result of homosexual practices. Women are more likely to become infected through heterosexual encounters or through intravenous drug use. Their life style may have caused parents or partners to abandon them. Denenberg (1990) deplored a scarcity of studies done on AIDS-infected women and stated that their clinical symptoms are often overlooked.

There are some AIDS-related problems that are especially serious for women. Often these women are single parents whose poverty and drug use contribute to their social isolation. One or more of their children may also be infected with AIDS, or the women may be pregnant at the time the diagnosis is made. Apart from their urgent medical needs, these women need counseling about pregnancies, present and future. They need immediate help in meeting the basic needs of their children. As they grow sicker, they can no longer manage to care for themselves or their children. They need help with childcare and assistance in making plans for the children after they die. These women grieve for their lost future, just as men do. Even though AIDS is progressively debilitating, the individual should participate in self-care and decision making as much as possible. Conferences that include the patient, partners, and parents should take place at frequent intervals. The goals of these meetings need not be specific; it is enough that they are a time to share concerns and communicate.

COUNSELING THE AIDS FAMILY

Invariably, the family of an AIDS-stricken person finds it hard to come to terms with the diagnosis. Relatives and friends may find it difficult to inform others of the nature of the illness. Even though they hold negative feelings toward the life style or sexual orientation of a son or daughter, parents may become very protective and defiant toward society. If they have avoided meeting the companions of a son or daughter until now, the parents may have to meet a lover or mate for the first time. The mother of a homosexual man may find it easier to become reconciled to her son than to his sexual partner. Occasionally, the mother of an individual with AIDS will see her son's lover as a rival for her ill son's affection. Their subsequent actions may then replicate the competing attitude of a hostile parent toward a son-in-law or daughter-in-law. Unless the dissension can be minimized, the competitive atmosphere will add to the turmoil of the household. Ideally, parents and other family members will rally and join with their son's partner in caring for the ill person. When parents allow the lover to share their grief and decisions, their own isolation is alleviated. As they learn to know their son's lover, they gain more understanding of their dying son and for the meaningful relationships in his life (Newman & Taylor, 1987).

AIDS AND SURVIVORS

The number of actual and projected deaths resulting from the AIDS epidemic is overwhelming, especially in gay communities and in the creative arts such as music, dance, theater, and design. This means that many individuals have suffered multiple losses as colleagues, companions, and lovers have succumbed. For some people, the epidemic has become a major catastrophe (Lennon et al., 1990). Govani (1988) described the experience of people who have lost two hundred people who were socially or professionally important to them. The result is that, for many survivors, grief and mourning are unending processes in which there is no time for recovery. Each death is met in the context of the deaths that went before and fear of the deaths that are to come. By the year 2000, over half a million AIDS-related deaths will have occurred, and millions of people will have faced multiple losses.

In a study of male and female homosexuals who had confronted multiple losses to AIDS, Cormack (1992) found that respondents monitored their reactions in an effort to achieve a balance between extreme (dysfunctional) engagement and extreme (dysfunctional) detachment. The balance is integrative, but it is always fragile and tentative. Several respondents expressed fear of moving too far in either direction of the continuum. In Cormack's (1992, p. 11) study, one of them explained, "Detachment works well for me, but I have to monitor it because if I become too detached, I become dysfunctional because I feel unreal, out of touch with what's happening and not connected, and that feeling can lead to depression."

Apparently, some survivors are able to protect themselves against overinvolvement while remaining concerned and committed. Yet many of them react to additional loss, real or anticipated, by shifting in the direction of extreme disengagement or extreme attachment. Functional detachment was obtained through behaviors such as getting away on weekends or trying to have a life that was not centered on AIDS. Cognitive mechanisms such as meditating, praying, or consciously distracting oneself were also used.

Self-protection maneuvers took several forms. Some respondents refused to start friendships with any seropositive individual who was symptomatic. Others regulated the amount of time they were willing to give to AIDS-stricken friends. Those who were unable to do this found themselves overextended and exhausted, as their involvement became dysfunctional. Contributing to the loss many survivors felt was the disappearance of their pre-AIDS habits and life styles. Reduced sexual freedom and the need for precautions that were often onerous, caused nostalgia for the free and easy life style of the past.

Rosenthal (1992) indicated that depression was more prevalent in gay communities during the 1980s than it is today. This is attributed to the concerted response of gay people to the epidemic. Many gay persons have become politically active and are involved in volunteer work for organizations such as Gay Men's Health Crisis, a New York-based advocacy and support group for seropositive individuals; Act-Up, an AIDS advocacy and protest group; and God's Love We Deliver, an organization that delivers meals to homebound AIDS people. Less community help is available in inner cities where multiple losses to AIDS are well known. Following the example of the Beth Israel Medical Center in New York, other clinics treating AIDS patients are beginning to offer bereavement programs for survivors.

COUNSELING BEREAVED SURVIVORS

Survivors who have lost several friends or relatives to AIDS respond in ways that are not always adaptive. Rosenthal (1992) reports that some survivors resort to "psychic numbing" that helps them avoid thinking about their losses. Some of them deny themselves the comfort of being with other people. They no longer answer the telephone lest someone tell them about another friend who has died or reentered a hospital. Some counselors believe the youthfulness of those who die and of those who survive makes the problem worse. Because their losses are recurrent and overwhelming, many survivors are afraid to express their sorrow for fear that it will immobilize them. Some of these survivors, who sit by the bedsides of dying friends, are also struggling with their own diagnosis, and wondering who will be left to comfort them when their turn comes.

The experience of losing one or more significant persons to AIDS often leads to feelings of impermanence and instability in all relationships. One approach is to encourage survivors to live in the present and to preserve a satisfying existence as long as possible instead of being overcome with grief. This is particularly appropriate if the survivors are themselves seropositive. Cormack (1992, p. 13) quoted one survivor who was struggling to formulate new goals and relinquish old ones. "What matters is whether we have enough presence of mind to notice the birds are singing and the sun is shining." Extreme involvement and extreme detachment may arrive in the aftermath of unresolved grief. Counseling should be directed to helping survivors find a middle ground where they can surrender those who have died without cutting themselves off from meaningful friends and support networks.

It is almost impossible to accelerate a grief process, but avoiding grief has negative effects. Traditionally, people in the United States have been urged to be "strong" instead of mourning openly. Yet survivors need to be able to weep, find other people who have undergone similar losses, and talk about those who have died. Rosenthal (1992) stated that reminiscing and exchanging memories does not drain survivors, but replenishes them. In Support group, survivors may be asked to bring some article that reminds them of their loss, display the article, and talk about its significance to the one who has died.

In bereavement groups, the ritualistic reading of the names of the dead can comfort survivors—witness the cathartic effect on families and surviving comrades produced simply by reciting the names of servicepersons lost in the Vietnam combat. Occasionally, in groups organized for people who have lost loved ones to AIDS, reading the names of the dead is accompanied by the steady beating of a drum (Rosenthal, 1992). These interventions are based on the idea that shared sorrow is diminished. Even though these strategies may seem an ordeal at the time, they leave the participants with a sense of release and greater willingness to get on with their own lives.

AIDS AND THE HEALTH CARE PROFESSIONAL

In the early 1980s, patients with AIDS were not often recognized in health facilities. Now, persons working in the health care professions can no longer ignore or avoid the large number of people with AIDS being cared for in clinics, general hospitals, hospices, and psychiatric centers. For a time, AIDS patients were identified as people who lived outside the mainstream of society. This early stereotype, plus the absence of definitive treatment or cure, has made the care of AIDS patients very difficult. Wallach (1989) reports that physicians, nurses, and other caregivers are not immune to anxiety about homosexuality, and the AIDS epidemic exacerbates this anxiety. Fear of contagion causes some members of health care professions to avoid or neglect persons suffering from AIDS. Wallach found that minority health caregivers are more troubled by the contagiousness of AIDS, more distrustful of information regarding safety measures, and more uneasy when caring for homosexual patients. Granted that this was a limited sample, the data suggest a need for educational programs especially designed for health care professionals educated abroad and not practicing in the United States.

Not every health care professional is capable of giving AIDS patients the compassion they so much need. If health care professionals are to meet ethical standards, they must acquire adequate knowledge of HIV and

AIDS. They must also identify in themselves any limitations or negativisms that might be detrimental to infected persons. Leukefeld (1989) lists a number of useful considerations for clinicians and practitioners.

- It is possible to establish rewarding and mutually beneficial relationships with persons who have AIDS.
- Working with an AIDS patient is very demanding and burnout is a constant threat. Access to educational programs, professional support groups, and AIDS network groups can be a sustaining force.
- Practitioners and clinicians should avoid excessive self-sacrifice and martyrdom. They should attend to their own needs and maintain interests in activities and recreation unconnected to their professional lives.
- It is important to examine one's feelings about AIDS, death, and dying. Practitioners and clinicians should expect to have feelings of despair and futility at times, even as they try to deal realistically with the AIDS-stricken person and the family.
- No health care professional should willingly become the sole care provider of a person with AIDS. Tasks and responsibilities should be distributed and shared to avoid feelings of engulfment and/or isolation.
- Practitioners and clinicians should take an active part in reducing prejudice and ignorance about AIDS. They should strive to eradicate boundaries regarding the allocation and distribution of services to persons with AIDS.

People in the health care system face problems in managing HIV-positive and AIDS-stricken persons who refuse testing or continue to engage in high-risk activities. Some states have passed "noncompliant carrier statutes" aimed at safeguarding the public. Unlike statutes that mandate reporting activities such as child abuse, these regulations make reporting discretionary. As a consequence, a clinical and legal impasse exists (Carlson et al., 1989). Sometimes the rights of patients seem to conflict with those of the health care professional. Hill (1991) describes an incident in which a nurse suffered a needle prick while treating a patient in a general hospital. The patient had not been tested for HIV and refused to submit to testing. According to the Centers for Disease Control, the risk of contracting HIV from one needle-stick exposure to contaminated blood is 0.03 percent. Since 1981, forty health care workers have become HIV positive as a result of occupational hazards; twenty-seven of these workers had suffered needle-stick injuries. Of the group of forty health care workers, three have developed AIDS. Knowing this, the nurse called the AIDS hot line in her states and followed the suggested protocol for needle sticks that occurred while working with untested blood. The nurse was dismayed to find that the patient refused HIV testing and that this was within his rights. Eventually, the patient did agree to testing and was found to be HIV positive. Follow-up showed the nurse to be HIV negative after one year, but she no longer works in the clinical setting and still feels that her own rights were considered secondary to patients' rights of confidentiality.

COUNSELING THE HEALTH CARE PROFESSIONAL

There is a curious inconsistency in people's attitudes toward those infected with the AIDS virus. In the past, infectious diseases such as scarlet fever and diphtheria caused entire households to be quarantined. Not many years ago, persons with active tuberculosis could be confined forcibly during infectious stages of their disease. In some respects, the stigma surrounding AIDS has operated to the detriment of persons caring for these patients, who may be placing themselves at risk when the HIV status of a patient is unknown. There is an apparent conflict between patient advocacy and the need to protect dedicated members of the health care profession.

Shubin (1989) stated that health care providers who have put their fears aside in order to care for AIDS patients sometimes find that their colleagues have trouble relating to them. Even though the colleagues know that AIDS cannot be transmitted through casual contact, they distance themselves from caregivers working with AIDS patients. The families of caregivers who have chosen to work with AIDS patients may make the burden greater. Some families repeatedly express worry that the caregivers may contract AIDS. They also are concerned about protecting themselves. The families warn caregivers to shower before coming home and not to bring home any garment that was worn while attending to patients. All these reactions mean that many caregivers working with AIDS patients must turn to one another for support. Some units offer organized support groups for these health care workers, but Shubin (1989) thought that it is the environment of the unit that is all important. Like everyone else, health care workers have different ways of dealing with stress. For some, a support group is helpful, but not for all. An important consideration, then, is that attending a support group is optional. Understanding and showing empathy from co-workers or supervisors on a day-to-day basis may make the difference between burnout and the ability to continue in these demanding clinical settings. Working with people one can trust, with whom one can weep for the AIDS victims and rage against their fate, is an outlet for many health care workers in this field.

When a general hospital in San Francisco opened an AIDS unit in 1983, the staff began to keep a log or journal containing the names of all the patients who had been cared for there before dying. Far from being morbid, the log was a way of remembering them. Victims continued their personhood and they did not become mere numbers. The staff reports that the names and the recollections they invoke is a solace for the staff.

People who take care of AIDS patients derive some emotional satisfaction, or else they could not continue. Many caregivers reach what Erikson (1963) called a state of "ego integrity" that overcomes despair. From a philosophical standpoint, these caregivers learn to accept death as an integral part of the life cycle. From a professional standpoint, they learn to concentrate on comforting the patients, not curing them. This might mean dealing with opportunistic infections such as pneumonia or meningitis, using nutritional supplements to delay or reverse declines in immune functioning as the infection progresses (Keithley et al., 1992), or welcoming the visits of a friend or lover whose companionship eases the patient's suffering.

Health care professionals who work mostly with AIDS patients have developed the following commandments (adapted from Shubin, 1989) for bedside caregivers and other staff members:

- Learn to say no to some of the requests made of you. Taking care of yourself is the first lesson AIDS caregivers must learn. In addition to clinical responsibilities, these caregivers are in demand as teachers and lecturers. Be selective in choosing these activities.
- Accept, intellectually and emotionally, what your limits are. Set a pace that is comfortable and will not push you to the breaking point, especially in the clinical setting.
- Realize that some patients will not always be compliant or accept your suggestions. Try to understand the underlying reasons without unduly blaming yourself.
- Do not make AIDS the center of your life. Take time off without feeling guilty.
- Take advantage of all sources of support—family, friends, colleagues, and groups.
- Be proud of the work you are doing. It is a testimony to your courage and professionalism.

A Citizens Commission on AIDS, operating in New York City and northern New Jersey, has developed a set of principles that employers and corporations working in those areas have accepted. The policy list contains the following principles, adapted from Noble (1992):

- People with AIDS or HIV are entitled to the same rights and considerations as other people with serious illnesses.
- Company policies should conform to relevant laws and regulations.

- Company policies should be based on the fact that HIV cannot be transmitted through ordinary contact in the workplace.
- Employers should provide accurate, up to date information on risk-reducing behavior.
- Employers should protect the confidentiality of an employee's medical status.
- HIV screening should not be a required element of pre-employment or routine medical examinations.
- In work settings such as clinics or hospitals where there is risk of HIV exposure, employers should provide adequate instruction and equipment to make sure that infection control procedures are instituted and maintained.

Professional and family members caring for persons with AIDS need to know that there is danger of infection from exposure to body fluids, and should be given extensive instructions on avoiding transmission. The American Red Cross maintains an Office of HIV/AIDS Education, 1709 New York Avenue N.W., Washington, D.C. 20006, phone: (202) 434-4074. Local American Red Cross chapters may also be contacted.

•CLINICAL EXAMPLE:
HIGH-RISK BEHAVIOR AND NEGATIVISM
IN AN HIV-POSITIVE MALE

> Kenny Johnson, a twenty-two-year-old heroin user, tested HIV positive, although he was symptom-free. He learned this when he was tested in a community-based drug program. The testing center guaranteed anonymity. Very little post-test counseling was given because Kenny was already participating in a drug rehabilitation program. He was strongly advised to disclose the results of his test to counselors in the drug program, but the testing center kept its promise of confidentiality.
>
> Kenny did not inform the drug program staff immediately, even though he was very upset by the test results. Two of his close friends had recently died of AIDS; Kenny was convinced that he would meet the same fate. He tried to commit suicide by overdosing on heroin. After lying unconscious in an alleyway, police found Kenny and took him to a general hospital in the city. Here, staff members found Kenny to be sullen and angry. He resented the efforts to save his life since he was going to die from AIDS anyway. Because he had been rescued only to face a worse death, Kenny threatened to take as many people with him as possible. He insisted that infecting other people was the best way to get back at whoever had infected him. He persistently endangered disease control precautions while in the hospital. He refused to remain in the hospital or to accept a residential drug

rehabilitation program. Hospital physicians sought legal advice, but were told that Kenny had the right to leave the hospital without medical authorization if he chose. The possibility of involuntary psychiatric commitment was explored, but the regulations in this area were even more stringent. Hospital staff had learned that Kenny was a bisexual who often engaged in prostitution to obtain money for drugs.

Social workers persuaded Kenny to go to a halfway house where he would receive some supervision and his behavior could be monitored. No suitable facility in the city was willing to accept Kenny because he would not agree to remain drug-free and sexually inactive. Kenny had a sister living in the neighborhood who had visited him a few times while he was hospitalized. Family meetings were arranged in the hope that Kenny could live with his sister and her husband. At first she was willing, but when she learned that Kenny was HIV positive, she reported that her husband and her mother-in-law would not let Kenny in the house. She also said that they insisted she not see her brother again. At this point, Kenny signed himself out of the hospital to live with a couple who were known drug users. Kenny and his friends had previously attended an outpatient drug program where they were known to share syringes and needles. This was a methadone maintenance program from which Kenny and his friends had dropped out as their methadone dosage was reduced.

Critical Guidelines

Following state regulations concerning HIV-positive status, hospital personnel notified the health department. Public health officials and community nurses tried unsuccessfully to discover where Kenny and his friends were living. Twice they were given addresses, only to find that the group had moved elsewhere. Although health care workers were concerned that Kenny would continue his drug habits and engage in sexual prostitution, there was little more that they could do. In all probability, Kenny's friends were HIV positive, but testing could not be arranged unless their whereabouts were known. Some ten months after Kenny disappeared from sight, an emergency ambulance brought him to the hospital. By this time he was emaciated and had oral lesions in his mouth and throat. It was clinically apparent that Kenny showed signs of ARC. This time he did not respond to medical treatment. The coroner determined that Kenny had died of an intentional or unintentional heroin overdose.

Kenny's case exemplifies the multiple problems due to his negativism, and indifference to his own welfare and that of others. Aftercare programs considered Kenny unsuitable because he was not only HIV positive, but he was also an unrehabilitated heroin user. Staff members in community programs refused to accept him because they wished to protect their vulnerable clientele. Kenny's sister led a stable life, but withdrew her offer of shelter when her own family expressed opposition.

This case illustrates the difficulties in dealing with HIV-infected persons under the current ambiguous regulations. Although official policies recommended informing others of Kenny's HIV status, there was no clear policy to enforce disclosure. Neither were there any regulations insisting on Kenny's compliance. The months when he dropped from sight were a time when he could have infected many other people. Health care personnel tried to convince Kenny of his obligations to the public, but balanced this against his right to confidentiality. This meant that no one was told of Kenny's test results without his knowledge and consent. Clearly, state regulations and community resources were inadequate in this situation.

SUMMARY

The effects of the AIDS-causing virus constitute the most formidable public health problem of the twentieth century. No longer limited to any one group, nation, or gender, the AIDS epidemic has spread worldwide within the last decade. Since no dependable cure is currently available, control of the epidemic depends largely on education and prevention. Infection is not transmitted through casual contact, but can be spread through exposure to body fluids of infected persons.

The virus has a latency period of up to ten years. Individuals who are seropositive harbor the virus, even though they may be symptom-free. These individuals are a hazard to others if they engage in unprotected sexual transactions. As the infection progresses, the immune system is depressed and individuals develop the AIDS ARC. This is marked by symptoms such as fever, weight loss, enlarged lymph glands, and recurrent bouts of opportunistic infections. A large percentage of individuals (30 percent) eventually develop AIDS. This disease is progressively debilitating, leading to intractable illnesses, culminating in death.

AIDS is both a chronic and a terminal disease. This means that AIDS-stricken individuals undergo prolonged suffering and disability. Friends and family members must watch helplessly as patients grow weaker. Patients require extensive treatment and compassion, and so do the persons who are involved in their care. This includes family, friends, volunteers, and professional health care workers. Many of these people have endured multiple losses as infected persons succumb to AIDS.

Many victims of the AIDS epidemic are young people in the prime of life. Their untimely deaths compound the difficulties of persons involved in their care. Bereavement counseling in various forms is increasingly available to survivors trying to deal with their grief. Counseling should be optional and adjusted according to the preferences of people propelled into crisis as a result of their experiences with AIDS victims. Variations in bereavement counseling are limited only by the needs of the participants and the skills of the group leaders. Health care professionals who deal with the AIDS epidemic constantly deal with depletion because of excessive demands made upon them. Many of these workers benefit from organized programs, but a large number have devised their own methods of helping themselves and their colleagues.

The first cases of AIDS were identified in the United States in 1981, although the virus was probably present in the population before that time. Statistics and other data on AIDS and HIV are continually revised as researchers continue their search for improved treatment and preventive measures. In the absence of definitive information, the only recourse is emphasis on education, especially among members of high-risk groups and among the large numbers of people, infected and uninfected, who have been damaged by the rampant AIDS epidemic.

REFERENCES

American Medical Association. "Prevention and Control of Acquired Immunodeficiency Syndrome: An Interim Report. *JAMA* 258(1987): 2097–2103.

American Psychiatric Association. "Aids Policy: Confidentiality and Exposure." *Psychiatric News* January 5, 1988, p. 27.

Booth, W. "CDC Paints a Picture of HIV Infection in the United States" *Science* 239(1988): 253.

Carlson, G.A., M. Greeman, and T.A. McClelland. "Management of HIV Positive Psychiatric Patients Who Fail to Reduce High Risk Behavior." *Hospital and Community Psychiatry* 40(1989): 511–514.

Centers for Disease Control. "Public Health Service Guidelines for Counseling and Antibody Testing to Prevent HIV Infection and AIDS." *Morbidity and Mortality Weekly Report* 36(1987): 509–515.

Chaches, E. "Women and Children with AIDS." In *Responding to AIDS: Psychosocial Initiatives,* edited by C.G. Leukefeld and M. Fimbres. Silver Springs, Maryland: National Association of Social Workers, 1987.

Cormack, B.J. "Balancing Engagement/Detachment in AIDS Related Multiple Losses." *Image* 24(1992): 9–14.

Curran, J.W., H.W. Jaffe, A.M. Hardy, et al. "Epidemiology of HIV Infection and AIDS in the United States." *Science* 239(1988): 610–616.

Denenberg, R. "Unique Aspects of HIV Infection in Women." In *Women, AIDS, and Activism,* edited by C. Chris and M. Pearls. Boston: South End Press, 1990.

Erikson, E.H. *Childhood and Society.* New York: Norton, 1963.

Flaskerud, J.H., and J. Thompson. "Beliefs about AIDS, Health, and Illness in Low Income White Women." *Nursing Research* 40(1991): 266–271.

Govani, L. "Psychosocial Issues of AIDS in the Nursing Care of Homosexual Men and Their Significant Others." *Nursing Clinics of North America* 23(1988): 749–765.

Henig, R.M. "Viruses in Unexpected Places." *The New York Times Magazine* November 29, 1992, 55.

Hicks, D.R., L.S. Martin, J.P. Getzhall, et al. "Inactivation of HTLV III/LAV Infected Cultures of Normal Human Lymphocytes by Nonoxynol-9 in Vitro." *Lancet* 2(1985): 1422–1423.

Hill, D. "Alone Out There." *Nursing 91* 21(1991): 43.

Keithley, J.K., J.M. Zeller, D.J. Szeluga, and P.A. Urbanski. "Nutritional Alterations in Persons with HIV Infection." *Image* 24(1992): 183–189.

Kubler-Ross, E. *AIDS: The Ultimate Challenge.* New York: Macmillan, 1987.

Lennon, M.C., J.L. Martin, and L. Dean. "The Influence of Social Support on AIDS Related Grief Reactions among Gay Men." *Social Science and Medicine* 31(1990): 477–484.

Leukefeld, C.G. "Psychosocial Issues in Dealing with AIDS." *Hospital and Community Psychiatry* 40(1989): 454–455.

Mishel, M. "The Measurement of Uncertainty in Illness." *Nursing Research* 30(1981): 258–263.

Mishel, M., and C.J. Braden. "Finding Meaning: Antecedents of Uncertainty in Illness." *Nursing Research* 37(1988): 98–103.

Mishel, M., and D. Sorenson. "Uncertainty in Gynecological Cancer: The Mediating Functions of Mastery and Coping." *Nursing Research* 40(1991): 167–171.

Newman, B.A., and E.H. Taylor. "The Family and AIDS." In *Responding to AIDS: Psychosocial Initiatives,* edited by C.G. Leukefeld and M. Fimbres. Silver Springs, Maryland: National Association of Social Workers, 1987.

Noble, B.P. "AIDS Awareness Goes to the Office." *The New York Times* December 6, 1992, F25.

O'Donnell, T.G., and S.L. Bernier. "Parents as Caregivers: When a Son Has AIDS." *Journal of Psychosocial Nursing* 28(1990): 14–17.

Perry, S.W., and J.C. Markowitz. "Counseling for HIV Testing." *Hospital and Community Psychiatry* 39(1988): 731–739.

Ragsdale, D., J.A. Kotarba, and J.R. Morrow. "Quality of Life of Hospitalized Patients with AIDS." *Image* 24(1992): 259–265.

Regan-Kubinski, M., and N. Sharts-Engel. "The HIV Infected Woman: Illness Cognition Assessment." *Journal of Psychosocial Nursing* 30(1992): 11–15.

Rosenthal, E. "Struggling to Cope with Losses in AIDS Rips Relationships Apart." *The New York Times* December 6, 1992, A1.

Saunders, J.M., and S.L. Buckingham. "Suicidal AIDS Patients: When Depression Turns Deadly." *Nursing 88* 18(1988): 59–64.

Shubin, S. "Caring for AIDS Patients: The Stress Will Be on You." *Nursing 89* 19(1989): 43–47.

U.S. Public Health. Report no. 103, vol. 3, supplement I. Washington, D.C.: National Institutes of Health, 1988.

Wallach, J.J. "AIDS Anxiety among Health Care Professionals." *Hospital and Community Psychiatry* 40(1989): 507–510.

Wechsler, H.J. *What's So Bad about Guilt?* New York: Simon & Schuster, 1990.

PART
FIVE

ATYPICAL
CRISIS

15

Post-traumatic Stress Reactions
War and Rape

*Nothing is calmer, more orderly than death. Chaos
is not very nice; loving chaos is dangerous, very very
dangerous. You can see that even in the streets these
days; it might be the end of us all, this love of chaos.
But then life is always more frightening, more dangerous than death is.*

Gabriella De Ferrari

The prototype of post-traumatic stress disorder (PTSD) may be found in
the returning Vietnam veteran, although the syndrome is probably as old
as warfare itself. In analyzing the nature of PTSD, it is helpful to examine
three factors: (1) the characteristics of the survivor, (2) the traumatic
experience, and (3) the social field in which the experience occurred. By
using this three-factor analysis, it is possible to explore the phenomenon
of PTSD beyond the experiences of the combat veteran.

PTSD can affect any person who has been subjected to stress or
trauma beyond reasonable human expectations. Victims of rape or assault, natural or human-derived disasters, or terrorism or harsh incarceration are all susceptible to PTSD. To avoid ambiguity, the American Psychiatric Association (1980, 1987) in 1980 and again in 1987 included the
diagnosis of PTSD in its *Diagnostic and Statistical Manual* (DSM-III and
DSM-III-R). *Post-traumatic stress disorder* is an extreme psychological reaction to overwhelming stress or trauma, and is characterized by certain
distinguishing features, which may appear separately or simultaneously.
One feature is the tendency to *relive* the event psychologically. The second
feature is "psychic numbing," which results in *anhedonia,* or the inability
to experience positive emotions. The DSM-III and DSM-III-R make it
clear that the syndrome is precipitated by events of such severity that
anyone experiencing it would have difficulty integrating them into everyday life.

The special problems of returning Vietnam veterans were first met
with skepticism, but Blair and Hildreth (1991) indicated that this attitude
was based on ignorance rather than indifference. The incidence of PTSD

among veterans of the Vietnam conflict ranged from a half million to one and a half million men and women who served (Walker, 1982).

Although the diagnosis of PTSD has been expanded to include not only combat veterans, but rape victims, battered women, and other victims of stress and trauma, there is some disagreement among clinicians concerning the syndrome. A number of professionals believe that persons with PTSD have pre-existing problems that stress exacerbated. This has contributed to the problems that veterans encountered in the 1970s when the diagnosis had not yet been officially recognized. However, as knowledge of the Vietnam experience penetrated professional circles, the syndrome began to receive proper attention. Moreover, knowledge of various aspects of PTSD broadened public and professional awareness of the adverse consequences that may follow any severe stress or trauma.

In addition to defining PTSD, the DSM-III-R lists the following five diagnostic criteria for PTSD (adapted from the American Psychiatric Association, 1987).

1. Exposure to a traumatic event or experience outside the usual range of human experience.
2. Reliving or reexperiencing the event in various ways, such as painful memories, intrusive and repetitious thoughts, dreams, nightmares, flashbacks, chronic anxiety, and dissociative episodes.
3. Persistent avoidance of stimuli associated with the traumatic event.
4. Persistent symptoms of arousal or reaction to stimuli associated with the traumatic event or experience.
5. Duration of symptomatology of at least one month, occurring at least six months after the traumatic event or experience.

The DSM-III-R indicates that, besides reexperiencing the trauma and the psychic numbing, at least two of the following symptoms must be present: hyperalertness, sleep disturbance, survivor guilt, impaired memory, difficulty in concentrating, and avoidance of activities that are reminiscent of the traumatic experience. Anxiety and depression, often accompanied by suicide ideation, are also frequent, along with low tolerance of frustration and explosiveness. Veterans sometimes reported idiosyncratic reactions. For instance, one veteran found that any red substance, such as tomato sauce, made him think of blood and immediately become nauseated. Another veteran reported that he had become a "speed freak" and "excitement junkie" who missed the challenge and danger of combat and tried to replicate it in civilian life.

The time frame of symptomatology is stipulated in the DSM-III-R (American Psychiatric Association, 1987). If symptoms occur within six months of the trauma and last no more than six months, the official diagnosis is *acute* PTSD. If the syndrome lasts more than six months, diagnosis is *chronic* PTSD. If onset occurs at least six months after the trauma, *delayed* PTSD is the proper diagnosis. Impairment can run the gamut from mild disruption of one's functioning to severe disruption in which almost every aspect of the person's life can be affected.

The symptom pattern in reaction to the trauma is quite striking. First, there is a tendency to relive the event in one form or another. The reliving may be through nightmares, intrusive thoughts, and/or almost obsessive ruminations. *Flashbacks,* the feeling of "being there again," and of reliving the event, set off by some seemingly neutral stimuli in the environment, are also a common phenomenon, especially among combat veterans. As an example, a veteran may notice similarities in terrain while on a camping trip with his family that take his thoughts and feelings too realistically back to a setting in Vietnam, bringing about a fast curtailment to a much-looked-forward-to vacation.

Trauma involves a range of experiences and feelings that includes fear, panic, guilt, anger, and pain, both physical and emotional. When one is traumatized, the normal inclination is to withdraw and/or escape both physically and emotionally. Children who badly burn their hands on an oven door will put some distance between themselves and the stove, give it a wide berth in the future, and may even develop a phobia toward the punishing object. People with PTSD have been burned; but it is their psyches, not their flesh, that is scarred. Like the burned children, they too would like to isolate themselves from the event and its emotional overlay; but the experience, with its many emotions and associations, is so complex that they cannot dissociate themselves from it without shutting down a good part of their emotional lives. If you no longer feel anything deeply, the unconscious logic goes, and you cannot be so deeply hurt again. Interpersonal relations can be profoundly affected. The things that the veteran once enjoyed hold no pleasure any longer, and the veteran's overall affect can appear blunted, even schizophrenic in extreme cases. It is important to note, however, that PTSD is classified as an anxiety disorder, not a psychosis.

THE DIAGNOSTIC DILEMMA

According to Jellenek and Williams (1984), the most frequent PTSD complication is substance abuse. This is particularly true of the Vietnam veteran partly because American military authorities dispensed various drugs. Amphetamines were used to stay awake; phenothiazines and other tranquilizers were used in combat for the first time. Alcohol was widely used, and even distributed to soldiers following an action. Marijuana was frequently used to reduce fear and stress. With this history, it was not surprising for Vietnam veterans to continue to use drugs after returning home. Newman (1987) cited the tendency of veterans with PTSD to medicate themselves for sleep problems, chronic anxiety, and harrowing recollections. Unfortunately, dependence on alcohol and other drugs caused veterans to be treated solely for substance abuse, while deeper problems were overlooked.

It is true that the PTSD symptoms may resemble those of other disorders. Sometimes PTSD is overlooked entirely; sometimes it is considered to be a secondary, rather than a primary, problem. Newman (1987) reported that the most frequent misdiagnosis of PTSD is personality disorder. This is probably a reflection of the traumatized veteran's inclination to distrust and antagonize others, particularly those in authority. The second most frequent misdiagnosis is psychotic disorder, usually paranoid schizophrenia.

Depression with a high risk of suicide has been identified as the most common symptom of PTSD. Other symptoms include poor impulse control, antisocial behavior, interpersonal distancing, and potential for violence. It was not until 1980 that the Veterans Administration authorized compensation and other benefits for persons afflicted with PTSD. Even then, applicants had to meet all the DSM criteria before compensation was paid. Blair and Hildreth (1991, p. 15) wrote,

> "The intensity of resistance and anger toward these patients by professionals can be most startling. Programs and plans of care are fraught with personal control issues, bias, and issues of pathological staff group dynamics."

The media have done much to sensitize the public and professionals to the rigors of the Vietnam combat experience. However, there continues to be some resistance to the validity of this diagnosis. *Malingering* is the term clinicians sometimes apply to these patients. Much of the resistance is attributable to the misperception that war wounds must be visible and physiological. Yet combat-related breakdowns have victimized soldiers in many different wars. In most instances, only the name of the breakdown was changed, as shown in Table 15–1. Percentages refer to those lost to further combat due to psychological trauma.

Sometimes it is difficult to discern from a veteran's history whether his condition is chronic or delayed in nature. Often, with the abatement of symptoms brought on by the exuberance of returning home, chronic symptoms may appear to be delayed in onset. At other times, there really is no symptomatology until several months or years post-trauma. In either case, most of what follows applies, and this author will use the term *delayed PTSD* to encompass both categories. This simplification also makes sense from a sociological point of view, since the word *delayed* may refer more to the veteran and society recognizing the problem later than to the appearance of the symptoms.

TABLE 15–1   Percentage of U.S. Armed Forces Lost to Service
Due to Combat-Related Psychiatric Disability

Conflict	Percentage Affected	Terminology
World War I	8 percent of armed forces	Shell shock War neurosis
World War II	37 percent of armed forces	Battle fatigue Combat fatigue
Korean War	25 percent in first years (later under 37 percent)	Post-combat psychiatric disorder
Vietnam War	12.6 percent of armed forces	Post-traumatic stress disorder

Source: Adapted from Rundell et al. (1989); Blair and Hildreth (1991).

A THREE-FACTOR THEORY

In trying to understand the Vietnam veteran with delayed PTSD, a holistic approach to the problem seems most helpful. When examining the effects of a traumatic event, it is important to look at the individual and whatever strengths or weaknesses he brings with him to the situation, at the nature of the stressor(s), as well as at the social context within which the traumatic event occurs.

The Warrior

Of great significance is the fact that the Vietnam soldier was between seventeen and twenty-five years of age, with an average age of less than twenty years (19.2). Among others, Wilson (1978) presented demographic data on the veteran, but with two and a half to four million men passing through Southeast Asia, it is difficult to speak of the average soldier and his strengths and weaknesses except in the most general of terms. It is in the most general of commonalities that a very significant factor emerges.

The average Vietnam veteran was in his late adolescence or early adulthood. In his theory of psychosocial development, Erikson (1968) explained that various stages in one's life required the resolution of specific key conflicts. For the adolescent or young adult, the task is to establish his sense of self, his identity, or else run the risk of role confusion and loss of self. That warrior of Vietnam was a young man in the midst of his own very important identity crisis.

One need only look back to one's late teens and early twenties to remember what it was like. Those of us who are products of a liberal arts education can recall our college days and the existential crises we experienced. Interacting with classmates whose beliefs and backgrounds were often quite different from our own; learning about the diverse, and often contradictory, philosophical, political, and theological systems of the world; trying to figure out who we were, what we wanted from life, where we were going. These were the important tasks we were undertaking, and their successful resolutions meant more than any college degree received in the process. Those young people who entered the job market after high school faced the same questions, only the answers had to be sought in the context of the marketplace. In either case, society stepped back, allowed youths to question and rebel, to try their wings, and to pull their lives together.

There was no psychological moratorium for the Vietnam veteran during which he could find himself. On the contrary, the military gave the young draftee training, camaraderie, and an imposed identity as a warrior. Unfortunately, he was ill-prepared for the brutality of a guerrilla war; so that even his identity as a warrior was ultimately severely shaken (Wilson, 1978). He returned home a loser in the minds of most Americans, and often in his own mind. More importantly, the veteran came face to face with destruction and death, according to Caputo (1977, p. xiii), "at an age when it is common to think of oneself as immortal." At the same time, the veteran had to confront a dark side of himself that most of us never need to see, a person who could kill and who sometimes even enjoyed doing it. How does one fit these primordial bits of information into a unified concept of self? Not only does combat delay identity integration, it also supplies the person with new data with which he has never been adequately prepared to deal. For many Vietnam veterans, the work of Erikson's fifth stage (resolving the identity vs. role diffusion conflict) has never been successfully completed.

For the veteran who did seek help early, or even within the last couple of years, through the Veterans Administration, it is not uncommon to find only meager reference to his military service in the clinical history, such as "Veteran served in Vietnam from this date to that, and was discharged on such and such a date." The clinical worker often asked nothing about what the soldier actually experienced there, and the veteran, who was often guarded and reluctant to talk about his feelings, was in no hurry to volunteer that information. In mental health facilities outside of the Veterans Administration, it is common to find no reference at all to the military history of the individual.

Therefore, what typically follows in the clinical assessment process should not be surprising. The veteran speaks of his distrust for people in general. He gives an erratic job history marked by confrontations with authority. He may be misusing, or has in the past abused, alcohol or drugs. His history includes violent episodes and possible arrests. When asked, and he usually is asked, if he ever hears things that others don't hear, or sees things that others don't see, he may answer "yes" to both and get too choked up or defensive to explain what are essentially flashback (not psychotic hallucinatory) experiences. He may give his presenting problem as depression or suicide ideation. Put this symptom picture together, and one of two diagnoses commonly will appear: character disorder or schizophrenia (paranoid, schizoaffective, or undifferentiated, depending on what symptom is most prevalent at intake).

If PTSD is misdiagnosed as schizophrenia, the treatment of choice tends to be medication, something to which many veterans take exception: one veteran being treated in a VA facility complained, "They gave me one pill in Vietnam when I went out on patrol to get me up, and another pill when I came back from patrol to get me down. I don't want anymore of their goddamn pills." If the veteran with PTSD is misdiagnosed as an antisocial personality, there really is no treatment for him, since sociopaths are not readily amenable to therapy and are often considered unpleasant folks with whom to deal. In either case, there is a man whose real problem has gone undetected and untreated, and whose self-concept as well as his reputation have been irreparably damaged by a haunting misdiagnosis. The misdiagnosis *is* haunting. The veteran has to deal with the fact that "the system" has labeled him "crazy" or sociopathic when he knows that he is neither. Moreover, trying to get compensation for a veteran in the Veterans Administration with delayed PTSD, especially if he has been misdiagnosed at any point in the past, can be a formidable task.

In many cases, the veteran's worst enemy is himself. One veteran who lost control of his temper went home and shaved his head for reasons he could not explain, but his behavior seemed an obvious act of self-punishment. Unable to work because of his PTSD symptoms, he refused to apply for public assistance, claiming it was demeaning and not worth the hassle. At the same time, he was living on the streets or off his family, and losing all respect for himself for doing so. His approach to life had become one of passive submission, marked by general underassertiveness with occasional explosive episodes. Such a pattern leads to more guilt, depression, and a self-defeating cycle of pity and more self-punishment.

Many veterans talk angrily of how they are portrayed in the media or thought of in the job market as "time bombs" waiting to explode. Ironically, this is precisely how many Vietnam veterans look on themselves. Their concern about losing control and committing violent acts is a strong emotional issue in group psychology. Many will avoid every situation where the potential for violence is even remotely present. A co-worker's hostility led one veteran to quit a well-paying job for fear of losing control and killing the man. For the angry veteran concerned with his potential to hurt others, a dangerous psychodynamic mechanism can occur: the rage may turn inward on the veteran in the form of suicide ideation and attempts. Sometimes the self-destructive methods and ideas of suicide are clear and direct, other times they are more subtle. A strong desire to join a brigade of international mercenaries, for example, is often a yearning for death, but at the direct hands of someone else in battle rather than at his own hand.

Lastly, guilt may be the biggest challenge to therapy. Survivor guilt, which could be called a guilt of "omission" because the veteran was excluded from the ranks of the dead while countless buddies were not, is the basis of haunting nightmares and ruminations. However, the guilt of "commission" for the deeds he has done is an even harder legacy with which to deal. Bourne (1972, p. 84) wrote, "Removed from the permissive and condoning environment of combat, many veterans reexamine their acts with horror when judged by the standards of their civilian environment to which they have returned."

Marin (1981) calls this feeling *moral guilt,* the pain of the human conscience for which a psychological term like *stress* seems grossly inadequate.

The Stressor: Combat

Before beginning an examination of the unique factors of the Vietnam conflict, it may be helpful to look briefly at the evolution of the concept of combat stress within the domain of military medicine. The history of American readiness for dealing with the psychological components of war is a history of unpreparedness. Bourne (1970) points to the Civil War, where a disorder called *nostalgia* was the first reference in U.S. history to the problem of combat fatigue or psychological breakdown under combat stress. Most people did not understand it, and no specialized treatment for the condition was available.

Out of World War I, with its constant shelling, emerged an acceptance of an organic basis for the disorder, which was appropriately called *shell shock.* Yet cases arose in soldiers not exposed to shelling, leading to moralistic judgments about the character and courage of these combat casualties. According to Boydstun and Perry (1980) in their history of military psychiatry, it was near the end of this first global conflict that an American, Thomas W. Salmon, developed a treatment program stressing immediate care near the front lines with the expectancy of speedy return to one's unit. Salmon's program was quickly forgotten in peacetime and had to be rediscovered in World War II, as well as in the Korean action.

Marin (1981) eloquently described the combat experience when he wrote:

> The world is real; the suffering of others is real; one's actions can sometimes irrevocably determine the destiny of others; the mis-

takes one makes are often transmuted directly into others' pain; there is sometimes no way to undo that pain—the dead remain dead, the maimed are forever maimed, and there is no way to deny one's responsibility or culpability, for those mistakes are written, forever as if in fire, in others' flesh (p. 74).

All warriors in history have had to deal with these undeniable truths and come to terms with them in their own way before going on with their lives. In many cases, the trauma of the events themselves as well as the emotional burden of accepting responsibility for them are lessened to some degree by the understanding and welcome extended to the returning warrior from his loved ones and by his society. As a participant in a "just" war with a "noble" cause, the returning soldier can more easily resolve the dissonance the combat experience and its legacy created.

For the two and a half to four million veterans who served in Vietnam, especially for the more than one million who saw combat, conditions needed to deal effectively with their experiences were noticeably absent. The nature of the warrior, the unique features of the Vietnam conflict, and the ambivalent attitude of America toward both created conditions that have impaired the readjustment of tens of thousands of Americans.

The reported incidence of acute combat disorders in Vietnam was quite low, as were all psychiatric casualties for that conflict (Bourne, 1970). The specific reasons for this misleading statistic will be discussed shortly. However, the number of chronic and delayed reactions being identified was overwhelming at times, and Egendorf et al. (1981) suggested that half of all Vietnam veterans have significant psychological problems related to their war experiences.

As part of the plan to prevent psychiatric casualties, twelve-month tours of duty were the general rule in Vietnam, interspersed with frequent rest and relaxation (R & R). When a man's date of expected return from overseas service (DEROS) arrived, he simply left his unit, only to be replaced by a new body. People came and went as individuals, wreaking havoc with unit cohesiveness and morale. It also led to what Wilson (1980) called the "survivor mentality," in which the goal of a veteran's war involvement was not to win the war, but rather to survive until his DEROS arrived.

Knowing he had only twelve months to serve "in country" and that then he would be recalled home seems to have been a crucial factor in producing the low psychological casualty rate figures. If a man is involved in a war for the duration, as was the case in World War II, psychological problems might be ignored or repressed for a while but eventually become unignorable. If, on the other hand, the soldier can see a light at the end of a twelve-month tunnel, he is in a better position to hold himself together, get his honorable discharge, and naively believe he can go home and leave the war behind.

In Vietnam, it was as easy to obtain drugs as cigarettes; and anyone with military experience knows of the availability and low cost of alcohol. Many veterans under stress medicated themselves with whatever substance was available. This medicating also had the effect of reducing the identification of many psychiatric problems and lowering the casualty figures in this way. Men with obvious alcohol and drug problems, and there were thousands, were labeled as "character disorders" (not stress reactors) and administratively discharged from the service as unsuitable for duty, presumably because of preexisting problems. Kormos (1978, p. 21) suggested that an "epidemic of combat reaction had been prevented only at the price of an epidemic of character disorder." The military failed to realize that for many Vietnam vets, drug abuse was simply the manifestation of a new form of psychopathology, along with other symptomatic problems like widespread insubordination and "fragging," the unhealthy and much-frowned-on policy of throwing hand grenades at one's own comrades.

There was no debriefing for the returnee, no working through experiences on the "slow boat ride home" with friends and comrades. As previously mentioned, a soldier was pulled from his unit when his date of expected return from overseas duty came up, and he might travel on a plane home with twenty other individuals from twenty different units. One veteran related how angry and guilty he felt on that plane, having "abandoned" his buddies whom he was leaving behind.

The Social Context: The Homecoming

In their exhaustive study of Vietnam veterans, Egendorf et al. (1981) found two pieces of data that relate to the impact of society on the adjustment of the veteran. First, only combat veterans serving after 1968 have a higher incidence of PTSD than their noncombat veteran peers. Secondly, during their first three years back from "Nam," many veterans showed erratic changes in occupational level, with a surprising downward trend during their second year home; this phenomenon was shown to be unrelated to PTSD. Explanations for this interesting data must be found by looking at Americans at home.

In 1968, America's attitude toward the war was really already bitter. The antiwar groups became more vocal and more demonstrative in their protests, and opposition to the war and its policies was growing, even within the government structure. The man-child soldier who had lost his friends in combat returned home to find he had lost many friends here also. To walk across a college campus wearing a fatigue jacket invited taunts and ridicule, along with accusations of "baby killings" and atrocities. A Vietnam veteran working in a local state-funded position trying to secure jobs for other returning veterans met with off-the-record comments from potential employers such as "Look, you seem to be all right, but these guys are too unpredictable, we just can't take a chance with them." The Vietnam veteran was seen and portrayed in the media, and still is in many areas, as a junkie, a psychopath, a schizophrenic, or "an accident waiting to happen." Whereas the door to jobs swung open for the returning World War II veteran, it was slammed in the face of the Vietnam veteran. This rejection led many to deny their veteran status on job applications and in conversations, and contributed to their anger and their reality-based paranoia. When asked about the reason for a noticeable limp acquired by courtesy of a Vietcong mortar barrage, one veteran used to reply with a smile: "I injured it falling off my motorcycle on the way to a peace demonstration in Washington."

In almost any conversation with a troubled Vietnam veteran, in every interview and in any publication addressing the veteran's dilemma, the conversation often turns to their homecoming, or, more precisely, their lack of a homecoming. They speak of having no parade on their return, a remark that leads to a great deal of misunderstanding and anger on the part of veterans of other wars. It is quite commonplace to run into World War II or Korean veterans who have no compassion for their Vietnam veteran brothers and who look upon them as a bunch of overgrown crybabies. "I never had no parade," is a common remark, "so what the hell is he crying about? He's no different." What they fail to realize is that the word *parade* is simply a metaphor for things like acceptance, support, and understanding. Vietnam veterans had enough dissonance about the war and their role in it without becoming recipients of any national frustration and guilt. Faced with outright rejection or just disinterest, many chose to withdraw and to keep their feelings hidden.

The social factor in the evolution of PTSD cannot be downplayed. Egendorf et al. (1981) offered statistics to show that veterans returning to close-knit families and small towns showed significantly less symptomatology than did their cohorts with little or poor family support in large urban areas. Social support for the former group helped smooth the transition by creating a supportive environment in which they could reintegrate their experiences.

There may be a temptation to cast the veteran in the role of victim or villain, sinner or saint; to do so would be an injustice, for he is none of these extremes. More often than not, he is a "survivor" traumatized by events and circumstances that would hinder the healthy emotional adjustment of any individual. Residuals of their war experience lingered and obstructed their civilian adjustment.

A Vietnam veteran made this statement years after returning home, which sums up his confusion and frustration with society:

> My generation and my father's generation—we were brought up to love America, to believe it was our responsibility to fight for America. Well, that's exactly what we did. But when we came home, they rejected us—and we were only doing what they wanted us to do and what we thought we had to do. And it hurts. . . .

The Vietnam veteran's perceived need to fight for every benefit that the government gives, the continued misdiagnosis of his problem, and the government's denial of his requests for compensation in favor of simply putting him on welfare—are all factors that deepen the hurt.

COUNSELING THE COMBAT VETERAN

Some years after the Vietnam War ended, it was evident that veterans were having major readjustment problems. Many large numbers of them were making no effort to find help within the Veterans Administration or even apply for benefits, yet many of them were jobless, had marital problems, and had police records of substance abuse or violent episodes. It was obvious that new types of programs were needed.

The organization known as Disabled American Veterans established a program known as Vietnam Veterans Outreach Program. Outreach centers were established in seventy cities across the country. Shortly afterwards, Congress authorized funding for counseling services for Vietnam veterans. Approximately ninety-one Veterans Administration outreach centers are now in operation. Staffed largely by Vietnam veterans and located where veterans live, not hidden away in large medical centers, the congressionally funded program and the Disabled Veterans program have been primary sources of counseling for veterans suffering from PTSD. Often, the initial contact a veteran makes to an outreach center is for employment or benefit advice. This ultimately leads to involvement in support groups or referrals to a mental health center.

Rap Groups

Until Vietnam veterans' groups were available, a mental health counselor might see a veteran in individual therapy with symptoms such as war-related nightmares or impulse control. In trying to relate symptomatology to war experiences, the counselor might meet evasion or silence. Veterans tended to adopt a "you had to be there in order to understand" attitude that inhibited exploring experiences that were still causing distress. This rationale for not talking about war experiences was removed when "rap" groups were established in which all members were Vietnam veterans.

The veterans themselves organized many of these rap groups. As Williams (1980, p. 45) explained, "Vietnam veterans are a group of survivors struggling to return to the mainstream of society." Much of their struggle began on their own, and later the Veterans Administration and Disabled American Veterans sponsored them. Without the presence of a professional counselor or facilitator, who may or may not be a veteran, the discussion in a rap group may not go beyond ventilation and catharsis. As long as the professional is a person not afraid to relate as a peer, to share and reveal his own experiences, he can make constructive contributions to the group. With the addition of a professional counselor or facilitator to the group, there is a significant shift from a rap group to a psycho-therapeutic group. Still, it is usual to retain the name *rap group* since therapy implies mental illness, an interpretation of their problems that veterans strongly resent.

Ziarnowski (1986) described important themes and issues arising in these groups. The themes arise within the context of sharing war stories and include guilt, anger, suicide ideation, distrust, lack of confidence, awareness of mortality, problems of daily living, and fear of committing violent acts. Unburdening these emotions has a cathartic effect, and the interest and solicitude of group members goes a long way toward rebuilding feelings of trust. For some veterans, this sharing of strong emotions and disclosing troubling events has too powerful an impact, and it is not uncommon to lose some members in the early stages of the group.

Gradually, other issues surface, still interspersed with war stories. Themes of mortality and distrust occur and recur periodically. Veterans who have been through combat and witnessed the death of buddies are stricken with their own vulnerability. One veteran confided in a group that he never sat anywhere, even in a fast food restaurant, unless he was near an exit with his back against the wall. Hearing this, other veterans acknowledged the same behaviors. Some seem to be forever on guard, looking over their shoulders, avoiding crowds, and carrying or sleeping with weapons hidden for their protection against unknown enemies.

Adjunctive Treatment

Group work seems to be the treatment of choice for most Vietnam veterans, but some veterans are better suited for individual therapy, and others in a group may require an individual session from time to time around a particular problem. Flexibility is always the mark of a good therapist. Of utmost importance is the realization that the veteran is part of a social network; if he is malfunctioning, it affects many people directly and indirectly who are involved with him.

For these reasons, it seems wise to have a partner's group available whenever a rap group is organized. The veterans' problems most directly affect the women in their lives. Couples therapy, conjoint family therapy, and community education programs—all are important alternatives and additions to the rap group approach.

If *cure* means the absence of symptoms, there is some doubt that it can be affected in delayed PTSD. Williams (1980) suggested making symptoms manageable as a realistic goal of psychotherapy. He is a firm believer in any pragmatic treatment program aimed at reducing or controlling the problems and issues outlined. Williams (1980) suggested four major goals to therapy with the Vietnam veteran: (1) help him control his anger, (2) help diminish his guilt, (3) aid him in expressing his emotions, and (4) help him back into the mainstream of society. To the last goal one might add, helping the veteran accept responsibility for actions within the social context in which they occurred, and encouraging in him an active orientation toward life instead of a passive, self-pitying one. How the therapist does this will depend on training, orientation, personality, flexibility, and clinical instincts. The one task in which the therapist might find that professional training is deficient is in dealing with the "moral guilt" issue. A second task for which training and upbringing leave the therapist ill-prepared is to listen, without displaying shock or disparagement, to stories of mutilated bodies, the stench of death, and the committing of atrocities.

Lifton (1973) suggested a strategy as old as the Church in tackling the "guilt" problem: face up to your responsibility, and perform some type of symbolic atonement as penance. Some may look on this approach as a neurotic one, a form of "undoing"; but it has been effective for centuries in the Church, and pragmatism looks like the approach of choice in this case. Some sort of active effort on a veteran's part to contribute constructively to the community or to other individuals may move him beyond crippling guilt.

The specialized programs for combat-related PTSD initially generated optimism about therapeutic outcomes. In contrast, Kolb (1986) and Perconte et al. (1989) have found considerable relapse and rehospitalization among veterans once considered to be greatly improved. Their findings suggested a pattern of chronicity that often develops among veterans with this disorder, and emphasized the importance of ongoing support and intervention. Treatment of these veterans is not likely to be successful if it is solely time-limited intervention. This has implications for offering more than brief crisis approaches. The veteran with PTSD may have some periods of relative adjustment interspersed explosive episodes. During these critical episodes, crisis intervention may be superimposed on the long-term program available to the veteran. Perconte (1987) described an optimum treatment program consisting of insight-oriented group psychotherapy, group desensitization techniques, behavior modification, individual and family counseling, and vocational counseling, all within the framework of partial hospitalization. Veterans attended sessions three days a week for about six hours each day. The comprehensiveness of the treatment program indicates that combat-related PTSD is neither transitory nor superficial.

RAPE TRAUMA AS CRISIS

Even though rape is a violent crime that occurs frequently, popular mythology conceals and protects it. Until recently, rape was thought to be a sexual crime, usually premeditated. Supporting this misconception were stereotypes of rape victims as seductive and manipulative. Such stereotypical constructs have worked to the disadvantage of rape victims. Rose (1986) criticized the idea of a sexually provocative victim, and the specific behavioral typology of rapists, claiming that they may add to the psychic trauma of the rape victim.

In studying the incidence of rape in populations with relatively low numbers of women, it was found that the occurrence of rape was unlikely, even though the male population might be experiencing considerable sexual frustration (Singhis, 1977). Lowenstein (1977) suggested that rape may be a means of releasing aggression against people for whom the rapist has a sense of fear or awe. The actual object of awe may be other men rather than women, but the rapist displaces his aggression to less powerful targets. This explanation coincides with the feminist viewpoint that because women are considered the property of men, acts of sexual aggression against women are a means of retaliation against other men. These psychodynamic explanations may be controversial, but they are conspicuous during wartime when the women of the enemy become targets of rape, much as the property of the enemy is looted and destroyed.

It is the contention of feminists that media representations of women as sexual objects rather than human beings subtly encourages rape. According to the Federal Bureau of Investigation (FBI), rape is an underreported crime, with the estimated number of reported rapes ranging from one in four to one in ten. These statistics mean that when fifty thousand rapes are reported yearly, the probable incidence is at least two hundred thousand. Supporting the idea that rape is an act of aggression is the fact that 70 percent of arrested rapists have previous criminal records for assault, robbery, and homicide, with rape often the accompaniment of other violent criminal acts (Tinklenberg et al., 1981; Groth et al., 1982).

The underreporting of rape crimes may be due, in part, to the victim's feelings of shame or humiliation. Until quite recently, rape victims who brought charges against their attackers found themselves in the role of accused as well as accuser. During the rape experience, the woman is in a state of panic during which she must make a quick decision on how much to resist. Her main concern is to stay alive. Since the rapist is usually stronger than the chosen victim, it is fairly easy to enforce submission. Many rapes are committed at gunpoint or after the victim has been overpowered physically or intimidated psychologically. Regardless of how much resistance the victim offered, the aftermath of rape finds her humiliated, confused, fearful, and enraged. These reactions do not abate quickly and may persist in extreme form for several years, complicating the interpersonal relationships of the victim's life.

Following the rape, victims have a sense of living in a dangerous, unpredictable world. Often, they become preoccupied with their own feelings of victimization and vulnerability. Some women are unable to resume normal sexual relationships with their chosen partners, either because of sexual revulsion or because of feelings of being unworthy. The victim's ability to work through the rape trauma depends, to a large extent, on the attitudes of caregivers, law enforcement officers, and significant persons in her life.

Sometimes the rape victim will engage in complete or partial denial for a lengthy period of time. One college senior confided her rape experience to a trusted instructor, accepted a referral for medical care, but refused further help until her final examinations were over and graduation was a certainty. Only then did the rape victim become willing to discuss the experience, confide in her parents, and begin to express her feelings. Such reactions are not atypical, and the individual selected to be the confidant of a rape victim should allow denial if the victim insists, while suggesting that counseling is advisable whenever the victim is ready to accept it. Almost always, denial is discarded after a short time, although rape victims often continue to limit the form and amount of help they are willing to receive.

Several studies have established the presence of a set of responses known as the *rape trauma syndrome* (Holmes & St. Lawrence, 1983; Becker et al., 1986). Although there is variation in responses, fearfulness, anxiety, and depression generally characterize the reactions of rape victims. According to Burgess and Holmstrom (1974), the rape trauma syndrome is composed of a reaction that evolves in two stages. In the first, acute stage immediately after the rape, victims are extremely anxious and afraid. This may last for a few hours to several weeks. Feelings of helplessness and depression that may last a lengthy period of time mark the rape victim's transition to the second stage.

Ellis (1983) proposed another reactive model. Ellis noted that fear, depression, and anxiety are present the first three months after a sexual assault. Relationship problems and sexual dysfunction may last from three months to a year or more after the assault. For instance, a sexual behavior that once was pleasurable in a consenting relationship may become repugnant because it triggers memory of the assault. Response to rape is neither uniform nor unidimensional, although some common-alities may be found. Therefore, the three-factor theory used to analyze experiences of the veteran can, with slight modification, be applied to the experiences of the rape trauma victim. The factors are: (1) attributes of the victim, (2) the traumatic event, and (3) the social context. These factors assist in assessing and counseling the rape victims.

THE RAPE VICTIM

The *National Crime Survey* (U.S. Department of Justice, 1985) reported those at greatest risk of being raped were young women between sixteen and twenty-four years of age. Women in this age group were two to three times more likely to be raped than were women as a whole group; this age distinction was virtually identical for white and black females. Sev-eral researchers have found that married and co-habiting women may face the most problems in dealing with the rape experience. A great many rape victims are reluctant to report the assault. This seems to be especially true of married and/or sexually active women who hesitate out of concern for their partner's reactions.

In an investigation of the experiences of 356 rape victims, Ruch and Chandler (1983) found that the level of support the husbands of married rape victims gave was usually inadequate. Like single rape victims living alone, married victims looked to friends, not to family, for emotional support. Single rape victims who lived with their family members re-ceived more support from their family than did married victims; single rape victims living with their family were less traumatized by rape than married victims or those who lived alone.

Women differ in their counseling needs after being raped. The wo-man's life stage and her life roles influence these differences. Acceptance and understanding make a great difference to a woman's adjustment, especially if support continues beyond a few weeks or months. The most serious reactions to rape trauma occur when the victim is "let down" or disappointed in her partner's attitude toward her. Women who already have an unsatisfactory relationship with their spouse or partner, are less disappointed when support is not forthcoming. These women quickly turn to others for understanding, and their adjustment is easier than for women who expected greater understanding from their spouse or partner.

The work of Amir (1971) demonstrated a propensity to blame the victim for the assault. His pioneer research showed that 19 percent of rape victims in the sample had police records, and "bad reputations" that contributed to their sexual victimization. However, in a study of adoles-cent rapists, Vinogradov et al. (1988) found that a large majority (88 percent) of the offenders said the victim's words or acts had not provoked the rape. Most offenders (70 percent) reported that they did not consider the victim to be sexually provocative, nor did they feel threatened by the victim. In suggesting that the victim may have invited or precipitated a rape, Amir noted that in 63 percent of rape cases in the study, both assailant and victim had been drinking. Vinogradov et al. (1988) discounted the notion that rape victims "ask for it," or send nonverbal messages that they are sexually available.

The victim's residence may be a consideration in being targeted. Many rapes are not premeditated nor thought out, but are committed when the assailant is engaged in other criminal activity, such as purse snatching, housebreaking, or burglary. The *National Crime Survey* (U.S. Department of Justice, 1985) has reported that one-third of completed rapes and one-fourth of attempted rapes take place in the home. Less than half of the completed rapes, but over half of the attempted rapes, take place in streets, parks, fields, playgrounds, parking lots, or garages. Despite the attention given to *date rape,* a woman is twice as likely to be raped by a stranger than by someone she knows (Divasto et al., 1984). However, it is possible that rape is less likely to be reported when the woman knows the assailant. The *National Crime Survey* statistics showed that 56 percent of victims reported the rape to the police when the assailant was a stranger, whereas only 45 percent did so when the assailant was an acquaintance or friend.

More often than not, rape is an intraracial event, with both victim and assailant members of the same race. The *National Crime Survey* reports indicate that when rapes are interracial, the offender is likely to be black and the victim white. At the same time, the likelihood of being raped is disproportionately greater for black women (Schneider et al., 1981). Rape is an extremely emotional issue and it is possible that, for various social, political, and economic reasons, less attention is paid to reporting and prosecuting assailants of black women. Vinogradov et al. (1988) stated that rape victims were targeted mostly because they were accessible and an assailant of superior strength could overcome them.

THE STRESSOR: RAPE TRAUMA

Studies of peak periods for rape reveal a high incidence occur on weekends and at night (Schneider et al., 1981). Two-thirds of all rapes and rape attempts occur at night, particularly between 6:00 P.M. and 12:00 A.M. Analysis of significant annual rhythms to rape occurrence shows that most take place in the summer or in the early fall. Studies of rapists have indicated that they are usually young men of urban background between the ages of sixteen and twenty-five years of age; many have records of prior arrests. Sex offenders often commit rape for the first time during adolescence, and there are high numbers of repeaters (Vinogradov et al., 1988).

Some experts allege that rape is often a planned event, but others point to distinct subgroups of rapists. One subgroup consists of *opportunistic offenders,* who commit rape without prior intent and only when the immediate situation makes assault possible. The opportunistic rapist is usually involved in various criminal activities, and the rape is almost an afterthought. Groth et al. (1977) saw rape as an aggressive, not a sexual act. Groth characterized *power rape* as premeditated and motivated by the rapist's need to control and dominate. His conceptual model defined the *anger rape* as unpremeditated and opportunistic, motivated by the rapist's chronic anger toward women. A third type, the *sadistic rape* is probably the most traumatic of all, since its purpose is to inflict pain and injury, and humiliation.

Although sexual intercourse may be of secondary importance, forced intercourse represents to the rapist and to the victim a violation of her most private self. Sadock (1985) wrote that one-third of rapists have erectile or ejaculatory dysfunction during the assault, therefore giving credence to the belief that the act of rape is aggressive rather than sexual. In instances of sadistic rape, the degradation of the victim increases the sexual excitement of the rapist. The girl or woman being raped believes herself to be in a life-threatening situation, especially if the assailant has a knife or a gun. The rapist may urinate or defecate on his victim, ejaculate into her face, or force objects into body orifices. The DSM-III-R (American Psychiatric Association, 1987) is cautious about linking rape to sexual sadism, but acknowledges the occasional association between rape and sexual sadism.

Statutory rape refers to intercourse between a male over sixteen years of age and a female under the age of consent. Age of consent ranges from fourteen to twenty-one years old, depending on the locality. Thus, a girl of fifteen and a young man of seventeen or eighteen may have a consensual sexual relationship, but in some jurisdictions the man could be held for statutory rape. Many forms of statutory rape are not assaultive and are truly sexual rather than aggressive acts. Unless the age difference between the male and female is great enough for the man to be considered a pedophile, statutory rape is not considered deviant or perverted. In general, the parents rather than the consenting girl file the charges of statutory rape.

THE SOCIAL CONTEXT: EXTERNAL SUPPORTS

Many women who have been raped exhibit symptoms of post-traumatic stress, which may be acute or chronic in nature. Few women emerge unaffected by the experience. Sadock (1985) reported a study of 130 women from fifteen to thirty months after being raped. More than half suffered sexual dysfunction, including inhibited orgasm, lack of sexual desire, and sexual aversion.

The victim deserves, but does not always receive, loving support from significant persons in her life. She also deserves respect from persons attending to her gynecological needs and from law enforcement personnel. When a rape victim has the courage to report the assault, she may be the object of innuendo and disbelief. This occurs less often than formerly, but when it happens, the woman feels as if she has been raped a second time. She is served best when physical and psychiatric care are offered in one location, and when these services are coordinated with those of law enforcement agents. Many metropolitan centers have a rape crisis team composed of women on call twenty-four hours a day. These team members receive special training and are sensitive to the physical and psychological trauma the rape victims have suffered. Group therapy, led by a facilitator, with members who have been sexually assaulted helps reduce the victims' sense of being unclean and demeaned. Group referrals should follow crisis work.

The feminist movement has worked to promote changes that have aided rape victims. Hiring policewomen has made reporting rape somewhat easier for the victim. Rape crisis centers and hot lines are available to provide immediate assistance and guidance. When a rape victim appears in court, she no longer must prove that she actively struggled and suffered physical injury. Testimony about the sexual history of the victim is not admissible in most states. These changes are undoubtedly helpful, but rape remains a severe trauma with lasting consequences for the victim.

More important than anything else is the behavior of husbands, parents, and significant others to the rape victim. Moss et al. (1990) emphasized the paramount importance of the husband's attitude. Sometimes the male partner fails to support the victim because of his own sense of being victimized by the assault. Another male partner who may initially have offered support, later has problems interacting sexually with the victim of the assault. Other male partners may engage in "blaming the victim," or assigning to the victim responsibility for being raped. Needless to say, these reactive patterns contribute to the victims' adjustment difficulties.

Brown and Prudo (1981) found that the marital relationship could either protect or endanger the psychological well-being of any woman in the aftermath of a stressful event such as rape. In particular, women who did not feel free to share their emotional concerns with a spouse or boyfriend were predisposed to depression following any stressful life event. Evidently, it is not the presence or absence of a relationship that protects or fails to protect, but the quality of support and understanding available within the relationship (Brown et al., 1986).

Moss et al. (1990) found that often the husband of a rape victim considered her depression and anxiety to be normal during the first days or weeks after the assault, and tended to reduce his expectations of her. As the victim's emotional problems continue beyond six to eight weeks, and she is unable to function as usual in the marriage and in the home, the spouse becomes impatient and angry. In such cases, marital counseling may be necessary to help the husband understand the victim's need for more time to adjust, and to monitor his demands on her. When a relationship becomes problematic after the assault, it may be advisable to include the spouse in the treatment and recovery of the victim. Intervention might include information about the usual impact of rape so that the victim's behavior is interpreted as normal rather than pathological.

COUNSELING THE RAPE VICTIM

The circumstances of the rape, the characteristics of the assailant, and the events that happened during the rape will all influence the victim's reaction. When and where was the victim approached? Where did the rape occur? Was the assailant known to her? Was she threatened? Did he have a weapon? Did she struggle? Guilt feelings about not resisting may add complications to the client's recovery process. What type of sex was demanded? For many women, the sexual aspect of the rape is highly distressing, especially if they have been forced to commit acts that are repulsive to them.

In order to provide appropriate treatment, it is necessary to determine the meaning of the sexual assault to the woman and her feelings about sex in general. The rape may create difficulties in the victim's present relationships and may stimulate doubt and fear about the possibility of future relationships.

The client's help-seeking behavior should also be explored. Where did the woman go for help? What was the encounter with the police like for her? How was she treated at the hospital? Is she considering pressing charges against the rapist? Who is available to help her? Who can she confide in? Who is she willing to tell about the experience? The social support systems of the victim can make the difference between successful resolution and continued fear and guilt.

The initial interview of the rape victim is of paramount importance in assessing the client's amount of psychological distress and in determining a plan of care. The purpose of the interview is to learn as much as possible about the incident and about the victim's reaction to it. Attention should be given to the victim's nonverbal responses. Her general appearance tells how she feels about herself, which helps to assess the severity of the distress and the loss of coping skills. She needs to be assisted in making decisions about whom and when she is going to tell about the experience, and who will make up her support system. By using available support systems, she can begin to regain the self-confidence needed to resume her normal life style. The victim should be encouraged to resume her normal style of activity as soon as possible, since delays only lead to difficulties later on.

The rape victim needs acceptance and empathy from practitioners, and from significant persons in her life. Most detrimental of all to the rape victim is the myth of the seductive female who misleads an unsuspecting male, or the manipulative female who shouts "Rape!" in order to deny her culpability for a sexual encounter. The feminist movement has done much to eradicate the ordeal victims who wish to bring charges against an alleged rapist must face. In most states the sexual experience of the rape victim is no longer a compelling issue, and in New York a prostitute has the right to press charges if sexual intercourse took place without her consent. Women no longer have to prove that they physically resisted the rapist but only that they did not consent voluntarily. Some states require women to attest to "earnest resistance."

Professional staff working in hospital emergency departments collaborate with rape crisis teams and act as liaison agents when a rape victim is brought in for treatment. Close work relationships between rape crisis workers and hospital staff members prevent the destruction of important evidence during the post rape examination and provide continuity of care for victims.

Rape is a traumatic event with great potential for precipitating crisis in victims and significant others. Because the reactions of family members and significant others to the assault are varied and unpredictable, it may not be advisable to notify anyone until the victim has given permission in this regard. Many rape victims need time to deal with their own feelings before being intruded on by well-intentioned friends or relatives. The reaction of the sexual partner involved with the victim prior to the rape is of crucial importance. If the partner is concerned primarily with the emotional state of the victim and offers unquestioning support, a state of severe disequilibrium in the victim may be averted. If a husband, father, or fiancé interprets the rape not as a crime against the victim, but as a violation of his own rights, the needs of the victim will not be met. Suggestions by family members, friends, or professionals that hint that the behaviors of the victim encouraged the assault will intimidate the victim and prolong self-recrimination.

Counseling following rape should be anxiety suppressive in nature, and directed toward reestablishing the victim's sense of worth and value. Informing the victim of her legal rights, helping her talk about the experience, and enlisting her cooperation in apprehending and prosecuting the rapist are measures that reduce feelings of helplessness. Even when the rapist is not apprehended immediately, participating in the activities of law enforcement agencies helps the victim to ruminate less about the experience. The same principles of fostering participation to reduce feelings of helplessness may be applied to the friends and relatives of the victim. As with other types of trauma, the development of crisis depends on the victim's perception of the rape event, the use of support networks, and the repertoire of coping mechanisms available to the victim and significant others.

The victim has most likely come to terms with the rape when her memories are less frequent and when the pain of the memories has decreased. A good sign is the resumption of a normal life style. Not all women will be able to settle the crisis completely or to attain the same level of acceptance. If progress stagnates, it may be necessary to reevaluate the available support systems to determine some of the difficulties the woman is encountering.

•CLINICAL EXAMPLE:
CRISIS FOLLOWING THE TRAUMA OF RAPE

Becky Walker had dinner with three female friends at a country inn. Because she was late for her appointment, Becky neglected to lock her car before meeting her friends. After finishing dinner she walked alone to the parking lot as her friends drove away. A man hiding in her car forced Becky at gunpoint to drive to a side road, where he raped her. In addition, she was forced to engage in acts of sodomy and fellatio. When her attacker finally left, Becky managed to drive her car home. Disheveled and hysterical, she told the story to her husband.

George Walker was shocked at the condition of his wife but was reluctant to report the incident to the police. He believed that Becky's failure to lock the car made her partly responsible and that her general behavior had been careless. Without saying it directly, George implied that Becky was at fault for allowing the rape to occur. His attitude prevented the intervention that both of them needed, and seriously impaired the marital relationship.

Critical Guidelines

Women who are sexually active and women without prior sexual experience all feel devalued by the rape experience. Many feel themselves changed in the eyes of others and may have trouble resuming customary sexual activities. The reactions of significant others and all persons providing treatment or counseling are extremely important.

The attitude of Becky's husband after she was raped intensified her distress. Figure 15–1 delineates reactions of the rape victim and her significant other, which lead to crisis. George's reluctance to report the rape to the police was understandable only if he feared his wife might be the object of unsympathetic

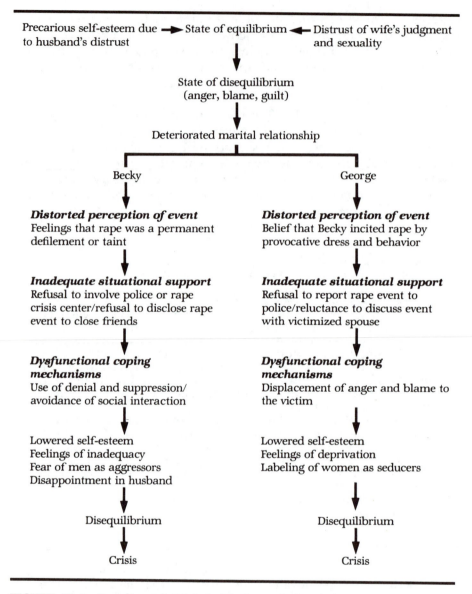

FIGURE 15–1 Paradigm of Crisis in Victim and Significant Other Following Rape. *Source:* Adapted from Aguilera and Messick (1978).

treatment. It should be noted that reporting a rape to the authorities instigates court proceedings only if the victim decides to bring charges. One advantage to reporting a rape, even when physical trauma is not excessive, is that the event is clearly labeled a criminal act and the woman is perceived as the victim of a crime, at least by the people who are most important to her. Failure to report a rape consigns the incident to an ambiguous and perhaps unmentionable category of events. Since discussing the experience with a supportive person helps most rape victims, the rape should not be an unreported incident or a forbidden topic unless the woman herself makes this decision.

SUMMARY

The psychological impairment many Vietnam combat veterans suffered contributed to our understanding of the phenomenon known as post-traumatic stress disorder (PTSD). It is generally accepted in professional groups that any catastrophic event beyond the normal range of human experience can precipitate the PTSD syndrome. This realization has led to more comprehensive programs for victims of war, torture, rape, terrorism, and harsh incarceration. A three-factor analysis, consisting of the victim, the stressful event, and the social context surrounding it, was used to discuss post-traumatic reactions of combat veterans and rape victims.

The patriotic adolescent who went off to fight the brutal war in Vietnam often returned home a disillusioned outcast. For many, the symptoms of delayed PTSD began to appear months or even years after they thought that they had put the worst behind them. Unable to explain their troubled thoughts and feelings, and unaware that thousands of other veterans were having similar adjustment problems, they began to believe that they were losing their minds. The majority were not "crazy" or psychotic. The symptoms they displayed are likely to appear in any individual exposed to unusual trauma (in this case, war). Given their age at the time, the unusual conditions of that war, and the social milieu to which they returned in this country, it is no surprise that Vietnam veterans are suffering stress-related symptoms, that their symptoms were delayed, or that help for the problem was so slow in coming.

The self-help "rap" groups and the outreach programs were of monumental importance in educating and assisting the veterans with the PTSD problem. Therapy, especially within a group setting, can be very beneficial in helping veterans control their symptoms and go on with their lives. Wives and family members should also be included in the education and therapeutic processes.

Americans were not there with support or understanding when the warriors, the survivors, came home. If Vietnam veterans are to successfully reenter the mainstream of society, it is time for us to do what should have been done a decade or so ago: CELEBRATE THEM HOME.

A first step has already been taken. From November 10 to 14, 1982, in our nation's capitol, America formally saluted its Vietnam veterans, living and dead. It matters little that the long, black memorial inscribed with the names of the 57,939 dead or missing Americans was paid for through private donations raised by the veterans themselves rather than by government proclamation. It is not important that the Vietnam veterans decided to throw themselves a "welcome home" party and to invite the rest of us to celebrate with them, instead of vice versa. It is really inconsequential that Presidents Reagan, Carter, Ford, and Nixon chose not to participate actively in the week's festivities. What does matter is that, for perhaps the first time in their post-Vietnam lives and in front of all America, veterans stood together again with their heads held high and often with tears in their eyes. Thanks to their persistence and courage, they made us all remember their patriotism and recognize their sacrifices. That one special week in Washington, D.C. does not close the book on Vietnam or its warriors. The *rituals* of welcome—the memorial, the speeches, and the parade—have finally been accomplished; but the *reality* of homecoming—the acceptance, the understanding, the benefits, and the educational and occupational opportunities—is yet to be fully realized.

The "homecoming" of rape victims often is disappointing. Some victims of rape receive gentle, considerate treatment from family, friends, and care providers. Unfortunately, this is not always the case. Improvements have been made in the way the media, the legal system, and care providers treat rape victims, but more are needed. Rape is an underreported crime because women fear that reporting rape will lead only to further victimization. This is an issue that continues to attract attention from activists in the women's movement. Their goal is to improve the social context that prevents rape victims from receiving the help to which their ordeal entitles them.

REFERENCES

Aguilera, D.C., and J.M. Messick. *Crisis Intervention: Theory and Methodology,* 3d ed. St. Louis: Mosby, 1978.

American Psychiatric Association. *Diagnostic and Statistical Manual of Mental Disorders, DSM-III.* Washington, D.C.: American Psychiatric Association, 1980.

———. *Diagnostic and Statistical Manual of Mental Disorders—Revised, DSM-III-R.* Washington, D.C.: American Psychiatric Association, 1987.

Amir, M. *Patterns in Forcible Rape.* Chicago: Chicago University Press, 1971.

Becker, J.V., L.J. Skinner, G.G. Abel, and J. Chicon. "Levels of Post Assault Sexual Functioning in Rape and Incest Victims." *Archives of Sexual Behavior* 15(1986): 65–74.

Blair, D.T., and N.A. Hildreth. "PTSD and the Vietnam Veteran: The Battle for Treatment." *Journal of Psychosocial Nursing* 29(1991): 15–21.

Bourne, P.G. *Men, Stress, and Vietnam.* Boston: Little, Brown, 1970.

———. "The Vietnam Veteran." In *The Vietnam Vet in Contemporary Society: Collected Materials Pertaining to the Young Veteran.* Washington, D.C.: U.S. Veterans Administration, Department of Medicine and Surgery, 1972.

Boydstun, J.A., and C.J.G. Perry. "Military Psychiatry." In *Comprehensive Textbook of Psychiatry,* 3d ed. edited by H.I. Kaplan, A.M. Freedman, and B.J. Sadock. Baltimore: Williams & Wilkins, 1980.

Brown, G.W., B. Andrews, T. Harris, Z. Adler, and L. Bridge. "Social Support, Self Esteem, and Depression." *Psychological Medicine* 16(1986): 813–831.

Brown, G.W., and R. Prudo. "Psychiatric Disorder in a Rural and Urban Population: Etiology of Depression." *Psychological Medicine* 11(1981): 581–599.

Burgess, A.W., and L.L. Holmstrom. *Rape: Victims of Crisis.* Bowie, Maryland: R.J. Brady, 1974.

Caputo, P.A. *Rumor of War.* New York: Holt, Rinehart and Wilson, 1977.

Divasto, P.V., A. Kaufman, L. Rosner, et al. "The Prevalence of Sexually Stressful Events among Females in the General Population." *Archives of Sexual Behavior* 13(1984): 59–67.

Egendorf, A., C. Kadushin, R.S. Laufer, G. Rothhart, and L. Sloan. *Legacies of Vietnam: Comparative Adjustment of Veterans and Their Peers.* New York: Center for Policy Research, 1981.

Ellis, E.M. "A Review of Empirical Rape Research: Victim Reactions." *Clinical Psychological Review* 3(1983): 473–490.

Erikson, E.H. *Identity, Youth, and Crisis.* New York: Norton, 1968.

Groth, A.N., A.W. Burgess, and L.L. Holmstrom. "Rape, Power, Anger, and Sexuality." *American Journal of Psychiatry* 134(1977): 1239–1243.

Groth, A.N., R.E. Longo, and J.B. McFadin. "Undetected Recidivism among Rapists and Child Molesters." *Crime and Delinquency* 28(1982): 450–458.

Holmes, M.P., and J.S. St. Lawrence. "Treatment of Rape Induced Trauma: Proposed Behavioral Conceptualization and Review of the Literature." *Clinical Psychology Review* 3(1983): 417–433.

Jellenek, J.M., and T. Williams. "Post Traumatic Stress Disorder and Substance Abuse in Vietnam Combat Veterans." *Journal of Substance and Treatment* 1(1984): 87–97.

Kolb, L.C. "Treatment of Post Traumatic Stress Disorders." In *Current Psychological Therapies,* vol. 23, edited by J.H. Masserman. New York: Grune and Stratton, 1986.

Kormos, H.R. "The Nature of Combat Stress." In *Stress Disorders among Vietnam Veterans: Theory, Research, and Treatment,* edited by C.R. Figley. New York: Brunner/Mazel, 1978.

Lifton, R.J. *Home from the War.* New York: Simon & Schuster, 1973.

Lowenstein, L.F. "Who Is the Rapist?" *Journal of Criminal Law* 162(1977): 37–42.

Marin, P. "Living in Moral Pain." *Psychology Today* November (1981):68–80.

Moss, M., E. Frank, and B. Anderson. "The Effects of Marital Status and Partner Support on Rape Trauma." *American Journal of Ortho-Psychiatry* 60(1990): 379–391.

Newman, J. "Differential Diagnosis in Post Traumatic Stress Disorder: Implications for Treatment." In *PTSD: A Handbook for Clinicians.* Cincinnati: Disabled American Veterans, 1987.

Perconte, S.T. "Efficacy of Partial Hospitalization Treatment of PTSD: Preliminary Results and Followup." *International Journal of Partial Hospitalization* 4(1987): 29–34.

Perconte, S.T., M.L. Griger, and G. Bellucci. "Relapse and Rehospitalization of Veterans Two Years After Treatment for PTSD." *Hospital and Community Psychiatry* 40(1989): 1072–1073.

Rose, D.S. "Worse than Death: Psychodynamics of Rape Victims and the Need for Psychotherapy." *American Journal of Psychiatry* 143(1986): 817–824.

Rundell, J.R., R.J. Ursano, H.C. Holloway, and E.K. Silberman. "Psychotic Responses to Trauma." *Hospital and Community Psychiatry* 40(1989): 68–74.

Ruch, L.D., and S.M. Chandler. "Sexual Trauma during the Acute Phase: An Exploratory Model and Multivariate Analysis." *Journal of Health and Social Behavior* 24(1983): 174–185.

Sadock, V.A. "Special Areas of Interest: Rape." In *Comprehensive Textbook of Psychiatry*, 4th ed., edited by H.I. Kaplan and B.J. Sadock. Baltimore: Williams & Wilkins, 1985.

Schneider, D.J., D. Blydenburgh, and G. Craft. "Some Factors for Analysis in Sexual Assault." *Social Science and Medicine* 15(1981): 55–61.

Singhis, S. "Note on Rape and Social Structure." *Psychological Reprints* 41(1977): 134.

Tinklenberg, J.R., P.L. Murphy, P. Murphy, and A. Pfefferbaum. "Drugs and Criminal Assaults by Adolescents: A Replication." *Journal of Psychoactive Drugs* 13(1981): 277–287.

U.S. Department of Justice. *National Crime Survey.* Washington, D.C.: U.S. Department of Justice, 1985.

Vinogradov, S., N.I. Dishotsky, A.K. Doty, and J.R. Tinklenberg. "Patterns of Behavior in Adolescent Rape." *American Journal of Orthopsychiatry* 58(1988): 179–187.

Walker, J.I., and J.O. Cavenar. "Vietnam Veterans: Their Problems Continue." *Journal of Mental and Nervous Disorders* 170(1982): 174–180.

Williams, T. *Posttraumatic Stress Disorders of the Vietnam Veteran: Observations and Recommendations for Psychological Treatment of the Veteran and His Family.* Cincinnati: Disabled American Veterans, 1980.

Wilson, J.P. *Forgotten Warrior Project. Part 1. Identity, Ideology and Crisis: The Vietnam Veteran in Transition. Part 2. Psychosocial Attributes of the Veteran Beyond Identity and Patterns of Adjustment: Future Implications.* Cleveland: Cleveland State University, 1978.

———. "Toward an Understanding of Posttraumatic Stress Disorders among Vietnam Veterans." *Testimony* before U.S. Senate Subcommittee on Veteran Affairs, Washington, D.C., May 21, 1980.

Ziarnowski, P. "Atypical Crisis: Delayed Stress Reaction." In *Crisis Counseling: A Contemporary Approach*, edited by E.H. Janosik. Boston: Jones and Bartlett, 1986.

16

Multiple Trauma
Victims, Families, and Caregivers

Perseverance is more prevailing than violence; and many things which cannot be overcome when they are together, yield themselves up when taken little by little.

Plutarch

Post-traumatic stress disorder (PTSD) is a syndrome that is often misdiagnosed in clinical settings. For years, the Diagnostic and Statistical Manual of Mental Disorders (DSM-I) stated that actual traumatic events may have a "temporary destabilizing effect," but that lasting pathology was due to deficient factors in personality. In the first edition of the Diagnostic Standard Manual of Mental Disorders, trauma was classified as a "transient situational personality disturbance," thus implying the trauma-related distress could only be temporary. Not until the 1980 publication of the DSM-III 3rd edition of the Diagnostic Standard Manual of Mental Disorders, did the American Psychiatric Association officially recognize the connection between enduring psychological distress and a traumatic event. Refer to Chapter 15 for additional information on post-traumatic stress.

Even now, the syndrome of post-traumatic stress is often unrecognized by clinical experts, despite its frequent occurrences. Boulanger (1990) noted a prevailing clinical failure to treat post-traumatic distress adequately. This failure was attributed to the tendency of many individuals to deny or avoid recollection of the trauma. Unless encouraged to do so, many did not describe or report their reactions to the event. Without opportunity and encouragement to express their emotions, some individuals did not process their memories in a cognitive way and failed to integrate their experiences. Major stress due to accidents, disasters, violence, and combat led to post-traumatic disorders in 20 to 30 percent of the victims (Kolb, 1989), largely because treatment was not available. The potential for trauma to precipitate crisis is considerable, and many trauma specialists believe that the magnitude of this potential has not been adequately recognized.

In this chapter, the impact of trauma will be explored as a potential cause of situational crisis, experienced simultaneously by different persons or groups of persons in response to the same event. Not only may the infliction of severe injury or trauma constitute a true crisis for the victim, but that same event may precipitate a crisis for the victim's family or significant others, and also may threaten the equilibrium of emergency service personnel responsible for the care of the severely injured or traumatized client. In this chapter, the potential for trauma to precipitate a crisis in these three populations—the victim, significant others, and care providers—will be discussed along with intervention techniques that may be used. A major portion of the chapter deals with the emergency service staff and their responses to severe trauma victims since this is an aspect of crisis intervention that is often overlooked.

The event of multiple trauma as a cause of situational crisis has not been extensively studied. It is, therefore, necessary to extrapolate findings from related crisis research. Such extrapolation is a valid approach since all life events, even the same life events, have unique meaning for the person experiencing them. Crisis intervention research has established that, because the precipitating event may vary and its meaning may be individualized for each participant, the same event may precipitate a crisis in one person, but not in another. There is, however, some universality of response to crisis across populations, and this commonality is the basis of crisis work. In all trauma there is the possibility of crisis not only for the victim, but also for other persons or groups of persons, particularly the family or significant other, and the initial caregivers, who are often members of the emergency department staff.

For many victims of trauma, especially polytrauma, the time immediately post-injury constitutes a pre-crisis state. The realization of the impact the trauma will have on the victim's life has not yet been reached. Professional intervention at this point can be of great importance. Pre-crisis and crisis episodes are periods when the victim experiences decreased defensiveness, increased openness, and diminished resistance to change (Puryear, 1980). If crisis intervention theory and principles are used in the pre-crisis state, an impending crisis may be avoided. Because of the proximity in time to the actual infliction of the trauma, initial caregiving generally falls within the pre-crisis period. In the hectic atmosphere of an emergency department, especially when the staff is caring for a multiple-trauma victim, there is a tendency to overlook the emotional needs of the client. Inclinations on the part of the client to view emotional needs as less important than the care of physical injuries reinforces this tendency. In adopting this attitude, many victims reflect the low priority the staff places on the emotional needs of the trauma victim. The emergency department staff must take the initiative to show trauma victims that: (1) the emotions they are experiencing are natural in the circumstances; (2) verbalization of fears and concerns is acceptable and will not be ignored; and (3) assistance is available to help clients deal with their feelings, fears, and concerns, either form the emergency department staff or from other sources to which they can be referred.

Because the probability is so great that cases of trauma, regardless of severity, will be followed by a crisis for the victim, the emergency department staff must be:

- Skilled in emotional assessment techniques.
- Able to assess the impact the trauma has for each victim relevant to social functioning and ability to cope.
- Knowledgeable in crisis intervention theory and techniques.
- Aware of hospital, professional, and community resources where the stressed client can receive additional or continued support.
- Supported administratively in their efforts to meet the emotional, as well as the physical, needs of the trauma victim.

TRAUMA AS CRISIS

Is trauma always a crisis for the victim? The answer lies in the definition of *crisis* as differentiated from *emergency* and the application of these terms to specific cases. Whitlock (1978) defined *emergency* as an "unforeseen combination of circumstances that calls for some kind of immediate action and specific treatment of various kinds." Medically, the action or treatment is necessary to save life or limb, or to prevent excessive morbidity. In general, any person who suffers major insult to one or more body systems will require immediate intervention to prevent mortality or excessive morbidity. Most trauma, especially multiple trauma, can be safely defined as an *emergency*. But is an emergency a crisis? Whitlock (1978) defined a *crisis* as a decisive turning point beyond which something crucial will happen. In the medical model, crisis is the point at which there is a change in the course of illness that indicates whether the prognosis will be remission or death. For some individuals, multiple trauma may remain an emergency rather than a crisis. For other individuals, minor trauma may not be an emergency in the strict sense of the term, but may precipitate a crisis for the victim, the family, and the caregivers. Much depends on the meaning of the event to all persons involved, their previous experiences in terms of stress, and the coping behaviors available to them. These phenomena are illustrated in the clinical examples that follow. An emergency may also be a crisis and a crisis may also be an emergency, but a crisis may exist without being an emergency and an emergency may exist without becoming a crisis.

For every crisis victim, some family members or significant others are likely to experience trauma to another individual as a personal crisis. For every multiple-trauma victim treated, there is the additional possibility that the demands made on the principal caregivers will precipitate a crisis for one or more of the care providers. A crisis precipitated by sudden trauma may result from strong, externally imposed forces that are unexpected, uncontrolled, and overwhelming. Rape, sudden death of a spouse, and accidental physical dismemberment are examples of trauma that often deteriorate into crises. The sudden, unanticipated quality of the trauma renders usual coping behaviors ineffective. Be it a precipitating event or a complication of an already-existing crisis, the meaning the event has for the persons involved must be recognized if planning and intervention are to be effective.

Classification of Crisis

Trauma may often be less a crisis in itself than an area in which other crises are manifested. In most instances, trauma is a hazard or precipitator of crisis. Physiologically, the specific injury can be a crisis when the injury represents a turning point for life or death. Emotionally, trauma may be a precipitator of crisis development or a complication of an existing crisis, either situational or developmental. There are six basic classes of crisis which may be located on a continuum of severity, with dispositional crises being the least severe (Burgess & Baldwin, 1981).

1. Dispositional crises
2. Crises of anticipated life transactions
3. Crises resulting from sudden traumatic stress
4. Maturational/developmental crises
5. Crises resulting from psychopathology
6. Psychiatric emergencies

A trauma experience, regardless of the actual event of physical injury, may worsen any of these six classifications. In this chapter, two clinical examples are presented at length. In one example, the physical injuries of the victim were not severe, yet a host of external factors along with the accident the victim experienced led to crisis. In the second example, there was a fatality that became a crisis for some, but not all survivors. The responses of caregivers in both instances are discussed.

To intervene effectively in a crisis, it is important to know the sequence of its appearance and eventual resolution. Baldwin (1977) identified the following distinct phases in the life span of an emotional crisis. Adaptive and maladaptive crisis resolution are compared.

Phase 1: Emotionally Hazardous Situation

- There is a rise of uncomfortable affect that signals disruption of homeostatic balance.
- This unpleasant affect produces motivation to reduce it and to return to a normal state of psychological homeostasis.
- Previously learned and used coping behaviors are brought to bear on the situation in attempts to reduce the unpleasant affect.
- In most instances, learned coping behaviors are successful in returning the individual to homeostatic balance in a short period of time.

Phase 2: The Emotional Crisis

- Previously learned coping behaviors are tried, but are found inadequate or ineffective as responses to the crisis situation.
- The unpleasant and uncomfortable affect intensifies, and cognitive disorganization increases over time.
- The individual is motivated to attempt new and/or novel coping behaviors or problem-solving techniques.
- The individual seeks out others for support and help in resolving the crisis.

Phase 3: Crisis Resolution

Adaptive Resolution:
- With help, the individual defines issues, deals with feelings, makes decisions, or learns new problem-solving or coping behaviors.
- Underlying conflicts represented in or reactivated by the crisis situation are identified and at least partially resolved.
- Internal and external sources of support are mobilized, and the individual's resources for resolving the crisis are defined.
- The unpleasant or uncomfortable affect is reduced, and the individual returns to at least a the fig
pre-crisis level of functioning.

Maladaptive Resolution:
- The individual does not seek or find adequate help to define issues, deal with feelings, make constructive decisions, or learn new problem-solving or coping behaviors.
- Underlying conflicts represented in or reactivated by the crisis situation remain unidentified and unresolved.
- Internal and external sources of support for the individual are not mobilized, and needed resources remain unavailable.
- The unpleasant and uncomfortable affect is reduced somewhat, thereby defusing the immediate crisis situation, and the individual returns to a less adaptive level of functioning than in the pre-crisis period.

Phase 4: Post-Crisis Adaptation

Adaptive Resolution:
- The individual becomes less vulnerable in a particular problematic situation because underlying conflicts have been resolved and will not be reactivated in such situations.
- The individual has learned new and more adaptive coping behaviors or problem-solving skills that can be used as responses to future stressful situations.
- The individual's general level of functioning may have improved, and personal growth and maturation have occurred.
- The likelihood of future emotionally hazardous situations of a particular type of developing into an emotional crisis is reduced.

Maladaptive Resolution:
- The individual remains vulnerable or becomes more vulnerable in particular problematic situations because underlying conflicts have not been resolved and will be reactivated in future, similar situations.
- The individual has learned maladaptive, self-defeating, or neurotic mechanisms to cope with stressful situations.
- The individual's general level of functioning may be reduced to a less adaptive level than in the pre-crisis period.
- The likelihood of future emotionally hazardous situations of a particular type developing into an emotional crisis is enhanced.

•CLINICAL EXAMPLE:
POST-TRAUMATIC REACTIONS OF A VICTIM AFTER MINOR TRAUMA

Karen Johncox, thirty-three years old, was driving to work alone when she lost control of her car and struck a tree. She was taken to the emergency department with multiple abrasions and a bruised eye. Karen was the mother of two children, sixteen-year-old Beth and fourteen-year-old Tony. Her husband, John, had died sixteen months earlier. Although Karen's injuries were superficial, she was extremely upset in the emergency department, where the police had taken her. She cried and repeatedly said, "It's too much—it's all too much." Her car had been damaged slightly but could still be driven. At Karen's request, a neighbor was called. The neighbor brought Karen's children with her to the emergency department. The neighbor's husband came along to drive Karen's car home.

Although statistics are unavailable, some trauma specialists believe that a significant number of motor vehicle accidents, especially those involving one car, may be the manifestation of conscious or unconscious desires for self-destruction. It may be asked whether Karen was precipitated into crisis by the added financial strain resulting from damage to her car and her absence from work, or were deeper psychological forces operating here? Perhaps Karen unconsciously saw injury as a valid excuse for relinquishing responsibilities that had become too overwhelming for her.

Karen's crisis, although not life threatening like John's, was no less significant. A crisis generally involves a loss or the threat of loss, or a radical change in the person's relationships with self, significant others, or a situation. Loss can occur through death, separation, change in status, or altered role relationships. Perceptions of loss, threatened loss, or change result in a temporary inability to cope, either because the stress is too great, because there is not adequate time or energy to mobilize necessary coping skills, or there is inadequate experience in coping. Karen never needed to cope with financial hardship prior to her husband's death nor to deal with legal problems related to her adolescent son. She had been suddenly catapulted from her familiar place as a dependent, protected woman to a position of assuming total responsibility for the family. Her automobile accident was an added financial and emotional strain that taxed her already-depleted coping resources. By the time Karen arrived in the emergency department, she was entering phase 3. By this stage, the tension has reached such a level internal and/or external resources must be mobilized to improve the situation. If the crisis is not resolved at or before this point, the client-victim will move into the manifestation of overt pathology seen in phase 4.

When Karen's children arrived at the emergency department with a neighbor, it was evident that while Tony appeared to have accepted his mother's trauma, Beth was not handling the situation well. Beth was so impassive that the neighbor asked the nurse to "look at" Beth to see if she was all right. Apparently, Beth had responded to the news of her mother's accident by complete silence and withdrawal. Careful interviewing revealed that Beth's perception of this event was distorted in its meaning for her. Beth feared that her mother's car had not been registered properly, that the police would be involved, and a report made in the newspaper. Her classmates at school already shunned her since police had arrested her brother some months earlier. She had not been asked to the annual dance yet and believed that she would not be invited because of her family's "criminal" record.

After her father's death, Karen had been forced to move the family to a less expensive home in another part of town. Beth now attended a different school and had not been able to see much of her best friend, who had lived next door to their former home. Through the problem-solving approach, Beth's perceptions and social supports should be assessed for their crisis potential. Although Beth and her mother perceived the trauma incident differently, both experienced a crisis state. Tony did not develop a crisis state in response to his mother's trauma. As the emergency department staff cared for Karen, they assessed her response to the accident as incompatible with, or inappropriate to, the degree of severity of her injuries. Continued investigation led to the realization that Karen might not be able to function effectively for a time after the accident.

Figure 16–1 contrasts the reactions of Karen's two children to their mother's accident. Note that Tony, who had been guilty of a minor legal infraction, rallied to his mother's support. In some respects, Tony identified with his mother because her accident was a police matter, just as his infraction had been. Neither Tony nor his sister had completely dealt with their feelings after their father's death. Tony, however, had found a congenial peer group in the new neighborhood, but Beth did not. Tony perceived his mother's accident as an opportunity to prove his worth to her. Beth considered the accident further proof of her mother's inadequacy.

Three significant factors determine whether an individual remains in a state of equilibrium or is propelled into crisis by trauma or any other stressful event. The significant factors are: (1) realistic perception of the event, (2) adequate situational support during the time of stress, and (3) an adequate repertoire of coping skills. Assessment of the three factors can provide a

Tony	Beth
↓	↓
Partial adjustment to father's death	Partial adjustment to father's death
↓	↓
Equilibrium (fragile)	Disequilibrium (anxiety and depression)
↓	↓
Tony (Karen's son)	Beth (Karen's daughter)
↓	↓
Undistorted perceptions of event	**Distorted perception of event**
Mother not seriously injured; guilty of minor legal infraction	Mother perceived as cause of further humiliation and ostracism
↓	↓
Adequate situational support	**Inadequate situational support**
Supportive peer group available after family relocated	Best friend unavailable after family relocation/supportive peer group lacking
↓	↓
Functional coping mechanisms	**Dysfunctional coping mechanisms**
Mother assisted Tony earlier/he is now eager to support mother	Withdrawal and isolation from family, peers, and social relationships
↓	↓
Resolution of problem	Continued anxiety and depression/no resolution
↓	↓
No crisis	Crisis

FIGURE 16–1 Paradigm of Crisis in Family Members After Minor Trauma. *Source:* Adapted from Aguilera and Messick (1978).

foundation for problem solving and for crisis resolving. It was Karen's lack of situational support and her unpracticed coping skills that caused her to overreact to her minor accident. These two deficiencies distorted her perception of the event, which led to crisis.

Critical Guidelines

When an individual comes to an emergency department with minor injuries, good physical care will likely be given. However, when the same individual becomes extremely upset, the chances are that emotional distress will receive less solicitude. This is unfortunate, since the emotional distress is often a cry for help from an individual who no longer feels in control. In Karen's case, her children's problems also needed attention. Her son's delinquent behavior and her daughter's unhappiness were linked to the family's loss of the husband and father. This entire family needed counseling, as their reactions to an apparently inconsequential accident revealed.

Rather than discharging Karen after minimal care, the emergency department staff should assess her response to her situation. Instead of criticizing Karen's behavior, the staff should allow her to express feelings generated by the trauma and to discuss individual perceptions of the traumatic event in addition to her own.

The generic level of crisis intervention uses supportive listening, but may include environmental manipulation. While some cases of trauma crisis may parallel other crisis reactions, especially those following a significant loss, the crisis of trauma has not been studied enough to associate a particular pattern of response with it. One or more types of intervention in the generic approach are appropriate to selected trauma victims.

- Providing general supportive measures that are appropriate in crisis situations.
- Assisting the client to be more objective by encouraging a review of a present situation. This approach may not be appropriate initially if the client needs to ventilate feelings.
- Encouraging the client to work out adaptive resolutions; identifying crisis as something that could happen to anyone; exploring constructive actions available to the client.
- Manipulating environment selectively while assisting the client to make changes and develop support network.
- Providing anticipatory guidance, thus aiding in the prevention of future difficulties.

Of the two general types of intervention, modified anxiety-provoking approaches would generally be appropriate only for the trauma victim whose reaction is disproportionate to the severity of the injuries. If denial is being used, the emergency room staff must persuade the trauma victim to face reality, unless, of course, the denial seems crucial to the psychological integrity of the victim. In interventions with Karen, she should be dealt with as an adult with adult responsibilities by introducing constructive actions she can take. Granted, it would appear that it is the realization of her responsibilities that is overwhelming Karen, but it is actually her distorted perception of those responsibilities that impedes her progress. The key to helping Karen is not to do anything for her that she could do for herself. Encourage her to make the necessary phone calls to arrange for repairs to her car and to notify her boss, providing, of course, that she is physically able to perform these activities. The caregivers should remind Karen of her ability to manage, and help her to identify people who can offer her support. Allowing a client to deny all need for help aids in avoiding reality. The well-meaning emergency department staff member, by making the necessary phone calls or acting as intermediary for Karen, may actually promote her regression into a pattern of dependency. Having her take constructive, productive actions promotes self-confidence and indicates that there are many aspects of this situation that she can handle and over which she has control.

Environmental manipulation appears to be extremely appropriate for crisis work with trauma victims. In addition, the caregiver should enact a supportive role consisting of careful and active listening, which provides reassurance that the victim is not alone. Environmental manipulation may involve removing excessive responsibility from the client or removing the client from a demanding environment. Neither of these is a full solution to the problem, but can be helpful temporarily. In Karen's case, admission to the hospital for a short period of observation might provide time in which to rally her psychological strengths. On the other hand, hospitalizing her might promote regression and dependence, besides increasing her financial burdens. While environmental manipulation is no guarantee of adaptive crisis resolution, it can promote a sense of competence in some individuals.

TRAUMA AS CRISIS FOR SIGNIFICANT OTHERS

For every individual experiencing an emotional crisis, there is at least one significant other involved directly, indirectly, or symbolically. For the emergency department staff, the immediate reaction of the significant other to the trauma event is often difficult to handle because of the other duties of the staff. In most cases, the significant other or family member either accompanies the trauma victim to the hospital for care, or is summoned to the emergency department and is present during the initial caregiving phase. Whereas the emergency department staff may view the arrival of a trauma victim as a routine event, they must remember that each victim is a member of a system composed of family or significant others who will be drastically affected by the infliction of trauma on one of their members.

The number of family members who will be affected and the degree to which each will be affected are rarely obvious to the emergency department staff. Whereas a traumatic injury may not constitute a crisis for the victim, one or more family members may interpret it as such. Fear of unknown consequences is extremely difficult for family members to endure, and it is incumbent upon staff members to explain necessary procedures and provide some accurate information to the waiting family.

For significant others and family members as well as victims, trauma as a situational crisis does not occur in isolation, but is superimposed on additional developmental or functional conflicts that may already have taxed resources to the utmost. When trauma to one member does result in crisis for the family, the crisis usually pertains to actual or anticipated dismemberment (loss of one of the members), often in combination with demoralization (loss of status). According to Phipps (1980), three categories of family crises are:

1. *Dismemberment.* Loss of a member.
2. *Accession.* Addition of a member.
3. *Demoralization.* Loss of status.

Crisis intervention in emergency departments is a form of primary psychiatric prevention, and to be optimally effective it must be instituted at the earliest possible point in the interaction of the client with the caregiving system. Among the positive aspects of crisis intervention in the emergency care setting, Hankoff et al. (1974) identified the following:

- With regard to logistics and economy of effort, the emergency department is an ideal site for a program of crisis intervention. The population of emergency care seekers contains a high percentage of clients at risk to develop crisis states as a result of physical and psychological trauma.
- Emergency service personnel have an orientation toward immediate assistance.
- The emergency department is a common portal of entry into the caregiving system, permitting the earliest recognition of clients at risk for crisis development, and thus is a most desirable point for intervention/prevention.

Hankoff et al. (1974) also recognized several negative factors that hinder the development of crisis intervention in the emergency department setting:

- The general orientation of the emergency department staff is toward overt action in response to specific medical emergencies.

- Emergency clients are moved through the emergency department as rapidly as possible to make room for incoming emergencies.
- Opportunities for direct follow-up emergency department staff are restricted.
- The emergency nature of many cases emphasizes and encourages the development of rapid assessment techniques. Making more-exploratory assessments for personal difficulties would require a marked change in pace.
- Increasing use of emergency facilities for nonurgent needs or as a primary care substitute has led emergency staff to view anything other than the most obvious emergent conditions as a referable case. Psychological emergencies are sometimes grouped with nonurgent medical conditions for referral and care at a later date.
- By making nonessential demands and asking questions, the emergency service staff often sees the relatives of emergency clients as burdens rather than as participants affected by the trauma.

It is relevant here to examine the feasibility of offering crisis work in the climate of the busy emergency department. Hankoff et al. (1974) reported the success of such a program at Misericordia Hospital Medical Center, Bronx, New York. The program used psychiatric staff as consultants and emergency department nurses as counselors to emergency service clients identified as entering crisis states. Crisis intervention in emergency departments is a form of primary psychiatric prevention, and to be optimally effective, it must be instituted at the earliest possible point in the interaction of the client with the caregiving system.

The Misericordia project demonstrated that emergency department staff can find the time and can be effective in crisis intervention. Two or three new patients per week were given crisis intervention with follow-up constituting one or two additional brief interviews, one or two phone calls, and, in some cases, a letter. Grief-stricken relatives of sudden-death victims were the most frequent recipients of crisis intervention in the Misericordia project, although a wide variety of individual types of crisis were seen. For many, the emergency room contact was the only occasion for intervention, whereas for others, referral for psychiatric treatment was required. In the cases of referrals, the relationship of trust that had developed between the client and the emergency department staff not only facilitated a smooth transition from crisis intervention to psychotherapy, but also provided the clients with an alternate source of assistance.

Baldwin (1978) developed a model for conceptualizing crisis intervention that has four stages applicable to the crisis of polytrauma. In each stage the therapist's affective and cognitive tasks are specified.

Stage 1: Catharsis/Assessment

Affective Tasks:
1. The therapist encourages the client to acknowledge and to express feelings that the crisis situation generated.
2. The therapist helps the client explore and to define the emotional meaning of the precipitating event that produced the crisis.
3. The therapist motivates the client to search for solutions. During the search, the therapist may provide direct help.

Cognitive Tasks:
1. The therapist helps the client to restore a realistic perspective of the crisis situation and to define viable options or courses of action available.
2. The therapist helps the client to conceptualize the precipitant and the psychodynamic meaning of the crisis situation that links the present to the past (when this component of a crisis is present).
3. The therapist elicits limited, but relevant, background information from the client to understand the crisis situation more fully.

Stage 2: Focusing/Contracting

Affective Tasks:
1. The therapist directs the client to an awareness of those feelings that impair or prevent use of adaptive coping behaviors in response to the crisis situation.
2. The therapist strives to develop a therapeutic alliance with the client, with emphasis on client responsibility for adaptive change and eventual crisis resolution.

Cognitive Tasks:
1. From the client, the therapist obtains agreement on a concise statement of the core conflict or problem that has produced the crisis.
2. Together, the therapist and the client, define a time and goal contract for the crisis resolution process.
3. The therapist and the client agree on a tentative therapeutic strategy or plan to attain the goals necessary for crisis resolution.

Stage 3: Intervention/Resolution

Affective Tasks:
1. The therapist defines and directly supports the client's strengths and adaptive responses to the crisis situation.
2. The therapist helps the client to work through feelings that support maladaptive coping responses (i.e., resistance) that prevent adaptive crisis resolution.

3. The therapist helps the client to respond directly and appropriately to the crisis situation in terms of both issues and feelings (i.e., direct communication with significant others involved is encouraged).

Cognitive Tasks:
1. The therapist teaches the client to develop new or more adaptive coping responses and problem-solving skills.
2. The therapist helps to define client progress in working toward stated goals for crisis resolution.
3. The therapist prevents diffusion of the therapeutic process away from the focal problem and the goals defined for crisis resolution.

Stage 4: Termination/Integration

Affective Tasks:
1. The therapist elicits and responds to termination issues, but does not prolong the therapeutic process because of them.
2. The therapist reinforces changes in coping behaviors and affective functioning, and relates these changes to adaptive resolution of the problematic situation.

Coping Tasks:
1. With the client, the therapist evaluates goal attainment or nonattainment during the crisis intervention process.
2. The therapist uses anticipatory guidance to help integrate adaptive change and to help prepare the client to meet future similar situations more adequately.
3. The therapist provides the client with information about additional services or community resources, or makes a direct referral for continuing therapy, as appropriate.

•CLINICAL EXAMPLE: CRISIS IN A SIGNIFICANT OTHER AFTER MAJOR TRAUMA

John Whitman was taken to the emergency room via ambulance following an accident in which his motorcycle struck an oncoming car. John had multiple fractures, deep lacerations, and contusions. He was thrashing about, screaming that he could not breathe. The emergency staff rapidly intubated him and mechanically ventilated him. Five minutes after intubation he had a cardiac arrest and could not be resuscitated. John's fiancée who was riding the motorcycle with him, was dead on arrival at the emergency room.

John Whitman's medical condition was a true emergency. He required immediate intervention to allow him to continue to live. In addition, John experienced a crisis that unfortunately ended in his death. John's crisis was a tension pneumothorax that the emergency room personnel did not correctly identify. The mechanical ventilation that the staff administered is contra-indicated in untreated tension pneumothorax. In John's case, the emergency situation deteriorated into a crisis partly because of the emergency measures that were taken.

John's mother and sister were notified that there had been an accident. They arrived at the same time as the parents of John's fiancée. Both families were taken to a quiet room and told that the two young people had died. The girl's father and John's sister, Sharon, viewed the bodies; the two mothers did not wish to do so. The fiancée's mother was tearful and distraught, but she seemed to turn to her husband. Sharon tried to comfort her mother, but was less successful. John's mother was tearless and seemed to be in a state of shock. "I can't believe it," she kept repeating. "What is going to happen next in this family?"

Although Sharon, too, was devastated by her brother's death, she rallied to help her mother in every possible way. In the past, she had often been her mother's mainstay, and she quickly assumed her familiar role. To herself she promised that her two boys would never have motorcycles, but she did not share this with her mother or the dead girl's parents.

John's mother was a widow and Sharon realized that her mother's pain was greater than her own. Happily married and the mother of two boys, Sharon drew comfort from knowing that her own two boys were safe at home. The victims were more central to the life of Alice, the mother than to the daughter. Neither woman engaged in blaming nor in perceptual distortion, but Sharon's mourning was facilitated by her husband and other supportive persons whom she used advantageously in accomplishing necessary grief work. Although Sharon accomplished adaptive grieving after her brother's death, her mother did not. John had lived at home with his mother; he and his fiancée planned to live with the older woman after their marriage. About seven years before John's accident, his father had succumbed to cancer after a long illness during which John's mother, Alice, had provided most of the care. Sharon had been somewhat shielded from the burden of her father's illness because she was already married and living in her own home. Only two years older than John, Sharon was fond of her brother and devoted to her mother. However, she did not feel alone and abandoned, as her mother did. Staff members observed that Sharon was more concerned for her mother than herself. When they found that John's mother was alone, they suggested that Sharon either go home with her mother or bring her mother to her home. The parents of the dead girl were overwhelmed by the accident, but they had each other for comfort. Figure 16–2 compares the crisis reaction of Alice, John's mother, with the adaptive grieving of Sharon, his sister.

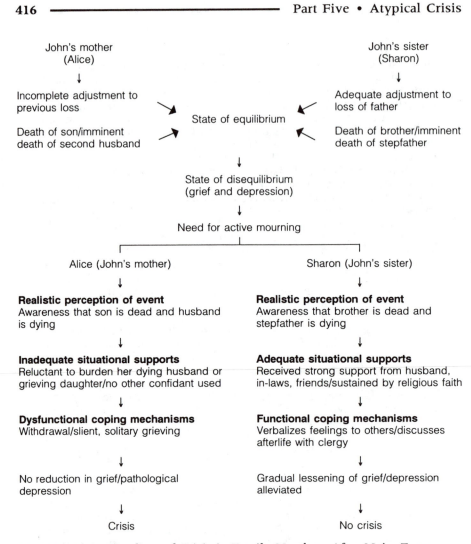

FIGURE 16–2 Paradigm of Crisis in Family Members After Major Trauma. *Source:* Adapted from Aguilera and Messick (1978).

Critical Guidelines

The death of two young people was difficult for emergency staff members to deal with. The death of John Whitman was especially harrowing. Not only had he been alive when he arrived at the emergency department, but he had been misdiagnosed. In all probability he would have succumbed to his injuries, but the staff wondered whether he might have survived if other measures had been instituted. The burden placed upon caregivers when rescue efforts fail is very heavy, even when they can assure themselves that everything possible was done on the patient's behalf.

Emergency staff members work under pressure. Saving lives and responding to medical needs is the first priority. After the death of John Whitman and his fiancée, staff members turned their attention to the families. It was apparent that the mothers, in particular, might need help in dealing with their unexpected losses. Without predicting difficulties, an emergency staff member suggested visits to respective family doctors within the next few days for both mothers; this time would inevitably be difficult for everyone. The staff emphasized the desirability of grieving and expressing one's feelings, and gave the phone number of the hospital mental health clinic, "Just in case anyone needs to talk in the next few weeks." Emergency room staff assured the family of their continued availability to answer questions the families might have.

In this busy emergency department, there was no formal mechanism for extending help to the families of trauma victims. If, later, the family in its grief communicated with the emergency staff, they would be received in a friendly fashion, and perhaps referred to a mental health facility. The lack of any program to assist families of trauma victims gave a message to caregivers that their responsibility began and ended with medical care for the victims. Unlike some emergency departments where there is a mental health consultant available, emergency staff had no one to consult when family members needed grief counseling or when personnel needed support for their feelings of discouragement.

COUNSELING SIGNIFICANT OTHERS

Each year, one out of every three Americans will suffer injury of traumatic proportions; 140,000 of them will not survive. Trauma kills more people between the ages of one year and thirty-four years than all diseases combined (Coolican, 1989). One hospital, in response to need, organized a Trauma Support Team (TST) consisting of nurses, doctors, chaplains, social workers, and volunteers. The team members are taught how to communicate with distressed families, how to impart information, and how to provide emotional support. Initially, the team operated only in the trauma department of the hospital but, as additional needs became apparent, an After Care Program was organized. This program offers long-term bereavement counseling to families that have suffered sudden, traumatic losses. It is even extended to the families of persons who are already dead upon reaching the hospital. The After Care Program is limited to families for whom death was unexpected, traumatic, and/or untimely.

After a referral, the bereaved family is sent a letter of condolence, which offers assistance as well. A phone call is made on the one-month

A BIBLIOGRAPHY FOR BEREAVED FAMILIES

We recommend the following books to families enrolled in our After Care Program. You might want to share this list with bereaved families.

For bereaved parents:
• *The Bereaved Parent,* by Harriet H. Schiff (New York, Crown, 1987). A sensitive and helpful resource, this book explores the feelings parents may have at the death of a child.
• *Song for Sarah: A Young Mother's Journey Through Grief, and Beyond,* by Paula D'Arcy (Wheaton, Ill., Harold Shaw Publishers, 1979). This poignant story is a mother's diary of the lives and accidental deaths of her young child and husband.
• *When Bad Things Happen to Good People,* by Harold S. Kushner (New York, Avon, 1983). A rabbi whose son died of a rare disease explores many of the questions and feelings surrounding the death of a child.

For parents and children:
• *The Tenth Good Thing About Barney,* by Judith Viorst (New York, Macmillan, 1988). A good introduction to death for children ages five through ten, this story tells how a young boy overcomes the sadness he feels when his cat dies by thinking of the ten best things about him.
• *A Summer to Die,* by Lois Lowry (New York, Bantam, 1979). A good resource for adolescent girls, this story is about the illness and death of a young girl's sister.
• *Death in the Family,* by James Agee (New York, AMSCO School Publications, Inc., 1970). This book, for parents and older children, tells how a young boy responds to his father's death.
• *Fall of Freddie the Leaf,* by Leo Buscaglia (New York, Slack, Inc., 1982). This warm and simple story tells how Freddie and his friends change with the seasons. It focuses on the delicate balance between life and death and may be helpful in explaining death to children.
• *Tiger Eyes,* by Judy Blume (New York, Bradbury Press, 1981). For girls age eight to seventeen, this book recounts the feelings of a daughter whose father has been murdered.

For widows and widowers:
• *But I Never Thought He'd Die: Practical Help for Widows,* by Miriam B. Nye (Louisville, Westminster John Knox, 1978). This guide may help widows, their children, friends, and pastors cope with death.
• *Widow,* by Lynn Caine (New York, Bantam, 1987). A young widow with two small children gives a personal and honest portrayal of widowhood.

General:
• *The Courage to Grieve: Creative Living, Recovery, and Growth Through Grief,* by Judy Tatelbaum (New York, Harper & Row, 1984). This book explores common feelings and reactions to the loss of a loved one. It's a good self-help book with creative suggestions for recovery and growth.
• *When Going to Pieces Holds You Together,* by William A. Miller (Minneapolis, Augsburg Publishing House, 1976). The author examines how helpful grief behaviors can be to the healing process.

For caregivers and friends:
• *How Can I Help? Stories & Reflections on Service,* by Ram Dass (New York, Alfred A. Knopf, Inc., 1985). This book—a guide for personal growth, inspiration, and wisdom—offers both practical and philosophical suggestions to those who wish to help.

Source: From Coolican (1989). Used with permission from *Nursing 89.* Copyright 1989 Springhouse Corporation. All rights reserved.

anniversary of the death, unless the family has already solicited help. Coolican (1989, p. 57) stated that "We've found that a personal call from a volunteer at this point is critical because until that time, families tend to be surrounded by relatives and friends. But then, a few weeks after the loss, they're left to grieve alone."

When it is appropriate, a referral may be made to a support group, or to a private therapist if the family desires. Many families do not understand the grief process and are alarmed by the emotional maelstrom they are experiencing. Many people need reassurance that what they are experiencing is normal, given their circumstances. The After Care personnel stay in touch with families up to two years after the death; termination is by mutual consent.

CRISIS FOR TRAUMA CAREGIVERS

Every emergency service care provider is at risk to experience a crisis state in relation to caring for the multiple-trauma victim. Caplan established that an emotionally hazardous situation can occur when a change in the individual's environment alters expectations of self in ways perceived to be negative. Trauma and polytrauma place unrealistic demands on emergency care providers that they feel compelled to meet. If the caregiver is unable to meet these unrealistic demands, and life-sustaining efforts prove unsuccessful, the caregiver may interpret death as a result of personal inadequacies. The result may be severe damage to the caregiver's self-esteem and feelings of competence.

A second aspect of trauma that may add to the caregiver's feelings of inadequacy is the interaction with the family or significant others of the critically or fatally injured victim. The caregiver is faced with the dilemma of trying to prepare the family to deal with probable death, while at the same time working diligently to save the victim. Standard ways of helping family members to cope with impending death, such as involving them in the care of the dying person or just having them present, are not feasible when dealing with the critically injured. Proved methods of assisting the patient to face death, such as allaying fears, allowing control of the environment, and promoting security through familiar objects, are not possible when dealing with a severely traumatized victim. Dealing with seemingly insurmountable obstacles in two crucial areas may significantly increase the caregiver's own susceptibility to crisis reactions.

Puryear (1980) identified five characteristics of a crisis state that can be readily associated with responses to polytrauma seen in certain emergency service personnel.

1. *Symptoms of stress.* Psychological and physiological signs associated with extreme discomfort, such as depression, anxiety, and gastrointestinal illnesses.
2. *Attitude of panic.* Feelings of inadequacy and helplessness, generally manifested by agitation, unproductive motor behaviors, or apathy.
3. *Emphasis on relief.* Being distracted from critical care by attending to the emotional stress of victims or family members; seeking relief not in problem solving, but in ineffectual behaviors, such as emphasizing minor details or seeking rescue by others.
4. *Lowered efficiency.* Continuing to function but with marked inefficiency; using inefficient, restricted problem-solving strategies.
5. *Limited duration.* With the maximum duration of a crisis being time limited, reequilibrium is inevitable. Whether crisis is followed by a higher or lower level of functioning is due to the adaptive or maladaptive coping mechanisms that were used.

•CLINICAL EXAMPLE: CRISIS IN A TRAUMA CAREGIVER

The situation in which John Whitman died shortly after arriving at the emergency department was especially hard for one staff member, a young and relatively inexperienced emergency nurse. What compounded her turmoil were the questions she had in her mind about the treatments administered just before the young man died.

As the only emergency care nurse on duty, Jan West knew that help would be needed. She summoned the supervisor to assist her, but she had reservations about the supervisor's ability to function in this type of critical situation. Jan had been working in the emergency department for only nine months and was concerned that her own skills would not be sufficient to care for the victims. In addition to the supervisor, a newly hired emergency room physician was present to assist with the injured persons, but Jan had never observed the physician in this type of situation. Jan believed that the management of the trauma in the emergency room proved inadequate in the sense that lives were lost (distorted perception of the situation). Jan had never faced this situation before (insufficient repertoire of learned coping techniques). She perceived the death of John as a direct result of her own incompetence and that of people designated to assist her (distorted perception). In an attempt to reduce the discomfort she felt, Jan asked to be reassigned to the geriatric service. In doing this, she believed she would not jeopardize lives with her incompetence (maladaptive resolution). This withdrawal from any future encounters with young, severely injured victims not only left Jan vulnerable to similar situations, but also did nothing to restore her damaged self-esteem. Maladaptive resolution of crisis for a health worker in this situation is shown in Figure 16–3.

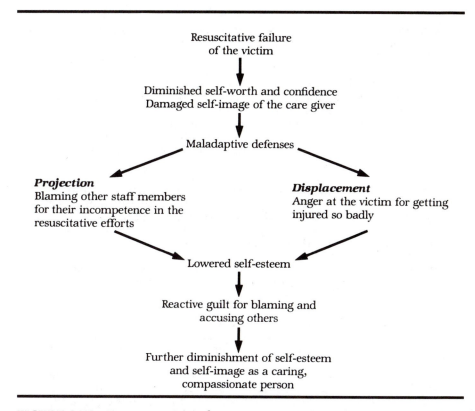

FIGURE 16–3   Trauma as Crisis for Caregivers. *Source:* Adapted from Aguilera and Messick (1978).

Critical Guidelines

Jan's understandable, but maladaptive, response to the crisis of trauma is common among caregivers in acute settings. The most common responses to crisis are anger, passivity, desperation, or denial, all of which are reactions that reflect feelings of anxiety and self-doubt (Puryear, 1980). Perceiving one's self as not being capable of helping others is damaging to one's self-image as a competent, capable, helping professional. To protect one's self-image, the caregiver may resort to blaming others openly for the failure of joint efforts. In addition, anger may be felt at the victim for being careless enough to be injured. Unfortunately, this global blaming leads to feelings of guilt that further damage one's self-image as a compassionate, understanding caregiver. The post-crisis adaptation of this nurse left much to be desired.

The caregivers know that when a trauma victim arrives in an emergency department, that victim's needs will disrupt usual tasks and responsibilities. Sometimes the trauma caregiver is willing and able to request additional personnel to assist. In most cases, this is an acceptable response. It alleviates the fears of personnel that they will be overwhelmed by demands of the situation. If caregivers are unexperienced in handling the type of injury that is presented, or if a disaster has sent large numbers of victims simultaneously to an emergency department, feelings of inadequacy arise and further impede staff efforts to cope. Helping efforts that do not produce desirable results may engender a crisis state in some caregivers. Crisis in caregivers may take the form of distancing themselves from colleagues or blaming other staff members for the trauma victim's failure to respond.

Caregivers cannot altogether avoid emotional reactions. Feelings of satisfaction and joy certainly prevail when the caregivers' hard work saves a life or prevents disability. Cognitive and objective evaluations of treatment administered to trauma victims are preferable and go far to avoid staff burnout. Such evaluations should be team focused, should avoid the scapegoating of any health team member, and should have the goal of improving care for other trauma victims.

Superimposed on or contributing to crisis response to trauma by emergency room personnel is the grieving process that the staff experiences each time a patient dies. Most individuals, survivors and caregivers alike, react to grief by progressing through stages of anger, depression, rationalization, and acceptance, but at different rates. Unlike the victim's family, there is a high degree of probability that the caregiver will be exposed to another trauma-related death before the preceding crisis has been resolved and the grieving process has been completed. With the period for crisis resolution estimated as six weeks and the intervals between trauma victims often much less than that, there is little opportunity for resolving the crisis before additional stress is introduced.

With emergency department staff, it may seem to be a single-trauma victim that triggers a crisis situation. In actuality, it may be that the failures and frustrations of managing trauma victims in the past are culminated in a single incident. Not all caregivers will be precipitated into a crisis by the advent of a trauma victim, nor will every staff member who has undergone a trauma-related crisis suffer subsequent crises related to trauma care. Two key concepts are especially appropriate to trauma-related crises in the emergency care staff. The first concept is that of *prevention of crises in this high-risk population*. The emergency department staff must be supported and assisted in various ways that increase and maintain self-esteem and feelings of control. Providing a nurturing, supportive environment for emergency caregivers is the primary level of crisis prevention. It is important to assist personnel in coping with the trauma situation. A comprehensive assessment and recording tool has been devised that can be used in the initial care of multiple-trauma victims. The tool promotes feelings of competence and control by not only serving to record assessment findings, but also by acting as a guide of assessments to be made. Accurate, complete assessment of the multiply injured client is essential if intervention is to be adequate and attentive.

The second concept relevant to the emergency department staff is that *success in coping with one crisis will increase the ability to cope with future crises.* Each trauma case must serve to increase the trauma nurse's intervention skills. If the trauma nurse is not assisted to cope with demands and personal feelings, eventual response to the advent of each trauma victim will be crisis with maladaptive resolution.

COUNSELING TRAUMA CAREGIVERS

Anxiety-provoking and anxiety-suppressive types of intervention are both applicable to the crisis caregivers experience in the face of, or aftermath of, caring for the multiple-trauma victim. Staff must be made to acknowledge the reality of situations that confront them. Not all trauma victims are salvageable, not because of inadequacies in care, but because of the nature and extent of injuries. The caregiver must be helped to be introspective and analytic, to express feelings verbally, and to oppose regressive or withdrawal tendencies. Personnel in crisis must be assisted to become objective observers of themselves, since learning about a problematic reaction will increase their power to deal with it. It is also appropriate to direct stressed staff members to sources of support and assistance, on a group or individual basis. There is tremendous social and peer pressure on emergency department and critical care staff to function under stress without acknowledging personal reactions. This attitude should be modified to reduce the stress providers of acute care experience. For emergency department personnel working under pressure, anxiety-suppressive strategies can be facilitative. Especially appropriate are permitting ventilation of feelings and reducing guilt or anxiety through reassurance. At times, the caregivers may need assistance in specific decision making, and techniques of anticipatory guidance are effective in avoiding future difficulties.

Environmental manipulation of one kind or another can be recommended. Environmental manipulation may include in-service programs that develop and maintain skills, and thereby alleviate feelings of inadequacy. Ambiguity regarding policies and procedures adds to the stress of caregivers working in acute care facilities. It is essential for staff members to understand what is expected of them and to have clear procedural guidelines. Such guidelines reduce the danger of litigation from dissatisfied clients, hold the caregivers to a consistent standard of practice, and help maintain clear communication among personnel members. The comprehensive Multiple-Trauma Record given in Figure 16–4 is an example of a detailed format that reduces ambiguity.

Adding competent support services is another example of environmental manipulation. Another consists of temporarily removing an individual caregiver from the acute care environment, even though there are

NAME _____ ADM. DATE ____ ADM. TIME ____

Wg _____ Vitals on Adm. B/P _____ P _____ R _____

Level consciousness
❏ Alert   ❏ Aphasic   ❏ Uncooperative
❏ Lethargic (sleepy, responds slowly or incompletely)
❏ Obtunded (arousable, sleeps deeply, indifferent)
❏ Responds to verbal stimuli appropriately
❏ Responds to painful stimuli appropriately
❏ Comatose (unresponsive)
❏ Decerebrate/Decorticate posturing   ❏ Symmetrical   ❏ Lateralized
❏ Positive Babinski   R ❏   L ❏
❏ Deep tendon reflexes   ❏ Present   ❏ Absent
Responds appropriately when asked   ❏ Location
❏ Day/date   ❏ Name
❏ Rapid changeability   ❏ Seizure activity
❏ Alert now/unconscious at scene   ❏ Agitated

Pupils/eye movements
❏ Equal
❏ Constrict briskly to light
❏ Consensual reaction present   ❏ Strabismus
❏ Unequal: R L greater than R L
❏ Accommodation equal
❏ Small but react—to light
❏ Nystagmus present
❏ Dysconjugate movement

Airway/respirations/breath sounds
❏ Apneic   ❏ Rapid, deep   ❏ Biot's
❏ Cheyne Stokes   ❏ Kussmaul   ❏ Apneustic
❏ Ataxic (irreg)   ❏ Normal (reg)
❏ Hypoventilation   ❏ Hyperventilation
❏ Rapidly changeable   ❏ Dyspnea
❏ Tachypnea   ❏ Bradypnea
❏ Respiratory rate _____/min.
❏ Endo-naso tracheal tube: Size _____

Breath sounds	*Right*	*Left*
❏ Diminished	_____	_____
❏ Rales	_____	_____
❏ Bronchii/wheeze	_____	_____
❏ Friction rub	_____	_____
❏ Egophony	_____	_____

Page 1   *Continued*

FIGURE 16–4   Emergency Record of Multiple Trauma

Allergies
Pertinent information

_____

- ❏ Wallet, purse, person checked for ID & other information
- ❏ Medic Alert tag
- ❏ Contact lenses
- ❏ Dentures
- ❏ Hearing aid

Treatment in progress on admission
- ❏ CPR   ❏ Airway, oral   ❏ O$_2$ via _____
- ❏ Backboard _____
- ❏ Splints _____

_____
_____

- ❏ Cervical collar   ❏ Other _____

Head/face
- ❏ Able to close eyes tightly and make teethbaring facial grimace
- ❏ Too badly traumatized to evaluate
- ❏ Periorbital ecchymosis without apparent direct injury   ❏ R   ❏ L
- ❏ Rhinorrhea   ❏ R   ❏ L
- ❏ Battle's signs   ❏ R   ❏ L
- ❏ Aural bleeding   ❏ R   ❏ L
- ❏ Otorrhea
- ❏ Lacerations _____
- ❏ Hematoma _____
- ❏ Abrasions _____
- ❏ Foreign bodies present _____
- ❏ Circumoral cyanosis _____

Heart sounds/cardiac rhythm
- ❏ Heart sounds loud/distant
- ❏ Heart sounds regular/irregular
- ❏ Monitor shows _____
- ❏ Heart murmur heard   ❏ Friction rub heard
- ❏ Paradoxical pulse
- ❏ Pulse rate _____ /min.

Chest
- ❏ Contusions _____   ❏ Paradoxical resp. _____
- ❏ Abrasions _____   ❏ Retractions _____
- ❏ Lacerations _____   ❏ Penetrating wound _____
- ❏ Hematoma _____   ❏ Subcut. emphysema _____
- ❏ Sucking wound _____

Page 2 _Continued_

FIGURE 16–4 _(continued)_

Abdomen
- ❑ Distension ❑ Rigidity ❑ Tenderness _____
- ❑ Pain: type _____
  - location _____
  - severity _____
- ❑ Bowel sounds hyperactive
- ❑ Bowel sounds absent/hypoactive
- ❑ Rectal bleeding/Amt. _____
- ❑ Emesis type _____ Amt. _____
- ❑ Mottled cyanosis of abdomen
- ❑ Penetrating wound _____
- ❑ Contusions _____ ❑ Abrasions _____
- ❑ Lacerations _____ Hematomas _____
- ❑ Cullen's sign present (bluish umbilicus)

Extremities
- ❑ Strong bilat. grip ❑ Quadriplegia
- ❑ Hemiplegia R ❑ L ❑
- ❑ Hemiparesis R ❑ L ❑
- ❑ Deformity _____
  _____
- ❑ Pain _____

- ❑ Contusions _____
- ❑ Lacerations _____
- ❑ Abrasions _____
- ❑ Hematoma _____
- Status of peripheral pulses
- ❑ Thready ❑ Bounding ❑ Not Palp. _____
- ❑ Slow ❑ Reg. ❑ Irreg. ❑ Rapid ❑ Weak
- Other Comments _____
- ❑ Other _____

Skin
- ❑ Cold/clammy ❑ Warm/dry ❑ Pale
- ❑ Jaundiced ❑ Flushed ❑ Cyanotic
- ❑ Burns _____
- ❑ Mottled _____

Page 3   *Continued*

FIGURE 16–4 *(continued)*

General

❏ Poor/vague recall circumstances of trauma, etc.
❏ Good recall
❏ First event recalled post trauma

❏ Date/time last food ingest _____
❏ Approx. time of trauma _____
❏ Brief Hx of trauma _____

❏ History of trauma not available
❏ Hx drug/alcohol ingestion _____

❏ Date last tet. tox. _____

Treatments/tests

❏ Uristix Dipstick moistened with aural or nasal drainage
❏ Blood Dextrostix _____
❏ Foley Catheter SZ _____
  amt. obtained _____
❏ Urine S/A _____ Urine S/G _____
❏ Hematuria   Gross ❏   Slight ❏
❏ Incontinence   Urine ❏   Feces ❏
❏ I.V.'s gauge needle _____
  Sites _____
  Solutions _____
❏ C.V.P. gauge cath. _____
  Site _____
  Initial reading: _____
❏ Subclavian gauge _____
  R side ❏   L side ❏
  Solution ❏
❏ Cutdown gauge cat. _____
  Site _____
  Solution _____
❏ N/G tube size _____
  Type & amount of drainage _____
❏ Tracheostomy size _____
❏ Chest tubes size _____
  Location _____
  Type/amt. drainage _____
❏ Temperature _____ Rectal/Axillary/Oral _____
❏ Splints _____

❏ Drsgs. _____

                                           Continued

FIGURE 16–4   *(continued)*

Medications given

_____ Time _____

_____ Time _____

_____ Time _____

_____ Time _____

❏ Pericentisis/peritoneal lavage _____

❏ Thoracentesis _____

_____

❏ Lab work _____

_____

_____

❏ X-rays _____

_____

_____

❏ Initially seen by _____ MD

Notes _____

_____

_____

_____

_____

_____

_____

_____ RN

Page 5

FIGURE 16–4 _(continued)_

inherent risks in this tactic. Patterned responses of emergency department staff to the care of severely injured persons have not been well enough documented to establish a generic response pattern on the part of caregivers. There is no doubt that emergency department personnel need programs and policies that will prevent the development of crises secondary to the urgent demands imposed by the setting. Many of the crisis experiences of emergency caregivers are replicated in staff members working in intensive care settings in which trauma is not externally imposed, but is part of an internal disease process. Therefore, similar interventions for all caregivers working in acute settings can be advocated.

SUMMARY

A crisis caused by sudden trauma usually follows from external causes that result in physical and psychological injury. There is often no direct correlation between the extent of physical damage and the extent of psychological distress. It is the perception of the victim and of others involved that determines the severity of the crisis reaction. For many victims of trauma, the period immediately following the injury is a pre-crisis state. If effective crisis intervention is available at this time, an actual crisis may be averted. Since trauma victims receive initial treatment from emergency workers, it is helpful if such workers have some knowledge of basic principles of crisis work. Anxiety-suppressing measures should be offered to trauma victims and their significant others during the early period of impact. Life-support measures take priority in the care of trauma victims; at the same time, knowledgeable emergency workers have the opportunity to implement primary prevention that may avoid a later crisis.

Because of their responsibilities, all emergency care providers are at risk of experiencing reactive crisis as they treat the victims of trauma. When life-support efforts are unsuccessful, the emergency care provider may feel personally responsible and professionally inadequate. Programs that alleviate these feelings are often necessary as crisis workers endeavor to meet the demands placed on them.

REFERENCES

Aguilera, D.C., and J.M. Messick. *Crisis Intervention: Theory and Methodology.* St. Louis: Mosby, 1978.

American Psychiatric Association. *Diagnostic and Statistical Manual of Mental Disorders 3rd ed.* Washington D.C.: American Psychiatric Association, 1981.

Baldwin, B.A. "Crisis Intervention in Professional Practice: Implications for Clinical Training." *American Journal of Orthopsychiatry* 47(1977): 659–670.

———. "A Paradigm for the Classification of Emotional Crises: Implications for Crisis Intervention." *American Journal of Orthopsychiatry* 48(1978): 538–551.

Boulanger, G. "A State of Anarchy and a Call to Arms: The Research and Treatment of Post Traumatic Stress Disorder." *Journal of Contemporary Psychology* 20(1990): 5–15.

Brown, D., and E. Witztom. "Recent Trauma in Psychiatric Outpatients." *American Journal of Orthopsychiatry* 62(1992): 545–551.

Burgess, A.W., and B.A. Baldwin. *Crisis Intervention: Theory and Practice.* Englewood Cliffs, New Jersey: Prentice-Hall, 1981.

Coolican, M. "Helping Survivors Survive." *Nursing 89* 19(1989): 52–57.

Hankoff, L.D., M.T. Mischorr, K.E. Tomleson, and S.A. Joyce. "A Program of Crisis Intervention in the Emergency Medical Setting." *American Journal of Psychiatry* 131(1974): 47–50.

Kolb, L.C. "Chronic Posttraumatic Stress Disorder: Implications of Recent Epidemiological and Neuropsychological Studies." *Psychological Medicine* 19(1989): 821–824.

Phipps, L.B. "Theoretical Frameworks Applicable to Family Care." In *Family-focused Care,* edited by J.R. Miller and E.H. Janosik. New York: McGraw-Hill, 1980.

Puryear, D.A. *Helping People in Crisis.* San Francisco: Jossey Bass, 1980.

Whitlock, G.E. *Understanding and Coping with Real Life Crises.* Monterey, California: Brooks/Cole, 1978.

PART
SIX

CRISIS PROGRAM PLANNING

17

Crisis Programs
Collaboration and Diversification

Things in life will not always run smoothly. Sometimes we will be rising toward the heights—then all will seem to reverse itself and start downward. The great fact to remember is that the trend of civilization is forever upward . . .

Endicott Peabody

It is probably useful to think of *crisis intervention* as the application of a special set of skills that members of the helping professions and interested lay persons can learn. At the same time, it is desirable to recognize that crisis counseling skills are somewhat unique and may require a shift in orientation for professionals who wish to develop expertise in this modality.

Among persons interested in crisis intervention, there should be strong belief in interdisciplinary and multidisciplinary cooperation, and conscious acceptance of the fact that crises may well occur at inconvenient times for the crisis worker.

For purposes of clarity, it should be noted that *multidisciplinary teams* involve groups of persons functioning according to the traditional tenets of their discipline, whereas *interdisciplinary teams* operate with a greater amount of shared functioning, even if this means adhering less to the accustomed behaviors of their respective disciplines. Crisis workers need to be aware of their personal strengths and weaknesses, in addition to knowing community resources well enough to ascertain which persons or agencies would be most helpful in dealing with the particular crisis that has been brought to the attention of the worker.

When a crisis arises, professionals, such as ministers, teachers, social workers, and attorneys, as well as members of the health care profession, emergency room staff, and ambulance crews, are all valuable sources of help. Because crises are so frequent, diverse, and pervasive, no effective source of help should be excluded or avoided merely to protect the territory of any discipline.

LESSONS FROM COMBAT

The experience of the military in dealing with combat crises contributed to our understanding of effective strategies. During World War I, the British evacuated battle-shock casualties to neuropsychiatric facilities far behind the front lines, often in England itself. This custom resulted in few soldiers being returned to duty and in the perpetuation or worsening of symptoms. The French treated their shock casualties at or close to the front lines and used aversive conditioning techniques to communicate to French soldiers that they were expected to return to active duty. Noting the different outcomes the British and the French obtained, Thomas Salmon, the officer in charge of the American Army's psychiatric program in northern Europe, tried to combine the compassion of the British with the outcome successes of the French. To do this, Salmon employed the concepts of *proximity, immediacy,* and *expectancy* (Cozza & Hales, 1991). His treatment was relatively brief and simple, consisting mostly of hot meals, a few nights of undisturbed sleep, and sympathetic listening.* Salmon's reorganization of American procedures for treating these casualties resulted in a 50 percent return to duty of shock casualties, with few relapses.

Unfortunately, Salmon's work was virtually ignored in World War II, until high numbers of psychiatric casualties forced the military to reinstitute formulations based on immediacy, proximity, and expectancy. Salmon's ideas were also used during the Korean and Vietnam conflicts (Ursano et al., 1989), with notable success. The following list describes Salmon's preventive formulations and their implications:

- *Immediacy.* Symptoms of combat shock should be treated as soon as possible.
- *Proximity.* Combat shock should be treated as close as possible to the region where the reaction occurred.
- *Expectancy.* Expectations should be conveyed that following a brief respite, customary tasks will be resumed.

Military psychiatry has contributed to crisis intervention in several ways. Among others, Hales (1987) noted that the community mental health movement of the 1950s used practices that the military had tested, since combat situations offered a natural laboratory. Battle-shock statistics of World Wars I and II demonstrated that external stress can cause emotional disequilibrium. In addition, prompt intervention offered in or near the stressful environment were able to prevent further regression and discourage chronicity (Cozza & Hales, 1991).

---

*Treatment was offered in proximity to combat areas, as soon as symptoms became evident, and with clear expectation that they would soon be alleviated.

SHARING THE TASK

By its very nature, crisis requires collaborative efforts that only crisis workers with some knowledge of their own constraints can organize. The involvement of more than one care provider relieves the potential for dependency, which is present in every crisis interaction. Depending on the nature and severity of the crisis, there are many individuals whose contributions to crisis work can be productive. It is in the interests of the client to recruit auxiliary care providers as soon as possible, although the initial worker may remain more or less active.

The skilled crisis worker will understand the importance of accepting all reliable providers of assistance and will encourage those in crisis to identify persons who might be helpful. The crisis worker may justifiably persuade the person in crisis to communicate with other family members or friends whose assistance is likely to alleviate the crisis. Rather than fostering the isolation of persons in crisis, the worker will do everything possible to help clients overcome their reluctance to establish or reestablish support networks.

Unless professional care providers are well versed in crisis theory, they are apt to be unwilling or unable to make suitable referrals to resources that may be more therapeutic than the best-intentioned professional. Any individual, professional or otherwise, who is experienced in crisis intervention is aware that crisis is not an issue that a single individual needs to handle.

The nature of crisis implies an adaptive or maladaptive resolution within a period of approximately two months. This does not mean, however, that only care providers who are involved throughout this time frame can offer crisis intervention. Ad hoc crisis intervention may consist only of permitting affective expression or identifying the cognitive and behavior distortion of those in crisis. Since crisis may be a complicating aspect of almost any human experience, therapeutic intervention should not be withheld merely because the care provider will be available for only a few days or even a few hours. Persons answering a hot line, for example, provide crisis intervention that is urgently needed and can be a conduit to other, more sustained intervention. Professionals working on an intensive care unit or in a hospice setting must frequently intervene to help families in crisis, along with meeting the essential needs of the seriously ill. The same may be said of a variety of situations in which crisis intervention is warranted, even when implemented by a care provider whose involvement does not continue for the duration of the crisis.

A subsidiary goal of crisis work is to maintain cooperation and collaboration among the crisis workers engaged in a common effort. This goal is often hard to achieve because many representatives of the helping professions see themselves as pivotal, regardless of the type of crisis being confronted. This observation seems particularly true of mental health professionals, who believe that their expertise in the area of emotional problems can be generalized to all types of crisis. It cannot be denied that attention to psychological reactions can substantially reduce the emotional residue of severe crises, but the multifaceted nature of crisis means that help from a variety of sources is often warranted. The addition of research scientists to the study of crisis theory is an important and valuable expansion of the crisis team (*The New York Times,* 1982).

INTERDISCIPLINARY COLLABORATION

A team organized some months after the collapse of a hotel in a midwestern American city provided an excellent illustration of interdisciplinary collaboration. The team worked under the auspices of the Human Skills Consortium, located in New Jersey, and consisted of a psychologist, a psychiatric nurse, a teacher of special education, a firefighter, and a paramedic, among others. The Human Skills Consortium was organized in response to a widely perceived need and has presented training sessions for emergency workers since its inception. The program, held for people who had been involved in the catastrophic collapse of a modern hotel, took the form of a twenty-hour marathon workshop designed to offer intensive training in crisis intervention. During the program, the team endeavored to give workshop participants an opportunity to consider answers to the following questions:*

What is a crisis?
Characteristics of people in crisis
Paradox of crisis as danger and opportunity

Why do people respond as they do to crisis?
Defensive vs. coping behavior
Egoism vs. altruism
Differentiation of needs
Needs of victims
Needs of caregivers

What are the significant features of crisis?
Grief process: grievers' perspective
Grief process: caregivers' perspective
Precipitators of crisis
Manifestations of crisis
Resolutions of crisis

*Joella Rand, R.N., Ph.D., a member of the collaborative group, provided data related to the marathon workshop and interdisciplinary team.

What intervention strategies are effective in crisis?
Assessment of clients' needs
Problem solving with the client
Implementing a plan for coping
Evaluating restored level of function

What is the impact of crisis work on personnel?
Subjective overinvolvement
Feelings of inadequacy
Feelings of guilt
Feelings of apathy and detachment
Feelings of anger
Burnout

The hotel disaster, like other catastrophes in recent times, served as a vital reminder of the current need for adequate numbers of people with varying skills, all of whom are trained and qualified in crisis intervention. Recurrent crises in the form of natural disasters, vehicle accidents, and nuclear contamination have caused more and more care providers to ask themselves, "If I were involved in a serious crisis event today, would I be able to handle it?" The question is relevant for professionals accustomed to dealing with standard emergency procedures, for paraprofessionals with official or quasi-official responsibilities, and for public-minded volunteers.

In training potential crisis workers, the marathon method is frequently used because the prolonged intensity builds up the stresses and pressures that the participants in a crisis must often face. A basic objective in a crisis workshop is to teach the personnel not to be harmful in the sense of judging themselves or others harshly. This means that crisis workers must learn to deal with strong emotion, their own and that of the victims or their families. The crisis worker needs to be reassured that feelings of frustration, ambivalence, guilt, or anger are normal in the face of crisis and no person involved can fully escape them. Leaders of the marathon workshop relied heavily on the technique of role portrayal. Situations were devised that were realistic and placed demands on the participants. Role portrayal is one of several techniques used in training crisis workers. A description of these techniques may be found in the section on training crisis hot line volunteers, which appears later in this chapter.

Even though the primary purpose of the workshop was to prepare participants for future crises, there was considerable discussion of the hotel disaster in which many had been involved. As might be expected, most of the participants were still working through the grief process, even though the tragedy had taken place some months earlier. When talking about some aspect of the workshop, the participants betrayed, with quivers in their voices, the lingering memories of the disaster. Although these workers had performed heroically, they were haunted by a sense of their helplessness. Terrible recollections of pieces of human bodies found in the disaster site continued to disturb them. For many workers, the experience was particularly painful because they sometimes found it necessary to cut through the bodies of the dead in order to reach survivors. Even though most of them were experienced rescue workers, they were accustomed to handling both the living and the dead respectfully, keeping bodies as intact as possible. Dismembering the dead, even to help survivors, was an act of violation for many of the workers.

Inability to avert tragedy was a poignant memory for some workers. One participant reported staying with an eleven-year-old boy while other workers labored to remove huge pieces of rock and debris that covered the child. After five hours of effort, the child was finally extricated from the rubble, only to die twenty minutes later in the arms of the worker who had been with him throughout the ordeal of the rescue effort.

MENTAL HEALTH WORKERS

The usual skills developed in the education and preparation of mental health professionals are often diametrically opposed to the skills necessary to deal with the crisis experience of a client with whom the mental health professional did not previously have an ongoing relationship. If the mental health professional abides by the usual forms of therapeutic intervention, the client in crisis may feel rejected and unaided. The overall approach to crisis intervention requires more activity and more directiveness on the part of the helper than is operant in other therapeutic modalities. The crisis worker needs to be more flexible in reference to the use of space and time than is common in other forms of therapy. In response to a client in crisis, the counselor may use touching, even to the extent of holding a distraught client who is in acute crisis. Admittedly, for some mental health professionals, the use of touch will be difficult and even problematic. If, however, the professional is comfortable with the use of touch, it can be a very effective technique.

The crisis worker also needs to be flexible regarding time factors. A client who is experiencing crisis will rarely fit neatly into a fifty-minute hour or a once-a-week schedule. It is not at all uncommon for a first crisis session to last from two to four hours, and for the next session to be scheduled later that day or for the next day. A person in crisis may need to be seen daily for several days, with the frequency of contact diminishing over the space of a few weeks. The main point is that persons in crisis need to know they can reach help at any time, even in the small hours of the morning if the need is urgent. This kind of flexibility and lack of structure may prove quite difficult for the qualified mental health professional who does not have an adequate grasp of crisis theory.

Another aspect of crisis intervention that is foreign to traditional mental health counseling is the acceptance of the client's dependency, which often accompanies initial crisis work. The crisis worker should be willing to accept temporary dependency without interpreting such phenomena as transference and countertransference. This dependency can be made acceptable by establishing a clear understanding that crisis work is a time-limited experience and that the client will return to a state of equilibrium in the foreseeable future.

EMERGENCY ROOM AND AMBULANCE WORKERS

An important consideration in collaborative crisis work is identifying special groups that are competent and skilled in handling certain types of crisis. Classic examples of this kind of group are ambulance crews and emergency room staffs. These are professionals and paraprofessionals who are exceedingly well trained in the medical aspects of acute crisis care. Because of the extreme importance of the medical emergency, these groups may not be altogether aware of the multifaceted nature of crises and therefore restrict their assistance to interventions that are entirely medical. Comprehensive training of medical professionals and paraprofessionals requires sensitizing them to the emotional components of a medical crisis, for medical personnel may overlook emotional threats as they concentrate on the life-threatening aspects of the experience. Similarly, mental health professionals and crisis center workers will benefit from specialized training in understanding the rudiments of acute medical care; the points of view of medical treatment teams; and the policies and protocols of ambulance crews, hospital emergency personnel, and police officers or firefighters.

Understanding the responsibilities of other care providers is necessary if the crisis worker is to help clients anticipate and accept essential medical procedures. Comprehending the rationale for certain treatments reduces anger and resentment at what may seem to be callous or indifferent attitudes on the part of medical specialists or rescue teams. Recognizing that crisis is a multidimensional situation enables the crisis worker to realize the value of interdisciplinary cooperation. Any programs designed to prepare crisis workers must emphasize collaboration between crisis workers with a mental health orientation and crisis workers with a physical health orientation. This kind of training can be accomplished by using experts from a variety of fields and disciplines, each of whom shares a special interest in crisis theory and practice.

HOT LINE AND CRISIS CENTER WORKERS

Paraprofessionals and volunteers who answer the thousands of crisis hot lines that have proliferated across the country probably deal with the majority of emotional crises. Almost every small city has at least one crisis line, and many urban areas have three or four competing or specialized hot lines. Almost all of these crisis hot lines share a common denominator—reliance on volunteers.

The total hours these volunteers provide may very likely surpass the total hours all paid mental health professionals in the country work. Almost all these hot lines are open twenty-four hours a day, seven days a week, and are answered by trained listeners functioning according to a pledge of confidentiality. Although the preparation and experience of volunteers varies considerably, there is consistent emphasis on not imposing one's own values, on ways to be helpful, on factors to be considered in assessing suicide risk, on interventions in suicide crises, and on familiarity with community resources to be used for referral (Hoff & Resing, 1982).

By and large, the people who volunteer to answer crisis hot lines are motivated by desire to help others and desire to gain knowledge and experience. They are often people to whom others turn in times of distress and who therefore believe they have an innate ability to help others. Some volunteers are individuals who have received help during a personal crisis, have successfully resolved the crisis, and now wish to offer assistance to others.

Many volunteers characteristically come to training sessions believing that they will be able to find "answers" for other people and that they can "solve problems" for others. Much of the initial training is devoted to active listening skills, to convincing the volunteers that they can neither solve problems nor find answers for other people, but can only help them discover their own solutions. Volunteers come to the training sessions expecting psychic rewards in terms of feeling good about their work and being liked by clients. Training programs must prepare volunteers for the frustration of dealing with situations for which there are no definitive answers, with the ambiguities that are often present in crisis situations, and with the regret that a crisis worker must endure when intervention is not successful. The importance of immediately accessible support and consultation for crisis hot line workers cannot be overstated. Such backup service is essential to quality control and to the emotional well-being of the workers.

PEER COUNSELING

The use of the peer counseling service began during the 1960s and 1970s, when the rise of counterculture influences challenged established values and life styles. The ability of mental health professionals to deal with the concerns of young people came into question, as did the responsiveness of established health care delivery systems to the special problems of youth. A notable innovation at the time was the use of peer counseling based on a client-centered model. In a number of institutions of secondary and higher education, selected young people were taught basic helping skills. Training programs usually emphasized a humanistic approach that advocated active listening, an empathetic relationship, and the dissemination of information.

A problem-solving model was adopted that attempted to define a problem, helped clients examine several alternative solutions, choose one, and proceed to act on the decision. Although inspired by sound motivation, peer counseling proved to have some deficiencies. Because client-centered intervention was considered paramount, little attention was given to the counselor's responsibility for establishing a contract and directing the sessions. Agreement regarding the time of meetings, the format of meetings, and the goal of meetings was reached largely through the initiative of the client. The client could return as often as needed, for as long as desired. No appointments were required for walk-in visits when the crisis center was open, and the hot line was always available.

There were advantages and disadvantages to peer counseling. The pattern of response offered immediate service to consumers and was compatible with youth values, particularly those that repudiated established methods of delivering service. Also acceptable was preoccupation with here-and-now reality rather than the past. Categorizing clients as mentally ill was considered to be dehumanizing and was avoided whenever possible. Despite these advantages, peer counseling, in many instances, was not successful. Young counselors lacked the knowledge and ability to set limits and to direct therapeutic sessions, thereby allowing the helping process to become unfocused and diffuse. Client dependency was inadvertently fostered by peer counselors who were unduly nurturing and protective. Excessive involvement with clients, the substitution of sympathy for empathy, and inattention to self-determination and the client's responsibility for growth impaired those peer programs that made inadequate provision for supervision of counselors and quality control of services. Peer counseling programs that proved durable were those that emulated the rigorous training and monitoring characteristic of most crisis centers.

TRAINING PROGRAMS

Early training sessions for volunteers combine didactic instruction with experiential learning. There are three major activities involved in experiential learning: role playing, role portrayal, and interpersonal recall.

Role playing is commonly used in training volunteers and is based on having one volunteer take the role of a client and a second volunteer take the role of the counselor, enacting an extemporaneous script improvised by the "client," with the group constituting the audience.

In contrast, *role portrayal* involves one of the trainers acting a simulated, circumscribed problem, using the therapeutic and acting skills of the trainer in order to show beginning crisis workers the mistakes and counterproductive interventions that novices are likely to make. By using the role portrayal technique, the trainer and the trainee can follow a designated script to some extent, allowing the audience to witness some of the natural mistakes that any trainee might make. One outcome of role portrayal is that the trainee "counselor" often does not realize that an untherapeutic intervention has been made until this is discerned and pointed out by the attentive audience. Suggestions from peers are usually less threatening than suggestions from the trainers, and audience participation adds to the interest of the proceedings.

The third training technique, *interpersonal recall,* is useful for ongoing training because it provides a form of feedback from the client whom the volunteer is counseling. Interpersonal process recall may be verbal or written. In either case, recall of the interpersonal transaction between counselor and client permits the interactional process to be reviewed by them both as they examine their internal reactions and establish the rationale for certain responses. Interpersonal process recall is a technique that can use authentic transactions, or augment role playing and role portrayal. However it is used, it is a technique that encourages self-analysis and facilitates self-instruction (Kagan et al., 1969).

The three experiential techniques just described are combined with group discussions and review of written and electronic recordings of actual crisis interventions. In the interests of confidentiality, it is essential that written permission be secured from clients whose conversations are used for educational purposes and that anonymity be preserved. The role portrayal technique does not threaten confidentiality, is adaptable, and can be used for the cross-training of members from various disciplines. Unlike role playing, which allows more leeway to the actors, role portrayal is relatively structured and affords trainers the opportunity to emphasize salient points.

SUPERVISION AND QUALITY CONTROL

The issues of support and guidance for crisis center volunteers are crucial. Of special importance is quality control, or maintaining high standards for services that crisis centers and crisis hot lines offer. The volunteers who answer crisis hot lines must deal with a wide range of problems, many of which have no easy or wholly satisfactory solutions. Supervisors and experienced professionals need to realize that volunteers may themselves be in crisis at the completion of some of the calls they answer. For example, there is great stress placed on volunteers who deal with seriously suicidal clients for whom no intervention seems effective. In addition, some angry clients typically use hot line services to vent their global anger on any available human being. Others will use the crisis hot line for prank calls that are mischievous or even obscene.

Because of the emotional demands of working on a hot line, volunteers need to have access to supervisors or backup professionals at all times. Just as the crisis of a client should not be ignored until it is convenient to respond, the crisis of a worker should not be overlooked at the conclusion of an emotionally charged call. Volunteers need support persons to whom they can turn for advice and reassurance whenever they feel the necessity for debriefing or for consultation regarding interventions that were just made. Even though one author of this chapter has supervised a hot line for more than ten years and has provided ongoing support to crisis hot line workers, volunteers have made very few inappropriate requests for help. The importance of immediately accessible support and consultation for crisis hot line workers cannot be overstated. Such backup service is essential to quality control and to the emotional well-being of the workers.

Another problem in maintaining esprit de corps among volunteer workers is the infrequency of positive feedback they receive. It is not only the clients served by the volunteers, but also the agencies to which volunteers make referrals that are lax in this respect. It is possible that agencies to which clients are referred may be restrained by respect for client confidentiality and therefore do not share developments with crisis workers. At other times, the agencies may be unaware that the client arrived at the agency as the result of a referral by a hot line crisis worker. Furthermore, the crisis volunteer usually receives less-than-adequate feedback from peers and from supervisors within the facility. Even when all working calls are recorded, and this is considered a desirable practice, a supervisor listens to only a small percentage of the calls a busy hot line facility takes. There is also an inclination to take therapeutic interventions for granted and concentrate on those that were less effective. This is a practice that sensitive supervisors avoid.

The most helpful way to monitor the performance of workers and to improve their skills is to record and listen to as many tape-recorded phone calls as possible. Routine monitoring of the calls permits analysis of difficult calls, provides supervision, and becomes a teaching method when selected calls are used for didactic instruction of one or more workers. Random monitoring of calls is less advisable than routine monitoring, but helps provide some degree of quality control.

Many of the issues around support for the workers and quality control for the work can be discussed at regular meetings that the volunteer and professional staff attend. Such meetings should be held at least monthly and more often if possible. Here the volunteers can be given opportunities to talk about some of their more difficult calls, to share ideas as to how calls might be handled, and to review selected segments of actual calls. Serious attention should be paid to the psychological satisfaction of volunteers working on a crisis hot line service, and planned activities need to be built into the training program to build morale and maintain high motivation. Certificates of service and other tokens of recognition are usually very meaningful to volunteer workers. Experienced and dedicated volunteers are the life supply of many crisis centers, and problems related to burnout or volunteer discontent must be acknowledged. Many of the larger, well-staffed crisis centers have a policy of assigning two or more volunteers to the same time schedule. This practice is very helpful in that volunteers can talk with one another and engage in mutual sharing after a difficult phone conversation. Even when two or more volunteers have been assigned to a shift, the need for prompt access to a supervisor or experienced professional cannot be avoided.

VOLUNTEERISM IN CRISIS WORK

Crisis intervention can often assist individuals to resume task-oriented behaviors and discard defensive reactions. It is this primary objective that benefits from the voluntary efforts of natural helpers in social settings, such as relatives, friends, teachers, and clergy. A distinction should be made, however, between the informal efforts of random individuals and the formal efforts of structured crisis teams, staffed by volunteers.

When the interventions of natural helpers fail, persons in crisis often avail themselves of assistance that diversified community programs offered, which rely on the work of volunteers as well as paid workers. Because some community workers, professional and otherwise, perceive *crisis intervention* as a catchall term applied to a host of therapeutic tactics, their understanding of specific principles may be vague. Collaboration is the rule rather than the exception in crisis counseling, but adequate preparation and supervision should be ongoing, especially for volunteers, regardless of their skills in other areas. In all crisis work, formal or informal, commitment to quality control and outcome evaluation is essential. Providing consultation and education to voluntary workers reinforces the idea that the work they perform is important.

•CLINICAL EXAMPLE:
PROTOTYPE OF VOLUNTARY CRISIS PROGRAMS

A voluntary crisis organization known as the Samaritans was founded in England in 1953 to help suicidal, despairing, and lonely people. Since then the organization has established branches in many countries, including the United States. Opened in 1974, the chapter in Boston follows the practices of the world-wide organization. The general policies of the organization are as follows:

Befriend the client as an equal, without engaging in discrimination or directive counseling.
Provide available help twenty-four hours a day.
Maintain complete confidentiality.
Select and train volunteer counselors with the utmost care.

At the Boston facility, about one hundred calls and visits are handled daily. The primary purpose of the organization is to help persons who are suicidal, but help is not restricted to these clients. If medical assistance is indicated and the caller consents, an ambulance will be sent. The police are seldom involved nor are calls traced except in unusual circumstances. Workers for the organization do not claim to save lives, but only to help callers avoid desperate measures, especially the finality of suicide, by suggesting means of relieving pain and frustration.

The problems callers describe are demanding and diversified. They include depression, endogenous or exogenous; loneliness and isolation; sexual problems; marital difficulties; physical illness or injury; financial worries; and psychiatric disorders. One feature of the program is called Special Befriending. This feature consists of assigning a particular volunteer to see a client outside the crisis facility for a limited time and purpose. The purpose might be to give support during the critical period of a divorce or the death of a loved one.

The organization insists on professional intervention whenever possible, and workers are discouraged from assuming tasks that are better left to others. When professional help seems advisable, the volunteer worker will try to persuade the client of the need, make the referral, and help the client with arrangements. A close liaison is maintained with mental health and social service agencies so that referrals proceed in two directions. Volunteers for the Samaritans refer clients to professionals, and professionals, in turn, make referrals to this crisis-oriented voluntary agency.

Volunteer Training. Careful selection and preparation of volunteers is the key to the success of the program. Applicants have at least two preliminary meetings with a selection committee, and only one applicant in three is accepted into the training course. The training course meets three hours a week for six weeks, and the volunteers are not taught rote answers or techniques. The aim is to prepare volunteers, emotionally and cognitively, for crisis work and for the calls they are likely to receive. Volunteers are asked to make a commitment to work one five-hour shift a week and one overnight shift a month, plus attending a monthly staff meeting. Three volunteers are assigned to each daytime shift, and two are assigned at night. Telephones are answered twenty-four hours a day, and the facility is open from 9:00 A.M. until 10:00 P.M. for people who wish to come in and talk. Volunteers are carefully screened for their personal qualities and aptitudes, without regard to sex, age, creed, or social status. Although not prepared in the professional sense, these volunteers are well trained and fully supervised with the help of professional consultants.

The Boston chapter is considered a charitable trust, so contributions to it are tax deductible. Thus far, funding has been provided by foundation grants and donations from businesses, insurance companies, and private citizens. Some financial support is obtained through public subsidies from the Department of Mental Health. Three directors, each with a designated area of responsibility, share administrative authority. A board of trustees meets as a body or in committee to deal with finances, public relations, and related issues. Additionally, staff and volunteers offer presentations and training programs to hospitals and clinics, nursing and social work schools, police groups, and other hot line and crisis centers (Samaritans, 1976).

SUMMARY

In crisis work there are few territorial barriers between experienced helpers, for the contributions of professionals, paraprofessionals, and nonprofessionals are all significant. There is a tendency, however, for some mental health professionals to concentrate on the emotional effects of crisis while overlooking urgent needs for medical intervention. At the same time, medical emergency workers may unintentionally cause psychological damage because of their preoccupation with physical trauma. It is essential then that the special skills of each group augment the skills of the others in order to prevent physical and psychological damage following the precipitation of crisis.

The importance of preparing individuals for crisis work cannot be stressed too much, and the experience in preparing and supervising volunteer crisis workers suggests several appropriate training tactics, such as marathon sessions and role portrayal. The impact of tragic disasters on crisis workers engaged in rescue operations is powerful and long lasting. Emotional support and opportunity for catharsis may be necessary intermittently for rescuers and survivors, even after considerable time has elapsed since the event.

Many crisis centers and crisis hot lines are staffed almost entirely by volunteer workers, whose interventions can only be as effective as the training programs used to prepare them. Training programs for volunteer crisis workers must warn them of frustrations encountered in dealing with situations for which there are no definitive answers, and also prepare them for the guilt they may experience when an intervention is unsuccessful. In addition to careful selection and adequate training of volunteer workers, crisis programs must strive for quality control through monitoring and supervising. Because of the rigors of crisis work, support for personnel is just as necessary as quality control. A clinical example that exemplifies admirable merging of selection, training, quality control, and community collaboration is found in the program of the Samaritans, a worldwide organization with a crisis center operating successfully in Boston since 1974.

REFERENCES

Cozza, K.L., and R.E. Hales. "Psychiatry in the Army: A Brief Historical Perspective and Current Developments." *Hospital and Community Psychiatry* 42(1991): 413–418.

Hales, R.E. "Community Psychiatry: Alive and Thriving in the Military." *Hospital and Community Psychiatry* 38(1987): 1259.

Hoff, L.A., and A. Resing. "Was this Suicide Preventable?" *American Journal of Nursing* 82(1982): 1106–1111.

Kagan, N., P.A. Schauble, A. Ressikoff, S.J. Danish, and D.R. Krothwohl. "Interpersonal Process Recall." *Journal of Nervous and Mental Disorders* 148(1969): 365–374.

Samaritans. *Mimeographed Report,* Boston, Mass. Samaritans, 1976.

The New York Times. "Hyatt Regency Disaster One Year Later." C1 July 5, 1982, C1.

Ursano, R.J., H.C. Holloway, and D.R. Jones. "Psychiatric Care in the Military Community: Family and Military Stressors." *Hospital and Community Psychiatry* 40(1989): 1284–1289.

Index